Stephanie Alexander AO is regarded as one of Australia's great food educators. Her reputation has been earned through her 30 years as an owner-chef in several restaurants, as the author of 15 influential books, and for her groundbreaking work in creating the Stephanie Alexander Kitchen Garden Foundation. Everything she has achieved and worked towards has been driven by her desire to break down anxieties about cooking, to emphasise the beauty of produce fresh from the garden and to promote the pleasures of sharing food around a table. Her fifth book, *The Cook's Companion*, is regarded as an Australian classic, and has sold over 500 000 copies. In 2013, this monumental work made its first appearance as an easy-to-use digital app. In 2014 Stephanie became an Officer of the Order of Australia in recognition of her work with the Stephanie Alexander Kitchen Garden Foundation. She was named Victorian of the Year in 2010 and, in 2012, appeared in the number one position on *Crikey* magazine's list of the most powerful people in Australian food. Her strong belief is that the earlier children learn about food through example and pleasurable hands-on experience, the better their food choices will be throughout life.

stephaniealexander.com.au

Dedicated with affection and gratitude to
Julie Gibbs, an extraordinary publisher.

The Cook's Table

Stephanie Alexander

Photography by Mark Chew

LANTERN

an imprint of
PENGUIN BOOKS

Sharing food experiences has always made me happier than anything else. Anticipation is part of this, and that includes planning the menu.

It also includes considering the setting for my dinner. Which tablecloth will it be – a very formal white linen cloth I bought in China many years ago, heavily embroidered with raised peonies, or a hand-blocked brilliantly coloured cotton cloth from Indonesia via Amsterdam, with its set of completely impractical organdy napkins in jewel-bright colours, or a subdued and classically pleasing soft grey linen cloth bought in the French town of Saint Remy whilst waiting for a cafe to open? And so on . . . And there are favourite and well-used jugs, plates and bowls, each with its own story and memory. Everything I own I use and am mystified at the concept that things should be saved for special occasions. Any meal with dear friends is a special occasion, as often as it can be managed.

And then there is the pleasure of the actual cooking. I am usually impatient to start cooking but, after years in a professional kitchen, I know to assemble ingredients first of all, doing as much measuring, sorting, washing and chopping as possible before actually picking up a pan. In planning my menu, I want to be away from the table as little as possible, so I have kept last-minute stovetop cooking to a minimum. I don't want to miss the best stories. I am hungry for the latest news and opinions. This is why in this book I have put effort into indicating what steps can be done in advance in the timetables that accompany every menu. And I always clean up as I go, so that in my open-plan kitchen/dining area my guests are welcomed into a clean and tidy space by a smiling cook, with glasses at the ready, wine chilled, eager for conversation.

This book has sprung from my desire to revisit memorable meals often enjoyed in equally memorable locations. Sometimes I am imagining some of the detail. Mostly the stories are true. Often the menus have been crafted after the event, always with the hope that they will bring pleasure to others and, above all, that the dishes described will be of course delicious and well balanced, but also will capture some of the essence of the celebration or location and be achievable by any interested cook.

There are 25 chapters, each having an introductory story before the menu and recipes appear. I have ranged far and wide, with stories drawn from close at hand, and others inspired by my travels. Family and friends weave in and out. There are many dishes originally enjoyed in France and Italy, and some that reflect the work of favourite authors. In recooking these dishes, I have remembered some very meaningful moments in my life.

Over the past 30 or even 40 years, I have been asked questions about all manner of topics relating to cooking, kitchens and edible gardening. I have tried to allay anxiety and answer every one of these questions in my earlier books, especially *The Cook's Companion* and the two volumes of *The Kitchen Garden Companion*. Over and over again, I realise how enjoyable and important it has been to my cooking life to have found knowledgeable and friendly suppliers. They have given me answers to my own questions and I have been able to pass them on. I urge all good cooks to seek out such friends. In contemplating one of these menus, or even a single dish, try to plan a visit to a farmers' market and you will be assured of the freshest herbs, fruit and vegetables. They are also an excellent place to locate some specialist items not always easy to find in larger stores, such as smoked eel or farmed venison to name just two.

One area I have never covered before is how to be organised when preparing a special menu for friends. It is well known that I trained to be a librarian before following my passion into the kitchen. Being organised and systematic is second nature to me, and many of my alumni in the hospitality world have instituted similar systems of worksheets and job lists as I used to do during the 21 years of Stephanie's Restaurant. I can laugh at myself but my list making was famous!

Here then can be found carefully compiled lists that will make any special dinner occasion smooth sailing. I have included a timetable of what to do when, and a list of ingredients required as a checklist. Items that need to be ordered in advance are indicated, wherever a process can be completed ahead of time it is noted, and reminders to check flowers, glasses and table linen and when to heat plates are not forgotten. Along the way there are hints or *trucs* that make the more complex dishes easier to follow. And the ingredient checklist ensures that you will not get part-way through a dish only to discover you have run out of coconut!

Every dish in this book can be successfully made by a careful home cook. Some require a bit more dedication than others but they are certainly not meant to emulate elaborate restaurant cooking. These menus are intended to give pleasure to those who love to cook and to share, who respect freshness and who therefore eat seasonally. Such foodlovers delight in using the best ingredients, be it a soft-leaved salad picked from a garden or a farmers' market, a free-range chicken or one of the outstanding extra virgin olive oils we are producing in Australia. While hopefully appealing to modern palates, my menus reflect my deep respect for traditional knowledge. I like to show the lineage of my recipes – whether they have been first found in a treasured volume or tasted in a simple or fancy restaurant, or been given to me by another foodlover. Each menu includes several dishes that complement each other. I am not especially interested in froth, foam, painted-on sauce, sprinkles on plates or towers of food but I do love the surprise of unexpected yet successful flavour and textural combinations.

I like to imagine that this book will lead to many wonderful parties around a table. Of course there will be times when the cook wants to make just one dish, not an entire menu. Thanks to an excellent index any individual recipe can be quickly located.

This book has been written during a time of great change at Penguin Books. It marks the end of a 25-year creative collaboration with publisher Julie Gibbs, and therefore has heightened significance for me. Julie and I have travelled together, eaten together in very simple settings, as well as some rather grand ones, and shared many marvellous moments. I hope there will be many more . . . As always, Julie has encouraged and supported me to the very last day, and I thank her for this and everything else from the bottom of my heart.

LATE SUMMER DINNER

A DINNER FOR 6

LULU'S
TOMATES PROVENÇALES

———

RED RICE PILAF
with FENNEL, PIPIS & MUSSELS

———

ROASTED DUCK
with PEAS, SAUTEED POTATOES
& BRAISED FLAT ONIONS

GREEN SALAD

———

GRILLED
APRICOT HALVES

LEMON-SCENTED VERBENA
ICE-CREAM

1

Two friends and I once shared a French adventure in the lovely southern town of Uzès. The town centre was classified as a protected zone in 1965, and many of the houses have been meticulously restored using local honey-coloured stone. The colours of the wooden shutters were delightful – dove-grey, sage green, old rose and the powdery-blue of plumbago. Late summer growth tumbled from window boxes and pots on balconies – geraniums, honeysuckle, roses. Walls were covered in flowering jasmine growing from tiny pockets of earth.

We rented an apartment, so daily trips to the market were a necessity as well as a delight. There were prodigiously sized multi-coloured heirloom tomatoes – yellow, red-black, pink satin and green – all curves and bumps. The biggest, meatiest ones just asked to be made into *tomates a la Provençale*, which I did often, following a recipe in one of my favourite books, *Lulu's Provençal Table* by the late Richard Olney, who was a great friend of the wine-making Peyraud family at Domaine Tempier in Bandol. The matriarch, Lulu, related her recipes to Richard, who captured them for posterity in this book. Without ever having met Lulu, I hear her exuberant voice in Richard's text. I have also been fortunate to have enjoyed several glasses of the superb peach-gold rosé from Domaine Tempier, an unforgettable wine. In this book, Richard paints the scene of innumerable relaxed and laughter-filled lunches set under shady grapevines. Lulu told him that 'everyone knows how to make *tomates provençales*' – well, maybe in Provence they do. With a crusty loaf and a fresh round or log of goat's cheese, this was our lunch on many days in Provence. On page 11 is her version, with a few tiny changes to reflect local ingredients.

The apricots, too, were sensational. It is years since I've tasted an apricot anywhere near those from the Uzès market; the apricot, more than any other fruit, says Provence to me. They seem to have absorbed the sunshine and their pink-gold blush is echoed in the cheeks of the market stallholders. On a much earlier holiday in Provence, noticing the most beautiful glowing and ripe apricots, I remember disagreeing with my companion and insisting we leave purchasing apricots until the very end of our shopping. Of course there were none left an hour later. A lesson learnt for future French marketing.

A handful of freshly picked parsley was included with every purchase, with a smile and wishes for a good weekend. I was interested to buy *tétragone de Provence*, described by the vendor as *épinards d'été*, and known here in the Antipodes as warrigal greens or New Zealand spinach (*tetragonia tetragonioides*). I blanched it quickly, then reheated it with garlic and butter, and found it tender and without any trace of the mouth-puckering oxalates common in those sampled in Australia – interesting. Even more interesting was unearthing a reference to this unusual vegetable in *The Alice B. Toklas Cook Book*, where Alice discovers what she refers to as *Tetredragon* or New Zealand spinach in her market at Bilignin, near the Swiss border in the 1930s. She was advised to feed this plant prodigiously with rich manure, and to only pick the young leaves, wash them and cook them in the water clinging to them, then, after draining, reheat them with either sour cream or butter. She describes them as deliciously tender. Recently I was served this leafy green in New Zealand, and it was tender and non–mouth puckering. I am convinced that the disagreeable level of oxalates in wild-gathered warrigal greens in Australia relates to lack of feeding due to our poorer soil.

At the fish stall, I bought tiny sweet mussels and clams no bigger than my thumbnail, known as *tellines*. I also bought some red rice hailing from the nearby Camargue, so I planned a soupy paella-type dish for dinner. The red rice was delicious; it developed the nuttiness of wild rice and a sweet flavour, retaining its rosy-pink colour.

There was convenience food too, but of a superior quality. Quail and chickens turned slowly on a spit were sold as soon as they were cooked. Into the bag also went some of the little potatoes and onions from the bottom of the spit, basted with the cooking juices. The smell was enticing and I found my mouth moistening in anticipation.

Another day we drove to the Camargue. I did not really believe we would see running white horses and flamingos in the salt marshes, but we did! Lunch at Sainte Maries-de-la-Mer offered a superb *soupe de poisson*, a robust and steaming bowl of red-gold soup that smelt of fresh shellfish served with crunchy ➤

croutons, and a spicy rouille paste. Every cafe offered plateaux of seafood, appropriate to this town, just metres from the sea.

We were recommended to try Le Tracteur, a modest restaurant located at the time on Avenue du Stade at nearby Sanilhac-Sagriès, for our farewell dinner. (Should you wish to go, Francophile friends recently told me that it has moved to quartier Bornègre, route d'Uzès, in the nearby village of Argilliers.) Our dinner was a delight. Parked outside the barn was an old Massey-Ferguson tractor. The prettily set outside tables were covered in Provençal cotton cloths, and were our first choice in the balmy weather. The food restored my faith in the existence of creative and surprising French food in out-of-the-way spots. It was brave and original, and the menu offered minimal choice. We had a delicious fresh peach salad with goat's cheese and chunky croutons, followed by a lovely roasted duck with braised flat onions and young peas in a spoonful of sticky sauce. Dessert was a knockout – grilled apricot halves with lemon-scented verbena ice-cream – those wonderful apricots again! We drove back to our little apartment just as the last of the light faded to a purple-pink sky, feeling very content.

So I had to repeat the dessert of grilled apricots with lemon-scented verbena ice-cream as a fitting finale here. I have a lemon verbena bush and use it mostly for tea, but ten leaves infused in the hot milk and cream made a very subtly scented ice-cream.

Lulu's *tomates provençales*

4 × 150 g ripe tomatoes *or*
2 × 250 g beefsteak-style tomatoes

2 teaspoons fine salt

extra virgin olive oil, for drizzling

PERSILLADE (BREADCRUMB
AND PARSLEY MIXTURE)

2 cloves garlic, peeled

4 tablespoons roughly chopped
flat-leaf parsley

⅔ cup (60 g) panko
breadcrumbs or day-old
coarse white breadcrumbs

freshly ground black pepper

It is not always easy for Australian cooks to find the huge meaty tomatoes ideal for this recipe. If you can, they are halved horizontally so each tomato yields two portions. The flavours are best if the tomatoes are served warm or at room temperature. Double the quantities if you have to buy smaller tomatoes as, after slicing off a 'lid', each one will be a single portion. The *persillade* keeps well for a day or two in the fridge. Scatter leftovers over fish to be grilled or other baked vegetables, such as halved eggplant (aubergines) or pumpkin (squash) pieces. A hungry person could easily eat two of these tomato halves as a first course, certainly if they were served as the main part of a simple lunch. Otherwise, serve four large halves or four whole smaller tomatoes per person. Reserve any extra for adding to a vegetable dish or simple braise as, after refrigerating for several hours, they will become rather soggy and be less appealing served as *tomates provençales*.

Preheat the oven to 220°C. Select a baking dish, which will also be the serving dish.

Cut the tomatoes in half horizontally. Using the handle of a teaspoon, remove most of the seeds to form pockets in each half. Very gently squeeze each half to release any remaining seeds. Settle the tomato halves in the baking dish and sprinkle evenly with the salt, then bake for 5 minutes.

Place a wire rack over a baking tray. Very carefully turn the tomatoes upside-down on the rack to drain, while you prepare the *persillade* filling. Finely chop the garlic and mix it with the parsley, then give a few more chops together. Place in a bowl with the breadcrumbs and pepper. Mix lightly with a fork.

Drizzle the baking dish with a little olive oil. Carefully settle the tomatoes hollowed-side up and spoon some of the *persillade* into the pockets, then spoon more over the top to cover the surface. Drizzle with olive oil and return to the oven for 20 minutes or until bubbling a little and golden brown on top.

Serve warm or at room temperature.

Red rice pilaf with fennel, pipis and mussels

2 tablespoons extra virgin olive oil

1 bulb fennel, cut into 1 cm dice
(to yield 1 cup [135 g]), fronds
and coarser outer stalks reserved

2 French shallots, finely chopped

2 cloves garlic, finely chopped

500 g black mussels, scrubbed
and 'beards' removed

300 g pipis or clams (vongole)

200 ml dry white wine

1 cup (200 g) red rice
(see page 513)

1½ cups (375 ml) Fish Stock
(see page 506) *or* water

½ teaspoon sea salt

50 g butter

freshly ground black pepper

2 tablespoons chopped herbs
(I use fennel fronds, flat-leaf
parsley and thyme)

This dramatic red rice, grown in France's Camargue region, tastes closer to wild rice than to any other long-grained rice I know. It is very sustaining, so portions do not need to be large. The same pilaf can be made with other long-grained rice, but it will probably take less time for the water to be completely absorbed. In the south of France, the pilaf I enjoyed also included some samphire, a salty vegetable that grows in marshy locales.

Heat the olive oil in an enamelled cast-iron or other flameproof casserole dish with a tight-fitting lid over medium heat and saute the fennel and shallot, stirring for 5 minutes or until softened. Increase the heat to high and cook for another 5 minutes so they take on a little colour. Add the garlic and stir for 1 minute.

Put all the shellfish, the wine and a few of the reserved coarser fennel stalks into a heavy-based frying pan with a tight-fitting lid. Cook, covered, over high heat for 5 minutes or until a gush of steam indicates the shellfish have opened. Tip the cooking juices through a fine-mesh sieve into a jug and reserve. Transfer the shellfish to a deep bowl, then cover with foil or a large plate to prevent them becoming dry. Rinse out the frying pan to be sure no sand or grit remains.

Add the rice to the fennel mixture and stir well. Tip in the reserved shellfish cooking juices and fish stock or water, then taste before deciding whether to add salt or not. Cover tightly, bring to the boil, then reduce the heat to low and place a simmer mat underneath. Cook for at least 25 minutes or until the liquid is absorbed. Taste and adjust for salt.

Preheat the oven to 110°C. Place 4 ovenproof serving bowls inside to warm.

Remove and discard the top shellfish shells. Heat the butter in a heavy-based frying pan over medium heat and add the shellfish. Shake to coat with butter until thoroughly hot.

Spoon the pilaf into the heated bowls and distribute the shellfish and buttery juices among them. Grind over some pepper and scatter with herbs, then serve.

Roasted duck with peas, sauteed potatoes and braised flat onions

1 × 2 kg duck, neck and wingtips removed and chopped into large pieces, then reserved

boiling water, as needed

2 tablespoons extra virgin olive oil

4 all-purpose potatoes, such as Nicola or desiree

sea salt and freshly ground black pepper

Braised Flat Onions (see page 17), to serve

Green Salad (see page 503), to serve

SAUCE

100 ml dry white wine

200 ml Chicken Stock (see page 505)

⅓ cup (80 ml) thickened cream

400 g young peas in the pod (to yield 150 g shelled)

There are a handful of food writers whose work not just makes me hungry, but who inform and inspire me, sending me straight to a market or the kitchen. British writer Simon Hopkinson is in my handful. For eight years Simon contributed outstanding food pieces to the UK newspaper *The Independent*. I did not know until I read the introduction to his book *Week In, Week Out* that he also contributed to the groundbreaking *Cordon Bleu Cookery Course* magazines, issued in monthly instalments in the 60s and 70s, as influential in its day as television cookery shows are today. I still have some issues, which are still exemplary pieces of work. Simon started me on this duck recipe (with the memory of the well-roasted Uzès duck an extra prompt). His version has cider and apples; mine has braised tiny onions and fresh peas. Given the contemporary interest in rare-grilled duck breasts, this is a very different experience. Two food-lovers might polish off the entire duck, but after an entree and with a sweet dish to follow, it is sufficient for four. (If you are concerned that it will be insufficient, buy two additional legs to roast, or roast two ducks and plan for leftovers.)

Preheat the oven to 180°C.

Remove the wishbone by pushing back the skin at the neck cavity and feeling with your fingers; use a small sharp knife. Using a skewer, puncture the duck skin all over the breast and around the thighs; do not puncture the flesh. Place on an upturned bowl in a very clean sink and slowly pour a full kettle of boiling water over the duck; the holes will open up and release some fat and the skin will visibly tighten. Dry the duck for at least 3 hours – I rest the duck on a wire rack over a tray in the refrigerator.

Meanwhile, rub the reserved neck and wing pieces with 1 teaspoon of the olive oil. Place in a flameproof roasting pan large enough to fit the duck and potatoes, then roast for 45 minutes or until well-coloured. Pour off any fat into a bowl and set the pan aside.

Par-boil the potatoes in a pan of lightly salted water for 10 minutes, then drain and leave until cool enough to handle. Peel and cut into large pieces. Set aside. ➤

recipe continues.

Increase the oven temperature to 220°C.

Rub the duck all over with the olive oil and sprinkle generously inside and out with salt and pepper. Place the duck on a roasting rack inside the roasting pan with the neck and wing pieces and roast for 20 minutes. Remove from the oven, reduce the temperature to 180°C and add the potatoes to the pan.

Roast the duck for another 1 hour, carefully pouring off any fat into the bowl every 20 minutes, then shaking the pan to ensure the potatoes are not sticking. During the last 20 minutes, reheat the braised onions in their sauce in an ovenproof frying pan and keep warm on one side of the stovetop until needed.

Bring a saucepan of lightly salted water to a simmer.

Test the duck by inserting a skewer into a thigh joint; it is ready when the juices run clear. Remove the duck from the oven and reduce the oven temperature to 120°C. Transfer the potatoes to a much smaller roasting pan and return to the oven to keep warm. As soon as you can handle the duck, use strong poultry shears to cut it in half by cutting along each side of the backbone and breastbone. Detach the legs, divide into thighs and drumsticks and place the pieces in the pan with the potatoes. Ease the breast halves away from the breastbone, then add to the pan in the oven. (The duck can now rest for 30 minutes, if that is more convenient.)

Meanwhile, to make the sauce, tip away all fat from the large roasting pan. Chop the backbone into 3 or 4 pieces and add to the pan. Heat over high heat, stirring. Deglaze the pan with the white wine, stirring and loosening all the stuck-on bits, then add the stock. Bubble together for a few minutes, then stir in the cream and simmer for 3 minutes; the sauce should have reduced slightly. Reheat the pan with the onions in their juices to reduce a bit more.

Strain the sauce through a very fine-mesh sieve into the onion pan and bring to a fast boil over high heat until the sauce is well reduced. Drop the peas into the pan of simmering water. Drain and add to the onions and sauce.

Slice the duck breasts on the diagonal. Divide the duck and potatoes among 4 warmed plates. Season the sauce to taste, if necessary. Spoon the onions, peas and sauce over, and serve.

Memorable Late Summer Dinner at Uzés

Braised flat onions

8 flat onions *or* small
pickling onions

40 g butter (truffle butter
would be even better)

1½ cups (375 ml) Chicken Stock
(see page 505)

sea salt and freshly ground
black pepper

**I have given the recipe for this separately, as they can be
completed hours before starting the duck on page 15. I have
long admired the flat onions displayed in French and Italian
markets and, until very recently, not grown commercially in
Australia. Now they sometimes appear at farmers' markets,
good greengrocers and at my local independent supermarket
too, often labelled *cipolline*, the Italian word for onions.
Their shape lends itself so well to braising and glazing, and
they seem to come in a wide variety of sizes, from about that
of a large button to as wide as a flat mushroom. The cooking
method is identical whatever the size; the time will vary,
however. When flat onions are unavailable, use the smallest
pickling onions you can find. If this dish is being served with
a grilled duck breast another time, you might like to turn the
rested duck breast in the onion pan juices. You could also add
a teaspoon more truffle butter, a pinch of chopped parsley or
other herbs. (See recipe picture on page 14.)**

Place the onions in a heavy-based saucepan and cover with
cold water. Bring to simmering point, then drain and run
under cold water. Peel, leaving the root ends intact.

Melt the butter in a small flameproof casserole dish with a lid
over medium heat. Roll the onions in the butter and add the stock,
then cook, covered, very gently over low heat for 15 minutes or
until a skewer slips easily into the onions without resistance; the
time will depend on their size. Do not add seasoning as the stock
will reduce greatly. (At this point, the onions and stock can be set
aside for an hour at room temperature or refrigerated if it will be
several hours or the next day before your main dish is ready to
serve.) Remove the root end from each onion.

To finish, place the dish over high heat and, watching closely,
shake, using a spoon to carefully turn the onions in the reducing
juices; they should be glazed and the pan juices well reduced and
sticky. Season very lightly with salt and pepper and serve.

Grilled apricot halves with
lemon-scented verbena ice-cream

12 apricots

½ cup (110 g) caster sugar

60 g unsalted butter

2 tablespoons Noilly Prat *or* Cognac

Lemon-scented verbena ice-cream
(see opposite), to serve

It goes without saying that it is only worth grilling apricots if they are of best quality and perfectly ripe. The fruit is never peeled. Apricots are quite acidic and need more sugar than other stone fruit. (See recipe picture on pages 20–21.)

Halve the apricots, put into a large bowl and sprinkle with the sugar. Leave at room temperature for 1 hour, by which time some juices will have formed in the bowl.

Place the butter in an ovenproof frying pan that will just fit the apricots in a single layer, then melt over medium heat. Lift the apricots from the sugary juices, reserving the juices, and place cut-side down in the pan. Leave the apricots to sizzle in the butter for 5 minutes or until the cut-side is golden and caramelised. Carefully turn, using a flexible spatula to keep the caramelised surface intact so the cut-side is uppermost. Spoon over the melted butter and the reserved sugary juices. Drizzle the apricots with a few drops of Noilly Prat or Cognac.

Preheat the oven griller heated to high setting, then grill the apricots for 1–2 minutes, so that the edges of each apricot half catch a little and become even more caramelised; a bit of scorch is even desirable! Cool a little before serving, as they will be very hot.

Serve with a scoop of lemon-scented verbena ice-cream.

Lemon-scented verbena ice-cream

1½ cups (375 ml) milk

½ cup (125 ml) thickened cream

½ cup (110 g) caster sugar

10 unsprayed lemon-scented
verbena leaves, washed

5 free-range egg yolks

The lemon-scented verbena bush is such a delight. It flowers right through spring and summer. The delicate sprays of pale-mauve flowers are held on long elegant arching stalks, perfect for a scented bouquet for a bedroom or bathroom. Do pick a spray to garnish each plate. Any extra ice-cream should be stored in a container with a well-fitting lid without too much extra space. It will be perfect for at least a week, probably much longer if it lasts that long. Always allow 30 minutes for the ice-cream to soften a bit before serving, if it has come straight from the freezer.

Place the milk, cream, half of the sugar and the verbena leaves in a small heavy-based saucepan over low heat to infuse for 1 hour, being careful not to reduce the volume of milk. Cool a little.

Using an electric mixer or hand-held electric beaters, whisk the egg yolks with the remaining sugar in a large bowl until light and foamy, then whisk in the strained warm milk and cream mixture, discarding the leaves.

Set up a bowl with a fine-mesh sieve resting over it before you start to cook the custard.

Rinse out the pan and pour in the milk mixture, then cook over medium heat for at least 10 minutes, stirring constantly with a wooden spoon, until the mixture thickens and coats the back of the spoon. (If you have a kitchen thermometer, 82–85°C is the temperature for a properly thickened custard.)

Strain the custard through the fine-mesh sieve into a bowl and cool completely in the refrigerator. Churn and freeze the mixture in an ice-cream machine according to the manufacturer's instructions.

Serve scoops of ice-cream with a spray or two of lemon verbena.

TIMETABLE FOR THE COOK

ONE WEEK BEFORE

- Plan to visit a farmers' market or a specialist greengrocer for super-special tomatoes (unless you have them in the garden)

TWO DAYS BEFORE

- Check **Ingredients List** and note what needs to be purchased
- Advise provedores of special requests (fresh duck/seafood)
- Check specialist equipment needed (sugar thermometer, ice-cream machine)
- Decide on table setting, including serving dishes
- Decide on wines – order if necessary
- Inspect tablecloth and napkins
- All shopping, including flowers
- Make ice-cream

DAY BEFORE

- Buy/collect shellfish and fish for stock, if making
- Make fish stock (or purchase best-quality stock)
- Make chicken stock (or purchase best-quality stock)
- Put bread onto a tray to dry a bit before making crumbs
- Chop 4 cloves garlic, store in bowl covered with extra virgin olive oil – refrigerate (see page 512)
- Pick parsley sprigs, wash, dry and cover – refrigerate in a paper towel–lined airtight container
- Blanch and braise flat onions – refrigerate with all juices

MORNING OF

Duck
- Scald duck, leave to dry 3 hours
- Parboil potatoes

Tomato dish
- Make *persillade*
- Prepare, bake and drain tomatoes
- Cover with *persillade* and place in gratin dish or baking tray

Mussels and pipis
- Rinse, remove beards, place in wide pan with lid

Green salad
- Wash, dry and crisp salad leaves
- Prepare dressing in bowl with crossed salad servers ready to toss before serving

Apricots
- Macerate apricots in sugar for 1 hour
- Cook apricots in butter
- Turn apricots and arrange in ovenproof roasting pan for last-minute grilling

- Chill wine, if appropriate
- Set table

AFTERNOON OF

Mussel and pipi pilaf
- Cook shallot, fennel and garlic for pilaf, stir in rice – do not refrigerate
- Steam mussels and pipis open, discard top shells, reserve strained juices, cover to prevent drying

Duck
- Place braised onions and juices in suitable pan for reheating

ONE HOUR BEFORE GUESTS ARRIVE

Note: The duck takes over 1 hour to cook, so this will occur while the dishes for the other courses are completed, served and enjoyed – a kitchen timer will be essential.

Duck
- Preheat oven to 220°C
- Place duck in oven for 20 minutes (set timer)
- Place pan with onions and juices on stovetop – do not heat yet
- Put pan of water on for peas

Mussel pilaf
- Bring fish stocks to simmer, add to pilaf and cook for 25 minutes (set timer)
- Place mussels and pipis in pan with butter

- Get changed

GUESTS ARRIVE

- Warm plates and serving dishes (see page 512)
- Stuffed tomatoes into oven for 20 minutes (set timer)
- Reduce oven to 180°C – place potatoes around duck and roast for 20 minutes (set timer)

DINNER IS SERVED

- Serve stuffed tomatoes
- Continue to roast duck for
  20 minutes (set timer)

SECOND COURSE

- Toss shellfish in pan with
  butter until bubbling
- Mix with hot rice
- Serve pilaf
- Meanwhile, pour off duck fat
  carefully, then roast for another
  20 minutes (set timer)

THIRD/MAIN COURSE

- Test duck with skewer –
  if cooked, remove from oven
  and leave to rest
- Potatoes back into oven –
  reduce oven to 120°C
- Cut duck into portions and
  make sauce
- Reheat onions and blanch peas
- Serve duck
- Meanwhile, remove ice-cream
  from freezer

DESSERT

- Preheat griller and grill apricots
- Serve apricots and ice-cream

INGREDIENTS LIST

PANTRY

- Sea salt
- Fine salt
- Australian extra virgin olive oil
- Red-wine vinegar
- Panko breadcrumbs
- Red rice
- Caster sugar

SPICE SHELF

- Black peppercorns

REFRIGERATOR

- Butter
- Free-range eggs
- Milk
- Thickened cream
- Good-quality purchased fish
  stock (if making homemade,
  see page 506)
- Good-quality purchased
  chicken stock (if making
  homemade, see page 505)

GREENGROCER/FARMERS'
MARKET (OR GARDEN)

- Flat-leaf parsley
- Thyme
- Lemon-scented verbena
- Garlic
- 4 × 150 g ripe tomatoes or 2 ×
  250 g beefsteak-style tomatoes
- 8 flat onions
- 400 g peas in pod
- 1 bulb fennel (save fronds)
- 2 French shallots
- 4 all-purpose potatoes,
  such as Nicola or desiree
- 12 apricots, as large as possible
- Selection of salad leaves

BUTCHER/POULTRY SUPPLIER

- 1 × 2 kg duck

FISHMONGER

- 500 g black mussels
- 300 g pipis or clams (vongole)

BAKER

- Day-old white loaf for
  breadcrumbs, if not using
  panko crumbs
- Bread for dinner

CELLAR

- Dry white wine for pilaf
  and duck
- Noilly Prat vermouth
  or Cognac for apricots
- Wine for the table
- Soft drink

VALENTINE'S DAY

A DINNER FOR 2

ONION-CHEESE PUFFS

MUSHROOM LASAGNE
with PORCINI

TROUT
with VERJUICE, SORREL & GRAPES

GREEN SALAD

BROWN-SUGAR
MERINGUES
with SALTED CARAMEL CREAM

CHRISTINE'S
ROSE-PETAL LIQUEUR

2

I claim to be the very first restaurateur to host a Valentine's Day menu in Melbourne. I searched and found the original handwritten menu, scattered with hearts, dated 14th February 1986. I would be interested to know if any restaurateur out there thinks they celebrated Valentine's Day any earlier than this.

In 1986, business was patchy and I was trying to think of enticing new ideas to bring in the crowds. I had always scorned the very idea of Valentine's Day – commercial rubbish imported from the United States – who had ever heard of it in Australia? Who had ever received a Valentine's Day card or bunch of roses? But undeniably, romance was a good story. And there were plenty of romantics out there who seized on the idea.

The following year there were many Valentine's Day dinners, and lunches in restaurants across Melbourne. Restaurants were full of tables for two – not necessarily good for business in fact, with a table of two occupying the place where usually there would be six or eight. By then, the public had been convinced that giving roses and chocolates and sending cards was the thing to do in mid-February. And, at Stephanie's Restaurant, we continued to rack our brains to think of 'romantic' food.

I must say the menu reads quite well from the vantage point of 2016, and the all-inclusive price is interesting! I toyed with the idea of reproducing the dishes here, but decided it should remain an historic document. The menu I propose instead is very suitable for any romantic occasion – a birthday or anniversary, or just to remind yourselves of how happy you are together. I have added a little sea salt to the caramel cream to reflect the current interest in this contrast of sharp saltiness and intensely sweet – leave it out if you prefer.

For the record, here is the menu for that first dinner.

Stephanie's Restaurant
Valentine's Day, 1986

————

1979 Vintage Pol Roger on arrival

The perfect match
Tomatoes and basil

Opal and cinnamon basils with red and yellow tomatoes
and Liquorice basil jelly
1983 Petaluma Chardonnay

Sweethearts
Crayfish hearts in a crayfish fumet and butter sauce
1983 Meursault 'Charmes' 1er cru Domaine Rene Monnier

A pair of love birds
Roasted quail, spiced pepper mix, noodles tossed
with cucumber and a pickled plum
1983 Seville Estate Pinot Noir

Three goat-y cheeses
With our buttermilk and rye bread
1983 Penfolds Magill Estate
- limited release -

Quince and angelica nougat icecream
Passionfruit caramel syrup
1984 Yalumba Heggies Botrytis Rhine Riesling

Coffee and tuiles
Victorian port muscat or Tokay

A heart to share
Chocolates handmade by Brendan Hill

All inclusive cost $85.00 per person

A year ago I was invited to participate in the Dunedin Writers and Readers Festival. I thoroughly enjoyed my first visit to this elegant city in New Zealand's South Island and met many interesting people, amongst them, potter Christine Boswijk, whose work is represented in major galleries in New Zealand and further afield. Christine is also an enthusiastic gardener and foodlover; she described to me some of the things she grows in what must be a most beautiful garden property. She makes a rose-scented liqueur, the recipe gleaned from an old Spanish cookbook, where it was claimed that it originated in the 11th century, originally made with roses from Valencia. When Christine sent me pictures of a lush pile of her own gorgeous Charles de Mills rose petals and her finished liqueur in stoppered glass bottles, I decided I simply must make it. I think a small glass of this fragrant rose-pink liqueur would be a most appropriate finish to a romantic dinner. Christine tells me she serves it on ice in the Depression-era glasses she collects.

My other concession to romance, and to heart-shaped anything, is to note that the butterflied trout, when presented on an oval platter, does look a bit like a heart. And if anyone can be persuaded to peel a grape for their loved one, Valentine's Day might be the perfect occasion!

Onion-cheese puffs

2 teaspoons extra virgin olive oil

½ small onion, finely diced

½ cup (150 g) Homemade Mayonnaise (see page 502)

1 tablespoon finely grated parmesan, plus extra to serve

2 tablespoons grated cheddar

2 tablespoons finely chopped flat-leaf parsley

sea salt and freshly ground black pepper

8 slices wholemeal or seeded bread

The quantities given will make far more than needed for two people – enough for eight in fact. However, as this delicious preparation freezes well, it is perfect to have on hand when a savoury treat is required at short notice. The cheese mixture can be frozen in a container as is, or already spread on the baked bread rounds. Plan to use them within a week or so, and bake them from frozen for best results (they may take an extra 5 minutes).

Preheat the oven to 180°C. Line a baking tray with baking paper.

Heat the olive oil in a small heavy-based saucepan, then saute the onion, covered, for 5 minutes or until well softened. Transfer to a bowl and leave to cool, then mix with the mayonnaise, cheeses and parsley and season with salt and pepper.

Remove the crusts from the bread, if you wish. Using a 4 cm round biscuit cutter, cut the bread into 32 rounds. Place on the lined tray and bake, without turning, for 10–15 minutes or until golden.

Preheat the oven griller to high. Spread about 1 teaspoon of the cheese and onion mixture on each round, right to the edge, then sprinkle with more parmesan and brown under the griller for 1–2 minutes.

Serve immediately.

Mushroom lasagne with porcini

10 g dried porcini

200 ml hot water

1 tablespoon extra virgin olive oil, plus extra for drizzling

30 g butter, plus extra for buttering and dotting

1 French shallot, finely chopped

½ cup (125 ml) Homemade Tomato Sauce (see page 502) or good-quality purchased tomato passata

250 g flat mushrooms, thickly sliced, including the stems

1 tablespoon chopped flat-leaf parsley

sea salt and freshly ground black pepper

175 g dried lasagne sheets, cooked (see page 501)

1 quantity Bechamel Sauce (see page 503)

90 g finely grated parmesan

freshly grated nutmeg

The quantities given here will fill a smallish lasagne dish (mine is 20 cm × 14 cm, which holds approximately 600 ml). The recipe could be doubled to serve 4–6 on another occasion. I frequently buy ready-made fresh lasagne sheets, however, I always precook them in boiling water, even though the packet says there is no need to. I find the pasta layers become thinner and more tender after an initial swim in boiling water.

Soak the porcini in the hot water for 30 minutes. Lift the porcini out, then rinse under cold water, pat dry and roughly chop. Set aside. Filter the soaking liquid through your finest mesh sieve lined with a damp sheet of paper towel over a bowl, reserving the liquid.

Heat the olive oil and butter in a large heavy-based saucepan over high heat and saute the shallot for 3 minutes or until soft. Add the porcini, reserved soaking water and tomato sauce and stir. Bring to the boil, then cover and reduce the heat to medium. Cook for 5 minutes or until the liquid has almost evaporated. Add the flat mushroom, then cook, covered, for 5 minutes. Increase the heat to high, add the parsley and season to taste with salt and pepper. Cook briskly, uncovered, stirring frequently for 6–8 minutes or until all the liquid has evaporated. Taste for seasoning and season if desired. Set aside.

Make the bechamel sauce, then stir in 40 g of the parmesan. Cook for a further 5 minutes on a simmer mat over low heat. Season to taste with salt, pepper and nutmeg. Keep warm or, if the assembly is delayed, warm the sauce briefly in a microwave-safe container in the microwave; it must be easily spreadable.

Preheat the oven to 200°C. Butter the lasagne dish very well and assemble as follows:

Layer One
Pasta, one-third of the mushroom mixture, one-quarter of the bechamel, one-quarter of the grated parmesan

Layer Two
Pasta, one-third of the mushroom mixture, one-quarter of the bechamel, one-quarter of the parmesan

Layer Three
Pasta, final third of the mushroom mixture, one-quarter of the bechamel, one-quarter of the parmesan

Layer Four
Pasta, rest of the bechamel, rest of the parmesan.
Dot with tiny pieces of butter.

Cover loosely with foil and bake for 30 minutes; remove the foil for the final 5 minutes. Leave the lasagne to rest for 10 minutes before cutting. (Providing the dish is suitable, leftover lasagne can be reheated in the dish in a microwave for about 2 minutes.)

Trout with verjuice, sorrel and grapes

6 small (pickling) onions *or* French shallots (whichever are the daintiest)

½ cup (125 ml) verjuice (see page 513)

12 large red grapes (peeled, if you wish)

1 × 400 g rainbow trout, skin on, butterflied

sea salt and freshly ground black pepper

1 tablespoon plain flour

2 tablespoons extra virgin olive oil

20 g unsalted butter

2 large handfuls trimmed sorrel leaves (central stalk removed), cut or torn into large pieces (if unavailable, use baby spinach leaves)

lemon wedges and Green Salad (see page 503), to serve

VERJUICE SAUCE

2–3 French shallots, very finely chopped (to yield 1 tablespoon)

1 sprig thyme

½ cup (125 ml) verjuice (see page 513)

2 teaspoons thickened cream

80 g unsalted butter

juice of ½ lemon

sea salt and freshly ground black pepper

Hopefully you have an obliging fishmonger who will butterfly the trout for you. This dramatic way of presenting the fish requires an oval serving dish. An oval frying pan is a great asset – even if it is not beautiful enough for service, it will make the cooking much easier. If the shallots you use for the sauce are pink, they will add a rosy hue. And I have to admit that I never peel the grapes!

Place the onions or shallots in a small saucepan and cover with cold water. Bring to the boil, then drain. Run under cold water, then peel. Return to the pan and cover with the verjuice, then cook, covered, over medium heat for 10–15 minutes or until tender; the time will depend on size. Drop the grapes into the pan and set aside.

To make the sauce, put the shallot, thyme and verjuice into a small heavy-based saucepan and simmer over medium heat for 5–8 minutes or until the verjuice has almost evaporated; the shallot will look very soft and moist. Add the cream and cook for 1 more minute. Reserve.

Meanwhile, preheat the oven to 110°C and place a heatproof serving plate and small ovenproof saucepan or jug inside to warm.

Season the trout with salt and pepper on both sides and dip into the flour, shaking off the excess. Heat the olive oil and butter together in a heavy-based ovenproof frying pan (oval for preference that fits the trout in 1 layer), over high heat until the butter has melted and the foam starts to subside. Place the trout in the pan, skin-side down, reduce the heat to medium and cook for 5 minutes. Using a wide egg lifter, turn the trout and cook for 2 minutes, then transfer, skin-side down, to the warm serving plate in the oven. Drop the sorrel or spinach into the buttery juices, increase the heat to high and stir for 2–3 minutes. Add the onions and grapes, then transfer to the oven.

Reheat the verjuice reduction and whisk in the butter. Add the lemon juice and taste for seasoning, then strain into the warm pan or jug.

Spoon the onions, grapes and sorrel or spinach around the fish and pour over the sauce or serve in the pan. Serve with lemon wedges to the side.

Brown-sugar meringues
with salted caramel cream

40 g light brown sugar

2 free-range egg whites (60 ml)

50 g caster sugar

SALTED CARAMEL CREAM

90 g caster sugar

90 ml water

1½ tablespoons espresso coffee

1 cup (250 ml) thickened cream

sea salt

These subtly-flavoured meringues are especially luscious when sandwiched with the caramel cream. Valentine's Day cooking presents a special challenge for the home cook, as one cannot make just four meringues or a tiny quantity of caramel cream. Leftover caramel cream can fill a sponge cake, or be served with poached fruit. It will keep in an airtight container in the refrigerator but will need to be used within a few days.

Preheat the oven to 120°C. Line 2 baking trays with baking paper.

Sift the brown sugar into a bowl and set aside. Using an electric mixer or hand-held electric beaters, beat the egg whites until soft peaks form. With the motor running, add one-third of the caster sugar at a time, beating well after each addition, until the whites are glossy and thick. With the motor still running, 'rain' in the brown sugar, as if it was polenta, until well combined.

Spoon or pipe tablespoon-sized blobs of meringue onto the trays, leaving space between; I use a spoon as I like the little swirls and peaks the spoon creates, so please yourself. (Alternatively, spoon heaped teaspoonfuls, if you are making tiny meringues.)

Bake the meringues for 50 minutes or until firm. Turn the oven off and prop the door open with a wooden spoon, then leave until the meringues are quite cold. Store in an airtight container.

To make the salted caramel cream, place the sugar and ¼ cup (60 ml) of the water in a small heavy-based saucepan. Bring to the boil over medium heat to dissolve the sugar, then increase the heat to high and boil for 5 minutes or until you have a medium–dark caramel; do not stir. Carefully pour in the coffee and remaining water, stirring, until the caramel is smooth again. Boil to reduce for 1 minute or until a drop looks and feels syrupy on a cold saucer. Leave to cool.

Using an electric mixer, whip the cream to soft peaks. Stop the motor and scoop all of the caramel over the cream. (If you do this with the motor running, all of the thick caramel will be spun onto the sides of the mixing bowl instead of on the cream.) Whip again until well blended and firm. Stir in a few flakes of sea salt.

Sandwich as many pairs of meringues as you wish to serve with a little caramel cream. Leave to soften for 30 minutes, then enjoy.

Christine's rose-petal liqueur

250 g unsprayed rose petals (from about 25 large fully opened roses)

2½ cups (400 g) pure icing sugar

1 cup (250 ml) water

1 teaspoon coriander seeds

600 ml vodka *or* grappa

Be warned – you need to start this recipe at least one month before you intend to serve it. The most important ingredient here is unsprayed, highly fragrant red or rose-pink roses. Lots of them! One of my favourites is Papa Meilland, but every rose fancier will have a favourite scented deeply-coloured rose variety. Christine says she has a hedge of Charles de Mills roses she uses for this each year. She serves her liqueur in some of her collection of etched Depression-era glasses. This distinctive glassware was mass produced for sale at extremely low prices during the Depression years in the United States. It was distributed as an incentive to purchase goods or services and is now highly collectable. My friend has not told me how long her liqueur lasts, but she mentioned she still had some from the previous season, so probably up to one year.

Gather the rose petals very early in the morning. Remove the white part of each petal with scissors, but do not wash them.

Place the icing sugar and water in a small heavy-based saucepan over low heat. Stir to dissolve the sugar, then maintain at simmering point for 5 minutes to make a syrup. Add the rose petals and coriander seeds. Cook over low heat for another 5 minutes. Remove from the heat and leave to cool.

Pour into a 2 litre capacity sterilised jar (see page 513) and add the vodka or grappa. Cover with a lid or plastic film to prevent dust or ants getting into the mixture. (If you have an ant problem, it is prudent to stand the jar inside another container half-filled with cold water to prevent them finding this sweet treat.)

Store in a cool, dark place for at least 1 month, then filter through something very fine, such as coffee filter paper. Transfer to a sterilised glass bottle or decanter with a stopper.

TIMETABLE FOR THE COOK

ONE MONTH BEFORE

Rose-petal liqueur
· Find 250 g spray-free fragrant
  red roses
· Snip white part of petals
· Infuse rose-petal liqueur

ONE WEEK BEFORE

· Check **Ingredients List** and
  note what needs to be purchased
· Advise provedores of special
  requests (butterflied large
  rainbow trout)
· Check specialist equipment needed
  (oval pan for cooking trout)

TWO DAYS BEFORE

· Decide on table setting,
  including serving dishes
· Decide on wines –
  order if necessary
· Inspect tablecloth and napkins
· All shopping, including flowers
· Make onion-cheese puff filling –
  refrigerate
· Make brown sugar meringues –
  store in an airtight container
· Filter rose-petal liqueur

DAY BEFORE

· Collect fish

Lasagne
· Make mushroom filling
· Make bechamel
· Grate parmesan
· Cook lasagne sheets
· Assemble lasagne in dishes –
  refrigerate

MORNING OF

Onion-cheese puffs
· Cut and bake croutons

Trout
· Prepare sorrel or spinach
· Squeeze lemon juice

Green salad
· Wash, dry and crisp salad leaves
· Prepare salad dressing in salad
  bowl with crossed salad servers
  ready to toss before serving

Meringues
· Make caramel cream
· Sandwich meringues
  with caramel cream

· Set table
· Chill wine, if appropriate

AFTERNOON OF

Trout
· Cook onions with verjuice,
  add grapes
· Make shallot and thyme reduction
· Measure butter for sauce

TWO HOURS
BEFORE COMPANION ARRIVES

· Assemble onion-cheese puffs
  on croutons
· Get changed

DINNER IS SERVED

FIRST COURSE

· Preheat oven to 200°C
· Grill croutons until bubbling

SECOND COURSE

· Bake lasagne at 200°C for
  30 minutes
· Remove lasagne and leave
  for 10 minutes
· Reduce oven to 110°C
  and warm trout plate
· Serve

THIRD/MAIN COURSE

· Cook trout
· Finish sauce and serve

DESSERT

· Serve meringues with
  rose-petal liqueur

INGREDIENTS LIST

PANTRY

· Sea salt
· Fine salt
· Australian extra virgin olive oil
· Red-wine vinegar
· Plain flour
· Caster sugar
· Light brown sugar
· Pure icing sugar
· Verjuice
· Tomato passata
  (or Homemade Tomato
  Sauce, see page 502)
· 175 g dried lasagne sheets
· 10 g dried porcini
· Espresso coffee beans

SPICE SHELF

· Black peppercorns
· Nutmeg (whole)
· Coriander seeds

REFRIGERATOR

· Unsalted butter
· Milk
· 260 ml thickened cream
· Free-range eggs
· 120 g parmesan
· Cheddar

GREENGROCER/FARMERS' MARKET (OR GARDEN)

· Flat-leaf parsley
· Thyme
· 2 large handfuls sorrel leaves
  or baby spinach leaves
· Selection of salad leaves
· 250 g edible rose petals (or
  petals from about 25 large
  fully opened unsprayed roses)
· 7 small (pickling) onions
· 4 French shallots
· 250 g flat mushrooms
· 12 large red grapes
· 1 lemon (plus an extra lemon
  if making mayonnaise)

FISHMONGER

· 1 × 400 g rainbow trout,
  skin on, butterflied
  (order in advance)

BAKER

· 8 slices wholemeal or
  seeded bread
· Bread for the table

CELLAR

· 600 ml vodka or grappa
· Wine for the table
· Soft drink

JAMAICAN
JERK
PARTY

A LUNCH FOR 8

BEEF PATTIES

———

BARBECUED
JERK CHICKEN

RICE & PEAS

CALLALOO
with SWEET POTATO

BAKED PLANTAINS
with MAPLE SYRUP

———

PINEAPPLE CHUNKS
with RUM

3   If you have a great barbecue, consider a jerk party – it will be lots of fun. Start with a hand-around tray of delicious beef patties, a hugely popular Jamaican snack, on sale at every beach shack and wherever people gather. A jerk party should be noisy and a bit crowded. It should be impossible to turn around without bumping into someone, ideal as a way of introducing people.

I tasted my first jerk chicken in Jamaica in the 60s, and my most recent one a few months ago at a great party in my daughter's yard. As her dad was Jamaican, she claims a special feel for the national dish. In between, I have tasted quite a few in Jamaica, ranging from absolutely delicious – juicy, spicy, just off the grill – to dry, stringy and cold. It is usual for a traditional dish such as this to have many versions, each one with its devotees who swear it is the true one. There is the dry rub school and the wet marinade school.

Said to have originated with the Arawaks, the indigenous inhabitants of the island, jerk chicken or pork is first marinated with a range of spices that must include plenty of pimiento (allspice), fiery Scotch bonnet chilli and usually black pepper as well. The pimiento tree produces the berries that we call allspice. I was told that, if the berries are picked green and soaked in rum, the drink is very good for stomachache. The leaves, when crushed, are highly aromatic, and the wood is considered essential for a proper jerk fire.

If you stop at a jerk shack along the roadside in Jamaica, make sure that your bit of jerk is just coming off the coals, so that you can count on juiciness, along with it actually having been cooked over the fire! Say no to an already chopped pile of fragments keeping warm on one side. Every jerk shack or stall will have a list of side dishes available. It will always offer rice and peas, and sometimes festival – a slightly sweet deep-fried stick of dough made from a mix of wheat and corn flours. It has to be said that festival is very solid, meaning filling and inexpensive, making it popular with locals.

On my last trip to Jamaica, my daughter and I happened upon a great jerk shack called Packy Pond – 'Boston-style', which was a reference to Boston Bay in the Parish of Portland, considered the island's 'best' jerk. Smiling, handsome Carl had an impressive coal fire burning in a traditional iron drum, split from top to bottom and turned on its side. Over the top of the fire was a metal grill. Dried pimiento branches fuelled the fire and were progressively pushed further into the fire as the first lot of coals crumbled. Iron pots were balanced directly on the coals. The chalked menu board offered tripe and beans; rice and peas; jerk pork; yams; curried goat; and callaloo, a green vegetable that we know as amaranth. We chose rice and peas, curried goat and some jerk pork with callaloo, eaten with a plastic spoon from a tin plate. I could only imagine that the owner-chef was catering to locals, as this track was way off any main road, located on a bone-shaking scenic route between the north coast and Treasure Beach. This jerk was one of the good ones.

Jerk chicken or pork makes great party food. It ought to be eaten with your fingers, or off a tin plate, preferably in someone's yard with reggae playing and Red Stripe beer available. Cook the rice and peas on page 53 in a rice cooker and leave on the table for self-service. We also like to roast some plantains dribbled with maple syrup (see page 56). If you can find amaranth, you could also add a big pot of callaloo. These leafy greens are available in Asian food stores. Mostly dark green, sometimes streaked with purple, in Jamaica callaloo is a popular soup ingredient. On many a jerk stall, I was offered a small bowl of the leaves simmered with onions, chillies and sometimes a bit of coconut milk or, as in the recipe on page 57, sweet potato.

There is a recipe in *The Cook's Companion* for a Jamaican sweet potato pudding, which is intriguing but very solid and sweet. It would be too heavy after this robust menu – a better finish would be chunked pineapple, natural or grilled, dribbled with a bit of rum (see page 58).

Beef patties

2 tablespoons olive oil

½ onion, finely chopped

2 cloves garlic, chopped

1 fresh small red chilli, finely
chopped (or more to taste)

200 g minced beef

2 teaspoons Indian-style
curry paste

2 tablespoons fresh breadcrumbs

6 whole allspice, coarsely crushed

1 teaspoon thyme leaves

100 g tomato paste (puree)

sea salt and freshly ground
black pepper

1 free-range egg

pinch fine salt

LARD PASTRY

1 cup (150 g) plain flour,
plus extra for dusting

1 cup (150 g) self-raising flour

2 teaspoons turmeric

2 teaspoons fine salt

100 g lard, at room temperature,
broken into 2 or 3 pieces

½ cup (125 ml) cold water

Although these look similar to empanadas, the pastry is quite different – more biscuit-like – and the filling is often very spicy indeed. I have used one chilli but you could double this for chilli lovers. While lard went out of favour for a while, the Allowrie brand has recently become available in larger supermarkets. Lard freezes very well, so extra blocks can be stored for another time.

To make the pastry, put the flours, turmeric and salt into a food processor and whizz to combine. Add the lard and pulse for about 30 seconds, then add the water and pulse to combine quickly. Tip onto a lightly floured workbench and knead to just bring together into a smooth dough. Flatten into a disc, wrap in plastic film and refrigerate to chill for 30 minutes or longer. Bring to room temperature for 15 minutes before rolling.

Meanwhile, prepare the filling. Heat half of the olive oil in a heavy-based frying pan over medium heat and saute the onion, garlic and chilli until the onion is soft. Drain in a sieve and discard the oil. Add the remaining olive oil to the pan and increase the heat to high. Saute the beef until browned, stirring to break up any clumps and ensure it browns evenly. Add the curry paste. Return the onion mixture to the pan, then add the breadcrumbs, allspice, thyme and tomato paste. Cook, stirring, for 3–4 minutes, then taste and adjust the seasoning. Set aside to cool.

Preheat the oven to 200°C.

Divide the pastry into 8 even pieces and roll each one on a floured workbench to form a 12 cm-long rectangle. Put a generous tablespoon of filling onto the centre of each pastry piece. Dampen the pastry edges with water, fold over to cover the filling, then trim to form a traditional half-moon or 'purse' shape. Press the edges together firmly with a fork. Whisk the egg with a pinch of salt.

Line a baking tray with baking paper, then place the patties on the tray and brush with beaten egg. Bake for 25–30 minutes or until golden brown. Eat warm or at room temperature.

Barbecued jerk chicken

2 kg free-range chicken pieces (drumsticks, thighs on the bone, with skin on)

1½ tablespoons extra virgin olive oil

JERK MARINADE

1½ tablespoons whole allspice

1½ tablespoons black peppercorns

1 teaspoon ground cinnamon

1 teaspoon ground nutmeg

1 tablespoon picked thyme leaves

6 spring onions, chopped (use the white part and most of the green)

3 small fresh red chillies or Scotch bonnet chillies (extra hot chillies for the serious chilli lover), finely chopped

1½ tablespoons dark brown sugar

3 teaspoons fine salt

¼ cup (60 ml) dark soy sauce

juice of 2 limes

1½ tablespoons extra virgin olive oil

This recipe is moderately hot. If you are unsure of the heat tolerance of your guests, perhaps keep the marinade moderate and have a purchased hot pepper sauce available for those who like it extra hot. All chillies need to be handled with care, so it is best to use disposable kitchen gloves when slicing or seeding them. Scrub your chopping board and knives and your hands really well and use a nailbrush to brush underneath your fingernails after handling them. I find a blender does a better job of reducing the ingredients to a paste than a food processor. While I prefer to barbecue this on a grill plate, in Jamaica it would be grilled on a flat sheet of iron, so please yourself. (See recipe pictures on pages 50 and 51.)

For the marinade, wrap the allspice and peppercorns in a clean dry tea towel and pound with a mallet or a heavy rolling pin to crush them both. Tip into a blender and add the cinnamon, nutmeg, thyme, spring onion, chilli, sugar, salt, soy sauce, lime juice and olive oil. Blend to form a coarse paste.

Scrape the marinade into a large glass bowl, add the chicken and, wearing disposable kitchen gloves, massage the marinade into the meat, making sure you also rub it underneath the skin. Cover and marinate in the refrigerator for at least 6 hours, or overnight. (I slip the marinated chicken pieces into a large oven bag and fold it closed, so that the aromas do not transfer to other things in the refrigerator.)

Preheat the oven to 180°C. Select a baking dish large enough to hold the chicken pieces in a single layer and add the olive oil.

Tip the chicken into the oiled baking dish, reserving any marinade still in the oven bag or bowl to brush on the chicken later. Bake for 45 minutes or until a skewer easily penetrates the thickest part of one of the thigh pieces. (It can be prepared to this stage 1 hour before barbecuing. Keep in a cool place, covered tightly to prevent insect attack. If longer, then refrigerate, allowing extra time on the barbecue for the pieces to become really hot in the centre.)

Just before serving, heat a barbecue to high heat, brush the chicken with any leftover marinade, then sear, turning for 15 minutes, until slightly charred and crisp on all sides and thoroughly hot right to the centre of each piece and the marinade is heated through. Serve at once.

Rice and peas

100 g red kidney beans
(these are the 'peas'), soaked
overnight in cold water

1 clove garlic, chopped

3 cups (750 ml) water

1½ cups (375 ml) coconut milk

2 tablespoons moist flakes coconut
(see page 512)

1 spring onion, finely chopped

1 generous teaspoon picked
thyme leaves

1 small fresh red chilli

sea salt and freshly ground
black pepper

1 cup (200 g) long-grain rice

**Rice and peas is a much-loved side dish for family meals in
Jamaica. There are many combinations of pulses and grains
such as this in countries where other forms of protein are harder
to come by, and much more expensive, so these dishes form an
important part of the traditional diet. Probably every cook in
Jamaica has a slightly different version. You will need to soak
the kidney beans overnight before proceeding with the recipe.
(See recipe picture on page 51.)**

Drain the soaked kidney beans and rinse under cold running water.
Put the kidney beans, garlic and water into a heavy-based saucepan
and bring slowly to the boil over medium heat. Reduce the heat to
low–medium and cook, covered, for 1½ hours or until the kidney
beans are tender, stirring from time to time to make sure there is
still water in the pan and the beans are not sticking.

Tip into a large bowl and add the coconut milk, coconut flakes,
spring onion, thyme and whole chilli, then season with salt and
pepper. Add the rice and stir to mix. Transfer the rice and bean
mixture to a rice cooker and set it to cook. (Alternatively, if you do
not have a rice cooker, return the mixture to the pan, then cover
and bring to the boil. Reduce the heat to low and cook for 20 minutes
or until all the liquid is absorbed.)

Serve in a bowl alongside the other dishes.

Callaloo with sweet potato

2 tablespoons extra virgin olive oil

1 large onion, finely diced

200 g sweet potato, peeled and cut into 1 cm dice

2 cloves garlic, finely chopped with 1 teaspoon fine salt

2 teaspoons picked thyme leaves

1 small fresh red chilli, seeded and thinly sliced

250 g amaranth *or* silverbeet leaves, coarsely shredded (weighed after removing the stems), well washed

½ cup (125 ml) coconut milk

freshly ground black pepper

Known as amaranth in Australia, callaloo is the name of a leafy green vegetable, as well as this moist side dish frequently served alongside jerk chicken or pork. Sold as *yin choy* in Asian vegetable markets, callaloo is also well known to Greek and Turkish cooks. It is very easy to grow. If you manage to locate the real thing, remove the leaves from the strong central stem, so you have 'bouquets' of leaves attached to small tender stems. The flavour is earthy and spinach-y, and said to be more tender than silverbeet. I wonder about that, as the silverbeet I grow is very tender indeed. Local West Indians have been asked where they buy their callaloo and the consensus is that they do not – they use silverbeet or spinach. If you wish to double the recipe you will need two very large frying pans. (See recipe picture on pages 54–55.)

Heat the oil in a wide (at least 24 cm) heavy-based frying pan over medium heat and add the onion. Cook, covered, over low heat until the onion has softened. Add the sweet potato, garlic, thyme and chilli. Stir to mix. Increase the heat to medium, then cook, covered, for 5–6 minutes, stirring at least once. Add the amaranth or silverbeet and any water still clinging to the leaves. Press a lid onto the bulging greens until they have wilted down, then uncover, stir and pour in the coconut milk.

Cook, covered, for 2–3 minutes or until the sweet potato and greens are tender. Taste for salt and season with pepper. Uncover and increase the heat to high to quickly reduce the liquid; the dish should be moist but not sloppy. Serve in a deep plate or bowl alongside the other dishes.

Serves 8

Baked plantains with maple syrup

4 plantains, skin yellow to brown

1 tablespoon olive oil

2 tablespoons water

½ cup (175 g) pure maple syrup

In Jamaica green plantains are fried and eaten as chips. Ripe plantains, where the skin is almost black, are not rotten as you might think, but are ready to be baked or fried as a side dish or made into a plantain tart. I have enjoyed flattened slices of half-ripe plantains fried in lard, called *tostades* in Mexico. Buy plantains well in advance of your party as they are almost always sold green. Having said that, the plantains I bought at a specialist shop supplying Melbourne's Spanish and Portuguese community were definitely yellow, with a few brown splashes. I wrapped them in newspaper and kept them at room temperature for a day or so to further ripen. They were delicious.

Over the years, readers have been astonished by the recipe in *The Cook's Companion* for a homely meatloaf baked with regular bananas, which was a family favourite when I was young. I now realise it would have been even better if Mum had access to ripe plantains! (See recipe picture on pages 54–55.)

Preheat the oven to 200°C.

Using a small, sharp knife, chop each plantain into 4 chunky pieces. Peel and discard half the skin from one side of each piece and put the pieces into a bowl, then tip in the olive oil. Stir to coat all sides, then transfer to a baking dish large enough to hold them in a single layer. Add the water to prevent them burning. Spoon over half of the maple syrup.

Bake the plantains for 15 minutes, then inspect and shake the dish to ensure they are not sticking. (The final cooking is best on the barbecue plate alongside the jerk chicken. As they will almost certainly stick to the barbecue plate, transfer them to a foil baking dish before the final drizzle with maple syrup. Do not move the pieces until you transfer them to the serving platter.)

Add the remaining maple syrup and bake or barbecue for a further 15 minutes, until tender and glazed.

Pineapple chunks with rum

1 ripe pineapple

rum, for drizzling

banana leaves, for serving
(optional)

Jamaica is famous for its rum, which comes in all types but is often overproof and very potent. I think a golden rum with plenty of flavour is best for this dish. On another occasion, these pineapple skewers could be grilled on the barbecue.

Remove the skin and all the eyes from the pineapple. Cut in half lengthwise, then cut each half into 4 sections, also lengthwise. Slice away the hard core and push each chunk onto a long skewer.

Arrange the skewers on a plate and drizzle the rum over. Arrange on a flat platter, perhaps lined with banana leaves for extra atmosphere. Serve.

TIMETABLE FOR THE COOK

TWO WEEKS BEFORE

- Check **Ingredients List** and note what needs to be purchased
- Check specialist equipment needed (wood-fired barbecue; disposable kitchen gloves)
- Advise provedores/suppliers of special requests (ripe plantains)
- Decide on wines, Red Stripe beer and West Indian rum – order if necessary

THREE DAYS BEFORE

- Decide on table setting, including serving dishes
- Inspect tablecloth and napkins (ensure adequate supply of napkins for sticky fingers)
- Inspect barbecue (clean if necessary) and check barbecue fuel
- Inspect outdoor furniture
- Contingency plan for rain?
- All shopping, including flowers

TWO DAYS BEFORE

- Chop 5 garlic cloves and cover with extra virgin olive oil (see page 512) – refrigerate
- Chop 4 small fresh red chillies – cover and refrigerate
- Chop 3 Scotch bonnet chillies – cover and refrigerate
- Make beef patty filling – refrigerate
- Make chicken marinade – cover and refrigerate
- Soak kidney beans overnight

ONE DAY BEFORE

- Make beef patty pastry
- Marinate chicken and refrigerate in oven bag
- Prepare callaloo (or silverbeet) and sweet potato
- Cook kidney beans
- Chill beer

MORNING OF

Plantains
- Bake plantain chunks – transfer to container for final glaze on barbecue

Beef patties
- Assemble and bake

Jerk chicken
- Bake, cool and cover chicken

Callaloo
- Cook amaranth or silverbeet and sweet potato

Beans and rice
- Assemble ingredients in rice cooker

Pineapple
- Cut pineapple and drizzle with rum

- Assemble drinks station and chill wine
- Set table

THIRTY MINUTES BEFORE GUESTS ARRIVE

- Preheat oven to 150°C and heat beef patties for 10 minutes (set timer)
- Turn barbecue on to high
- Flick rice cooker switch on
- Have serving plates and napkins ready
- Set out extra chilli sauce for chilli lovers
- Assemble pineapple skewers – cover and refrigerate
- Get changed

LUNCH IS SERVED ON PLATTERS FOR SELF-SERVICE

- Offer beef patties
- Barbecue chicken for 15 minutes, turning once – minimum poking or turning and serve
- Place dish of plantain chunks onto barbecue with chicken, then serve
- Heat callaloo and sweet potato and serve
- Serve rice and peas

DESSERT

- Serve pineapple skewers

INGREDIENTS LIST

PANTRY

- Sea salt
- Fine salt
- Australian extra virgin olive oil
- Indian-style curry paste
  (such as rogan josh)
- Plain flour
- Self-raising flour
- Moist flakes coconut
  (see page 512)
- Dark brown sugar
- Pure maple syrup
- Long-grain rice
- Tomato paste (puree)
- Dark soy sauce
- Dried red kidney beans
- 2 cups/500 ml coconut milk

SPICE SHELF

- Black peppercorns
- Allspice (whole)
- Ground turmeric
- Ground nutmeg
- Ground cinnamon

REFRIGERATOR

- Free-range eggs
- Lard

GREENGROCER/FARMERS'
MARKET (OR GARDEN)

- 6 hot fresh red chillies
  (Scotch bonnet variety
  the hottest of all)
- Thyme
- Garlic
- 4 ripe plantains,
  with yellow to brown skin
- 2 onions
- 7 spring onions
- 250 g amaranth or silverbeet
- 200 g sweet potato
- 2 limes
- 1 ripe pineapple
- Banana leaves (optional)

BUTCHER

- 200 g minced beef
- 2 kg free-range chicken pieces
  (drumsticks, thighs on-the-bone
  with skin-on)

BAKER

- Bread for the fresh breadcrumbs

CELLAR

- West Indian rum
- Red Stripe beer
- Wine for the table, if desired
- Soft drink

TOUR
DE
FORCE

A MENU FOR
SHOW-OFF COOKS

GOUGÈRES

CRAB COCKTAIL
with **FINGER LIME**

CARTA DA MUSICA

PIGS' TROTTERS
with **MUSHROOMS, HAM &
SWEETBREADS STUFFING**

with

DAMIEN'S ONION SOUBISE
& SIMPLE TOMATO SAUCE

GREEN SALAD

RASPBERRY
CURD CREPE LAYER 'CAKE'

4 This menu is intentionally challenging. After all, it is designed to impress; it involves picking crabmeat from the shell and dealing with sweetbreads and pigs' trotters. As the dessert course features raspberries, it places this menu in summer or early autumn, when there is a second crop of excellent raspberries in March and April.

I find it difficult to think of a better accompaniment to Champagne than warm cheese-studded gougères (see page 67). These traditional choux pastry puffs from Burgundy incorporate a generous quantity of gruyere. They are perfect for entertaining, as they have the significant advantage of being able to be made days in advance and frozen. The required quantity are then baked exactly when required.

Over the years, I have prepared crab in many ways: potted with mace-flavoured butter; wrapped in a ball of soused spinach and glazed with a shimmering crab jelly; bound with mayonnaise and sandwiched between compressed layers of puff pastry intended to shatter at the first touch of the fork; as a filling for tender pasta squares; whole in their shell with the full battery of bib, pick and mallet; I could go on . . . But the very best way of all is to buy a live crab, cook, chill, crack and pick it, then serve the exquisite flesh as a simple salad, almost unadorned.

On page 69 I have matched fresh, sweet crab with finger lime pearls. I successfully grew indigenous finger limes at my last house. Each finger lime, when picked ripe and split or sliced and squeezed, gives up a generous quantity of pearls of intense citrus flavour that pop in the mouth; perfect with oysters and also wonderful with fresh crab. Finger limes come in different colours – mine were pink. The amazing thing is that the entire fruit can be frozen and, when thawed, the 'pearls' are intact and just as crunchy as when they were first picked – although the skin looks a bit limp and worse for wear. Just as well, as my little shrub yielded more than 50 fruit.

Whether you are dressing the crabmeat with olive oil or mayonnaise, do it lightly to avoid crushing it. Have a pepper mill nearby and something crisp and crunchy – here I suggest the Italian specialty flatbread *carta da musica*. Many years ago, when I attended cooking classes in Venice with the late cookery writer Marcella Hazan, her husband, Victor, surprised the students each day with a regional product and told us its story. One day he carried in a pile of fragile *carta da musica*, the thinnest wafers of crispbread, each about the size of a small dinner plate, to be served alongside *salumi* (Italian cold cuts) or other antipasti. I have included a recipe that works for me on page 72, although I suspect it is not traditional.

Also years ago, I was invited to participate in a week's promotion of so-called modern Australian cooking at a London hotel, and I chose a menu that was a bit of a showstopper, with lots of complicated preparation. Very stupid really, especially as the promotion proved very successful and the demand for boned rabbit and boned pigs' trotters threatened to have me and my tiny team undone. But chef Bruno Loubet, now of Grain Store bistro in London, was newly in charge of the kitchen and he and his team all pitched in. Soon everyone was boning trotters. It was years later that Bruno told me he had worked for the great Pierre Koffmann at his London restaurant, La Tante Claire, whose specialty was a boned stuffed pig's trotter, so he could bone a pig's trotter in his sleep!

In the recipe on pages 74–75, the trotters start out split, thanks to your obliging butcher, so the boning is not nearly as difficult. The charm of the dish is the sticky, gelatinous character of the skin, contrasting with the softness of the mushroom and sweetbread stuffing under a crunchy coating, the whole offset with something sharp and piquant. Sauce tartare comes to mind, but I think this mayonnaise-based sauce could be too rich, especially when you have served the crabmeat bound with mayonnaise. Alongside instead is a fresh tomato sauce, blended till fairly smooth (see page 77). A bowl of creamy onion soubise (see page 76) can be offered as well.

Do serve a green salad after this rich main dish, preferably with an edge of bitterness from some witlof, radicchio or watercress – or all three!

Raspberries are as near to perfection as any fruit I know. For the layer 'cake' on page 80, the layers are thin crepes, providing another challenge for the cook to achieve perfect thinness and correct size. The raspberry curd is an exciting variation on the lemon curd I have used for this in the past.

Gougères

100 g gruyere *or* emmental
or other hard cheese, coarsely
grated or cut into thin strips

1 free-range egg yolk,
lightly beaten

CHOUX PASTRY

60 g unsalted butter

pinch of fine salt

¾ cup (180 ml) water

125 g plain flour, sifted

3 free-range eggs

**These cheese-flavoured, airy yet crunchy choux puffs are
a specialty of Burgundy. If you wish to make these in advance,
remember that they cook perfectly from frozen.**

To make the pastry, combine the butter, salt and water in a heavy-
based saucepan. Bring to the boil and remove from the heat. Add
the flour all at once, stirring to combine. Return the pan to medium
heat, stirring for 3 minutes or until the mixture dries out and starts
to leave the side of the pan. Transfer to a food processor or electric
mixer with the paddle attachment, then add one egg at a time,
incorporating each one before adding the next.

Preheat the oven to 200°C. Line a baking tray with baking paper.

Add three-quarters of the cheese to the pastry and stir to mix.
Transfer the dough to a piping bag fitted with a plain 1 cm nozzle.
Pipe 4 cm diameter rounds of dough onto the lined tray, leaving
5 cm gaps between them. Brush the top of each one with beaten
egg yolk and scatter with the remaining cheese.

Immediately transfer to the oven and bake for 10 minutes;
do not disturb them. Reduce the oven temperature to 180°C and
bake for a further 30 minutes. Serve at once. (If you are delayed,
the puffs can be held in a turned-off oven for 5–10 minutes.)

Crab cocktail with finger lime

8 blue swimmer crabs
(about 400–500 g each)
or 500 g ready-picked
cooked crabmeat

sea salt

ice cubes

1 cup (large handful)
very finely shredded salad leaves,
preferably including some red
and some green

extra virgin olive oil, for drizzling

lemon juice, as needed

½ cup (150 g) Homemade
Mayonnaise (see page 502)

2 finger limes *or* a slim wedge
of lime

coriander micro shoots (optional),
to serve

Carta da Musica (see page 72),
to serve

freshly ground black pepper

Years ago, I wrote in *The Cook's Companion*, 'Crabs are designed in such a way that to separate and extract the body meat from each nook and cranny has to be regarded as a labour of love. This is why a picked salad of absolutely fresh crabmeat is one of the greatest treats for all crustacean lovers.' It is also why it is best to get all the cracking and picking out of the way hours before your guests are due. I have suggested two different ways of presenting this delicacy. As a somewhat retro crab cocktail or as a salad pure and simple, with a garnish of Australian finger lime and Japanese pickled ginger.

When I tested this, I bought four medium-sized blue swimmer crabs, each weighing around 400 g. I extracted 250 g pure meat, a generous serve for four, and an adequate portion for six, given the other dishes to follow; you will need more here as you are cooking for eight. As a shortcut, you can buy already-picked crabmeat from reputable fishmongers, sold in plastic bags. It will be frozen and should be removed from its wrapping and placed on a plate lined with paper towel, then slowly thawed in the refrigerator. In some markets, you may be able to get freshly picked crab that has been vacuum-packed. I would need to be convinced that the meat had been picked in the last twelve hours. At my own exceptional fishmongers, they sometimes sell freshly cooked crabs, already cracked into pieces, which have been cooked that day.

Chill the crabs in the refrigerator or freezer for 30 minutes.

Bring a large heavy-based saucepan of very well salted water to the boil. Plunge in the sleepy crabs. Bring the water back to the boil, and cook, allowing about 6 minutes for every 500 g whole crab. Lift the crabs into a bath of iced water and leave to cool completely. Lift out the crabs and transfer to a baking tray lined with a thick layer of paper towel to absorb any liquid and refrigerate until you are ready to pick.

Cover a workbench with an unused unscented plastic rubbish bag and set out a heavy mallet, a pair of kitchen scissors, a couple of bowls (one for the meat and one for shell fragments) and maybe a skewer. ➤

recipe continues.

(Perhaps start playing your favourite music as this next stage will take time.) First, break off all the legs. Prise off the top shell. Discard the feathery gills. Cut the body of each crab into quarters. Crack the large claws with a heavy mallet and pull the meat away from the tough membrane. Cut along the small legs with scissors, then break them in half and extract the meat. Using the skewer and your fingers, retrieve every fragment of meat from each section of the body, being careful not to include fragments of cartilage, which is extremely easy to do. Place the retrieved crabmeat in a paper towel-lined bowl in the refrigerator and clean down the area, washing the workbench very well.

Dress the shredded leaves sparingly with olive oil and lemon juice. Select 8 pretty glasses. Half-fill with shredded lettuce. Mix the crab meat lightly with the mayonnaise and pile it evenly on top of the lettuce. Squeeze some pearls from the finger lime on top of every cocktail, and snip and scatter the coriander shoots over.

It would be a nice idea to offer a bowl of extra mayonnaise for the truly appreciative mayonnaise lovers.

Put the *carta da musica* on a plate or into a basket on the table for guests to break into pieces to use as a scoop.

Crab salad variation

To serve this as a simple, yet sublime salad, omit the mayonnaise and shredded leaves dressed with extra virgin olive oil and lemon juice. Instead, make a nest of choice salad leaves on 8 chilled plates. Place the crabmeat in a small bowl, season with sea salt and freshly ground black pepper, then sprinkle on a little fruity extra virgin olive oil – enough to just moisten – and add a squeeze of lemon juice. Spoon the crabmeat evenly into the nests of leaves. Put a pile of finger lime pearls on each plate and one or two slices of Japanese pickled ginger.

Tour de Force

Carta da musica

1 cup (150 g) plain flour,
plus extra for dusting

½ cup (80 g) fine semolina

1 teaspoon sea salt

150 ml lukewarm water

There are many different recipes for these in print claiming to be the only way. I am not going to claim authenticity, but this recipe and technique works brilliantly for me. *Carta da musica* are traditionally sold as round wafers. I find it far easier to achieve the paper-thin texture by rolling the dough through a pasta machine, which results in more elongated pieces. Your crackers will then be rectangular. Alternatively, you could cut the rolled dough into 12 cm to 14 cm rectangles, then cut each rectangle in half on the diagonal to make a rough triangle.

Place the flour, semolina and salt in a food processor and whizz to combine. With the motor running, pour in enough water to make a softish dough. Transfer to a lightly floured workbench and knead lightly for 5 minutes to form a firm and pliable ball. Cover with a clean, dry tea towel and leave to rest for 10 minutes.

Preheat the oven to 230°C. It is easiest to have 2 baking trays ready, so that each piece of rolled dough can be put onto a cold tray.

Divide the dough into 6 balls, then, working one at a time, roll each ball to the thinnest setting on a pasta machine; you should roll one ball, bake it, and then roll the next one, as the rolled dough will quickly dry out while waiting to be baked. (Each length of dough will probably need to be cut across to make 2 pieces that will fit on your baking tray.)

Lay the long, thin sheets of dough on an ungreased baking tray and bake for 2–3 minutes; the dough will lift and bubble. Open the oven and carefully flip the sheets onto the other side. Bake for another 2 minutes; the sheets will be pale gold. Tip them onto a wire rack, then repeat until all the sheets are rolled and baked.

Carta da musica are best served pretty well straight from the oven; certainly within a few hours of baking.

Serves 8

1/3 cup (80 ml) red-wine vinegar

3 sprigs thyme

3 fresh bay leaves

1 teaspoon black peppercorns

4 pigs' trotters, split in half
lengthwise (have the butcher
do this)

Onion Soubise (see page 76),
Simple Tomato Sauce (see page
77) and Dijon mustard, to serve

MUSHROOM, HAM AND
SWEETBREAD STUFFING

250 g free-range chicken breast
fillet, roughly chopped

2 free-range egg whites

sea salt and freshly ground
black pepper

150 ml thickened cream

250 g sweetbreads (to yield 150 g
trimmed), veal for preference

100 g butter

2 large onions, chopped

300 g button mushrooms, chopped

200 g ham, diced

1 tablespoon chopped thyme

3 tablespoons chopped
flat-leaf parsley

TO COAT AND SERVE

1½ cups (105 g) panko breadcrumbs

100 g butter, melted

Pigs' trotters with mushroom, ham and sweetbread stuffing

Pied de cochons

This dish is truly a *tour de force* and will need to be started two days before the dinner to allow for shopping as well as preparation. Your butcher will certainly need advance notice regarding sweetbreads, and maybe trotters as well. The basic stuffing recipe was used to fill a tripe *boudin* (sausage) at Stephanie's Restaurant. As mentioned on page 65, these trotters are split and stuffed, so the boning is much less fraught. As the trotters are split lengthwise, there is no need to laboriously work the skin away from the bones as they are conveniently exposed instantly. It still requires a cook with nimble fingers who enjoys the nitty-gritty of challenging preparation. If sweetbreads prove unobtainable, proceed without them. All the stuffing elements should be chilled before adding to the trotters. (See recipe picture on page 78.)

Combine the vinegar, thyme, bay leaves and peppercorns in a heavy-based saucepan large enough to accommodate the trotters. Reassemble the split trotters, wrap each one in muslin and tie with kitchen twine, then place them in the pan. Add enough water to just cover. Weight with a heavy heatproof plate, then cover and slowly simmer over low–medium heat for 3½–4 hours or until a metal skewer slides through the muslin and skin without resistance. Unwrap and separate the trotters. Leave the trotters until just cool enough to handle them; it is more difficult to remove the bones from cold trotters. Reserve the cooking liquid.

Using very clean hands, remove as many bones as possible, leaving the toe bone in place. You may end up with something raggedy but do not despair as the stuffing will fix it. Line a non-stick baking tray with baking paper. Place the boned trotters on the tray skin-side down. Season well with salt and pepper. Cover with plastic film and refrigerate while you make the stuffing.

First make a chicken mousse. Process the chicken in a food processor until finely chopped. With the motor running, work in the egg whites until shiny. Season with salt and pepper. Transfer to a bowl, cover with plastic film and refrigerate until chilled.

Return the chilled mousse to the cold processor, then, with the motor running, pulse in the cream. Transfer to the bowl, cover with plastic film and chill until needed.

Meanwhile, soak the sweetbreads in salted water for 1 hour. Drain and rinse, then place in a heavy-based saucepan with some of the reserved trotter cooking liquid and bring to simmering point. Simmer for 15 minutes, then transfer to a shallow bowl or plate and put another plate on top. Weight to press the sweetbreads and refrigerate until cold. Remove the weight and plate, peel away any membrane and unsightly bits and cut into small pieces.

For the onion mixture, melt the butter in a heavy-based frying pan over medium heat and saute the onion for 5 minutes or until golden. Add the mushroom and cook for a few minutes. Increase the heat to high to evaporate any excess liquid. Season lightly with salt and pepper, then scoop into a bowl and refrigerate until chilled.

All stuffing elements should be cold before combining. Place the onion and mushroom mixture, sweetbreads, ham, thyme, parsley and salt and pepper in a bowl and stir together. Tip in the chicken mousse and work together, using a spatula. Divide the stuffing evenly among the trotters, mounding it up a little. Cover the tray with plastic film and refrigerate.

Preheat the oven to 220°C.

Process the panko in a food processor until fine crumbs form, then place in a container that is large enough that the trotters won't be crowded when you crumb them. Place the melted butter in a shallow plate large enough to bathe each trotter in. The trotters need to be handled delicately as you spoon the butter generously over them. Using a large spoon, spoon over the crumbs, gently shaking off the excess. Return each coated trotter to the paper-lined tray. Drizzle the last of the butter onto the coated trotters.

Roast the stuffed trotters for 45 minutes or until golden brown.

Serve with a spoonful each of the simple tomato sauce and onion soubise, and offer Dijon mustard alongside.

Damien's onion soubise

500 g onions, peeled
(weight after peeling)

120 g unsalted butter

1 tablespoon extra virgin olive oil

sea salt and freshly ground
black pepper

few drops sherry vinegar

It was my friend and colleague Damien Pignolet who convinced me that an onion soubise was a delicious accompaniment to many meat dishes. This recipe is based on the one in Damien's marvellous cookbook *French*. Soubise basically consists entirely of onions. It is not a gluey mix of white sauce and onion, as was my childhood experience of onion sauce cooked to a puree that was uninspiring and often chalky – certainly not light – in texture. This sauce, to be served with the rich pigs' trotters on pages 74–75, is very light in body, and could be enriched with a spoonful of double cream. It can also be further reduced if you wish.

Slice the onions in a food processor. Place in a large heavy-based saucepan and cover generously with cold water. Bring slowly to the boil over low heat. Drain in a colander and press down on the onion well to extract as much moisture as possible.

Sweat the onion in the butter and olive oil in a medium-sized enamelled cast-iron or other flameproof casserole dish with a tight-fitting lid over low heat for 30 minutes, stirring from time to time. Taste a piece of onion; it should be completely soft.

Preheat the oven to 120°C.

Cover the onion directly with a piece of baking paper, then put on the lid. Transfer to the oven to cook for 1 hour, stirring once or twice.

Blend the onion mixture in a food processor or blender, then season to taste with salt and pepper; a blender will result in a smoother preparation than a food processor. A few drops of sherry vinegar will add a welcome piquancy.

Serve warm. (The sauce can easily be made up to 2–3 days in advance, then gently reheated in a microwave.)

Simple tomato sauce

500 g ripe tomatoes

boiling water, as needed

50 g unsalted butter

1 tablespoon extra virgin olive oil

1 onion, diced

1 clove garlic, chopped

10 basil leaves

sea salt and freshly ground
black pepper

This fast to make, fresh-tasting sauce is quite light in body. You can reduce it further if you want a thicker sauce. Here it is intended to go with the rather rich stuffed trotters on page 74, but it has many more uses, such as with pasta or shellfish or added to a minestrone-type vegetable soup.

Remove the cores from the tomatoes and make a cross at the other end. Place in a deep bowl and cover with boiling water, then leave for 2–3 minutes or until the skins start to lift. Drain and run the tomatoes briefly under cold water. Peel, discarding the skins. Halve and squeeze out most of the seeds, then roughly chop.

Heat the butter and olive oil in a heavy-based saucepan over medium heat for 3 minutes or until frothing. Add the onion and saute for 5 minutes or until soft and golden. Add the garlic, tomato and basil. Season lightly with salt and pepper and cover with a lid, then cook for 15 minutes. Uncover the pan, cool the tomato mixture a little, then process in a food processor or blender until smooth. (A food processor will leave some texture in the sauce. It will be completely smooth if pureed in a blender.) Taste and adjust the seasoning.

If made in advance, reheat just before serving the main course.

Serves 8–10

Raspberry curd crepe layer 'cake'

raspberries, to serve

CREPES (MAKES 8–10)

30 g butter, plus extra for cooking

pinch fine salt

1¾ cups (430 ml) milk

1 cup (150 g) plain flour

2 free-range eggs

RASPBERRY CURD

400 g raspberries (to yield 1 cup [250 ml] puree)

3 gelatine leaves (see page 512)

1 tablespoon boiling water

6 free-range egg yolks

½ cup (110 g) white sugar

100 g unsalted butter, softened

CREAM LAYER

2 gelatine leaves

1 tablespoon boiling water

600 ml thickened cream

FRUIT 'ICING'

3 gelatine leaves

200 ml apple or grape juice

175 g raspberries (to yield 100 ml puree)

ice cubes

For many years, I made a lemon curd crepe layer 'cake' and it was always popular. Tender crepes and unsweetened cream meant that it was not super sweet and the acidity of the lemons – in this version, raspberries – makes a delightful final note after a big dinner. This can be made 48 hours in advance and kept covered in the fridge until 15 minutes before serving.

The raspberries are first whizzed to a puree in a food processor, then this puree must be forced through a fine-mesh sieve over a bowl to extract all seeds. This needs to be done with some effort or else there is a danger that quite a bit of the usable raspberry is discarded with the seeds in the sieve. I use a smooth wooden pestle to help it along; the back of a strong nylon spatula can also be used. (See picture of the 'cake' on page 79.)

To make the crepe batter, warm the butter, salt and milk in a small heavy-based saucepan over low heat until the butter has melted. Put the flour into a bowl and make a well in the centre. Break the eggs into the well and work in some of the flour. Add the warm milk mixture and whisk until smooth. Refrigerate for 2 hours before cooking. The consistency should be like thin cream; if not, thin with more milk.

To make the raspberry curd, puree the raspberries in a blender, then press through a fine-mesh sieve over a bowl, pressing firmly to remove all the seeds (which will be discarded) to extract as much of the puree as possible. Soak the gelatine leaves in a bowl of cold water for 5 minutes or until softened. Squeeze to remove any excess water and drop into a small bowl with the boiling water. Swish to dissolve completely. Using a whisk, electric mixer or hand-held electric beaters, whisk the egg yolks and sugar until well combined but not frothy. Tip into a heavy-based stainless-steel saucepan over medium heat and add the butter, dissolved gelatine and raspberry puree. Bring to simmering point over medium–high heat, stirring constantly for about 5 minutes. As soon as the first bubbles appear, remove from the heat while still stirring. Leave to cool.

For the cream layer, soak the gelatine leaves in a bowl of cold water for 5 minutes or until softened. Squeeze to remove any excess water and drop into a small bowl with the boiling water. Swish to dissolve completely. Add the dissolved gelatine to the cream, then, using an electric mixer or hand-held electric beaters, whip until it holds firm peaks. Set aside until needed.

Heat a crepe pan over medium heat, then wipe with a piece of buttered paper towel. Lift the pan from the heat, ladle in some of the batter, then swirl quickly to spread it thinly to the edge of the pan. Return the pan to the heat and cook for 1 minute. After 1 minute, lift the outer edge of the crepe with a flexible spatula and flip the crepe, using your fingers or the spatula. Cook the other side for less than a minute; this is so quick and you want the other side to be just cooked. Immediately slide the crepe onto a dry tea towel. Continue with the remaining batter until all the crepes are cooked. You need the best 7 of them; your first one will not be the best.

To assemble the 'cake', place the base of a 20 cm springform cake tin on a baking tray lined with baking paper. Cut out a template of the base on baking paper. Cut the crepes to the exact size of the template. Start the layering process on the base of the cake tin, first with 1 crepe, one-third of the curd, another crepe, one-third of the cream, then another crepe. Repeat layering the remaining curd, crepes and cream, finishing with a crepe. Place the side of the springform tin in position, close firmly, then refrigerate the cake for 1 hour for it to firm and the cream and curd to set.

Meanwhile, make the 'icing'. Soak the gelatine in a bowl of cold water. Heat 2 tablespoons of the apple or grape juice in a small heavy-based saucepan to boiling point and drop in the squeezed gelatine leaves. Whisk lightly to dissolve. Combine with the rest of the juice and the raspberry puree, then transfer to a stainless-steel bowl. Set the bowl over a second stainless-steel bowl containing crushed ice or ice cubes. Gently turn the top bowl, stirring the mixture gently – you do not want to create bubbles. When the mixture starts to thicken and look syrupy, gently pour the 'icing' over the cake and return to the refrigerator to set for another hour.

Cut into wedges using a knife dipped in hot water, then serve with extra raspberries, if desired.

TIMETABLE FOR THE COOK

TWO WEEKS BEFORE

- Check **Ingredients List** and note what needs to be purchased
- Advise provedores of special requests (pigs' trotters and sweetbreads, live crabs, finger limes)
- Visit fishmonger – check whether they will cook the crab the day before or will you have to cook it? Alternatively, do they sell really fresh crabmeat already picked and vacuum-packed?

THREE DAYS BEFORE

- Check specialist equipment needed (paddle attachment for electric mixer, crepe pan same diameter as selected springform cake tin)
- Decide on table setting, including serving dishes
- Decide on wines – order if necessary
- Inspect tablecloth and napkins
- All shopping, including flowers
- Collect trotters and sweetbreads

Gougères
- Make and pipe – freeze in an airtight container

Trotters
- Make tomato sauce – refrigerate in an airtight container
- Make onion soubise – refrigerate in an airtight container

TWO DAYS BEFORE

- Pick, wash and dry parsley – refrigerate in a paper towel-lined airtight container

Trotters
- Make chicken mousse – refrigerate
- Trim sweetbreads – refrigerate
- Cook onion and mushroom mixture – refrigerate
- Chop ham – refrigerate

Crepe layer 'cake'
- Make crepes – refrigerate
- Make raspberry curd – refrigerate
- Whip cream – refrigerate
- Assemble – refrigerate

DAY BEFORE

Crab cocktail/salad
- If serving crab cocktail rather than salad, make mayonnaise

Trotters
- Cook for 3½–4 hours (set timer)
- Bone, place on baking paper–lined baking tray and cover – refrigerate
- Soak and cook sweetbreads (use some trotter cooking liquid), then press – refrigerate
- Combine stuffing ingredients
- Stuff and coat trotters
- Drizzle with extra butter and cover – refrigerate

Crepe layer 'cake'
- Make and pour on topping – refrigerate

MORNING OF

Crab cocktail/salad
- Collect live or cooked crab
- Cook if necessary, chill and pick crabmeat
- Place picked crab on paper towel–lined plate and cover well – refrigerate
- Prepare garnish

Green salad
- Wash, dry and crisp salad leaves
- Prepare dressing in bowl with crossed salad servers ready to toss before serving

Crepe layer 'cake'
- Carefully ease away ring of springform tin

- Set table

AFTERNOON OF

Carta da musica
- Make dough
- Bake – store in an airtight container

- Chill glasses for crab cocktail, if required
- Chill wine, if necessary
- Get changed

ONE HOUR BEFORE GUESTS ARRIVE

Crab cocktail/salad
- Assemble crab cocktail
- Set out *carta da musica*
- Put extra mayonnaise into jug at room temperature

Trotters
- Place Dijon mustard in a bowl on the table

FIRST COURSE

- Preheat oven to 200°C
- Bake gougères (plan 45 minutes before serving)
- Serve

- Meanwhile, increase oven temperature to 220°C
- Bake trotters for 45 minutes (set timer)

SECOND COURSE

- Serve crab cocktail/salad

THIRD/MAIN COURSE

- Reheat soubise and tomato sauce
- Serve trotters with spoonful of soubise and spoonful of tomato sauce
- Toss and serve green salad

DESSERT

- Put hot water into jug, then dip in a very sharp knife to cut crepe cake
- Place slices on plates on their side
- Offer extra raspberries, if desired

INGREDIENTS LIST

PANTRY

- Sea salt
- Fine salt
- Australian extra virgin olive oil
- Red-wine vinegar
- Sherry vinegar
- Dijon mustard
- Plain flour
- Fine semolina
- White sugar
- 8 gelatine leaves
- Panko breadcrumbs

SPICE SHELF

- Black peppercorns
- White peppercorns or Tabasco

REFRIGERATOR

- Milk
- 660 g unsalted butter
- 750 ml thickened cream
- 100 g gruyere or emmental or other hard cheese
- 13 free-range eggs
- 200 ml apple or grape juice

BUTCHER/DELICATESSEN

- 4 pigs' trotters, split in half lengthwise (order in advance)
- 250 g free-range chicken breast fillet, skin off
- 250 g sweetbreads (to yield 150 g trimmed), veal for preference
- 200 g ham

GREENGROCER/FARMERS' MARKET (OR GARDEN)

- Flat-leaf parsley
- Thyme
- 3 fresh bay leaves
- Basil
- Coriander micro shoots (optional)
- Garlic
- Large handful salad leaves (some red, some green)
- Selection of salad leaves
- 600 g onions, plus 3 large onions
- 300 g button mushrooms
- 500 g ripe tomatoes
- 1 lemon
- 2 finger limes or 1 lime
- 600 g raspberries

FISHMONGER

- 8 raw blue swimmer crabs (about 400 g each) or 500 g ready-picked cooked crabmeat

BAKER

- Bread for the table

CELLAR

- Wine for the table
- Soft drink

BIRTHDAY PARTY

FOR A TEENAGER

A PARTY FOR 10

SPICY PORK EMPANADAS

SILVERBEET & RICOTTA
CANNELLONI
with ANCHOVY & SAGE FRITTERS

PARSLEY HAM TART

BOWL OF RADISHES & CHERRY TOMATOES

YOGHURT FLATBREAD
with GARLIC BUTTER

GUACAMOLE

———

STRAWBERRY CRUSH
ICE-CREAM

CHOCOLATE & PUMPKIN SEED BISCUITS

FRUIT PLATTER

5

It is a long time since I've had any teenagers of my own,
but I do spend part of every summer in the company of some
delightful teenagers. I am impressed by their prodigious appetites,
willingness to try anything at all and their interest in a previously
unencountered taste or texture. I have great hope for them and
it does stir one to making a bit of an effort when there is every
likelihood of praise.

I decided the food for a birthday party for teenagers should be
portable, preferably hand-held or, at the most, requiring a small
plate and napkin. This allows the host to set out a very colourful
table, with the dishes arranged on big bold platters, including an
eye-catching display of fresh seasonal fruit. It is a well-known bit
of folk wisdom that a bowl of fruit is often left untouched, but if
fruit is presented as slices of melon, pyramids of berries, wedges
of peach and nectarine, halved passionfruit etcetera, there is far
more interest. Plan to also offer a jug of freshly squeezed juice –
watermelon with a few strawberries added is delicious,
as is freshly squeezed orange juice.

Depending on the teenagers present, the flatbread on page
96 could become an ice-breaking communal activity of rolling,
slapping on the barbecue and brushing with the garlic and herb
butter. The flatbreads can be torn into pieces and used as scoops
for self-service from a big bowl of guacamole (see page 97).

The empanadas on page 89 are small pies or pasties popular in
Argentina and other South American countries, and also in Spain.
They vary considerably – for example, I have seen recipes where
the pastry is delicate and made with extra virgin olive oil, while
other recipes use lard (rendered pork fat) as the fat, resulting in
a more substantial dough. Some are filled with minced or chopped
beef or lamb or pork, while others are filled with salted codfish.
Usually the filling is a little bit spicy. Sometimes they are baked
and other times deep-fried.

You could double the ingredients for the parsley ham tart on
page 94 and make two tarts. One tart with ham as specified and
one where ham is replaced with a similar quantity of poached

smoked fish, or plainly cooked spinach if there will be non–meat eaters attending. Or you could make one tart and use either poached or smoked fish or spinach in the filling instead of ham.

I haven't mentioned a green salad or a cheeseboard. Include them if you like, however, a well-dressed green salad is not so easy to eat with one hand – but it is your teenager's party so they should decide. A bowl of cherry tomatoes and a big bowl of washed radishes will add something fresh and crunchy to the buffet table.

In the early years of my work for the Stephanie Alexander Kitchen Garden Foundation, there were quite a few fundraising events aimed at raising awareness as well as funds. Sydney chef Sean Moran is well known for his delightful restaurant Sean's Panaroma at Bondi. He and I participated in the Bondi Primary School Fundraiser in 2011, as did the Foundation's NSW Ambassador, chef and friend Kylie Kwong. Kylie served perfectly soft-boiled eggs with salads of organic vegetables. I made a very successful silverbeet and ricotta cannelloni (see pages 90–91), which I garnished with deep-fried sage leaves sandwiched with an anchovy fillet (see page 92). Sean then served a magnificent strawberry ice-cream, which I have never forgotten.

Which brings me to dessert. At a certain point in the party it is a good idea to clear away the savoury debris. I have already mentioned the fruit bowl and how it can look so sumptuous. Alongside is a platter of the chocolate and pumpkin seed biscuits on page 103 and a chilled bowl of Sean's aforementioned strawberry crush ice-cream (see page 100).

Spicy pork empanadas

¼ cup (60 ml) extra virgin olive oil

250 g lean minced pork

1 onion, finely chopped

100 g preserved piquillo peppers (see page 512), well drained and roughly chopped

3 cloves garlic, crushed

3 tablespoons roughly chopped flat-leaf parsley

1 teaspoon fennel seeds, ground using a mortar and pestle

½ teaspoon hot chilli paste (see page 511)

1 tablespoon Homemade Tomato Sauce (see page 502) *or* good-quality commercial tomato passata

1 teaspoon smoked sweet paprika

1 free-range egg, lightly beaten

EMPANADA DOUGH

1⅓ cups (200 g) plain flour, plus extra for dusting

50 g coarse polenta, plus extra for rolling

sea salt

2 tablespoons extra virgin olive oil

40 g butter, melted

2 tablespoons fino sherry

¼ cup (60 ml) water, as needed

I have enjoyed empanadas in both Spain and Argentina and they were very different. In Spain, my favourites had a salted codfish and egg filling and a delicate pastry mixed with some fino sherry. Then I went to a cooking class in Buenos Aires where we were shown a very different spicy beef filling and a much more solid pastry, made with lard. Every street stall in Buenos Aires sold empanadas, some filled with beef but just as many contained pork. I have tried to bring together all my favourite bits in this recipe.

To make the dough, put the flour, polenta and a pinch of salt into a food processor and whizz to blend. Mix the olive oil, butter and sherry. With the motor running, add the oil mixture to the flour mixture, then gradually add the water – you may not need it all – and process until the mixture forms a ball. Transfer to a workbench dusted with flour and knead for 1 minute. Wrap in plastic film and set aside for at least 1 hour while you make and cool the filling. (The pastry can be made several hours before filling or the day before – just bring it back to room temperature before rolling.)

Heat a large heavy-based frying pan over medium heat and add half of the olive oil. Add the pork and stir with a wooden spoon to break it up well, cooking until evenly lightly browned all over. Tip into a bowl. Add the remaining oil to the pan and saute the onion, piquillo peppers and garlic over medium heat, stirring for 3 minutes or until softened. Cook for a few more minutes, then add the parsley, fennel seeds and chilli paste. Return the pork to the pan, add the tomato sauce or passata and paprika and cook, stirring frequently for 5 minutes. Taste and adjust for salt and spiciness.

Preheat the oven to 220°C. Line a baking tray with baking paper.

Dust the workbench with polenta. Divide the dough into 12 even balls and roll each one to form a round about 12 cm in diameter. Divide the pork filling among the rounds. Brush the edge of each round with the egg wash, then fold over to make a half-moon shape. Seal the edges well with a fork. Place each empanada on the lined tray. Brush all over with egg wash. Bake for 10–15 minutes or until browned. Cool before taking your first bite!

Silverbeet and ricotta cannelloni

20 g butter, plus extra for buttering and dotting

2 tablespoons extra virgin olive oil

1 large onion, finely chopped

1 quantity Bechamel Sauce (see page 502)

500 g silverbeet (to yield 400 g trimmed and 200 g cooked), stems removed, leaves washed well

500 g fresh, firm ricotta, drained

150 g finely grated parmesan

sea salt and freshly ground black pepper

freshly grated nutmeg

PASTA

1⅓ cups (200 g) plain flour

2 free-range eggs

This recipe looks long and complicated but it really is manageable if you follow the steps. Every component can be made up to two days ahead of the party, and assembling the cannelloni in a good looking dish that can be taken from the oven to the table can also be done in advance. All that is needed on the day is to put the covered cannelloni into the oven.
On pages 32 and 334 I have included lasagne recipes where the pasta layer uses commercial pasta sheets; you could do that here. However, learning to make fresh pasta is a very useful skill and is great fun. It's also an excellent way of involving the whole family in the kitchen. (See recipe picture on page 93.)

To make the pasta, process the flour and eggs in a food processor until a dough forms. Leave to rest for at least 30 minutes. Using a pasta machine, roll the dough to the second thinnest setting. Cut into ten 14 cm squares. Bring a large stockpot of well-salted water to the boil and have a bowl of ice-cold water and a tray lined with a dry tea towel alongside. Drop several pieces of the pasta into the boiling water. Cook for 2 minutes, then scoop out and place immediately in the ice-cold water. Remove and spread carefully on the dry tea towel without overlapping, to prevent them sticking and tearing. Cover with plastic film and set aside. Repeat until all the pasta is cooked.

Heat the butter and olive oil in a small heavy-based frying pan over medium heat, then add the onion and saute for 5 minutes or until very soft and pale golden. Transfer to a bowl and set aside to cool.

Keep the bechamel sauce warm or, if the assembly is delayed, warm the sauce briefly in a microwave; it must be easily spreadable.

Bundle the silverbeet leaves together and cut into 2 cm-wide ribbons. Drop them into a heavy-based saucepan over medium heat with a splash of water, stirring to ensure they do not stick to the pan. Cover and cook for 2–3 minutes or until wilted. Drain well, then squeeze to remove excess liquid; you should have about 200 g.

Add the silverbeet, ricotta, two-thirds of the parmesan and two-thirds of the bechamel sauce to the onion. Season with salt, pepper and freshly grated nutmeg.

Butter a baking dish that will comfortably hold 10 cannelloni (mine is 30 cm × 24 cm).

Preheat the oven to 180°C.

To assemble, take each piece of pasta and spoon one-tenth of the silverbeet filling on top, spreading the filling a bit and leaving a 1 cm border around the edges. Tuck in the sides and roll loosely to enclose the filling. Place the rolled cannelloni, seam-side down, in the buttered dish, taking care not to pack the cannelloni too tightly. Continue until all the pasta and filling are used. Cover with the remaining bechamel sauce and scatter with the reserved parmesan. Dot with extra butter.

Bake for 30 minutes or until the cannelloni are bubbling and the top is golden. (If you have refrigerated the prepared and filled cannelloni, then this will take a bit longer – more like 50 minutes.)

Serve with the anchovy and sage fritters on page 92 alongside.

Anchovy and sage fritters

40 large sage leaves

1 free-range egg white,
lightly whisked just enough
to break the gel

10 anchovy fillets in olive oil,
halved lengthwise

vegetable oil, for deep-frying

CORNFLOUR BATTER

60 g cornflour

¼ cup (60 ml) cold water

1 free-range egg white,
lightly whisked just enough
to break the gel

These sage and anchovy fritters are absolutely delicious, but they are a last-minute touch. Decide whether they will be part of the party plan or perhaps reserved for another occasion, when the cannelloni might be the main course for a dinner for four or six friends.

Using a pastry brush, brush each sage leaf with egg white and 'sandwich' with half an anchovy fillet and a second sage leaf. Press firmly, transfer to a baking tray, then cover with plastic film and set aside until required. (The fritters are fine for an hour or so at room temperature. If the weather is very hot, store them in the refrigerator to prevent excessive drying out.)

Just before serving, make the cornflour batter. Place the cornflour, water and egg white in a bowl and whisk to combine; the batter should drip from your fingers and appear translucent. (It will settle if it stands for any length of time and will need to be whisked again just before using.)

Heat vegetable oil for deep-frying in a deep heavy-based frying pan over high heat until it registers 170°C on a deep-fry thermometer. Test the oil with a drop of batter; it should sizzle and turn golden almost immediately. Dip the fritters into the batter, drain off the excess and carefully place in the hot oil; do not crowd the pan. Turn the fritters to brown the other side. Lift the fritters out with a skimmer or slotted spoon, allowing excess oil to drain into the pan. Drain on paper towel.

Serve alongside the cannelloni.

Parsley ham tart

plain flour, for dusting

1 quantity Shortcrust Pastry
(see page 508)

2 tablespoons extra virgin olive oil

2 large onions, finely chopped

200 g lean ham, diced

½ cup (handful) flat-leaf parsley,
roughly chopped

1 free-range egg, plus 1 egg yolk

200 ml thickened cream

¼ cup (30 g) coarsely
grated gruyere

sea salt and freshly ground
black pepper

This tart will be very popular. It is packed with good things, so the wedges can be quite modest in size. If you have many non–red meat eaters, it makes sense to poach a fillet of Shetland cod or other smoked fish in milk and then flake it into the mixture instead of the ham. Do be generous with the parsley. If you are serving this for lunch or a lighter main meal, it serves six to eight.

Dust the workbench with a little flour and roll out the pastry until 5 mm thick, then use it to line a 22 cm flan tin with a removable base. Chill for 30 minutes. Line the tart tin with baking paper and fill with baking weights or dried chickpeas.

Preheat the oven to 200°C. Blind-bake the tart case for 20 minutes, then cool and lift out the weights and baking paper.

Reduce the oven temperature to 180°C.

Heat the olive oil in a small heavy-based saucepan over medium heat, then saute the onion for 10 minutes or until soft. Mix in the ham and parsley.

Place the egg, egg yolk, cream, gruyere and salt and pepper to taste (be cautious with the salt as the ham will be quite salty already) in a bowl and whisk to mix well. Tip the onion/ham mixture into the egg/cream mixture and mix well.

Pour into the tart case and bake for 25 minutes or until the filling is golden and has risen slightly.

This tart is best served warm or at room temperature.

Yoghurt flatbread
with garlic and herb butter

1⅔ cups (250 g) self-raising flour,
plus extra for dusting

2 teaspoons baking powder

250 g natural Greek-style yoghurt

2 teaspoons sea salt

GARLIC AND HERB BUTTER

150 g unsalted butter,
diced and softened

2 cloves garlic, finely chopped
to form a paste

¼ cup (small handful) flat-leaf
parsley, roughly chopped

There are so many ways to make flatbread – yeast or no yeast and no leavening at all or some baking powder; various types of flour; and ways of folding and flattening the dough and different ways to cook it. I watched a woman making the simplest flour and water flatbread in a village in Rajasthan in India. Her flour was, of course, unbleached with bits of the bran still intact. She baked the patted-out discs straightaway on a tiny fire fed with sticks and, as soon as a bread was toasted and slightly charred, she spread it with pure white butter made from buffalo milk. It tasted wonderful.

This version is a bit more refined, but nonetheless delicious. The flatbreads should be cooked just before serving, as they will harden if kept warm in the oven. The garlic and herb butter is optional. (See picture on pages 98–99.)

Place the flour, baking powder, yoghurt and salt in a food processor and pulse until you have a dough. Knead the dough on a workbench lightly dusted with a little flour for 1 minute or so to bring it together. Put the dough into a floured bowl, cover with a damp tea towel and set aside at room temperature for 30 minutes (do not leave for too long as the surface will start to dry out after an hour or so, especially in hot weather).

Meanwhile, to make the garlic and herb butter, combine the soft butter, garlic and parsley in a small bowl.

Just before serving, heat a heavy-based frying pan over high heat (or fire up the barbecue flatplate). Dust a clean workbench and rolling pin with flour. Divide the dough into 8–10 even pieces and roll them out into 16 cm diameter rounds. Working in batches, cook the dough rounds on your hot, dry pan or barbecue flatplate for a couple of minutes on each side, until slightly puffy and a bit charred.

Immediately spread the gorgeous herby garlic butter on top of each one and serve in a pile on a wooden chopping board, so that everyone can help themselves. Serve warm.

Guacamole

3 large, perfectly ripe avocados, halved and seeded

juice of 2 limes or 1 lemon

1 large ripe tomato or 2 medium tomatoes, cut into 1 cm dice

3 tablespoons coriander leaves, washed, dried and roughly chopped

1 teaspoon finely chopped fresh long red chilli (seeded or not, depending on heat preferred)

3 spring onions, finely chopped

sea salt

Yoghurt Flatbread (see opposite), to serve

This classic preparation is always popular, and especially delicious on just-cooked flatbread, warm from the frying pan or barbecue. (See picture on pages 98–99.) There are many variations: smooth or chunky; with tomato or not; lots of chilli, no chilli; and so on. This is my favourite, and is reprinted here from my well-known work *The Cook's Companion*. Sometimes I keep the hollow avocado shells and pile the finished guacamole into them.

Scoop out the flesh from the avocado shells, reserving the shells, if desired, for serving.

Roughly chop the flesh and transfer to a large bowl. Add the lime or lemon juice, tomato, coriander, chilli, spring onion and salt to taste and mix gently with a large metal spoon. Taste for seasoning; guacamole should be well balanced between rich and creamy, sharp and tangy.

Serve with the flatbread.

Strawberry crush ice-cream

2 × 250 g punnets best-quality strawberries, washed and hulled

190 g caster sugar

1½ cups (375 ml) thickened cream

ice cubes

4 free-range egg yolks

I do not get to Sean's Panaroma Restaurant at Bondi nearly as often as I would like but, whenever I do, I enjoy lovely, original food. He is a great chef and a good friend and I am delighted that he let me 'borrow' his recipe for strawberry crush ice-cream, published in his wonderful book, *Let it Simmer*. Sean serves his ice-cream sandwiched between delicate meringue shells. You will need to have an ice-cream machine to make this. Like all homemade ice-creams, this is best eaten within a week of making.

Place the strawberries in a bowl and mash with one-third (65 g) of the caster sugar until just coarsely pureed. Set aside.

Place the cream in a small heavy-based saucepan and bring to the boil over medium heat. Have on hand a fine-meshed sieve resting over a heatproof bowl, sitting inside another large bowl with a layer of ice cubes in it to cool the custard swiftly the moment it's cooked.

Meanwhile, using an electric mixer, whisk the egg yolks with the remaining caster sugar until pale, then pour in the boiling cream. Whisk briefly, then place the pan over low heat and cook, stirring constantly with a wooden spoon for 8–10 minutes, until the custard thickens enough to coat the back of your spoon; it is imperative not to let the custard boil as it will scramble, yet it should congeal slightly at the base of the pan.

Strain the custard through the strainer into the bowl sitting over the bowl of ice cubes, then stir in the crushed strawberry mixture. Leave to sit over the ice to chill. When cold, churn and freeze in an ice-cream machine according to the manufacturer's instructions.

Chocolate and pumpkin seed biscuits

125 g unsalted butter

25 g caster sugar

60 g soft brown sugar

⅔ cup (100 g) self-raising flour

100 g rolled oats

75 g bittersweet/dark chocolate
(70 per cent cocoa solids),
roughly chopped

50 g pumpkin seed kernels (pepitas)

**An excellent recipe. These biscuits have plenty of crunch
and are not very sweet. Use the very best dark chocolate
as the quality will be noticed.**

Preheat the oven to 170°C. Line a baking tray with baking paper.

Place the butter and sugars in a food processor and process until
light and fluffy. Add the flour and oats and pulse to mix, then add
the chocolate and pumpkin seeds. Pulse briefly to just combine.

Roll the dough into 3 cm diameter balls, then place on the baking
tray, leaving room between for the biscuits to spread. Flatten slightly
with the back of the spoon.

Bake for 15–20 minutes or until the biscuits are golden brown.
Transfer to a wire rack and leave to cool completely. Store in an
airtight container for up to 1 week.

TIMETABLE FOR THE COOK

ONE WEEK BEFORE

- Check **Ingredients List** and note what needs to be purchased
- Check equipment needed (deep-fry thermometer, ice-cream machine)

THREE DAYS BEFORE

- Decide on table setting, including serving dishes
- Check barbecue (clean if necessary) and check fuel
- Inspect tablecloth and napkins
- Check outdoor furniture
- Decide on drinks – fruit cup, freshly squeezed juice
- All shopping, including flowers
- Make and wrap shortcrust pastry for the tart – refrigerate

TWO DAYS BEFORE

- Make ice-cream – freeze
- Make chocolate biscuits – store in an airtight tin

DAY BEFORE

Empanadas
- Make and wrap dough – refrigerate
- Make filling – refrigerate

Cannelloni
- Make components (pasta, bechamel and silverbeet filling)
- Assemble in dish and cover – refrigerate

MORNING OF

- Make garlic and herb butter
- Juice fruit – refrigerate
- Set table

Empanadas
- Assemble – refrigerate

Parsley ham tart
- Blind-bake tart shell
- Make filling – refrigerate

AFTERNOON OF

Anchovy and sage fritter components
- Prepare

Guacamole
- Make – refrigerate

Parsley ham tart
- Preheat oven
- Fill and bake

Fruit platter
- Prepare fruit

TWO HOURS BEFORE GUESTS ARRIVE

- Bake empanadas in a preheated 220°C oven
- Trim radishes, wash and leave in water
- Spoon strawberry ice-cream into balls, place on a baking paper–lined tray and return to freezer
- Make flatbread dough
- Get changed

Anchovy and sage fritters
- Assemble

ONE HOUR BEFORE GUESTS ARRIVE

Cannelloni
- Bake in a preheated 180°C oven
- Cook anchovy and sage fritters – keep warm near stove

- Set table for self-service – ensure there are enough napkins, plates (more than 1 each)
- Put jugs of water and fruit juice onto table
- Cut parsley ham tart into 10–12 wedges and place on a platter on the table
- Put guacamole bowl onto table
- Put radishes and cherry tomatoes into serving bowls on table
- Display fruit on table (in background at this time)

DISHES ARE SERVED ON PLATTERS FOR SELF-SERVICE

Empanadas
- Return to still-warm oven for 10 minutes (set timer) – place in cloth-lined basket to stay warm

Cannelloni
- Adult help on hand to serve cannelloni
- Place anchovy and sage fritters near cannelloni

Flatbread
- Roll and cook flatbreads on a heavy pan or the barbecue (guests may like to help)
- Brush cooked flatbreads with garlic and herb butter and stack

DESSERT

- Remove savoury dishes
- Place clean plates and/or dessert bowls on table
- Serve strawberry ice-cream balls in a pretty bowl or glasses
- Serve biscuits
- Move fruit display to centre of table

INGREDIENTS LIST

PANTRY

- Sea salt
- Fine salt
- Australian extra virgin olive oil
- Oil for deep-frying, such as vegetable oil or grapeseed oil
- Plain flour
- Self-raising flour
- Cornflour (wheaten)
- Baking powder
- Caster sugar
- Brown sugar
- Rolled oats
- Coarse polenta
- Piquillo peppers
- Tomato passata *or* Homemade Tomato Sauce (see page 502)
- 50 g pumpkin seed kernels (pepitas)
- Anchovy fillets in olive oil
- 75 g bittersweet/dark chocolate (70 per cent cocoa solids)

SPICE SHELF

- Black peppercorns
- Fennel seeds
- Hot chilli paste
- Smoked sweet paprika
- Nutmeg (whole)

REFRIGERATOR

- Milk
- Butter
- Free-range eggs
- 250 g natural Greek-style yoghurt
- 500 g ricotta
- 30 g gruyere
- 150 g parmesan
- 600 ml thickened cream

GREENGROCER/FARMERS' MARKET (OR GARDEN)

- Flat-leaf parsley
- 40 large sage leaves
- Coriander
- 1 fresh long red chilli
- Garlic
- 4 onions
- 3 spring onions
- 500 g silverbeet
- 3 large ripe avocados
- 2 limes or 1 lemon
- 2 tomatoes
- Radishes
- Cherry tomatoes
- Selection of salad leaves (optional)
- 500 g strawberries
- Seasonal fruit selection for platter

BUTCHER/DELICATESSEN

- 250 g lean minced pork
- 200 g lean ham

CELLAR

- Fino sherry for empanadas
- Drinks for the table

A DINNER
❧ OF ❧
MEMORIES

A DINNER FOR 6

SALMON CARPACCIO
with SALT COD & TOMATO

———

DAMIEN'S
SAFFRON FISH
VELOUTÉ

———

SWORDFISH
with OLIVE & CAPER SALSA

GREEN SALAD

———

ANNIE'S
APPLE CARAMEL
TARTLETS

6

This menu brings together a mixture of recollections, mostly from the 80s. I am comfortable that all of these dishes stand up well to the passage of so much time, and will be enthusiastically received today.

For the first course, best-quality sashimi-grade raw fish is served as a carpaccio with a tiny bit of grated unsoaked salted codfish, ripe tomatoes and basil leaves. Using raw salted codfish as a condiment on raw fish was an exciting taste when I first encountered it in the Restaurant Troisgros (now called La Maison Troisgros) in Roanne, France, back in the early 80s. Salted codfish (*baccala*) is sold in food stores catering for Spanish, Portuguese and Italian clients; you will only need a very small piece. I have garnished the fish with tiny segments of lemon flesh. If you have access to Australian indigenous finger limes, which ripen over the warmer months in the southern states, the pearls from one of these would be sufficient for two or three portions.

The soup course evokes one of many memorable evenings with my friend Damien Pignolet. Damien and Josephine Pignolet owned and cooked at the incomparable Claude's Restaurant in Woollahra, where fortunate diners enjoyed some of the finest food offered anywhere in the world at that time. Josephine died in an accident in 1987, and her memory continues in the annual Josephine Pignolet Award, bestowed upon an up-and-coming chef deemed sufficiently talented and dedicated to receive the prestigious title of Young Chef of the Year. Damien is a peerless French cook with a reverence for the classics, and he is a stickler for correct technique.

In my notebook for 1988, it says we enjoyed this soup together with a 1982 Corton-Charlemagne – I have never forgotten the perfection of the match. The wide soup plates are important, so that the colour and shape of the fish can be appreciated, and they must be warmed before pouring in the finished soup. Velouté means 'velvety', which is the special charm of this soup.

The swordfish course reminds me of another fine Sydney restaurant from the 80s, Oasis Seros, where the kitchen was operated by the brilliant and inventive chef Phillip Searle. I think it must have been my first taste of swordfish, and I was captivated by its meaty yet juicy texture and the fact that it was cooked medium–rare. Phillip topped his swordfish with deeply caramelised onion and sat it on a flowing puree of potato – still a wonderful combination. Here I have added a caper and olive salsa that needs to be tossed in a pan with extra virgin olive oil so it is thoroughly warmed when spooned onto the fish.

Those cooks with a second oven will have an advantage when preparing this menu, as the serving plates and bowls need to be heated at a low temperature, while finishing the tartlets requires a hot oven again. I have tried to suggest ways to manage this in the accompanying timetable on page 121.

Since the time of Oasis Seros, we have become more aware of overfishing, and swordfish stocks have been considered at risk. *Australia's Sustainable Seafood Guide* gives swordfish an amber 'Eat Less' ranking. You can find more detailed information at sustainableseafood.org.au.

In 1992, I visited the gardens of Hatfield House in Hertfordshire, and marvelled at the avenues of 'John Downie' crabapples. The fruit is more lozenge-shaped than round, and its skin colour was a brilliant scarlet splashed with gold. It can be eaten as a fresh fruit, although it is still quite sharp. During the same holiday I ate a crabapple tarte tatin at Woolley Grange, a delightful Jacobean manor house converted to a very friendly hotel–restaurant, just 11 or so kilometres from Bath at Bradford-on-Avon. Inspired, I bought 'John Downie' trees for my own garden and, although I made several excellent tartes tatin over the years, I have never been convinced that my trees were the same variety as those I admired in England.

At a 2015 Ladies Night Dinner, bringing together three former colleagues from Stephanie's Restaurant, there were many memories shared. Nicky Riemer of Union Dining served her version of my duck galantine (see page 439) with pickled cherries; Natalie Paull of Beatrix Bakes served the crispest cannoli shells filled with soft goat's curd and slow-roasted peppers; and Annie Smithers of du Fermier, knowing of my fondness for crabapples, served individual crabapple tarte tatin tartlets. Annie has discovered another variety of crabapple called Huonville with very large fruit that is rosy–almost-ruby-red, right to the core. Each tartlet had just one of these baked crabapples on it, served with a scoop of lemon-verbena ice-cream. Annie's tartlets were very special indeed.

Salmon carpaccio
with salt cod and tomato

1 × 400 g centre-cut sashimi-grade salmon fillet, pin-boned, skinned and trimmed of any dark flesh, placed in the freezer for 30 minutes only

1 large ripe tomato *or* 2 smaller tomatoes, cut into 5 mm dice

2 finger limes, pearls removed *or* 1 lemon, peeled and segmented (see page 511), then finely chopped

100 g piece of salt cod (or the smallest piece you can buy) (optional)

fruity extra virgin olive oil, for drizzling

20 small basil leaves, torn

hot sourdough toast, to serve

DRESSING

3 spring onions, trimmed and very thinly sliced, including some of the green section

2–3 small fresh red chillies, seeded and very thinly sliced

1 teaspoon coriander seeds, toasted and crushed using a mortar and pestle

juice of 1 lemon

There are a few rules to follow when serving raw fish. The first is to be certain you are buying the freshest possible fish; the second is that the knife you use is very sharp. I have a wooden mallet I use to tap out the slices of raw fish, protected between two sheets of plastic film. Unlike metal mallets, my wooden mallet has a smooth, flat surface so it doesn't break up whatever is being pounded; the flat side of a meat mallet can be used, with minimum force, instead.

The plates should be chilled before you start slicing the fish; just ensure they are free of smudges as it will be hard to wipe the plates once the fish is portioned. When ordering your salmon, ask for it to be pin-boned and skinned, including removing any dark flesh; 50–60 g per person is sufficient, given the dishes to follow.

If you cannot obtain salt cod, use the best-quality sea salt for this dish. But do try to find it as it is a marvellous combination! A piece of salted codfish will last for months if kept in a dry place (not the refrigerator), so it can be purchased weeks in advance.

Chill 6 clean serving plates in the refrigerator.

Cut the salmon into 5 mm-thick slices. Put 2 or 3 slices inside a clean freezer bag or between 2 pieces of plastic film and gently flatten them. Arrange the slices on one of the chilled plates. Continue until you have 6 plates with a rosette of slices on each. Cover the plates with plastic film and return to the refrigerator until you are ready to serve. (The covered plates can chill in the refrigerator for a couple of hours without any deterioration.)

To make the dressing, place the spring onion, chilli, coriander seed and lemon juice in a small bowl and stir to mix. Set aside.

When ready to serve, remove the plates from the refrigerator and peel away the plastic film. Scatter each plate with a portion of tomato and finger lime pearls (or lemon flesh). Spoon over some of the dressing. Slice the salt cod very thinly with a sharp knife onto a plate; expect it to crumble. Drizzle each portion generously with some beautiful olive oil, scatter over the basil leaves and sprinkle with the shaved salt cod, if using, or season with sea salt.

Serve at once with the hot toast.

Damien's saffron fish velouté

1 litre Fish Stock (see page 506)

pinch of saffron threads

6 small red mullets or other small fish, scaled, cleaned and filleted (to yield about 300 g fillets)

3 small leatherjackets or other small fish, scaled, cleaned and filleted (to yield about 300 g fillets)

6 scallops, roe intact or not, as you prefer, trimmed of any black intestinal threads

sea salt and freshly ground black or white pepper

freshly grated nutmeg

BEURRE MANIE

20 g butter

¼ cup (35 g) plain flour

LIAISON

3 free-range egg yolks

½ cup (125 ml) thickened cream

When Damien Pignolet made this soup for me, he used red mullet and leatherjacket. Red mullet is not always available, but its pretty pink skin and sweet flesh make it an ideal choice. Leatherjackets were common in my childhood, when Dad caught them regularly on fishing outings in Western Port Bay. I rarely see them in Victoria these days and, when I do, they are always skinned; the skin is like leather and cannot be eaten. One never wants to be too prescriptive in naming varieties of fish for soups or stews, as local availability varies. Choose fillets of roughly similar thickness so they poach in the same time; fillets with differently coloured flesh or skin or shapes will add interest. When the best local Australian scallops are available, I slip one into each portion. The serving dishes are important. They should be ovenproof, shallow and wide *assiettes creuses* (see page 511).

To prepare the beurre manie, rub the butter into the flour. Set aside.

Pour the stock into a wide heavy-based frying pan and bring to simmering point over medium heat, then add the saffron. Leave to infuse for a few minutes.

Preheat the oven to 110°C. Heat 6 wide, shallow heatproof soup bowls in the oven, as well as a heatproof plate to keep the fish warm.

Poach the fish (and scallops, if using) in the saffron-scented stock for 5 minutes or until just cooked through. Transfer to the plate in the oven to keep warm. Return the stock to the boil and whisk in small pieces of beurre manie (about the size of a pea) to thicken the stock. Taste it and adjust the seasoning with salt and pepper. Simmer, covered with a piece of lightly buttered baking paper to prevent the soup reducing too much, for 5 minutes.

Meanwhile, make the liaison. Whisk the egg yolks and cream together in a heatproof bowl. Add a ladleful of soup to the egg and cream mixture, then whisk to combine well. Reduce the heat to low (use a simmer mat, if necessary) and pour the egg and cream liaison into the pan. Stir for 1 minute; the texture should be velvety.

Divide the fish and scallops, if using, among the hot soup bowls and pour the soup evenly over, then grind a little pepper and grate a little nutmeg on top. Serve at once.

Swordfish with olive and caper salsa

12 waxy potatoes
(Kipfler or similar), peeled

sea salt

extra virgin olive oil, for drizzling
and cooking

6 × 180 g swordfish *or* tuna steaks

freshly ground black pepper

500 g small green or yellow
(butter) beans, trimmed

4 tablespoons coarsely chopped
flat-leaf parsley

1 tablespoon finely chopped chives

OLIVE AND CAPER SALSA

finely grated zest and juice of
1 lemon

20 green Sicilian olives,
pitted and quartered

20 kalamata olives, pitted
and quartered

1½ tablespoons capers in brine,
drained and patted dry with
paper towel

⅓ cup (80 ml) extra virgin olive oil

freshly ground black pepper

**This dish is very speedy to cook, so all the components should
be ready before you start cooking the fish. As the ingredients
all say 'Sicily' to me, choose big, round, bright green Sicilian
olives. You can use tuna steaks instead of swordfish, if you prefer,
although they are sold twice as thick as swordfish, so will need
to be cooked a little longer.**

To make the salsa, place the lemon zest, lemon juice, olives, capers
and olive oil in a bowl and stir well to combine. Taste and season with
pepper. Cover with plastic film and set aside at room temperature for
at least 1 hour to allow the flavours to develop. Set aside.

Preheat the oven to 110°C. Heat 6 serving plates and a large
plate for the swordfish steaks, if you have to cook them in batches.

Cook the potatoes in an ovenproof saucepan of lightly salted
simmering water for 15–20 minutes, depending on size, until tender.
Drain, slice thickly, return to the pan and add a few drops of olive oil,
then shake gently to coat. Transfer the pan of potatoes to the oven.

Bring a small heavy-based saucepan of lightly salted water to
the simmer. Keep warm.

Heat a chargrill pan or large heavy-based frying pan over high
heat. (Even better if you have the space and equipment to heat
2 pans, so all the fish can cook at the same time.) Brush both sides
of the swordfish steaks with olive oil and season lightly with salt and
pepper. Add the steaks to the pan/s and reduce the heat to medium–
high. Cook the steaks for 3 minutes on each side for medium or
until cooked to your liking. Transfer to the warmed plate and
cover loosely with foil to keep warm. If necessary, repeat with the
remaining swordfish steaks.

Meanwhile, cook the beans in the pan of simmering water for
10 minutes or until just tender. Eat one to test for the perfect tender
bite without any squeak! Drain and set aside.

Place the potato pan over low heat, add the reserved salsa, the
drained beans, parsley and chives and toss together. Divide the potato
evenly among the warmed plates, cover with the fish, then spoon
over the salsa mixture and serve.

Annie's apple caramel tartlets

1 packet all-butter puff pastry
(I use Carême all-butter puff pastry)

plain flour, for dusting

6 small eating apples

double cream or Lemon-scented
verbena Ice-cream (see page 19),
to serve

CARAMEL

1 cup (220 g) caster sugar

1 cup (250 ml) water

60 g unsalted butter

Of course, these sweet little tartlets are really miniature tartes tatin, but when the apples selected are crabapples, they deserve their own identity. This recipe is very closely based on one in Annie Smithers' lovely book, *Annie's Garden to Table*. Most cooks will use more readily available apples, so the instructions are for regular eating apples. Should you happen to have large suitable crabapples, you will need to halve them, then remove the seeds and cores, either with a sharp knife or a very sharp, small melon baller. They do not need to be peeled. And, very roughly, four to five crabapples is the equivalent of one small eating apple.

The size of the dish selected is critical as it determines how many sections of apple will fit and what size each section will be – a half, quarter or an eighth. I think you should peel an apple, halve it, remove the core and have a trial run with your chosen dish. I used shallow 8 cm round ceramic dishes. Annie uses 8 cm-diameter round-based toughened glass dishes. Tart tins with removable bases are not suitable.

Unroll the puff pastry onto a floured workbench and roll it until 5 mm thick. Invert one of your chosen moulds onto the pastry sheet and cut out rounds 2 cm diameter larger than the mould for the base of the tarts. Transfer the pastry rounds to a baking tray lined with baking paper and chill in the refrigerator.

To make the caramel, assemble everything you will need near the stove – the moulds on a baking tray, the sugar, the water, the butter and a whisk. Melt the sugar with ½ cup (125 ml) of the water, stirring until the sugar has melted, then boil the syrup without touching over medium heat for 7 minutes or until it becomes a rich toffee colour. Add the remaining ½ cup (125 ml) water and the butter, standing back as the mixture will hiss and spit. Reduce the heat to low and whisk the caramel until smooth.

Evenly pour the caramel into each mould to generously coat the bottoms. There will be caramel left over, which is intended. Set aside; it will become quite thick but can be easily reheated.

Preheat the oven to 180°C. ➤

recipe continues.

While the caramel cools, prepare your apples. Peel, halve and core, then arrange a bottom layer of apple in each caramel-lined mould, with the largest piece rounded-side down. Fill in and around it with any smaller pieces, if there is still space. Top with a second large piece, rounded-side up.

Bake the apple until soft; this will vary depending on the variety of apple. Mine took 40 minutes to test tender when inserted with a fine skewer. Leave to cool for 5 minutes. (The tartlets can be prepared hours before dinner to this stage. Keep covered with a clean cloth at room temperature.)

Increase the oven temperature to 200°C.

Place a round of puff pastry over each mould and return the tartlets to the oven for 15 minutes or until the pastry is golden and risen. Remove from the oven very carefully – hot caramel causes a nasty burn. (If the pastry lids have risen to great heights, which can happen with the wonderful Carême pastry, just press them down very gently with a dry tea towel for 1 minute.)

Leave to stand for 3–4 minutes, then invert the moulds onto serving plates. Leave for 1 minute before removing the moulds. (Alternatively, the tarts can stand for 30 minutes, then be reheated for 5 minutes, if that is more convenient.)

Re-warm the remaining caramel in the pan over low heat for 2 minutes, then spoon extra caramel over each tartlet.

Offer the very best cream or a scoop of lemon-scented verbena ice-cream to go with these delicious tartlets.

TIMETABLE FOR THE COOK

TWO DAYS BEFORE

- Check **Ingredients List** and note what needs to be purchased
- Check specialist equipment needed (apple tartlet moulds)
- Advise provedores of special requests (fish and scallops)
- Decide on table setting, including serving dishes
- Decide on wine – order if necessary
- Inspect tablecloth and napkins
- All shopping, including flowers
- Collect fish for stock, if making
- Make fish stock (or purchase good-quality stock)
- Thaw pastry for tartlets in refrigerator overnight

DAY BEFORE

- Finely grate zest and juice of lemons – refrigerate
- Pit and quarter olives – refrigerate
- Wash and pick parsley sprigs, cover – refrigerate in a paper towel-lined airtight container
- Chill wine, if necessary

Fish soup
- Make beurre manie
- Reduce fish stock

Apple tartlets
- Select moulds
- Cut a test apple to see how it fits best in a mould
- Roll and cut tartlet pastry lids – refrigerate

MORNING OF

- Chop parsley and snip chives
- Collect fish and scallops (if using)
- Portion fish fillets, place on a wire rack over a plate – refrigerate
- Trim scallops (if using)

Carpaccio
- Place salmon in freezer for 30 minutes only (set timer)
- Slice and flatten salmon – refrigerate
- Section lemon flesh or squeeze finger lime pearls
- Slice salted cod with sharp knife, then cover (do not refrigerate)

Swordfish/tuna
- Prepare vegetables
- Slice spring onion and chilli
- Toast and coarsely crush coriander seeds

- Set table

AFTERNOON OF

- Preheat oven to 180°C

Carpaccio
- Chill plates

Fish soup
- Infuse fish stock with saffron

Swordfish/tuna
- Mix salsa ingredients – do not refrigerate

Green salad
- Wash, dry and crisp salad leaves
- Prepare salad dressing in salad bowl with crossed salad servers ready to toss before serving

Apple tarts
- Make caramel and line moulds, reserving pan of extra caramel
- Cut apples to fit moulds and bake

ONE HOUR BEFORE GUESTS ARRIVE

Apple tarts
- Preheat oven to 200°C
- Place puff pastry lids over apple tarts and bake for 20 minutes (set timer)
- Remove tarts carefully, gently press excessively puffed pastry with a dry tea towel and leave on the tray

THIRTY MINUTES BEFORE GUESTS ARRIVE

- Adjust oven temperature to 110°C
- Warm soup plates, main plates and serving dish for resting cooked fish (see page 512)

Swordfish/tuna
- Remove swordfish/tuna from refrigerator and brush with olive oil, season and cover

Carpaccio
- Divide among chilled plates, if not already done
- Mix dressing ingredients

Fish soup
- Assemble fish in saffron stock on stove ready for poaching
- Whisk yolks and cream together in a heatproof bowl – set on side of stove

DINNER IS SERVED

FIRST COURSE

- Garnish carpaccio – add dressing, codfish and final drizzle of olive oil, then serve

- Meanwhile, prepare to serve third/main course

- Cook potatoes for 15 minutes (set timer)
- Drizzle with olive oil and transfer pan to oven
- Put pan of lightly salted water on for beans

SECOND COURSE

- Remove heated soup plates from oven, leaving plate for cooked fish
- Poach fish, portion into warm bowls, finish soup
- Ladle into bowls, season with pepper and freshly grated nutmeg and serve

THIRD/MAIN COURSE

- Heat pan/pans for cooking swordfish or tuna
- Remove potato pan from oven and set on stovetop
- Remove main course plates from oven and increase oven temperature to 200°C
- Cook beans until tender, drain
- Sear fish for 3 minutes each side, transfer to warmed main course plates
- Add salsa ingredients, beans, parsley and chives to potatoes, beans and parsley
- Shake together gently and spoon over fish steaks
- Toss and serve green salad

DESSERT

- Return tartlets to oven for 5 minutes (set timer)
- Carefully invert tartlets onto serving plates
- Re-warm extra caramel and spoon over apple
- Offer tartlets with cream

INGREDIENTS LIST

PANTRY

- Sea salt
- Fine salt
- Australian extra virgin olive oil
- Red-wine vinegar
- Plain flour
- Caster sugar

SPICE SHELF

- Black peppercorns
- Coriander seeds
- Saffron threads
- Nutmeg (whole)
- White peppercorns (optional)

REFRIGERATOR

- Milk
- Unsalted butter
- Thickened cream
- Free-range eggs
- 1 litre good-quality purchased fish stock (if making homemade, see page 506)
- Green sicilian olives
- Kalamata olives
- Capers in brine
- 1 packet all-butter puff pastry
- Double cream or Lemon-scented verbena ice-cream (see page 19)

GREENGROCER/FARMERS' MARKET (OR GARDEN)

- Flat-leaf parsley
- 20 small basil leaves
- Chives
- Sprig lemon verbena leaves (optional, if making ice-cream)
- Selection of salad leaves
- 1 large ripe tomato or 2 smaller tomatoes

- 2 lemons
- 2 finger limes (or an extra lemon)
- 3 spring onions
- 2–3 small fresh red chillies
- 12 waxy potatoes, such as Kipfler
- 500 g small green or yellow (butter) beans, trimmed
- 6 small eating apples

FISHMONGER

- 1 × 400 g centre-cut salmon fillet, pin-boned, skinned and trimmed of any dark flesh
- 100 g piece salt cod (*baccala*) (or the smallest piece you can buy; optional)
- 6 small red mullets or other small fish, scaled, cleaned and filleted (to yield about 300 g fillets)
- 3 small leatherjackets or other small fish, scaled, cleaned and filletcd (to yield about 300 g fillets)
- 6 scallops, roe intact or not, as you prefer (optional)
- 6 × 180 g swordfish or tuna steaks
- Trimmings from mullet and other fish (optional)

BAKER

- Sourdough bread

CELLAR

- Wine for the table
- Dry white wine for stock (optional)
- Soft drink

FROM THE

VEGETABLE GARDEN

A DINNER FOR 6

SLOW-ROASTED
Peppers & Fennel

Gnocchi Fritti

Green Salad
with GARLIC CROUTONS
& PRETTY PETALS

Gözleme
with GREEK BASIL,
SILVERBEET & FETA

Roasted Pumpkin
with SAGE & AMARETTI PANGRATTATO

———

Chocolate Budino

7

As I write this in late summer, almost autumn, the pepper (capsicum) bushes are still laden, there are still eggplants (aubergines), the very last of my tomatoes adorn the straggly bushes (some still green), and the herbs and leafy crops are still giving generously.

Why not take the opportunity to involve the children and cook a colourful meal together? It will be a special thrill for your children to cook with you. I have worked with young children in schools for many years now, as they learn to grow and cook some of their own food. I can vouch for their competence and enthusiasm – they love to do stuff! These students want to chop, stir, slice, roll or mix. They make pasta, carefully dry salad leaves, and handle food processors and knives, as well as rolling pins. These young kitchen gardeners are accustomed to harvesting produce from their own gardens, so their dishes are almost always vegetarian. They are also accustomed to making something delicious from small quantities, as their harvest often has to offer tastes for 20 classmates. Not a worry for a family, but it does mean that fritters, flatbreads, dips, pie fillings and soups are often on the menu. Combined with eggs from happy chickens, spices, herbs and cheeses, all manner of good things can be made.

In my small garden I have a flourishing tiny-leaved Greek basil plant, as well as the more usual floppy-leaved variety. I prefer to use the large floppy leaves to make pesto and survey my filled jars with pride. My friend Janni Kyritsis told me a lovely story regarding Greek basil. As a child in Greece he remembers that every household grew this variety in emptied food tins on kitchen windowsills. The breeze blew the scent indoors through the open windows. The basil was picked at the end of summer and hung to dry all winter. It was also dipped in holy water and shaken in church during the service, presumably to add its scent there too. I wanted to use it so it found its way into the filling for *gözleme* on page 130. These Turkish pastries are traditionally made by filling hand-rolled dough sheets with a range of toppings – in this case freshly picked silverbeet leaves – then sealing and cooking them over a grill.

Although some of my peppers are still green, I picked a few last week to bring inside and, to my surprise, they reddened in a few days. I will combine some of these peppers with a purchased bulb of fennel. I was served a delicious compote of slowly stewed, meltingly soft red and green peppers with a little side plate of puffy hot *gnocchi fritti* (fried dough, see page 129) in a local cafe recently. A note of caution here – deep-frying and anything to do with boiling water are moments when an adult needs to be supervising if children are assisting in the kitchen.

The pumpkin patch has to be one of the most successful and generous crops in many of the school gardens I visit. One does tire of pumpkin soup, although I can enjoy quite a few pumpkin scones (see page 201)! A great culinary triumph of the Italian city of Modena is a combination of sweet pumpkin, crisp sage and butter, with the tantalising extra note of crumbled amaretti biscuits (trust me) usually found as a pasta filling. With a bit of a twist, the flavours can also work as a dish without the pasta. On page 132 I roasted slices of pumpkin and have added some of these flavours at the end. This combination also makes a successful topping for bruschetta.

Of course, a meal from the garden is not complete without a great leafy salad, given a bit of crunch with some roughly torn sourdough croutons. If the garden permits, a scattering of pretty petals – borage, calendula, heartsease (viola) and/or chive blossoms – are wonderful additions.

You can decide whether you serve this lovely meal as a procession of dishes, once known as *service á la Russe*, or whether you copy what happens in many kitchen garden classrooms, where service is *à la Française*, and everything comes to the table at once on platters (often colourful and mismatched), so it is a personal decision in what order one eats what.

Then, after such a splendid vegetarian meal, it would be appropriate to offer small portions of a luscious Italian chocolate budino, a rich, creamy Italian custard-like dessert (see page 135).

Slow-roasted peppers and fennel

2 red peppers (capsicums),
stem ends and seeds removed

2 yellow peppers (capsicums),
stem ends and seeds removed

1 bulb fennel, quartered, then cut
into long 1 cm-thick slices

2 fresh bay leaves

4 cloves garlic, peeled

generous sprig of thyme

½ cup (125 ml) extra virgin olive oil

sea salt and freshly ground
black pepper

This meltingly soft yet intensely flavoured dish can be enjoyed in many ways. Here it is served as a first course with fried *gnocchi fritti* alongside. On another occasion, the vegetables would make a delicious bruschetta topping, could be part of an antipasto plate, used as an omelette filling, or offered as the vegetable accompaniment to simply grilled fish. It is nicest if the cook has peeled the peppers before cooking. The finished dish can be gently reheated if needed to be warm. (See recipe picture on page 126.)

Preheat the oven to 150°C.

Cut the peppers along their natural grooves to make 2–3 cm-wide pieces. Using a speed peeler (sometimes called an asparagus peeler) and a loose zigzag motion, peel off as much of the skin as you can.

Place the peppers, fennel, bay leaves, garlic, thyme and olive oil in a heavy-based flameproof casserole dish (enamelled cast-iron is perfect). Stir to make sure all the vegetables are coated with oil. Cover tightly and bake for at least 3 hours. Inspect to see if the vegetables are completely soft and just starting to caramelise. If they are soft but still swimming in the oil, transfer the casserole to the stovetop over high heat and, watching carefully, cook for 5–10 minutes, shaking the casserole dish regularly to prevent sticking. (If they are not soft and starting to caramelise at the edges, bake for another 20 minutes, then check again.)

Season with salt and pepper, then tip all the vegetables and oily juices into a serving dish. Serve warm or at room temperature.

Gnocchi fritti

1 teaspoon instant dried yeast

½ cup (125 ml) lukewarm water

2 cups (300 g) plain flour,
plus extra for dusting

1 teaspoon sea salt

40 g butter, melted

50 ml iced water

600 ml extra virgin olive oil,
or as needed, for deep-frying
(see page 501), plus extra for
greasing

sea salt

salumi, to serve (optional)

These puffs are delicious with all sorts of salty *salumi* (Italian cold cuts), with a plate of olives or, as served here, alongside softly stewed, oily vegetables. They are best eaten immediately after they are fried. (See recipe picture on page 126.)

Leftover rolled dough can be kept for an hour or so closely covered with plastic film to prevent it drying out. Fried *gnocchi fritti* are not nice if they sit around for any length of time, but a second batch of freshly fried ones would sometimes be very welcome. Alternatively, any excess *gnocchi* can be frozen in an airtight container, and will still puff up when deep-fried straight from the freezer. Do use quality oil for deep-frying and check the temperature with a thermometer; it should be at 170°C. To minimise the amount of olive oil needed, select a small deep heavy-based saucepan and be prepared to fry several batches. If you use a wide pan you will need a lot more oil.

Dissolve the yeast in the water until it looks a bit bubbly.

Put the flour and salt into a food processor and whizz to blend. Mix the melted butter with the dissolved yeast mixture. With the motor running, add the butter/yeast mixture and the iced water. Process until the mixture starts to form a ball. Remove the dough; it should feel soft and pliable.

Knead the dough on a floured workbench for 5 minutes or until it feels a bit sticky but elastic. Place in an oiled bowl, cover with plastic film and leave at room temperature for 1 hour or until doubled in size.

Place the dough on a workbench lightly dusted with flour, then roll to about 5 mm thick. Using a pizza cutter, cut into 4 cm squares.

Preheat the oven to 120°C and place a baking tray inside to keep batches of *gnocchi fritti* warm while the next lot are frying.

Heat olive oil for deep-frying in a small deep heavy-based saucepan to 170°C. Fry 3–4 dough pieces at a time for 3 minutes or until puffed and golden brown on both sides. Using a slotted spoon, transfer the hot *gnocchi fritti* to paper towel to drain for 2–3 minutes, then transfer to the tray in the oven to keep warm. Sprinkle with a little salt before serving. Continue until all are fried.

Serve warm with *salumi*, if desired.

Gözleme with Greek basil, silverbeet and feta

150 ml lukewarm water

1 scant teaspoon instant dried yeast

pinch of fine salt

½ teaspoon caster sugar

1½ cups (225 g) plain flour, plus extra for dusting

1 tablespoon extra virgin olive oil, plus extra for brushing

lemon wedges, to serve

FILLING

10–12 leaves freshly picked silverbeet *or* chard leaves

2 tablespoons chopped Greek basil *or* dill, marjoram *or* regular basil

125 g feta, crumbled

sea salt and freshly ground black pepper

The challenge is to roll the dough as thinly as the Turkish women I saw. My first Istanbul *gözleme* was filled with blanched chopped nettles and curd cheese. Back home, I was especially pleased with the one I filled with chard leaves freshly picked from my garden. The dough balls can be refrigerated for up to three days, covered with plastic film to prevent them drying out. Leave for 30 minutes at room temperature before rolling and cooking.

Combine the lukewarm water, yeast, salt and sugar in a jug. Stir with a fork. Cover, then stand in a warm, draught-free spot for 5 minutes or until bubbles form on the surface.

Sift the flour into a food processor. Add the olive oil to the yeast mixture. With the motor running, add the liquid mixture to the flour and process briefly to form a soft dough. Turn the dough onto a lightly floured workbench. Knead for 5 minutes or until elastic. Cut the dough into 6 even portions. Place on a greased baking tray or in a lightly oiled bowl. Cover with a clean tea towel. Stand in a warm, draught-free spot for 30 minutes or until the dough looks puffed and has more or less doubled in size.

Meanwhile, make the filling. Wash and dry the silverbeet or chard leaves and roll them together, then thinly slice. Place in a bowl and mix with the herbs.

Dust a workbench with flour. Roll each piece of dough into a 22 cm diameter round. Place one-sixth of the leaves over half of each round. Top with one-sixth of the feta and season with salt and pepper. Fold the dough over to enclose the filling. Press the edges together to seal. Carefully place on a baking tray lined with baking paper without touching, to prevent them sticking or tearing.

Heat a large heavy-based frying pan (or the clean flat plate of your barbecue, which means they can all cook at once) to medium. Brush one side of each *gözleme* with a little olive oil and flip into the pan or onto the flatplate. Cook for 2–3 minutes or until golden, then brush the uncooked side with olive oil. Flip over and cook for 2–3 minutes, until golden and crisp.

Cut into wedges, then serve immediately with lemon wedges alongside.

Roasted pumpkin with sage
and amaretti pangrattato

750–800 g Kent or butternut pumpkin (squash), cut into 1.5 cm-thick slices

2 tablespoons extra virgin olive oil, plus extra for brushing and drizzling

2 cloves garlic, bruised

18 sage leaves

sea salt

AMARETTI PANGRATTATO

2 cloves garlic, finely chopped

2 tablespoons pumpkin seed kernels (pepitas)

½ cup (60 g) panko breadcrumbs *or* coarse fresh breadcrumbs

3 amaretti biscuits, crumbled

finely grated zest of 1 lemon

few shakes of chilli flakes

⅓ cup (25 g) finely grated parmesan

1 tablespoon extra virgin olive oil

½ teaspoon sea salt

Select your favourite type of pumpkin – I like both Kent and butternut very much. Both have skins that bake to a slightly chewy texture that I also enjoy, but you can peel the pumpkin if you prefer. If you plan to eat the skin, wipe it before starting to cut the slices. The pangrattato features amaretti, an Italian biscuit flavoured with apricot kernels or almond kernels, which add a very distinctive, if faint, taste of bitter almonds. The biscuits are widely available in supermarkets; the most authentic are made by Italian companies. Any leftover pumpkin makes a delicious pizza topping, or can be added to a pasta dish or frittata.

Preheat the oven to 220°C. Line a baking tray with baking paper.

Put the pumpkin and olive oil into a bowl and turn to ensure that all sides are coated. Place on the lined tray, then add the garlic. Bake for 30 minutes, turning halfway, or until tender and blistered.

To make the pangrattato, place the garlic, pumpkin seeds, panko, amaretti, lemon zest, chilli, parmesan, olive oil and salt in a bowl and mix lightly; you don't want to compact this mixture. Scatter the pangrattato thickly over each pumpkin slice.

Brush the sage leaves with extra olive oil and place a few on each pumpkin slice. Bake for a further 5–8 minutes or until the topping is golden and starting to bubble.

Using an egg lifter or similar, pile the pumpkin slices onto a serving platter, give a final drizzle of olive oil and a sprinkle of salt, and serve warm or at room temperature.

Chocolate budino

70 g good-quality
Dutched cocoa, sifted

½ cup (110 g) firmly packed
brown sugar

2 tablespoons caster sugar

2 tablespoons cornflour

pinch of salt

2 cups (500 ml) milk

100 g bittersweet/dark chocolate
(70 per cent cocoa solids),
finely chopped

½ teaspoon pure vanilla extract *or*
1 teaspoon liqueur, such as Cognac,
Armagnac *or* Grand Marnier

softly whipped cream or pouring
cream, to serve

**This fascinating dessert tastes impossibly rich and yet it is made
without cream, eggs or butter. The quality of the chocolate and
the cocoa are important. And I like to serve it with a puddle of
pouring cream or softly whipped cream on top. My friend and
colleague Lauraine Jacobs from Auckland alerted me to this
recipe and I have since made it many times. Lauraine tops her
budino with chopped roasted hazelnuts.**

Place the cocoa, sugars, cornflour and salt in a bowl and whisk with
1 cup (250 ml) of the milk until smooth. Transfer to a heavy-based
saucepan and add the chocolate, then whisk over medium heat until
the chocolate has melted and the mixture is glossy and smooth (use
a spatula occasionally to scrape down the side, ensuring no mixture
lodges in between the saucepan's base and side). Add the remaining
milk and cook, whisking constantly, for 5 minutes or until the pudding
is thick and smooth and large bubbles are popping on the surface.
Working quickly, remove the pan from the heat and whisk in the
vanilla extract or liqueur.

Immediately pour the pudding mixture evenly into six 100 ml-
capacity serving glasses or bowls (or four 150 ml-capacity serving
glasses or bowls).

Serve the budino warm or chilled. A skin will form quickly on
the surface; if you want to avoid this, press plastic film directly
onto the surface as soon as you pour it into the glasses or bowls.
Serve topped with cream.

TIMETABLE FOR THE COOK

FIVE DAYS BEFORE

- Check **Ingredients List** and note what needs to be purchased
- Plan to visit a farmers' market, if available

TWO DAYS BEFORE

- Check specialist equipment needed (deep-fry thermometer)
- All shopping, including flowers
- Decide on table setting, including serving dishes
- Inspect tablecloth and napkins
- If barbecuing *gözleme*, check barbecue is clean and check fuel
- Decide on wine – order if necessary

DAY BEFORE

Gözleme
- Make dough, cover with plastic film – refrigerate

- Make amaretti pangrattato

MORNING OF

- Peel and prepare peppers (capsicums)
- Prepare fennel
- Slice pumpkin, coat with oil and arrange in baking dish
- Chill wine

Gözleme
- Prepare silverbeet filling

Budino
- Make, cover with plastic film – decide whether to chill or not?

AFTERNOON OF

Pepper and fennel dish
- Preheat oven to 150°C
- Bake for 3 hours (set timer)

Gnocchi fritti
- Make dough

Gözleme
- Cut lemon wedges

Green salad
- Wash, dry and crisp salad leaves and greens – refrigerate
- Prepare dressing in bowl with crossed salad servers ready to toss before serving

- Set table

TWO HOURS BEFORE GUESTS ARRIVE

Pepper and fennel dish
- Remove from oven – keep at room temperature

Gözleme
- Fill and fold

Pumpkin
- Adjust oven to 220°C and bake for 30 minutes (set timer) – keep at room temperature

Gnocchi fritti
- Reduce oven temperature to 120°C and place tray inside
- Roll and cut dough
- Assemble pan for deep-frying with thermometer, olive oil, slotted spoon and paper towel-lined tray for draining

ONE HOUR BEFORE GUESTS ARRIVE

- Get changed
- *Gözleme* – heat barbecue
- Warm plates and serving dishes (see page 512)
- *Gnocchi fritti* – fry 3–4 per person at 170°C and transfer to lined tray in oven

DINNER IS SERVED

FIRST COURSE

- Divide warm peppers and fennel into bowls
- Place hot *gnocchi fritti* on central platter

SECOND COURSE

- Host absent to cook *gözleme* in one hit on hot barbecue
- Cut *gözleme* into wedges or slices and place on central platter for self-service
- Platter with lemon wedges on table
- Finish pumpkin dish – put back into 200°C oven with pangrattato and sage leaves for 5–8 minutes (set timer)

THIRD COURSE

- Serve pumpkin on individual plates
- Toss and serve green salad

DESSERT

- Put cream onto budino and serve

INGREDIENTS LIST

PANTRY

· Sea salt
· Fine salt
· Australian extra virgin olive oil
· Red-wine vinegar
· Plain flour
· Cornflour (wheaten)
· Instant dried yeast
· Caster sugar
· Brown sugar
· Panko breadcrumbs (or bread
  for coarse fresh breadcrumbs)
· Pumpkin seed kernels (pepitas)
· Amaretti biscuits
· Good-quality Dutched cocoa
· Bittersweet/dark chocolate
  (70 per cent cocoa solids)

SPICE SHELF

· Black peppercorns
· Chilli flakes
· Pure vanilla extract

REFRIGERATOR

· Butter
· Milk
· Pouring cream
· 125 g feta
· 25 g parmesan

GREENGROCER/FARMERS' MARKET (OR GARDEN)

· Fresh bay leaves
· Thyme
· Greek basil (or dill, marjoram
  or regular basil)
· 18 sage leaves
· Garlic
· 2 lemons
· 2 red peppers (capsicums)
· 2 yellow peppers (capsicums)
· 1 bulb fennel
· 10–12 silverbeet or
  chard leaves
· 800 g Kent or butternut
  pumpkin (squash)
· Selection of salad leaves
· Edible flowers

BUTCHER/DELICATESSEN

· *Salumi* (Italian cold cuts;
  optional)

BAKER

· Bread for dinner
· Sourdough for croutons

CELLAR

· Wine for the table
· Soft drink
· Cognac, Armagnac or
  Grand Marnier, for dessert

PUGLIA
CUCINA
POVERA

BUT DELIZIOSA

A DINNER FOR 6

CHILLI, FENNEL SEED & OLIVE OIL
TARALLI

MUSSELS
with A CRUNCHY CRUST

BOWL OF OLIVES

———

ORECCHIETTE
with RAPINI

———

FISH
BAKED ON LEMON LEAVES
with A CRUMB & LEMON ZEST CRUST

GREEN SALAD

———

PUGLIAN BOWL
OF FIGS & GRAPES

ESPRESSO BISCUITS

8

I was excited to visit Puglia for the first time with some of my favourite food-loving adventurers. The land is bare and dry, speaking of a harsher life than in the North of Italy. The beautiful stone walls edging the fields are a by-product of this rugged land, and much stone clearing had to occur before it could be cultivated. The olive trees are quite different from those seen elsewhere in Italy. Here they have thick, gnarled trunks, often more than 50 cm in diameter, and with bushy tops quite unlike the pruned, shapely trees of Umbria and Tuscany.

Our first few days were spent at Il Frantoio, an excellent example of the *agriturismo* destinations (farm stays on working farms) that dot Italy today. These *masseria* (farms) are required to serve a high percentage of food produced on the property. At breakfast, the fruit was either persimmon, tiny green figs with crimson centres, peeled prickly pear, grapes or oranges. Sweet dishes were often made with almonds and lemons harvested from the property.

Il Frantoio's owner was very entertaining and a passionate Pugliese. He announced one evening, 'Do not think that the cooking of Puglia is just orecchiette with broccoli and a mixed grill. Our history goes back 700 years. And did you know that only 80 per cent of pasta is boiled; 20 per cent is fried?' We were then served a dish of unadorned fried borage pasta, which reminded me that the cooking of Puglia is definitely *cucina povera* (cooking of the poor). I preferred the following evening's pasta made with spelt flour tossed with chopped zucchini (courgette) flowers and a touch of saffron. My favourite dish of all was a chickpea roulade (*farinata*) filled with tiny green beans, chopped chicory and ricotta.

From this base camp, we visited some wonderful towns. I particularly enjoyed an outstanding lunch at Taverna della Gelosia in the old town of Ostuni, which commenced with an exceptional parade of antipasti: a white bean puree topped with cooked chicory; *lampascioni* (translated as wild onions but in fact wild hyacinth bulbs); deep-fried zucchini flowers; tiny-shaped fresh ricotta served with a dollop of caramelised onion; grilled peppers (capsicum); eggplant parmigiana; and more and more.

Puglia Cucina Povera *but* Deliziosa

Next came the most exciting fresh pasta dishes, each one served in a 'basket' made of the hard Puglian semolina bread. The combinations were: cavatelli with zucchini, mint and pine nuts; *fenescecchie*, a special Puglian-style macaroni (made by rolling small discs of pasta around a thin metal rod like a knitting needle), with wild fennel, almonds and herbs; and orecchiette with rapini and anchovy.

Then we moved on to a gracious and historic villa in tiny Tricase Porto, just about the southernmost tip of Puglia. Sitting on the shady *loggia* (veranda), you looked down the sweeping driveway to the sea wall and beyond to the Adriatic. Next landfall Greece. This was our home for a week. Day and night we were soothed by the sighing of the breeze through the tall pines. Tricase Porto has a tiny boat harbour dotted with brightly painted fishing boats. A walk around the sea wall revealed villa after villa, layered up the hillside. So many families must summer here – we could imagine how different our sleepy Tricase Porto might be in July and August.

We made expeditions to nearby Castro to buy the morning's catch from the spotless fish shop, cut into the stone of the hillside about 100 metres from the sea. We bought eight *orata* (a type of bream) and, after scaling and gutting, the proprietor took a bucket and drew seawater to sluice the fish. This seawater, five metres from a harbour full of fishing craft, ran as clear as tap water. Later that night, I baked the fish on lemon leaves with a crust of the most laboriously worked breadcrumbs – I put oven-baked hunks of bread into a plastic bag wrapped in a tea towel and bashed them with a wine bottle, sifted this through a coarse plastic sieve, then mixed it with garlic and lemon zest. Alongside were waxy potatoes baked with rosemary and olives. The perfect finish was a platter of ripe figs and bunches of sweet purple grapes. I bought espresso-flavoured biscotti at the local bakery, which were a perfect accompaniment to a glass of Primitivo di Manduria Dolce Naturale, the deliciously sweet DOCG (*Denominazione di Origine Controllata e Garantita*) dessert wine from the area.

For our last day, we visited stunning Lecce and admired the highly decorated cathedral and beautiful cloisters. We lingered here, then drove back to the villa via a narrow coastal road. The brilliant-orange sun sank slowly, leaving behind a lavender twilight with the pines and olives as dark silhouettes.

Chilli, fennel seed and olive oil *taralli*

1½ cups (225 g) strong plain bread flour, plus extra for dusting

¼ teaspoon instant dried yeast

1 × 25 g sachet tomato paste (puree)

¾ teaspoon sea salt, plus extra to sprinkle

½ teaspoon dried chilli flakes, plus extra to sprinkle

¾ teaspoon fennel seeds

1½ tablespoons extra virgin olive oil, plus extra for brushing

1½ tablespoons dry white wine

90 ml lukewarm water

bowl of olives (such as Sicilian green olives), to serve

These hard little fennel-flavoured biscuits are the perfect nibble to accompany an aperitif. (See recipe picture on pages 142–143.)

Place the flour, yeast, tomato paste, salt, chilli flakes and fennel seeds in a food processor and whizz for a few seconds to mix. Combine the olive oil, wine and water and, with the motor running, add to the flour mixture and process until a ball forms. Turn the dough out onto a floured workbench and knead for 3–5 minutes or until smooth and elastic.

Roll the dough into a sausage shape and cut in half to make 2 logs. Cut each log into 1 cm-thick slices and roll each one into an 8 cm-long rope. Join the ends together and place on baking trays lined with baking paper; you should have about 30 *taralli*. Set aside for 1 hour.

Preheat the oven to 190°C. Bring a saucepan of water to the boil and, working in batches, boil the *taralli* for 1 minute or until they float. Remove with a slotted spoon, transfer to a wire rack and leave to cool.

Return the *taralli* to the lined baking trays, brush with extra olive oil and scatter with extra chilli flakes and salt. Bake for 30–40 minutes or until dark golden. Cool and store in airtight containers for up to 1 month.

Serve with a bowl of olives alongside.

Serves 6

Mussels with a crunchy crust

24 black mussels, well scrubbed and bearded

½ cup (125 ml) dry white wine

6 tablespoons coarsely chopped flat-leaf parsley

½ cup (35 g) fresh white breadcrumbs

¼ cup (20 g) grated pecorino

1 clove garlic, very finely chopped

freshly ground black pepper (or ½ teaspoon very finely chopped small fresh red chilli)

extra virgin olive oil, for drizzling

These delicious mussels are an ideal addition to the antipasto table. Here they are served alongside the *taralli* and a bowl of local olives (see picture on page 143). On another occasion, this amount would make a starter for two or three. The mussels can be eaten with fingers but do be careful as the shell edges can be very sharp – maybe serve with teaspoons or small forks.

Place the mussels in a wide heavy-based frying pan with a lid and pour on the wine. Cook, covered, over medium heat for 5 minutes or until a gush of steam tells you the mussels are opening and cooked. Immediately transfer the opened mussels to a plate, reserving the liquid, and, as soon as they're cool enough to handle, remove and discard the top shells. Inspect every mussel to make sure there are no bits of 'beard' left.

Mix the parsley, breadcrumbs, pecorino, garlic and pepper or chilli in a bowl. Strain the mussel juice through a fine-mesh sieve lined with muslin or paper towel. Add enough of the strained juice to make a moist mixture. Evenly spoon the breadcrumb mixture over each mussel, covering it completely.

Preheat an oven griller to very hot. Transfer the mussels to a baking tray. Generously drizzle with olive oil and grill for 5 minutes or until golden and just starting to look bubbly; not for too long or the mussels will toughen.

Serve at once.

Orecchiette with rapini

sea salt

500 g dried orecchiette
(see page 512)

¼ cup (60 ml) extra virgin olive
oil, plus extra for drizzling

2 cloves garlic, thinly sliced

8 anchovy fillets in olive oil,
chopped

1–2 small fresh red chillies,
seeded and thinly sliced

5–6 cups (5–6 large handfuls)
trimmed rapini

freshly ground black pepper
(optional)

This is probably the dish most closely associated with Puglia. To make this dish outside the region, it is first necessary to identify what rapini is. It has many names, including *cimi di rape* or broccoli *raab* and will most likely be found in an Italian-owned greengrocer. Bunches are often huge and ungainly, including the thick lower stems, which are inedible. You need to sort the thin stems with leaves and clusters of yellow flowers attached, then cut these into 10–12 cm lengths. It is very easy to grow; however, in my experience, it needs to grow rapidly to avoid stringiness. The flavour is somewhere between broccolini and chicory, always with an element of bitterness that is part of its charm. The orecchiette takes longer to cook than the greens, so put them on first – it's their resilience, combined with the bitterness of the rapini, which makes such a great combination.

Preheat the oven to 110°C and place 6 pasta bowls inside to warm.

Put a large heavy-based saucepan (mine is 8 litre capacity) of well-salted water on to boil. Drop in the pasta and bring back to the boil, stirring once or twice to keep the pasta from sticking.

Meanwhile, heat the olive oil and garlic in a heavy-based frying pan over medium heat, stirring for 1 minute or until the garlic is just pale-gold. Immediately drop in the anchovy and, using a wooden spoon, crush to a paste. Add the chilli, remove the pan from the heat and set aside.

Taste the pasta and, if a few minutes from being al dente, drop in the rapini. Cook for a further 5 minutes, then taste a stalk. If it is tender and the pasta is al dente, drain in a colander or continue to cook until al dente. Return the pasta and rapini to the hot pan and tip in the anchovy and chilli sauce. Stir to mix.

Tip evenly into the warmed pasta bowls. Season with a little salt, add a drizzle of olive oil and grinding of pepper for extra spice, if desired, then serve.

Fish baked on lemon leaves
with a crumb and lemon zest crust

½ cup (125 ml) extra virgin
olive oil

6 waxy potatoes, such as
Kipflers *or* Dutch creams,
washed and cut on the diagonal
into 1 cm-thick slices

12 unsprayed lemon leaves,
washed and dried (avoid the
oldest and most leathery)

12 slices lemon

6 × 180 g thick white fish cutlets

sea salt and freshly ground
black pepper

2 fresh small red chillies

Green Salad (see page 503),
to serve

CRUMB AND LEMON ZEST
CRUST

¾ cup (50 g) fresh
white breadcrumbs

finely grated zest of 2 lemons

2 cloves garlic, very finely chopped

3 tablespoons coarsely chopped
flat-leaf parsley

sea salt and freshly ground
black pepper

extra virgin olive oil, for drizzling

**In Puglia we made this dish with *orata*, a very firm fleshed
fish. At home, I have made it with thick mackerel cutlets and,
on another occasion, with snapper cutlets. Select an oval or
rectangular baking dish that comfortably holds the fish with
quite a bit of room to spare for the potatoes. The finished dish
can be brought to the table for self-service; ideal if lunch is to
be served from a long buffet outdoors.**

Preheat the oven to 180°C. Brush a baking dish (mine is oval
and approximately 32 cm × 26 cm) with a little of the olive oil.

Cook the potato in a pan of simmering water for 5–8 minutes.
Drain and set aside.

Brush the lemon leaves and lemon slices with olive oil and place
in the dish. Place the fish cutlets on top, leaving gaps between them.
Tuck the potato slices in between the fish, then poke in the chillies.
Drizzle the fish and potatoes with most of the olive oil and cover
tightly with foil. Bake for 15 minutes.

Meanwhile, prepare the crust. Place the breadcrumbs, lemon
zest, garlic, parsley and salt and pepper in a small bowl and mix to
combine. Moisten with the remaining olive oil.

Remove the fish from the oven and remove the foil; it will
not be fully cooked. Turn the fish over, lift the lemon slices from
underneath and place them over the potato; they will caramelise
during the next cooking stage. Scatter the crust evenly over the
fish and spoon the pan juices over the crust.

Increase the oven temperature to 200°C. Return the fish and
potato to the oven for a further 8–10 minutes or until the crust is
golden and the fish is cooked through. Meanwhile, warm 6 serving
plates (see page 512).

Serve at once, with a green salad to the side.

Puglian bowl of figs and grapes
with Espresso biscuits

I do love the simple beauty of a still-life of fruit on a beautiful wide platter. Few things are more sensual than ripe figs, their skins almost bursting, and I would opt for a mixture of green and red grapes. In Puglia, the fruit display was determined by what was in the orchard or nearby. It may well have included pomegranates, persimmons and mulberries or prickly pears, depending on the season.

Ripe prickly pears are very sweet, but first-timers need to be warned about the prickles in the skin. They are almost always carefully peeled in the kitchen, away from the dining table, using a sharp knife and holding the fruit with a fork. The peels are dropped straight into the compost bin, as it is astonishing how a small number of prickles from the skins can find their way onto your hands if the fruit has been peeled on a chopping board. If you have access to freshly harvested almonds, scatter a few handfuls amongst the fruit. And there are always local biscotti to enjoy at this stage in the meal, dipped in sweet wine or not, as you prefer. (See recipe picture on pages 150–153.)

Espresso biscuits

125 g unsalted butter, slightly softened

¼ cup (55 g) caster sugar

125 g plain flour, plus extra for dusting

25 g finely ground espresso roast coffee beans

These biscuits require finely ground coffee beans *not* instant coffee or coffee essence; their granular crunch is part of the charm. The dough needs to be chilled well before baking. It can either be rolled using a silicone pastry mat and cut into shapes or rolled into a cylinder, then sliced and baked as required.

Using an electric mixer or hand-held electric beaters, cream the butter and sugar. Add the flour and coffee and mix just until blended; do not overmix. Gather the dough together and press into a 4 cm-diameter roll or flatten into a disc. Wrap in plastic film and refrigerate to chill thoroughly.

Roll the dough into a log on a lightly floured silicone mat, then flatten slightly. Place on a baking tray lined with baking paper, then chill in the refrigerator for 15 minutes. Cut into 5 mm-thick slices. Alternatively, roll the dough out and cut into shapes – stars, fingers or anything you fancy.

Preheat the oven to 170°C. Bake the biscotti for 15–20 minutes, until firm to the touch and pale golden around the edges. Cool on the tray. Store in an airtight container.

TIMETABLE FOR THE COOK

THREE DAYS BEFORE

- Check **Ingredients List** and note what needs to be purchased
- Visit specialist Italian supplier for special requests (rapini; fruit, including prickly pear, grapes, persimmons, mulberries, figs season permitting)
- Pick unsprayed lemon leaves from your own (or a neighbour's) tree

TWO DAYS BEFORE

- Decide on table setting, including serving dishes
- Decide on wines – order if necessary
- Inspect tablecloth and napkins
- Complete all shopping, including flowers
- Order fish and mussels

DAY BEFORE

- Dry chunks of bread overnight for crumbs

Taralli
- Make dough
- Cook and cool – store in an airtight container

Orecchiette
- Trim and wash rapini – refrigerate

Espresso biscuits
- Make dough – refrigerate
- Bake and cool – store in an airtight container

MORNING OF

- Collect seafood – remove fish from packaging, place on a wire rack over a plate – refrigerate
- Make crumbs for fish and mussels
- Wash, dry and chop parsley for fish and mussels
- Slice 2 cloves garlic, cover with extra virgin olive oil (see page 512)

Mussels
- Grate pecorino

Orecchiette
- Chop anchovies
- Seed and chop chillies, cover

Fish
- Finely grate zest of 2 lemons
- Cut 2 lemons into 12 slices
- Wash and cook potato
- Assemble fish and potato on lemon leaves
- Mix crust

Green salad
- Wash, dry and crisp salad leaves
- Prepare salad dressing in salad bowl with crossed salad servers ready to toss before serving

AFTERNOON OF

Mussels
- Scrub and steam open
- Mix crust
- Assemble stuffed mussels on baking tray

- Chill wine, if applicable
- Set table

GUESTS ARRIVE

- Put large pan of salted water on for orecchiette
- Warm pasta plates (see page 512)

DINNER IS SERVED

ANTIPASTO/FIRST COURSE

- Set oven griller on high
- Grill mussels for 5 minutes (set timer)
- Place olives, *taralli* and mussels on table for self-service (offer napkins for oily fingers)

PASTA/SECOND COURSE

- Cook pasta for 10 minutes (set timer)
- Make anchovy and chilli sauce for rapini and pasta
- Add rapini to pasta and cook for another 5 minutes (reset timer)
- Drain pasta and rapini, shake well, return to empty pan
- Tip in anchovy and chilli sauce, toss
- Serve in warm bowls
- Warm main course plates (see page 512)

MAIN/THIRD COURSE

- Preheat oven to 180°C
- Bake fish for 15 minutes (set timer)
- Remove fish, turn and add crust, lightly cover and leave on workbench
- Increase oven temperature to 200°C
- Return fish to brown for 8–10 minutes (set timer)
- Toss and serve salad

DESSERT

- Assemble fruit platter and offer espresso biscuits

INGREDIENTS LIST

PANTRY

· Sea salt
· Fine salt
· Australian extra virgin olive oil
· Strong plain flour
  (for making bread)
· Plain flour
· Dried yeast
· Caster sugar
· Tomato paste (puree)
· Orecchiette
· Anchovy fillets in olive oil
· Espresso coffee beans

SPICE SHELF

· Black peppercorns
· Chilli flakes
· Fennel seeds

REFRIGERATOR

· Unsalted butter
· Pecorino
· Olives (such as Sicilian
  green olives)

GREENGROCER/FARMERS' MARKET (OR GARDEN)

· Flat-leaf parsley
· 5 small fresh red chillies
· Garlic
· 4 lemons, plus 12 unsprayed
  lemon leaves
· 6 waxy potatoes, such as
  Kipflers or Dutch creams
· 2 bunches rapini
· Selection of salad leaves
· Figs
· Grapes
· Other seasonal fruit to
  serve with espresso biscuits
  and coffee

FISHMONGER

· 24 black mussels
· 6 × 180 g thick white
  fish cutlets

BAKER

· Bread for breadcrumbs
· Bread for the table

CELLAR

· Dry white wine for *taralli*
  and mussels
· Sweet wine for biscuits
· Wine for the table
· Soft drink

SUNDAY
BRUNCH

A BRUNCH FOR 12

PROVENÇAL OMELETTE

Layer 'cake'

with TAPENADE
& HOMEMADE TOMATO SAUCE

BLUE-EYE

Trevalla–Brandade Croutons

Sausage

IN BRIOCHE

JACK'S

Stunning Cos Salad

from SOUTHERN OCEAN LODGE

———

Cheeseboard

SOUR CHERRY & RHUBARB

Yeast Tart

9

Sunday brunch has a special charm. If the weather is kind it can be enjoyed outdoors. Guests are relaxed, the day still stretches ahead, and brunch encourages an informal selection of dishes that can all be set out more or less at the same time so the cook can also be relaxed. I like to serve dishes that are at their best when less than piping hot, and even one or two that are cold. At my place, it is the time when I spread out my most colourful cloth and favourite platters. Self-service is mandatory. Brunch is also a good moment to offer condiments – spiced fruits such as quinces or plums, interesting mustards or fruit pastes.

I have hosted many brunches in my time, so deciding on this selection was hard. One is never sure how many of the guests will have already eaten breakfast. Most I suspect, so I tend to nominate eleven as my brunch hour, and I rarely serve 'breakfast-y' dishes such as fried eggs, although I think it is a lovely idea to offer freshly squeezed orange juice, with some sparkling wine available for those who feel like starting with a Buck's Fizz. I suppose I am assuming that it is really an early-ish lunch. I will not eat again until quite late, and then only very lightly.

The closest to breakfast cookery is my layer 'cake' of savoury omelettes, which I first encountered in a small cafe in Provence under its Provençal name, *créspeou*. Served with a fresh tomato sauce, it is very delicious. The layers can vary depending on what is in season. Croutons piled with a tangy brandade of lightly salt-cured blue-eye trevalla add crunch and get the taste buds tingling.

Recently I was fortunate enough to participate in an event on Kangaroo Island known as Feastival and, as my reward for collaborating on a dinner and hosting a marvellous demonstration by local schoolchildren, I was offered a night's stay at the stunning Southern Ocean Lodge. What an amazing place it is – superlatives fail. Considered one of the great hotels in the world, every room and all the public spaces have uninterrupted views of the Southern Ocean and, if you leave the ocean-side doors open as I did, you sleep with the sound of crashing waves and wake to a glorious

view of the dawn turning the massed clouds pink. But back
to brunch. Chef Jack Ingram served the most delicious lunch
and it is the entree I want to copy here – a sectioned small cos
lettuce drizzled with Kangaroo Island extra virgin olive oil and
generously scattered with a 'crumble' of toasted breadcrumbs,
lemon zest, parsley and grated parmesan. Alongside was a spoonful
of beautiful mayonnaise – so simple and fresh.

Almost all the chopping and preparing is done the day
beforehand. And for the sausage in brioche, buy a fat European-
style boiling-type sausage from a butcher familiar with this style
of smallgood or, if such a purveyor is not available, make your
own (see page 507). In summer it is best to make the brioche the
day before and refrigerate it overnight; it will need to be taken
from the fridge as soon as you wake up to give it time to recover.
If your brunch is an autumn or winter affair, it is sufficient to
leave the dough in a covered basin in an unheated room.

You will also need to prepare the very simple yeast dough for
the sour cherry tart, either the day before or early in the morning,
but the filling can be ready to go. Depending on the time of year,
the filling could be gooseberries, rhubarb or sweet cherries or,
as here, a combination.

Brunch is a good time to serve a cheeseboard with no more
than three varieties (see picture on pages 170–171). I prefer bread
to crackers, but a thoughtful host will offer both.

Provençal omelette layer 'cake'

Crespeou

Homemade Tomato Sauce
(see page 502), to serve

SILVERBEET OMELETTE

300 g silverbeet *or* chard leaves,
stems removed

ice cubes

3 large free-range eggs

sea salt and freshly ground
black pepper

2 tablespoons extra virgin olive oil,
plus extra for drizzling

1 clove garlic, chopped

TOMATO OMELETTE

400 g ripe tomatoes

1 teaspoon fine salt

3 large free-range eggs

sea salt and freshly ground
black pepper

¼ cup (60 ml) extra virgin
olive oil, plus extra for drizzling

1 clove garlic, chopped

1 tablespoon basil leaves, chopped

The 'cake' consists of three separate omelettes that are stacked to form a cake, which is then 'iced' with a simple tapenade mixture. I like to accompany this with a ribbon of fresh tomato sauce and brandade croutons.

For the silverbeet omelette, wash the silverbeet leaves, blanch for a few seconds in a pan of boiling water, then plunge into iced water. Squeeze first with your hands, then wrapped in a cloth. Slice thinly and set aside. Break the eggs into a bowl, season with salt and pepper and whisk lightly. Heat a heavy-based frying pan with a generous drizzle of olive oil over medium heat. Saute the garlic for a moment, then add the leaves. Toss until well mixed and fragrant. Tip into the egg mixture and mix very well together without delay.

Heat the olive oil in a 20 cm non-stick omelette pan over medium heat. Tip in the egg and silverbeet mixture; it should sizzle and the edge should start to puff up. Reduce the heat to low, then cover with a saucepan lid and cook for a few minutes. Remove the lid and, if the omelette looks just a bit moist but not runny, shake the pan to ensure that the omelette is not sticking, then invert it onto a plate. Add a dribble more oil to the pan, slide the omelette back in for a few seconds to finish the other side, then slide onto the serving plate.

For the tomato omelette, core the tomatoes and cut a cross on the other end. Plunge into a pan of boiling water for a minute. Lift into cold water, then peel. Halve, squeeze out the seeds and cut into 5 mm dice. Mix with the salt and place in a sieve over a bowl, then set aside for 1 hour.

Break the eggs into a bowl, season with salt and pepper and whisk lightly.

Heat a heavy-based frying pan with half of the olive oil over medium heat. Saute the garlic for a moment, then add the tomato. Stir to mix. Cook for 5 minutes or until the tomato has given up all its liquid. Add the basil. Tip into the egg mixture and mix very well.

Heat the remaining olive oil in the omelette pan over medium heat. Tip in the egg and tomato mixture; it should sizzle and the edge should start to puff up. Reduce the heat to low, then cover with a lid and cook for a few minutes. Remove the lid and, if the ➤

recipe continues.

ZUCCHINI OMELETTE

1 clove garlic

1 tablespoon flat-leaf parsley

¼ cup (60 ml) extra virgin olive oil, plus extra for drizzling

½ onion, thinly sliced

300 g zucchinis (courgettes), cut into 5 mm dice

3 large free-range eggs, lightly beaten

sea salt and freshly ground black pepper

omelette looks just a bit moist but not runny, shake the pan to ensure that the omelette is not sticking and invert onto a plate. Add a dribble more olive oil to the pan and slide the omelette back in to cook for a few seconds, then slide it on top of the silverbeet omelette on the serving plate.

For the zucchini omelette, chop the garlic and parsley finely together. Heat half of the olive oil in a heavy-based saucepan over low heat, then cook the onion, stirring from time to time with a wooden spoon, for 3 minutes or until softened and translucent. Transfer the onion to a small plate. Saute the zucchini in the pan over high heat for 5 minutes, tossing so it does not stick. Stir in the garlic and parsley mixture, cook for another minute, then stir in the onion. Tip into the egg mixture and mix very well together without delay.

Heat the remaining olive oil in the omelette pan over medium heat. Tip in the egg and zucchini mixture; it should sizzle and the edge should start to puff up. Reduce the heat to low, then cover with the lid and cook for a few minutes. Remove the lid and, if the omelette looks just a bit moist but not runny, shake the pan to ensure that the omelette is not sticking and invert onto a plate. Add a dribble more olive oil to the pan, slide the omelette back into the pan for a few seconds, then slide it on top of the 2 omelettes on the serving plate.

Leave the omelette stack to cool, then 'ice' it with tapenade.

Makes about ½ cup (160 g)

Tapenade

150 g pitted black or green olives

2 anchovy fillets in olive oil

1 tablespoon capers (salted or in brine), drained

2 tablespoons extra virgin olive oil, plus extra if needed

freshly ground black pepper

Process the olives, anchovies, capers and olive oil in a food processor to form a coarse paste, then season with pepper.

Use to 'ice' the omelette layer 'cake'.

Blue-eye trevalla–brandade croutons

1 × 300 g piece blue-eye trevalla

sea salt

½ teaspoon black or
white peppercorns

1 fresh bay leaf

a generous sprig thyme

1 French shallot, roughly chopped

2 cloves garlic, sliced

1½ cups (375 ml) milk

150 g potatoes, peeled
and roughly chopped

¼ cup (60 ml) extra virgin olive oil

CROUTONS

1 baguette, thinly sliced on
the diagonal

extra virgin olive oil, for brushing

Brandade de morue is a Provençal dish of salt cod pureed with olive oil and milk or cream; sometimes it also includes mashed potato and garlic. Here I've substituted home-salted blue-eye trevalla for salt cod; you will need to do this the day before serving. The French word *brandade* derives from the Provençal *brandado*, which comes from *brandar*, that is, to shake or stir and, by extension, to pound. Before the days of food processors, making brandade would have required a lot of physical effort.

Place the fish on a plate and sprinkle both sides generously with salt. Transfer to a colander standing over the plate to catch the juices and refrigerate for 24 hours.

The next day, place the peppercorns, bay leaf, thyme, shallot, garlic and milk in a heavy-based saucepan and bring to simmering point. Add the fish; if there is not enough liquid to cover it, add a little water. Cover the pan with the lid and poach over low heat for 10–15 minutes or until quite tender. Cool in the liquid for a few minutes, then transfer to a baking tray, discard the skin and any bones and flake the flesh. Strain the milk, discarding the solids, and set aside.

Meanwhile, cook the potato in a saucepan of simmering water until tender. Press the potato through a potato ricer into the bowl of an electric mixer fitted with a paddle attachment. Add the flaked fish and beat until very smooth. With the motor running, gradually add a little of the reserved poaching liquid, alternating with the olive oil; the finished mixture should be very smooth and creamy. Taste for seasoning and adjust if necessary.

To prepare the croutons, preheat the oven to 200°C. Brush the baguette slices with olive oil and place on a baking tray, then bake for 10 minutes or until golden and crisp at the edges. Cool.

Spread the brandade onto the croutons and serve with wedges of the layered omelette 'cake' and the tomato sauce (see picture on page 160).

Sausage in brioche

Saucisson en brioche is a glamorous variation on the perennially popular sausage in a hunk of bread. In this case, the bread is a buttery brioche dough – easy to make and always impressive. The sausage can be one of several varieties of European-style sausage intended for simmering in stock with sauerkraut or lentils, or serving in a salad or with hot potatoes, as opposed to thinner sausages intended for grilling, barbecuing or pan-frying. Boiling sausages are dense in texture and can take up to 1½ hours to cook. Any good butcher or delicatessen with a European clientele will be able to provide such a sausage. An Italian butcher will have a *cotechino* in the colder months. A French or Swiss butcher will have a range of suitable sausages, possibly including a *saucisson de Lyons*. (If not available, I have included a recipe on page 507 for a homemade sausage that is a reasonable substitute.)

The only *truc* (trick) to guaranteed success is to make sure you wrap the still-warm sausage in the risen brioche dough. If the sausage has been refrigerated and is cold it will not adhere to the dough, so your finished *saucisson en brioche* is likely to have a gap between the sausage and dough. A refrigerated cooked sausage can, however, be warmed in a pan of simmering water for 15 minutes before wrapping in the dough. (See recipe picture on pages 166–167.)

fine salt

1 × 650–700 g purchased boiling
sausage (see opposite) *or* Pork
and Pistachio Boiling Sausage
(see page 507)

1 free-range egg yolk,
lightly beaten

Dijon mustard and preserved
fruits, to serve

BRIOCHE DOUGH

30 g caster sugar

1 cup (250 ml) milk

2 teaspoons instant dried yeast

6 free-range egg yolks,
lightly beaten

3⅓ cups (500 g) plain flour

1 teaspoon fine salt

150 g unsalted butter, chopped,
plus extra for buttering

Start the brioche 4 hours before the brunch. Heat the sugar and milk in a small heavy-based saucepan to lukewarm. Sprinkle over the yeast and leave for 10 minutes to froth. Add the egg yolk and mix lightly with a whisk or fork.

Sift the flour and salt into the bowl of an electric mixer fitted with a dough hook. Form a well in the centre and pour in the yeast mixture. Beat well, then add the softened butter in several lots, beating well after each addition. Continue to beat until the dough is shiny, smooth and comes away cleanly from the side of the bowl. Transfer to a lightly buttered bowl. Cover with a damp cloth and leave to rise in a warm place, away from draughts, for 2–2½ hours or until doubled.

Meanwhile, bring a wide deep pan of lightly salted water to simmering point. Prick the sausage with a fine skewer in a few places to prevent the skin bursting. Immerse the sausage in the water and simmer gently for 1½ hours. Leave the sausage in the warm water until you are ready to wrap it in the brioche dough, then lift it from the liquid and peel away and discard the skin.

When the dough is well risen, knock it down in the bowl and proceed to wrap the warm sausage. Line a baking tray with baking paper. Place the dough on the lined tray, then press the brioche dough into a rectangle about 30 cm long × 15 cm wide × 1 cm thick. Centre the sausage on the dough lengthwise, then bring up the sides to cover the sausage, overlapping by 1 cm. Roll the sausage over so that the seam is underneath. Pinch the ends firmly together. Brush the entire log with the lightly beaten egg yolk. Leave in a warm draught-free place for 20 minutes to recover.

Preheat the oven to 200°C.

Bake for 10 minutes, then reduce the temperature to 180°C and bake for a further 10–15 minutes or until the brioche is golden brown. Leave to rest for 10 minutes before cutting.

Using a serrated knife, cut the sausage in brioche into thick slices. Offer mustard and any preserved fruits you might have in the pantry in small bowls alongside.

Jack's stunning cos salad
from Southern Ocean Lodge

6 small cos lettuce *or* 6 witlof

PARMESAN CUSTARD

ice cubes

2 free-range eggs, plus 2 egg yolks

300 ml thickened cream

100 g finely grated parmesan

sea salt

GRIBICHE

2 free-range eggs

1 tablespoon capers
(salted or in brine)

2 tablespoons chopped
flat-leaf parsley

finely grated zest of 1 lemon

2 tablespoons extra virgin olive oil
(I use an Australian brand)

sea salt and freshly ground
black pepper

Southern Ocean Lodge is a luxurious hotel facing the Great Southern Ocean in a remote part of Kangaroo Island, South Australia. I was fortunate enough to stay there and chef Jack Ingram served me this crisp, creamy and crunchy salad. He has generously given me the details and, since then, the salad has delighted my friends and me many times. (See recipe picture on pages 166–167.) Jack used very small cos lettuce, which is a perfect choice. Sometimes I have used halved witlof, both the green and the ruby-red variety. At Southern Ocean Lodge Jack served a dollop of mayonnaise on the side of the plate; this is optional.

Wash the cos or witlof, keeping them whole. Drain well, then wrap in a thick, dry tea towel and refrigerate.

To make the custard, put a handful of ice cubes into a stainless-steel bowl and leave on a workbench. Set a heavy-based saucepan half-filled with water over medium heat; it will need to be the right size so that a second stainless-steel bowl fits over the hot water without it touching the bowl.

Whisk the eggs and yolks lightly together in the second bowl. Set aside. Place the cream and parmesan in a small heavy-based saucepan over medium heat and bring to the boil, stirring. Immediately whisk the simmering cream and cheese mixture into the egg mixture. Place the bowl of egg and cream mixture over the pan of hot water and continue to whisk for a few minutes, until the custard thickens; watch carefully as this will only take a few minutes. Immediately remove the bowl from the heat and place over the ice cubes. Whisk until the custard is cold. Scrape the custard into a small airtight container and cover, then refrigerate for up to 2 days.

To start the gribiche, hard boil the eggs, then leave to cool. Peel. Using the back of a dessert spoon, separately press the whites and yolks through a coarse-mesh sieve into separate airtight containers and cover, then refrigerate for up to a day.

LEMON CRUMBLE

60 g unsalted butter

½ cup (35 g) panko breadcrumbs

1 clove garlic, finely crushed

2 teaspoons extra virgin olive oil

2 teaspoons finely grated
lemon zest

1 tablespoon lemon juice

1 tablespoon finely chopped
flat-leaf parsley

To make the lemon crumble, line a plate with a double sheet of paper towel. Melt the butter in a wide heavy-based frying pan over medium heat and saute the crumbs, stirring constantly until golden brown. Stir in the garlic, olive oil, lemon zest and juice and parsley. Tip onto the paper-lined plate to cool and absorb any excess butter and oil.

Just before serving, finish the gribiche. Mix together the capers, parsley, lemon zest, olive oil and egg whites and yolks and season with salt and pepper.

To serve, select wide dinner plates. Halve the cos or witlof lengthwise. Trim away the bases if necessary, taking care to keep the leaves together. Place a cos or witlof half, cut-side up, on each plate. Generously spoon on some parmesan custard, then a generous quantity of the gribiche and finally the lemon crumble. Serve at once.

Sour cherry and rhubarb yeast tart

750 g sour cherries (to yield
500 g pitted), stems removed and
pitted (reserve 1 tablespoon pits)
or preserved sour cherries
(see recipe introduction)

¾ cup (165 g) white sugar,
plus 1 tablespoon extra

juice of 1 lemon

½ bunch rhubarb stalks, sliced into
3 cm lengths (to yield ½–¾ cup
stewed rhubarb)

2 tablespoons soft brown sugar

⅓ cup (80 ml) water

½ cup (60 g) ground almonds

1 free-range egg yolk, beaten
with 1 teaspoon water

double cream, to serve

YEASTED PASTRY

125 g plain flour, plus extra
for dusting

30 g caster sugar

1½ teaspoons instant dried yeast

¼ cup (60 ml) warm milk

1 free-range egg yolk

2 drops pure vanilla extract

¼ teaspoon ground cinnamon

25 g butter, softened

**This lovely free-form tart is very versatile. Make it as one 28 cm
tart or double the pastry recipe and make six 10–12 cm diameter
tarts. I have had great success with buying preserved pitted
sour cherries in syrup when fresh cherries are not available.
The bottling syrup can be reduced to glaze the finished tart.
(See recipe picture on pages 170–171.)**

To make the pastry, place the flour in a food processor. Mix the
sugar, yeast and warm milk in a bowl and set aside for 5 minutes
or until frothy. Stir until creamy. Whisk in the egg yolk, vanilla
and cinnamon. With the motor running, slowly add the milk/yeast
mixture to the flour, then immediately add the softened butter.
As soon as a soft dough has formed, stop the motor, scrape the
dough onto a floured workbench and knead lightly. Place in
a clean bowl, cover with a cloth and leave to rise for 30 minutes.

If using fresh sour cherries, wrap the reserved pits in a piece of
muslin and smash, then tie the corners to make a secure bundle.
Place the fresh or preserved cherries, bundle of pits (if using), sugar
and lemon juice in a heavy-based stainless-steel saucepan (the pits
add a subtle almond flavour). Bring to a simmer, stirring once or
twice. Simmer for 5 minutes. Drain the cherries in a sieve resting
over a bowl, reserving the syrup. Return the syrup to the pan and
boil over high heat to reduce by three-quarters; watch closely as this
may only take 5 minutes or so.

Place the sliced rhubarb in a heavy-based stainless-steel saucepan.
Add the brown sugar and water. Bring to a simmer, stirring once or
twice, then simmer, covered, for 5 minutes or until the rhubarb is
quite soft. Drain the rhubarb in a sieve resting over a bowl, reserving
the syrup. Return the syrup to the pan and boil over high heat
to reduce by three-quarters; watch closely as this may only take
5 minutes or so. Combine the rhubarb and cherries. Combine the
rhubarb syrup with the cherry syrup.

Preheat the oven to 200°C. Line a 30 cm pizza tray with baking paper.

Roll out the dough on a lightly floured workbench to form a rough 28 cm round. Place it on the lined tray and press out to the edges of the tray with your fingers. Scatter the ground almonds over, leaving a 3 cm border. Spoon the cherry and rhubarb mixture over the almonds. Fold the pastry edges over the edge of the fruit. Brush the folded edge with the beaten egg wash and scatter with the remaining white sugar. Spoon some of the reduced syrup over the fruit.

Bake the tart for 15 minutes. Reduce the oven temperature to 180°C and bake for another 10–15 minutes or until well browned and the base is cooked through. Slide the tart onto a wire rack and leave to cool a little.

Slide onto a serving platter and drizzle with the rest of the reduced syrup. Serve warm or cold, sliced, with double cream.

TIMETABLE FOR THE COOK

ONE WEEK BEFORE

- Check **Ingredients List** and note what has to be purchased
- Advise provedores of special requests (boiling sausage or brined pork shoulder)
- Check specialist equipment needed (mincing, paddle and dough hook attachments for electric mixer, optional)

THREE DAYS BEFORE

- Decide on table setting, including serving dishes
- Check outdoor furniture
- Inspect tablecloth and napkins
- Decide on wine – order if necessary
- All shopping, including flowers
- If making sausage, season – refrigerate overnight

TWO DAYS BEFORE

Omelette 'cake'
- Make tapenade – refrigerate
- Make tomato sauce – refrigerate

Brandade
- Salt fish – refrigerate overnight

Sausage in brioche
- If making sausage, mince pork – refrigerate overnight

Cos salad
- Make parmesan custard – refrigerate

Sour cherry and rhubarb yeast tart
- Poach sour cherries and/or rhubarb

DAY BEFORE

Brandade croutons
- Make brandade – refrigerate

Sausage in brioche
- If making sausage, form and poach – refrigerate

Omelette 'cake'
- Prepare vegetables for layers
- Place in separate airtight containers – refrigerate

Cos salad
- Wash, dry and crisp baby cos (or witlof)
- Prepare eggs for gribiche – refrigerate

- Chill wine, if necessary

EARLY MORNING OF

Sausage in brioche
- Make brioche

Omelette 'cake'
- Make all omelette layers – cool and stack (refrigerate if hot weather)
- 'Ice' omelette stack with tapenade

Cos salad
- Make lemon crumble

Sour cherry and rhubarb yeast tart
- Make and wrap pastry

- Set table

MID-MORNING OF

Sausage in brioche
- Punch down brioche
- If using bought sausage, simmer for 1–2 hours
- If using homemade sausage, simmer for 30–45 minutes

Cos salad
- Cut and bake croutons

Sour cherry and rhubarb yeast tart
- Prepare filling
- Assemble
- Bake

ONE HOUR BEFORE GUESTS ARRIVE

- Wrap sausage in brioche, brush with eggwash, leave to recover
- Preheat oven to 200°C

- Get changed

BRUNCH IS SERVED

Brioche
- Bake for 10 minutes (set timer)
- Reduce oven temperature to 180°C and bake a further 10–15 minutes (set timer)
- Serve

Omelette 'cake'
- Cut into wedges and serve with tomato sauce alongside

Brandade croutons
- Pile brandade onto croutons and serve

Cos salad
- Finish gribiche
- Assemble and serve

Cheeseboard
- Assemble and serve

Sour cherry and rhubarb yeast tart
- Cut into slices and serve
- Offer double cream

INGREDIENTS LIST

PANTRY

· Sea salt
· Fine salt
· Australian extra virgin olive oil
· Red-wine vinegar
· Plain flour
· Caster sugar
· Brown sugar
· White sugar
· Dried yeast
· Panko breadcrumbs
· Dijon mustard
· Anchovy fillets in olive oil
· Ground almonds
· Preserved spiced fruits, such as quinces, plums
· Preserved sour cherries in syrup (optional)

SPICE SHELF

· Black peppercorns
· White peppercorns
· Nutmeg (whole)
· Ground cinnamon
· Pure vanilla extract

REFRIGERATOR

· 250 g unsalted butter
· Milk
· 300 ml thickened cream
· Double cream
· 100 g parmesan
· Selection of 3 cheeses for cheeseboard (1 soft; 1 blue; 1 hard)
· 2 dozen free-range eggs
· 150 g pitted black or green olives
· Capers (salted or in brine)

GREENGROCER/FARMERS' MARKET (OR GARDEN)

· 1 fresh bay leaf
· Basil
· Flat-leaf parsley
· Thyme
· Garlic
· 300 g silverbeet or chard leaves
· 1.4 kg ripe tomatoes
· 300 g zucchinis (courgettes)
· 1 onion
· 1 French shallot
· 2 potatoes (150 g)
· 1 orange
· 6 small cos lettuce or witlof
· 3 lemons
· 750 g sour cherries (to yield 500 g stemmed and pitted cherries) or 500 g preserved sour cherries in syrup
· ½ bunch rhubarb

BUTCHER

· 1 × 650–700 g boiling sausage (cotechino or other variety)

Or, if making your own sausage:
· 1 kg boneless pickled pork shoulder
· 300 g hard back fat

FISHMONGER

· 1 × 300 g blue-eye trevalla fillet

BAKER

· Baguette for croutons
· Bread for the table

CELLAR

· Wine for the table (sparkling wine if s erving Buck's Fizz)
· Freshly squeezed orange juice (if serving Buck's Fizz)
· Soft drink

AUTUMNAL
ITALIAN
LUNCH
IN A
SUBURBAN FARM

A LUNCH FOR 4

CROSTINI
with **NEW-SEASON OLIVE OIL & GARLIC**

———

SPAGHETTI
with **SHELLING BEANS, ZUCCHINI TOMATOES & POTATOES**

———

LAMB CUTLETS
OVER AN OLIVE-WOOD FIRE
with **SALMORIGLIO**

ZUCCHINI FLOWER FRITTERS

GREEN SALAD

———

APPLE, PEAR & GRAPE
AUTUMN PIE

10

I paid a long overdue visit to my friends Lina and Tony Siciliano at Villa Varapodi, Rose Creek Estate in suburban Keilor. We first met at a farmers' market several years ago, and I was astonished by their produce and wanted to know more. They have created a piece of paradise in Keilor. The land was purchased in the early 80s and every stick, plant, terrace and fence has been created and built almost exclusively by Tony and Lina; son Angelo has a special interest in the vineyard.

Nowadays, first-time visitors pinch themselves once they stroll down the driveway and see the established vineyard, olive grove, laden fruit trees, chicken run and unbelievably extensive vegetable garden. Many people plant and maintain productive gardens. What is so astonishing here is the extent; at last count there were 400 olive trees, over 3000 vines and 17 fig trees!

Lina and Tony farm their property as their parents would have done in Calabria. The work is unrelenting and exhausting to contemplate, and these two are no spring chickens. The quality of everything they produce is outstanding, be it olive oil that wins prizes everywhere; a delicious rosé, amongst other wines; the only cedro tree (an unusual citrus grown for its thick rind, which is candied) I have ever seen outside of Italy; and rows and rows of numerous varieties of tomato, eggplant (aubergine), zucchini (courgette), beans and herbs. Everything is organic and, of course, Lina bottles and dries her produce and saves seeds. The product range from her vast tomato crop is almost unbelievable: passata; sundried tomatoes; sundried tomatoes stuffed with a mix of capers, basil, oregano and garlic; fresh sauce; pickled vegetables; and, naturally, every day throughout the long tomato harvest, they are consumed fresh. The same energy and enthusiasm are applied to every crop, be it olives or grapes. Lina told me she had to sell a house in her village in Italy to pay for the olive oil press that produces such outstanding oil.

Our lunch was sensational. We started with crunchy crostini spread with a little garlic and herbs, and bathed generously in Villa Varapodi's new-season green olive oil, an oil of outstanding aroma and flavour. Lina then prepared an intriguing dish of potatoes, beans, basil, tomatoes and spaghetti cooked in a single pot so that the juices formed a perfect rose-gold sauce.

Lina then built an impressive fire in her back garden barbecue using prunings from the olive trees and grapevines. They flared quickly and in half an hour had burned down to coals. Lina's cutlets still had a cap of fat on them and the bones had not been scraped, as most butchers seem to do nowadays. The small amount of fat sizzled on the coals and contributed a delectable smoky crispness to the cutlets, and the meat left on the bone cooked to a delicious golden brown. It had been years since I had tasted anything as good! These succulent grilled lamb chops were spread with Lina's *salmoriglio* (a pungent Italian herb sauce of oregano, garlic, black pepper and olive oil commonly drizzled over grilled meat or fish), accompanied by fritters made from a handful of brilliant zucchini flowers.

Rather wistfully, Lina wonders how they can ensure the survival of Villa Varapodi. Will anyone be prepared to work as she and Tony have done and still do? It is an important question; they are actually custodians of a living museum. Very few young people, including those concerned about future food security and aiming for self-sufficiency, can approach the level of understanding these two have of growing conditions, managing micro-climates, respecting traditions they understand so well, passed on to them by their parents and, above all, of joyfully appreciating what their land offers them and their children. I would like to see their extraordinary knowledge valued and, in some way, passed on to a new generation. But 'How?' is the question.

As we sat on the veranda, the table laid with a crisply ironed embroidered cloth, under a canopy of vines with wine, oil and food all produced from the estate, we could well have been in an Italian village, instead of 17 kilometres from the Melbourne CBD.

Crostini with new-season olive oil and garlic

good-quality fresh bread
with a good crust and
firm crumb, such as ciabatta

garlic, finely chopped

flat-leaf parsley, coarsely chopped

Rose Creek Estate Villa Varapodi
Olive Oil, for drizzling

Lina and Tony Siciliano are very generous. From time to time, they open their wonderful estate to help a charity and, very recently, my not-for-profit Kitchen Garden Foundation was the beneficiary of such a day. What fun it was. Hundreds of enthusiastic visitors came to look and learn. Garden tours were organised throughout the day. The magnificent wood-fired oven was fired up, fuelled by prunings from the olive trees. Forty kilos of pizza dough was transformed into hundreds of wonderful crisp-bottomed pizzas. Every visitor was welcomed with a crostini that showed off their award-winning new-season olive oil to perfection.

Cut slices from the loaves, at least 1 cm thick. Scatter with a little garlic, a shower of chopped parsley and a generous drizzle of olive oil.
    Enjoy!

Spaghetti with shelling beans, zucchini, tomatoes and potatoes

2–3 potatoes (about 300 g total), peeled and cut into bite-sized pieces

3 litres water

500–600 g scarlet runner *or* other runner-type green beans, topped, tailed and cut into 5 cm lengths

2 small green zucchinis (courgettes), halved lengthwise, then quartered

½ cup (70 g) shelled fresh borlotti beans (optional)

1 bunch basil (if purchased), *or* several stems from the garden

sea salt

300 g spaghetti (I use No. 5 Barilla)

⅓ cup (80 ml) extra virgin olive oil

2 cloves garlic, chopped

2–3 ripe tomatoes, cut into bite-sized pieces

Lina cooked this dish, known as *pasta e vajenja*, for me in very late summer, when we picked the very last of her summer beans. We also picked a variety of green bean unknown to me, which would usually be left to dry completely, then be shelled for use in winter soups and stews. Lina called these beans *madamola*, but warned that the word might be dialect – borlotti beans would be a perfect substitute. Lina shelled the beans and only the inner bean was added to the dish, whilst the more usual scarlet runner green beans were broken into sections.

Cook the potato in a large heavy-based saucepan in the 3 litres simmering water for 10 minutes or until semi-cooked. Add the beans, zucchini, shelled borlotti beans, if using, 1 whole stem of basil, 2 tablespoons salt and the spaghetti to the pan. Cook for 5 minutes.

Meanwhile, heat the olive oil in a small heavy-based saucepan over medium heat and add the garlic, then stir until pale-gold. Add the tomato, a pinch of salt and a generous handful of roughly shredded basil leaves. Cook over low heat for 2 minutes or until the juice from the tomato starts to run (be sure not to overcook it).

Once the spaghetti is al dente, drain half the water from the pan, reserving some of the cooking water. Return the pan to medium heat and mix in the tomato sauce; the mixture should be very moist at this point. Add a little of the reserved cooking water if the dish is too dry. Check the seasoning and adjust if desired. Continue to cook for another 2 minutes; the dish is the correct consistency when it settles softly into each pasta bowl and the sauce looks creamy and a lovely red-gold colour.

Add a final drizzle of olive oil (preferably Villa Varapodi), then serve.

Lamb cutlets over an olive-wood fire with *salmoriglio*

12 lamb cutlets (order in advance and ask your butcher to leave the cap of fat intact and not scrape the bones clean)

sea salt

extra virgin olive oil, for drizzling

Zucchini Flower Fritters (see page 187) and Green Salad (see page 503), to serve

SALMORIGLIO

2 cloves garlic, finely chopped

½ cup (handful) flat-leaf parsley stems, finely chopped

2 tablespoons dried oregano (I use the dried long stalks of oregano wrapped in plastic sleeves)

juice of ½ lemon

½ cup (125 ml) Villa Varapodi extra virgin olive oil

sea salt

I have enjoyed dishes with the Italian sauce *salmoriglio* several times, mostly spooned over grilled meat or fish, but I was never quite sure what the word meant. While there is certainly salt, the primary ingredients are extra virgin olive oil, freshly squeezed lemon juice and herbs. It is the choice of herbs that distinguishes one cook's *salmoriglio* from another. The *salmoriglio* Lina served me over her incomparable lamb cutlets included flat-leaf parsley and some oregano. Some cooks mix this sauce to a paste with a mortar and pestle. Lina prefers a loose mixture that can be spooned over the meat. If you have leftover sauce, toasted crusty bread smothered in *salmoriglio* is also a great side dish. If you wish to cook this for more people, allow for two cutlets per serve and double the *salmoriglio* ingredients.

Heat an ovenproof serving dish either in a 110°C oven or, as Lina does, on one end of the barbecue where it will be sufficiently warmed by the fire.

Leave the cutlets at room temperature while the fire burns to coals (or the barbecue heats to very hot, if you do not have a wood-burning barbecue).

Grill the lamb for 4–5 minutes, then turn and grill for another 4–5 minutes on the other side. Sprinkle with salt while the cutlets are on the grill.

To make the *salmoriglio*, using a fork, mix the garlic, herbs, lemon juice, olive oil and salt to taste in a bowl.

Transfer the cutlets to a hot serving dish and spoon over some of the *salmoriglio*. Offer extra sauce at the table. Serve with the zucchini flower fritters and green salad alongside.

Zucchini flower fritters

2 handfuls zucchini (courgette) flowers

extra virgin olive oil, for shallow-frying

sea salt and freshly ground black pepper

BATTER

2 tablespoons self-raising flour

2 tablespoons plain flour

½ cup (125 ml) soda water, as needed

Lina gathers these brilliant male zucchini flowers in huge bunches in late summer and into autumn. These fritters are marvellous, and so easy. They can also include one or two tiny zucchini, if chopped very finely.

Check the flowers for ants, then pull the petals away from the green calyx. Dip in cold water and pat dry with paper towel.

To make the batter, place the flours in a bowl and mix with enough of the soda water to form a creamy batter. Tear the petals into pieces and drop into the batter.

Place olive oil to a depth of 5 mm in a small heavy-based saucepan over medium heat. Working in batches, fry spoonfuls of the batter and petal mixture, turning after a minute, until golden and crisp. Remove from the pan and drain on paper towel.

Sprinkle with a little salt and pepper, then serve at once.

Apple, pear and grape autumn pie

2 large eating apples

2 large ripe pears

200 g seedless red grapes
(weighed after stemming)

2 tablespoons liqueur of choice
(I used Poire William)

plain flour, for dusting

1 quantity Sweet Shortcrust Pastry
(see page 508), removed from the
refrigerator 1 hour before rolling

1½ tablespoons cornflour

⅓ cup (4 tablespoons) homemade
chunky quince preserve *or*
preserved fruit pieces (optional)

1 free-range egg yolk, beaten

double cream, to serve

ALMOND MIXTURE

75 g caster sugar

100 g ground almonds

60 g unsalted butter

The idea for this pie came from a cutting from a 1982 issue of an Italian food magazine I found amongst my files. The picture showed a crisp crust bursting with autumn fruits. I cannot imagine why it took me more than 25 years to make it, but it did, and it married well with the flavours I enjoyed at the Siciliano's table.

For the almond mixture, place the sugar, ground almonds and butter in a food processor and process to form a paste. Scrape into an airtight container, cover and refrigerate until needed.

Peel the apples and pears, remove the cores and cut into 1.5 cm dice. (The fruit should weigh 600 g.) Place the apple, pear and grapes in a bowl and drizzle over the chosen liqueur. Stir to coat all the fruit and leave to macerate at room temperature for at least 1 hour (or overnight in an airtight container in the refrigerator).

Preheat the oven to 210°C. Choose a 22 cm flan tin with a removable base.

On a lightly floured workbench, roll out the larger disc of pastry until 5 mm thick and use to line the tin. Loosely cover the pastry base with the almond mixture; do not press it onto the pastry, just pinch on dollops to cover the base (the paste absorbs most of the fruit juices, preventing the pastry from becoming soggy).

Sift the cornflour over the fruit and stir to mix through evenly. Add the quince or fruit preserve, if using. Spoon the fruit over the almond mixture.

Brush the edges of the pastry with the beaten egg yolk. Roll out the second piece of pastry on the lightly floured workbench until 5 mm thick, then settle over the fruit to form the lid. Seal the edges very well by. Brush the lid with the egg yolk and cut 2–3 slits to allow steam to escape.

Bake the pie for 35 minutes, checking after 25 minutes in case the pie is browning too much; if necessary, reduce the oven temperature to 190°C.

Leave the pie to cool on a wire rack until you can easily remove the ring. Serve wedges warm or at room temperature, with double cream.

TIMETABLE FOR THE COOK

ONE WEEK BEFORE

- Check **Ingredients List** and note what needs to be purchased
- Advise provedores of special requests (order lamb cutlets from your butcher with fat cap left on and bones not scraped)
- Check specialist equipment needed (hinged grill pan useful for turning a lot of cutlets at once – Italian suppliers sell them)

TWO DAYS BEFORE

- Decide on table setting, including serving dishes
- Decide on wines – order if necessary
- Inspect tablecloth and napkins
- Inspect barbecue (clean if necessary) and check fuel – wood or gas?
- Check outdoor furniture
- All shopping, including flowers

DAY BEFORE

Spaghetti dish
- Shell beans – refrigerate in an airtight container
- Cut green beans or runner beans – refrigerate in an airtight container
- Cut zucchini – refrigerate in an airtight container
- Cut tomatoes – refrigerate in an airtight container
- Cook garlic/extra virgin olive oil/ tomato/salt and basil mixture – refrigerate in an airtight container

Autumn pie
- Make pastry – refrigerate
- Make almond mixture – refrigerate
- Cut all fruit, drizzle with liqueur – refrigerate in an airtight container

MORNING OF

- Chill wines, if appropriate
- Pick produce from garden, if available
- Chop lots of parsley – set aside
- Chop 10 cloves garlic and cover generously with extra virgin olive oil (see page 512)
- Squeeze lemon juice
- Set table

Crostini
- Cut bread and wrap in plastic film

Spaghetti dish
- Peel and cut potatoes – store in a bowl of water
- Start cooking

Lamb cutlets
- Make *salmoriglio*

Autumn pie
- Prepare, bake and cool

Green salad
- Wash, dry and crisp salad leaves
- Prepare salad dressing in salad bowl with crossed salad servers ready to toss before serving

ONE HOUR BEFORE GUESTS ARRIVE

- If using wood-fired barbecue, start big wood fire to burn down to coals
- Brush bread with garlic and oil, scatter with flat-leaf parsley
- Gather, rinse and dry zucchini flowers
- Take cutlets out of refrigerator
- Get changed

GUESTS ARRIVE

- Warm pasta bowls and serving plates (see page 512)

LUNCH IS SERVED

FIRST COURSE

- Finish and serve crostini

SECOND COURSE

- Add potato, beans and spaghetti to pasta dish
- Finish and serve pasta dish

THIRD/MAIN COURSE

- Grill cutlets, turn after 4–5 minutes (set timer), season with salt and grill for a further 4–5 minutes
- Serve cutlets from central platter
- Pass around *salmoriglio*
- Mix, cook and serve zucchini flower fritters
- Toss and serve green salad

DESSERT

- Cut pie into wedges and offer double cream

INGREDIENTS LIST

PANTRY

· Sea salt
· Fine salt
· Australian extra virgin olive oil
· Red-wine vinegar
· Plain flour
· Self-raising flour
· Cornflour (wheaten)
· Caster sugar
· Spaghetti
· Homemade chunky quince preserve or jam or preserved fruit pieces
· Ground almonds

SPICE SHELF

· Black peppercorns
· Dried oregano

REFRIGERATOR

· Unsalted butter
· Free-range eggs
· Double cream

GREENGROCER/FARMERS' MARKET (OR GARDEN)

· Flat-leaf parsley
· Basil
· Garlic
· Flat green beans
· Scarlet runner beans or fresh borlotti beans (if available)
· 2 small zucchinis (courgettes)
· Zucchini flowers
· 2–3 waxy potatoes (about 300 g)
· 2–3 tomatoes
· 1 lemon
· Selection of salad leaves
· 2 large eating apples
· 2 large ripe pears
· 200 g seedless red grapes

BUTCHER

· 12 lamb cutlets (order with cap of fat intact and bones not frenched)

BAKER

· Ciabatta loaves for crostini
· Crusty loaf for the table

CELLAR

· Liqueur of choice for tart (I used Poire William)
· Wine for the table
· Soda water
· Soft drink

AFTERNOON
✻ TEA ✻

AFTERNOON TEA
FOR 8–10

WASHINGTON
CURRANT POUND CAKE

DATE & WALNUT LOAF

PUMPKIN SCONES

JOAN CAMPBELL'S
NEENISH TARTLETS

JAM & CREAM-FILLED
SPONGE CAKE
with ROSE-GERANIUM LEAVES

11

What has happened to afternoon tea? I admit it is difficult to find the right moment for a proper afternoon tea. I revert to the influence of my British forebears when I think about afternoon tea. There should be freshly baked scones, something with cream, definitely cake, and possibly a pie.

I once had afternoon tea at The Ritz in Piccadilly, London. Considered a very smart thing to do but ultimately I found it unsatisfying – piped music, men in morning suits, dainty cakes and even daintier sandwiches, being stared at by passers-by until I felt that I was having tea on the stage. I had a much more enjoyable cream tea at the Chelsea Physic Garden. Founded in 1673 by the Society of Apothecaries, it is the second oldest botanical garden in England. For years I wanted to visit the Garden and had never found them open. Until, on a glorious Bank Holiday, I was in luck. The gardens are fascinating; the plants are grouped, named and described to show how they are or were used, especially for medicinal purposes. On this day, the crowds came to admire, to picnic or to just sit and contemplate. The Embankment Gate is not the official entry point and its sign read, 'This gate is only opened for Royalty and for manure'!

The Chelsea Physic Garden also has a delightfully eccentric cafe. Plenty of goodwill and smiles but no system that I could see. The tables were set under a marquee with scalloped edging that fluttered in the breeze. On every table was a beautiful full-blown rose. The scene resembled the set of *Midsomer Murders*; I expected Joyce Barnaby to be serving the teas. I remember a compote of poached stone fruit in an orange blossom syrup. A good friend has described a celebrated chocolate cake she enjoyed there but it was not to be seen on the day I visited.

My grandmother baked a flat scone with currants every evening for my grandfather. Not a scone as we know it and I now suspect it was a Singing Hinny, after reading *The Farmhouse Kitchen*, by Mary Norwak, wherein she lists a marvellous array of yeasted and non-yeasted scones and buns, each one sounding more delicious than the one before. Grandfather's Singing Hinny was made with a mix of butter and lard and was said to sing as it sizzled on the flat top of a fuel stove. Reading about Devonshire splits, baps, bannocks and Sally Lunns, not to mention the humble cheese scone, as well as tea breads, drop scones and crumpets sent me to the shops to buy currants, yeast, lard and buttermilk. But there is another problem. A batch of any one of the above will probably make at least 10. Who is going to help me eat them? They are definitely best eaten just-baked and the temptation is to eat too many. If only I played cards, or even tennis, maybe a plate of scones would be the perfect offering.

I also wonder whether high tea still exists in genteel English country homes. Long ago I stayed with such a family in Somerset and marvelled at this curious but delicious meal that seemed to be neither afternoon tea nor dinner and yet was copious and served at around 5 p.m. Supper, which was nothing much, followed at around 9 p.m. The best and warmest seats near the fire were taken by the dogs.

And these days, when I visit France, I want to eat those glistening fruit tarts, custard-filled eclairs and sandwiched macarons but usually I am planning to eat a big meal in the evening and I have to pass by regretfully – besides I generally would have just had lunch!

A friend who lives on a sheep farm in Gippsland, Victoria, says that a substantial afternoon tea is still expected during shearing season, and another friend says the same about her experience with fruit picking. Both activities really require hard physical labour, and that is really the crux of the matter; very different from spending the morning reading, writing or attending meetings. Still, sometimes on holidays, after a long walk on the beach, a really good spread is justified and enjoyable, perhaps followed much later by a bowl of soup. And anytime at all anyone can whip up a batch of scones, even if fancier items need a bit more planning.

Washington currant pound cake

2 cups (300 g) plain flour

1 teaspoon baking powder

¾ teaspoon freshly grated nutmeg

pinch of fine salt

250 g unsalted butter

1¾ cups (385 g) caster sugar

4 free-range eggs

½ teaspoon pure vanilla extract

¾ cup (180 ml) milk

200 g currants (*or* 125 g currants and 75 g Craisins)

Madeira *or* oloroso sherry, for drizzling (optional), and to serve

This makes a very substantial cake that keeps very well. The recipe was published in a food magazine in 1989 and I found it among my collection of clippings. It was attributed to the late Millie Sherman, a renowned chocolate maker and cake baker who operated her own business, Otello, in Sydney for many years. Millie advised that this cake should be kept in an airtight container for three days before serving. I do wonder whether she might have drizzled it with a bit of the Madeira or oloroso sherry, as we might do with a Christmas cake! The quantities given in that recipe made an enormous cake and I have reduced them by one-third. And I confess that I did not wait for three days before sampling.

Preheat the oven to 180°C. Butter a 1.5 litre-capacity 22 cm gugelhopf mould (or butter and line a 20 cm round cake tin with baking paper).

Sift the flour into a bowl with the baking powder, nutmeg and salt. Set aside. Using an electric mixer or hand-held electric beaters, cream the butter and sugar until pale. Add the eggs, one at a time, beating well after adding each one. Add the vanilla and continue to beat until the batter is smooth, light and fluffy.

Using a wooden spoon, stir one-third of the flour mixture into the butter/egg mixture and add half of the milk. Repeat with another one-third of flour and the rest of the milk. Finish with the rest of the flour. Mix only until the ingredients are combined. Stir in the currants. Transfer to the prepared cake mould or tin.

Bake on the centre shelf of the oven for 1 hour 20 minutes or until a skewer inserted in the middle of the cake comes out clean. Cool the cake in the mould or tin on a wire rack for 15 minutes, then turn out directly onto the rack to cool completely. Store in an airtight container. Drizzle with a little Madeira or sherry the next day, if desired.

Serve sliced, with a glass of choice Madeira or maybe an oloroso sherry.

Date and walnut loaf

180 g plain flour

2 teaspoons baking powder

½ teaspoon salt

½ teaspoon bicarbonate of soda

50 g soft brown sugar

80 g pitted fresh dates (weight after pitting), roughly chopped

50 g shelled walnuts, roughly chopped

¼ cup (90 g) black treacle

20 g butter

150 ml milk

butter, for spreading

Older recipes for date loaf suggest that the cook only had access to very dry dates needing a long preliminary soaking. Nowadays, fresh dates are imported from Israel and other places. They have been frozen for transportation but arrive in our fruit shops soft and glistening.

Preheat the oven to 160°C. Butter and line a 3 cup-capacity (750 ml) loaf tin with baking paper.

Sift the flour with the baking powder, salt and bicarbonate of soda. Mix in the brown sugar, dates and walnuts, then, using your fingertips, mix together to ensure that the date and walnut pieces are evenly distributed.

Warm the treacle, butter and milk in a small heavy-based saucepan over low heat until the butter has melted. Stir the warm liquid into the flour mixture and mix with a wooden spoon to form a fairly thick, smooth batter. Pour into the prepared tin and smooth over the surface.

Bake for 40–45 minutes or until the loaf is well risen and firm to the touch and a skewer inserted in the centre comes out clean. Turn onto a wire rack and remove the paper. Leave to cool completely. Store in an airtight container.

Slice with a serrated knife, place on a serving plate and serve spread with butter.

Pumpkin scones

350 g (to yield 1 cup
[400 g]) mashed peeled,
seeded pumpkin (squash)

fine salt

2 cups (300 g) self-raising flour,
plus extra for dusting

40 g butter, softened

2 tablespoons soft brown sugar

1 free-range egg, lightly beaten

milk, for brushing tops

butter, marmalade or chutney and
good-quality cheddar, to serve

It had been raining all weekend and I was getting restless. Making a batch of scones seemed like a good idea, and there was a chunk of pumpkin (squash) in the refrigerator. I am not sure whether other countries have taken to pumpkin scones as we seem to have here in Australia. It is important to choose a variety of pumpkin that cooks dry, such as Kent or butternut. Some cooks add spice, and that would be a nice idea too, especially cinnamon. Pumpkin scones are best served generously buttered, and I like them also with homemade marmalade or chutney and a good cheddar cheese. They will be welcome on any afternoon tea table.

Cut the pumpkin into bite-sized pieces and cook in a saucepan of lightly salted simmering water for 15 minutes or until tender. Drain the pumpkin and tip back into the pan, then place over low heat for a minute or two to be sure there is no liquid remaining. Crush with a potato masher and transfer to a measuring cup to check that you now have 1 cup pumpkin mash.

Preheat the oven to 200°C. Line a baking tray with baking paper.

Put the flour and a pinch of salt into a large mixing bowl and give a quick whisk. Rub in the butter with your fingertips. (Alternatively, put the flour, a pinch of salt and the butter in a food processor and quickly pulse, then transfer to a bowl and proceed with the recipe.)

Mix the pumpkin with the sugar and egg. Tip into the flour mixture and bring together quickly, using either your fingers or a wooden spoon. (Do not use the food processor for this, as it is easy to overwork the dough and the scones will toughen.) Tip onto a floured workbench and give the scone mix a quick pat, then push to bring it together; it should be about 2.5 cm thick.

Cut the dough into 12 rectangles, squares or wedges (alternatively, dip a 4 cm diameter scone cutter in extra flour and cut out 12 rounds). Brush the tops with a little milk and bake for about 15 minutes. Wrap the scones in a clean dry tea towel to keep warm and soft.

To serve, split the scones and either butter them or offer a good homemade marmalade or chutney and slices of good-quality cheddar.

Joan Campbell's neenish tartlets

125 g ground almonds

2 tablespoons pure icing sugar

⅓ cup (50 g) plain flour,
plus extra for dusting

pinch of salt

1 free-range egg, lightly beaten

FILLING

200 g unsalted butter

150 g pure icing sugar

pinch of salt

1 tablespoon liqueur Muscat *or*
Tokay, Madeira *or* port

VANILLA ICING

½ cup (80 g) pure icing sugar, sifted

pinch of fine salt

2 teaspoons unsalted butter

few drops pure vanilla extract

1 tablespoon milk

CHOCOLATE ICING

½ cup (80 g) pure icing sugar, sifted

pinch of fine salt

2 teaspoons unsalted butter

2 teaspoons good-quality
Dutched cocoa

3 teaspoons boiling water,
as needed

The origin of neenish tarts is unclear – some claim they have a German heritage. They are a favourite in cake shops, but can be stodgy and overly sweet. These dainty tartlets are based on the recipe from a great Australian foodie, the late Joan Campbell (one of the most revered former food editors of *Vogue Entertaining*), in her book *Bloody Delicious!* Joan was a great friend and I miss her voice roaring down the telephone, communicating good sense and scurrilous gossip in equal measure.

For the tart cases, process the almonds, icing sugar, flour and salt in a food processor for a few seconds until well mixed. Add the egg and process until the dough forms a ball. Wrap in plastic film and refrigerate for 30 minutes.

Preheat the oven to 180°C.

Roll the dough out very thinly on a lightly floured board or silicone sheet, then, using a 7 cm round biscuit cutter, cut out 15–20 rounds to line small tartlet tins. Bake the tart cases for 12–15 minutes, until crisp and pale-biscuit coloured. Remove from the tins and cool on a wire rack.

For the filling, place all the ingredients in the cleaned food processor bowl and process until white and creamy. Fill the cold pastry cases, smoothing the surface. Chill for at least 15 minutes before proceeding with the icing.

To make the vanilla icing, process all the ingredients in the cleaned food processor to a spreadable consistency. Spread the icing over one half of the surface of each tart. Allow it to set before icing with the chocolate icing.

To make the chocolate icing, process the icing sugar, salt, butter and cocoa in the cleaned food processor, adding enough boiling water to make a spreadable consistency. Be cautious – you will need very little water.

Spread the remaining halves with the chocolate icing. Allow the icing to set, then store in an airtight container in the refrigerator. Remove 15 minutes before serving. The tarts will keep in an airtight container in the refrigerator for 1 week or more, if necessary.

Jam and cream–filled sponge cake with rose-geranium leaves

1 cup (220 g) caster sugar

7 free-range eggs, separated

½ teaspoon pure vanilla extract

½ cup (75 g) plain flour

½ cup (75 g) potato flour

pinch of fine salt

5–7 unsprayed rose-geranium leaves, washed and dried (optional)

raspberry *or* strawberry jam, for spreading

300 ml thickened cream, whipped

pure icing sugar (optional), for dusting

This is an unusual sponge cake. It includes potato flour as well as wheat flour but no fat, and results in a cake with a rather substantial texture compared with the usual feather-light style sponge cake. Somehow it feels more 'country kitchen' than its fluffier cousin. It is baked for a long time at a low temperature. Once filled and stored in an airtight cake tin in the refrigerator, this cake still tastes good after several days.

Preheat the oven to 160°C. Butter, flour and line the base of a 26 cm springform cake tin.

Using an electric mixer or hand-held electric beaters, beat the sugar, egg yolks and vanilla at high speed until the mixture is pale and has tripled in bulk. Sift the flours and salt and fold in gently. Transfer the mixture to a large mixing bowl.

Wash, cool and thoroughly dry the mixer bowl and the whisk. Beat the egg whites until stiff but not dry. Vigorously whisk one-third of the egg white into the stiff batter to loosen it, then lightly fold in the rest.

Turn the batter into the cake tin. Arrange the rose-geranium leaves lightly on top, if using. Bake for 50 minutes or until the cake is light golden and a skewer inserted in the centre comes out clean. Turn off the heat and leave the cake to rest in the oven with the door propped open for 10 minutes. Remove and leave to cool in the tin, then turn out onto a wire rack to cool completely.

The cake is best served split in half horizontally (see opposite), spread with raspberry or strawberry jam, then topped with a generous quantity of stiffly whipped cream. Settle the second half on top and refrigerate for 1 hour before serving. Dust generously with icing sugar, if you wish.

TIMETABLE FOR THE COOK

THREE DAYS
BEFORE THE AFTERNOON TEA

- Check **Ingredients List** and note what needs to be purchased
- Make Washington currant pound cake

TWO DAYS
BEFORE THE AFTERNOON TEA

- All shopping, including flowers
- Decide on table setting, including serving dishes
- Inspect tablecloth and napkins
- Decide on tea, coffee, juices
- Drizzle wine on pound cake, if desired

Neenish tarts
- Make cases and filling, then fill – store in an airtight container in the refrigerator

DAY BEFORE
THE AFTERNOON TEA

Scones
- Cook and mash pumpkin

Pound cake
- Drizzle wine over, if desired

Date and walnut loaf
- Prepare and bake

Neenish tarts
- Make vanilla icing and chocolate icing, then ice tarts – refrigerate

Sponge cake
- Prepare, bake and cool

MORNING OF

Sponge cake
- Split and fill with jam and cream – refrigerate if weather is warm

- Set table

TWO HOURS
BEFORE GUESTS ARRIVE

Pumpkin scones
- Prepare and bake
- Assemble cheese and chutney

Date and walnut loaf
- Slice and butter

ONE HOUR
BEFORE GUESTS ARRIVE

- Remove neenish tarts from refrigerator
- Remove sponge cake from refrigerator
- Put cakes onto plates
- Dust sponge cake with icing sugar, if desired
- Fill kettle and milk jugs
- Have coffee plungers ready

- Get changed

AFTERNOON TEA IS SERVED

- Everything placed on table to make a beautiful and generous display for self-service

INGREDIENTS LIST

PANTRY
- Sea salt
- Fine salt
- Plain flour
- Self-raising flour
- Potato flour
- Baking powder
- Bicarbonate of soda
- Caster sugar
- Soft brown sugar
- Pure icing sugar
- Black treacle
- 200 g currants (or 125 g currants/75 g Craisins)
- Ground almonds
- Good-quality Dutched cocoa
- Marmalade or chutney
- Raspberry or strawberry jam
- Tea selection
- Espresso coffee beans

SPICE SHELF
- Nutmeg (whole)
- Pure vanilla extract

REFRIGERATOR
- Milk
- 600 g unsalted butter
- 300 ml thickened cream
- Good-quality cheddar
- 13 free-range eggs

GREENGROCER/FARMERS' MARKET (OR GARDEN)
- 350 g pumpkin
- 80 g pitted fresh dates
- Shelled walnuts
- Unsprayed rose geranium leaves (optional)

CELLAR
- Liqueur Muscat (or Tokay, Madeira or port)
- Madeira or Oloroso sherry

MOTHER'S
DAY
LUNCH

A LUNCH FOR 6

RUSSIAN SALAD CANAPES

———

POTATO PANCAKES
with SMOKED EEL, HORSERADISH CREAM
& BEETROOT RELISH

———

SAFFRON-MARINATED
LAMB RUMP
with SLOW-COOKED PEPPERS
& FARRO & SPINACH PILAF

GREEN SALAD

———

HUNGARIAN CHOCOLATE CAKE

12 My mother was very dismissive of Mother's Day. She would say 'commercial nonsense', and my memory is that she didn't show more than a cursory interest in the handcrafted cards we created for her. I believe she was hoping to dissuade us from spending our modest pocket money on some eminently disposable object. As the years rolled by she did relax and enjoy a family dinner on this day, especially once there were grandchildren, so it became really a Mother's and a Grandmother's Day. But lavish gifts were not expected and not given. A pretty bunch of flowers was always well received.

There is a little story attached to each course of this dinner.

We all have our favourite 'Mum' moments; not surprisingly, mine are often to do with food. Many Melburnians will remember with affection the extraordinary department store Georges. Home of the most beautiful and the most expensive, it exuded stylish luxury, from its velvet-pile carpet in the entrance to the tucked-away Regency Café, I think at the back of the third floor. My mother never bought clothing or accessories from Georges – far too expensive – but her idea of an exceptional outing was to take me to the Regency Café for lunch. The waitress, perhaps server would be more appropriate, wheeled a trolley to the table. We always ordered the chicken salad, because from underneath the cloth on the trolley's lower level would emerge a large sauceboat of perfect hand-mounted golden mayonnaise, which was ladled over the chicken in generous dollops. How delicious it was. Mum and I both knew the difference between this wonderful sauce and mere salad cream.

The starter of Russian salad on page 213 is another wonderful way to show off good mayonnaise. It is also an excellent dish to engage grandchildren in cutting and mixing, then handing around the little canapes while guests assemble and presents are opened. The next generation is much more gracious about accepting gifts on this special day.

The first course of potato pancakes with smoked eel (see page 214) is always a crowd-pleaser. I have eaten a more extravagant version topped with house-smoked salmon and garnished with black truffles at Georges Blanc's restaurant at Vonnas in Burgundy. As far as I know, Georges is still circulating in his dining room at the age of 73. The restaurant, originally called Les Mères Blanc, opened in 1872, and was managed by three generations of Blanc women. Young Georges took over in 1981 – the restaurant achieved its three Michelin stars that year and has never lost them. Nowadays I believe the restaurant kitchens are managed by his sons Frédéric and Alexandre. What a dynasty! My memories are from the early 80s and I recall, above all, the flowers, not just in the restaurant but in the entire town square, which is virtually all part of the Georges Blanc empire.

Several years ago now I was asked to contribute to the popular The World's Longest Lunch event that is part of the Melbourne Food and Wine Festival. Each March over 1000 people gather at a designated venue – in this case all along the perimeter of the Fitzroy Gardens – to enjoy food, wine, conversation and a very festive atmosphere. I created the grilled lamb rump dish on page 220 to be served with farro and slow-roasted peppers (capsicums). Mum would have loved this. She enjoyed grilling lamb and roasting peppers on the barbecue. I can picture her now stripping the skin from the peppers and dropping them into a bowl of olive oil, garlic and red-wine vinegar. She would never have heard of farro, but could well have decided on a dish of slow-cooked barley.

And for Mum's dessert, in our family history European cakes rich in nuts, chocolate and liqueur were always a treat. Mum's friendship with post-war refugees led to wonderful dinner parties where her Austrian, Czech and Hungarian friends might well have brought along a cake such as this. I first tasted this Hungarian chocolate cake, called *Rigó Jancsi*, at a cake shop in Lygon Street, Carlton, long since swallowed up by an unbroken streetscape of cafes and fashion boutiques. But in my student days, when an essay was looming and I was looking for another excuse to procrastinate, a trip to Lygon Street for a cake was a favourite outing. Nowadays, Melburnians might head to Acland Street or to one of a growing number of specialist bakers.

Makes enough for 24

Russian salad canapes

½ cup (150 g) Homemade
Mayonnaise (see page 502)

finely grated zest and juice of
½ lemon

1 × 150 g free-range chicken
breast (or even better, a roasted
breast of guinea fowl), skin on

Chicken Stock (see page 505) *or*
water, as needed

1 large waxy potato, peeled

2 carrots, peeled

1 handful green beans, trimmed

1 large dill pickle, cut into
5 mm dice

2 tablespoons chopped
flat-leaf parsley

1 tablespoon chopped dill

sea salt and freshly ground
black pepper

1 baguette, cut into thin slices *or*
witlof spears

extra virgin olive oil, for brushing

The origin of this salad seems connected to the introduction of French chefs to Russia during the 19th century. Russian salad is often shaped into a multi-coloured pyramid on a buffet table, secured by the generous addition of real mayonnaise. The ingredients depend on availability and, in springtime, asparagus tips, sweet young peas and young turnips would be delightful. When the salad is part of a buffet table I still serve this as a pyramid, often surrounded by crisp witlof spears. Here, I pile the salad onto toast cut from a baguette and baked quickly till crisp in a hot oven. Cool the toast before spooning on the salad and offer the additional mayonnaise alongside for those who like to add a bit extra. All the vegetables should be cooked close to serving time, so that they can be spread out to cool before being mixed with the mayonnaise; the salad should not be chilled.

Just before compiling, mix the mayonnaise with the lemon zest and juice in a small bowl.

Poach the chicken in a pan of simmering light stock or water for 10 minutes or until just cooked through. Leave to cool in the liquid, then discard the skin and cut the meat into 1 cm dice. Cool.

Meanwhile, cook the potato in a pan of simmering water for 15 minutes or until cooked, then cut into 1 cm dice. Cool completely. Cook the carrots in a pan of simmering water for 6–8 minutes or until tender, then cool and cut into 1 cm dice. Cook the green beans in a pan of simmering water for 5 minutes or until tender but not squeaky. Cool and cut into 1 cm lengths.

To assemble, put the chicken, vegetables, dill pickle and herbs into a large bowl. Mix lightly and season with salt and pepper. Add just enough of the lemon mayonnaise to bind; serve the rest in a small bowl alongside the salad.

Preheat the oven to 200°C.

Brush the baguette slices with olive oil, then place on a baking tray and bake for 3–5 minutes or until golden and crisp. Cool.

Spoon the Russian salad onto a platter surrounded by the baguette toasts, then serve.

Potato pancakes with smoked eel, horseradish cream and beetroot relish

250 g potatoes, peeled and cut into 4 cm chunks

pinch of fine salt

2 tablespoons milk

2 tablespoons plain flour

1 large free-range egg, plus 2 egg whites (60 ml)

2 tablespoons thickened cream

sea salt and freshly ground black pepper

1 tablespoon chopped flat-leaf parsley

2 teaspoons chopped chives, plus extra to serve

clarified butter (see page 511), for cooking

200 g fillets of smoked eel, skin removed and cut into 4 cm lengths

Beetroot Relish (see page 217), to serve

creme fraiche (optional), to serve

HORSERADISH CREAM
(OPTIONAL)

½ cup (125 ml) thickened cream

1 tablespoon finely grated fresh horseradish *or* 1 tablespoon well-drained purchased horseradish

sea salt

At Georges Blanc's restaurant at Vonnas near Lyon, one can experience these potato pancakes at both ends of the meal; as a starter with smoked fish as here, or as a dessert, sprinkled with sugar. Australian vacuum-packed smoked eel has become readily available at fishmongers and farmers' markets. If the eel has already been filleted, it is ready to use, while a whole one will need to be skinned (you will need to buy a 400 g piece). This is easy as the tough skin just peels away from the flesh. Prise the fillet away from the bones and slice it into whatever-size pieces you prefer. Keep the skin to rewrap any unused portion of eel and use the eel within three days. If you can't find fresh horseradish, use commercial horseradish, sold in jars, or simply omit the horseradish cream and top with creme fraiche instead.

To make the horseradish cream, if using, lightly whip the cream. Fold the fresh or purchased horseradish into the cream. Season with a little salt and set aside.

Cook the potato in a saucepan of lightly salted simmering water for 10 minutes or until tender. Drain and press through a potato ricer or a fine-mesh sieve into a bowl. Add the milk and beat with a wooden spoon. (A perfectionist cook would push the preparation through a coarse-mesh sieve again to remove any last small lumps to ensure a smooth texture.) Cool for a few minutes.

Sift the flour over the potato mixture and work in well with a wooden spoon. Add the whole egg and unbeaten egg whites. Whisk until completely smooth. Stir in the cream and taste for seasoning, then season with salt and pepper as desired. Add the parsley and chives.

Film a non-stick heavy-based frying pan with clarified butter. Heat over medium heat and drop tablespoonfuls of the batter into the pan; the little pancakes will form themselves into rounds about 6 cm in diameter. Cook until the tops start to blister, then turn over; the pancakes should look beautifully golden with crisp edges. Cook for another minute or so and keep warm until all are cooked. Serve at once.

Serve the pancakes on a warm plate or plates (see page 512) topped with a spoonful of beetroot relish, the eel and a spoonful of creme fraiche or horseradish cream, scattered with extra chopped chives.

Beetroot relish

2 red beetroot (about 400 g)

2 tablespoons extra virgin olive oil

1 tablespoon water

2 teaspoons red-wine vinegar *or* vino cotto (see page 513)

sea salt and freshly ground black pepper

I have made this with both golden and red beetroot at different times. The golden beetroot looks particularly lovely against the smoked eel but is less generally available. Red beetroot is probably more dramatic. Do wear disposable gloves when handling red beetroot, as it stains. Serve this hot as a vegetable side dish, or warm or at room temperature as part of an antipasto selection, or to accompany any smoked or cured fish dish.

Peel the beetroot and grate using the shredding disc of a food processor or the coarsest side of a box grater. Place in a stainless-steel saucepan with the olive oil and water and cook, covered, over medium heat, stirring from time to time, for 10 minutes; the beetroot will still have a slight crunch to it. Remove the lid and boil over high heat for 2–3 minutes or until the liquid has evaporated. Add the vinegar or vino cotto and season to taste with salt and pepper.

Leave to cool, then serve. Leftovers can be stored in an airtight container in the refrigerator for up to 1 week.

Saffron-marinated lamb rump with slow-cooked peppers and farro and spinach pilaf

3 onions, peeled

½ teaspoon saffron threads

2 tablespoons boiling water

6 × 200 g trimmed lamb rumps

sea salt and freshly ground black pepper

extra virgin olive oil, for cooking

1 teaspoon sumac

mint leaves and sumac (optional), to serve

Green Salad (see page 503), to serve

SLOW-COOKED PEPPERS

3 red peppers (capsicums)

2 yellow peppers (capsicums)

½ cup (125 ml) extra virgin olive oil

3 cloves garlic, peeled

1 fresh bay leaf

FARRO AND SPINACH PILAF

1 cup (150 g) farro (see page 511)

sea salt

2 tablespoons extra virgin olive oil

15 mint leaves, chopped

1 large bunch spinach, stems removed and washed *or* 500 g baby spinach leaves

60 g butter

freshly ground black pepper

Buy six lamb rumps if serving six people, and expect to have some lamb left over. I suggest using a meat probe, which is a thermometer that makes cooking meat to a precise point foolproof; they are available from all cookware suppliers. Both the peppers and farro can be fully prepared the day before and reheated, which is advisable, as preparing the peppers takes several hours. I cooked them with their skins on, as the long cooking makes the skins very soft, so they can easily be lifted from the flesh. If you prefer, you can peel each pepper segment before cooking, using a speed peeler (also called an asparagus peeler). (See recipe picture on pages 218–219.)

Place the onions in a food processor and process for several minutes until you have a very sloppy puree. Pour into a fine-mesh sieve and press with the back of a spoon to extract as much liquid as possible; discard the solids. Soak the saffron threads in the boiling water. Combine the saffron water with the reserved onion liquid in a large glass or stainless-steel bowl and add the lamb. Cover with plastic film and marinate in the refrigerator for at least 8 hours, turning once or twice.

To make the slow-cooked peppers, preheat the oven to 150°C.

Cut the peppers in half, remove the seeds and membrane, then slice the flesh into thick strips. Place in a roasting pan with the olive oil, garlic and bay leaf. Cover tightly with foil or a lid and roast for at least 2 hours or until the peppers are really soft. Once cool, the skins can be lifted away from each strip, if you wish. Set aside with any roasting juices until needed, or refrigerate if prepared the day before.

To make the pilaf, rinse the farro under cold running water until the water is clear, then drain. Place in a heavy-based saucepan and barely cover with cold water. Add a good pinch of salt, then bring to the boil over high heat. Reduce the heat to low, then cook, covered, for 20 minutes or until the farro is just cooked but still nutty in the centre. Drain well. While still warm, stir in the olive oil and mint.

Meanwhile, wash and stem the spinach. Place in a heavy-based saucepan with the butter and wilt over medium heat for 3–4 minutes or until collapsed into a buttery mass. Immediately transfer to a food processor and process to create a buttery puree, then stir this through the warm farro. Check the seasoning and season with salt and pepper, if desired. Set aside. Just before serving, gently reheat in the pan.

Preheat the oven to 220°C.

Season the lamb with salt and pepper. Heat a little olive oil in an ovenproof frying pan over high heat, then seal the lamb well on all sides. Transfer to the oven to cook for 8 minutes or until a probe thermometer inserted in the thickest part of a rump registers 55°C. Leave to rest for 10 minutes or so until the lamb registers 60°C on the thermometer. Sprinkle with sumac. Slice thickly, reserving the resting juices to add to the roasted peppers as they reheat. (Reserve the less attractive lamb slices for a salad the next day.)

When ready to serve, reheat the peppers, adding all the juices from the resting lamb.

To serve, place a portion of the farro and spinach on each plate, arrange a piece of lamb on top, then spoon the peppers around. Scatter with extra mint and perhaps an extra sprinkle of sumac. Serve with the green salad alongside.

Using frozen spinach

When making the pilaf, you can replace the fresh spinach with 120 g frozen pureed spinach. To do this, thaw the spinach completely in a sieve set over a bowl, then discard any liquid. Place the spinach in a heavy-based saucepan with the butter and wilt over medium heat. Puree as above and combine with the cooked farro.

Hungarian chocolate cake

Rigó Jancsi

½ cup (90 g) bittersweet/dark chocolate (70 per cent cocoa solids), roughly chopped

180 g unsalted butter, softened

½ cup (110 g) caster sugar

4 free-range eggs, separated

½ cup (75 g) plain flour

CHOCOLATE FILLING

285 g bittersweet/dark chocolate (70 per cent cocoa solids), roughly chopped

350 ml thickened cream

⅓ cup (80 ml) kirsch

⅓ cup (110 g) preserved sour cherries *or* 3–4 chopped marrons glaces (optional)

CHOCOLATE GLAZE

200 g bittersweet/dark chocolate (70 per cent cocoa solids), roughly chopped

½ cup (125 ml) very strong espresso

100 g unsalted butter, chopped

The story goes that Rigó Jancsi was a Hungarian gypsy violinist who, in 1896, fell in love with an aristocrat who reciprocated and ran away with him. The affair did not last but the recipe for this luscious chocolate mousse cake he supposedly created has endured in many versions. (See picture on page 223.)

Butter a 32 cm × 23 cm Swiss roll tin and line the base and sides with baking paper.

Preheat the oven to 180°C.

Place the chocolate in a heatproof bowl that fits snugly over a saucepan of simmering water, making sure the base of the bowl does not touch the water, then heat until the chocolate has melted. Remove the bowl, stir and leave to cool for a few minutes.

Using an electric mixer, cream the butter with half of the caster sugar until light and fluffy. Add the melted chocolate and mix well, then add one egg yolk at a time, beating well after adding each one. Transfer the mixture to a large bowl. Wash and dry the electric mixer bowl and whisk.

Beat the egg whites until soft peaks form. Continue beating, adding the rest of the caster sugar until stiff peaks form. Lighten the chocolate mixture using one-third of the egg white mixture. Fold firmly to incorporate. Fold in the rest of the white. Sift the flour over the mixture and fold it in lightly but thoroughly.

Pour the batter into the prepared tin and smooth the top. Bake for 12–15 minutes or until the cake feels firm in the centre; do not overcook. Leave to cool on a wire rack for a few minutes, then turn out onto a baking tray lined with baking paper.

Meanwhile, to make the filling, place a heatproof bowl over a saucepan of simmering water over medium heat, taking care that the bowl does not touch the water. Place the chocolate and cream in the bowl, then stir to melt the chocolate until the mixture is combined and quite smooth. Stir in the kirsch. Remove the bowl from the pan and chill in the refrigerator for 45 minutes or until quite cold. Transfer to the bowl of the electric mixer and beat until it thickens and is lighter in colour. Fold in the cherries or marrons glaces, if using.

When the cake is cold, cut it in half lengthwise. Place one half on a tray wider than the cake (to catch drips from the final glaze).

Spread the filling over the bottom half; it should be at least 2 cm high. Settle the top half over the filling and neaten the edges with a spatula. Chill the cake while you make the glaze.

To make the glaze, combine all the ingredients in a heatproof bowl over a saucepan of simmering water over medium heat, taking care that the bowl does not touch the water. Heat until the chocolate has melted, then stir until the mixture is well combined and very smooth.

Pour the glaze slowly and evenly over the top of the cake, allowing it to run down the sides. Refrigerate to set the glaze.

To serve, using a very sharp knife dipped in hot water, cut into serving pieces.

TIMETABLE FOR THE COOK

TWO DAYS BEFORE

- Check **Ingredients List** and note what needs to be purchased
- Advise provedores of special requests (eel)
- All shopping, including flowers
- Decide on table setting, including serving dishes
- Inspect tablecloth and napkins
- Decide on wine – order if necessary
- Make mayonnaise – refrigerate

DAY BEFORE

Potato pancake
- Make batter, press plastic film right down on surface – refrigerate
- Make beetroot relish

Lamb
- Marinate
- Prepare spinach leaves – refrigerate
- Rinse and drain farro – refrigerate
- Slow-cook peppers – refrigerate

Chocolate cake
- Make and cool
- Make filling
- Make glaze
- Fill and glaze cake – store in an airtight container

- Chill wine, if necessary

MORNING OF

Russian salad canapes
- Poach chicken breast and cool – refrigerate

- Set table

AFTERNOON OF

Russian salad canapes
- Cook all vegetables, cool and mix with mayonnaise – cover and leave at room temperature
- Slice baguette – cover with plastic film

Potato pancakes
- Skin and portion eel – refrigerate

Green salad
- Wash, dry and crisp salad leaves – refrigerate
- Prepare salad dressing in salad bowl with crossed salad servers ready to toss before serving

Lamb
- Seal

TWO HOURS BEFORE GUESTS ARRIVE

Russian salad canapes
- Toast baguette slices

Farro pilaf
- Prepare and cook
- Chop mint

Chocolate cake
- Remove from refrigerator

ONE HOUR BEFORE GUESTS ARRIVE

- Preheat oven to 100°C
- Cook potato pancakes and keep warm
- Get changed

LUNCH IS SERVED

CANAPES

- Top canapes with Russian salad or spoon salad onto a platter and add baguette slices
- Serve
- Warm plates (see page 512) before setting oven to 220°C

FIRST COURSE

- Remove pancakes from oven and increase oven temperature to 220°C for cooking lamb
- Top pancakes with beetroot relish and eel
- Serve

SECOND/MAIN COURSE

- Roast lamb for 8 minutes (set timer)
- Reheat peppers
- Reheat farro pilaf
- Rest lamb
- Slice and serve lamb with farro and peppers
- Toss green salad and serve

DESSERT

- Slice cake and serve with cream

INGREDIENTS LIST

PANTRY

· Sea salt
· Fine salt
· Australian extra virgin olive oil
· Red-wine vinegar
· Vino cotto
· Plain flour
· Caster sugar
· Dill pickles
· 150 g farro
· 600 g bittersweet/dark chocolate (70 per cent cocoa solids)
· Espresso coffee beans

SPICE SHELF

· Black peppercorns
· Saffron threads
· Sumac

REFRIGERATOR

· Milk
· Unsalted butter
· Clarified butter
· Free-range eggs
· Creme fraiche or horseradish cream
· 515 ml thickened cream
· Preserved sour cherries or 3–4 chopped marrons glacés

GREENGROCER/FARMERS' MARKET (OR GARDEN)

· Flat-leaf parsley
· Dill
· Chives
· Mint
· 1 fresh bay leaf
· Garlic
· 350 g waxy potatoes
· 2 carrots
· 1 handful green beans
· 1 lemon
· Fresh horseradish
· 2 red beetroot (about 400 g)
· 3 onions
· 3 red peppers (capsicums)
· 2 yellow peppers (capsicums)
· 1 large bunch spinach or 500 g baby spinach leaves (or 120 g frozen pureed spinach)
· 2 witlof (optional)
· Selection of salad leaves

BUTCHER

· 1 × 150 g free-range chicken breast
· 6 × 200 g trimmed lamb rumps

FISHMONGER

· 200 g smoked eel fillets

BAKER

· Bread for the table
· Baguette

CELLAR

· Wine for the table
· Kirsch
· Soft drink

PERU

IN THIN AIR

A DINNER FOR 6

PLANTAIN CRISPS
with SPICED SALT

———

CEVICHE
with LECHE DE TIGRE

———

BRAISED
LAMB SHANKS
with CORIANDER & QUINOA
with PEAS

———

CUSTARD APPLE
& GINGER MOUSSE
CANNOLI
with TROPICAL FRUIT SALAD

13   I started to feel breathless within five minutes of getting off the
plane at Cusco in Peru, the starting point for travellers intending
to visit the lost city of Machu Picchu, high in the Andes. Cusco is
3000 metres above sea level. Altitude sickness is very debilitating
and we heard many stories of its arbitrary nature – one member of
a family succumbs, the others do not. I had three days of misery.
Skull-numbing headache, nausea, scarlet face, breathlessness,
no energy at all, and then it was over. Coca tea is claimed as
a remedy – not sure it helped but nor did the pills I was given.
I threw them away and waited for it to pass. And it did.

The adventure to Cusco was preceded by a week in downtown
Lima (at sea level!), with several day trips into the surrounding
countryside. Fields of quinoa were grown in partially crumbling
terraces, still in use where the Incas had built them 500 years
previously. Every village had impressive piles of yellow corn laid
out to dry.

I wanted to experience as much Peruvian cuisine as I could.
I started the day with fresh prickly pear and corn tamales.
As we drove into the countryside, we stopped to look at the
oven-baked potatoes and roasted guinea pigs (called *cuy*) for
sale at roadside stands. I just did not feel brave enough to try
one – and they did look very dry. I decided that another popular
roadside option of beef heart on a skewer was also not for me –
I have awful memories of once trying, in London in the 60s,
to make a beef heart edible by slow-braising it. I failed. The meat
was tough and leathery, the juices acrid and the flat smelt bad for
days afterwards. I did buy two roasted potatoes, one with pink
flesh and one with yellow flesh, both tasting similar and rather
mealy in texture, with a smoky flavour imparted by the simple
clay oven.

Ceviche is more my style – it is ubiquitous in Peru, with the
best places claiming to have the ultimate version of the marinade
called *leche de tigre* or 'tiger's' milk. Recipes for this vary widely –
some call for evaporated milk, or even cream, or very specific

quantities of different chillies. The constants are very fresh fish, lime juice, red onion, chilli and salt.

I love raw fish and in Lima, then later Cusco, it came chunked with lots of thinly sliced raw red onion and lime juice, usually with a substantial wedge of caramelised sweet potato on the side – surprising to our eyes and palate. Chef Diego de Muñoz later explained that the lime juice, mingled with juices from the fish, red onion and ever-present chilli, makes this *leche de tigre*. The liquid is so popular it is sometimes served as a drink alongside the fish! It is even said to cure hangovers. Just as popular as ceviche is *tiraditos*, where the fish is thinly sliced as the Japanese do for sashimi. It appears in all manner of guises, perhaps with a sauce made from yellow or red chillies, or a fruit-based puree. The constant menu item *causa* is a potato stuffed or sandwiched with something else. Peruvians delighted in telling me that there are hundreds of varieties of potato – including white, yellow, orange and purple, and that a variety is carefully selected depending on how you wish to cook it.

I was introduced to *chicha morada*, a non-alcoholic drink the colour of cherry juice made from purple corn, flavoured with cinnamon and lime. And it did not take me long to sample the very famous cocktail pisco sour. Pisco is a powerful grape spirit usually served diluted with lime juice and sugar syrup, with a teardrop of bitters to finish. Very refreshing. Locals told me that the saying is 'one is never enough but three is too many'. Very wise.

In simple restaurants, the portions were always enormous, accompanied by a generous serving of some sort of starchy food. And on the table for nibbling, and with every order of pisco sour, was a bowl of something crunchy, frequently roasted large corn kernels known as *cancha*. Many times, despite our best intentions, we simply could not manage a dessert.

At one restaurant, three of us were presented with an enormous baked fish, I estimated at least two kilos in size. It was described as a type of rockfish, *chita* (Peruvian grunt fish, for which I cannot find any other name, although its shape was similar to that of a snapper). Its skin had been rubbed with salt so that it baked crisp. It had been basted with lots of butter, and was scattered with many thin slices of lightly fried garlic. Alongside were fat chips of yucca, a popular tuber, which were delicious and reminded me of Jamaican roasted breadfruit, as well as a dish of plain rice. ➤

At another restaurant, I loved my grilled baby goat chops, rubbed with a herb and chilli paste and accompanied by a huge helping of fried potato cake. At the same meal, one of my friends was quite overwhelmed by a cast-iron pot holding at least two cups of cooked green rice, studded with all manner of vegetables and braised duck. The green came from coriander, which is a much-loved flavour in Peru, and was used over and over again in dishes we tasted. The lamb dish on page 240 of this menu is a good example.

Some young chefs have started to gain attention by lightening traditional dishes, whilst still respecting, embracing and celebrating the ethnic diversity found all over Peru. The results are outstanding. One of Lima's best-loved and most highly regarded restaurants is Rafael. Chef Rafael Osterling greeted me with enthusiasm and boosted my ego by enquiring why I stopped writing a column for *Australian Gourmet Traveller* magazine. At the time of writing this, I had stopped contributing two years earlier but nonetheless I made sure that the magazine's editor knew she had a great fan in Lima, Peru.

At Rafael, I adored my dessert of pomegranate and custard apple *tumbao*, a colloquial word usually applied to music that has a sensual rhythm. I guess eating creamy smooth custard apple could well be described as a sensual experience. The dessert was presented in a cannoli shell.

At Astrid y Gastón, I met chef Diego Muñoz, who worked in Australia for several years and loves my home country, so my little group was greeted warmly. We asked Diego to send out some of his favourite dishes. I had just one request – please could he include guinea pig. I was to leave Peru the next day and felt ashamed that I had still not overcome my worry about trying it. The guinea pig was the triumph of the meal. Described as 'confit guinea pig with fried cassava' it was absolutely delicious, like a small parcel of rich and buttery suckling pig with the crispest, crunchiest skin that crackled as we sliced into it.

Eating is an emotional experience and there will be many who are uncomfortable with the idea of eating guinea pig. I would simply say that these animals are raised as food in a part of Peru unsuitable for grazing large animals. Guinea pigs are herbivores, like sheep or cattle, and it does not seem very different from raising chickens and then eating them. Vegetarians may disagree.

And in between this eating, we went to Machu Picchu. Its terraces are familiar from photos but the achievement of being there and climbing at least part of the way will be a special memory forever. The city was looked for but never found by the Spaniards. As one guide book says, the Inca civilisation may not have survived the Spanish conquest, but its architecture did. It is hard to believe the rock terraces date from as early as the 13th century through to the 15th century. And it is also incredible to contemplate how Hiram Bingham must have felt when he 'discovered' this ancient city in 1911.

The stone steps are irregular and have been polished with time and human traffic. I found the climb hard on the thighs, made even more challenging by the thin air and a recent hip replacement. My daughter reminded me that many years before she did the six-day trek to the site, arriving at the wooden gate at the highest point at dawn, and then had two hours to marvel and explore as the sun rose over this magical place, before the first bus-conveyed travellers arrived.

Plantain crisps with spiced salt

1 teaspoon sea salt

shake of cayenne pepper

¼ teaspoon ground cumin

¼ teaspoon smoked paprika

¼ cup (60 ml) extra virgin olive oil

1 green plantain

These irresistible snacks will not last long – hide them until they have cooled a little. You must obtain a completely green plantain, a very large and heavy banana variety readily available in food stores catering to either Latin American, Spanish, Portuguese or African clientele. If none is available, buy an absolutely green banana; the crisps will still be possible, although the flavour is not as good.

Plantain skin is very hard and does not peel like a regular banana. To prepare, use a sharp knife to score the skin from the top to the bottom (not too deeply) in three places, then strip the skin away. The slices should be no more than 2 mm thick, so I recommend using a vegetable mandoline.

Cooking the crisps requires close attention. It is inevitable that some will brown faster than others, so the cook needs to be on hand with a spatula and a tray lined with paper towel to remove the crisps as soon as they are ready. They lose their just-baked crispness after two or three hours, so make them and eat them without delay.

Mix the salt and spices in a wide bowl. Add the olive oil and whisk lightly to just combine.

Line 2 baking trays with baking paper and line a third tray with paper towel.

Preheat the oven to 180°C.

Using a mandoline, cut the plantain into 2 mm-thick slices; the slices are quite delicate so be very gentle with them. Carefully slide each slice through the seasoned oil and place on the lined trays; do not overlap.

Bake for 15 minutes, then check; the slices will lift and dance around a bit. It is likely that those at the edges of the trays will have crisped up first of all, so transfer these to the paper towel–lined tray. Return the trays to the oven and cook for another 5 minutes, then inspect again – the crisps can go from not quite done to burnt in a few minutes, so do not go far away!

Leave to drain and cool, then serve in a napkin- or paper towel–lined basket or on a platter.

Ceviche with *leche de tigre*

1 × 500 g super-fresh fillet firm
white fish (blue-eye trevalla,
snapper, mulloway), skin removed
or 1 × 300 g fillet firm white fish,
skin removed and 1 × 200 g piece
sashimi-grade tuna

1 teaspoon sea salt

¾ red onion, halved and
very thinly sliced

ice cubes

1 sweet potato, peeled and
cut into six 1 cm-thick slices

handful coriander sprigs,
well washed, for scattering

1 lime, cut into 6 wedges

LECHE DE TIGRE MARINADE

½ cup (125 ml) lime juice
(approximately 4 limes)

100 ml fish stock (good-quality
purchased stock is fine here)

50 g fish trimmings from the
ceviche (the very thin or ragged
edge of the chunk of fish)

1 × 10 cm stick celery, thinly sliced

10 g ginger, peeled and chopped

1 clove garlic, chopped

2 teaspoons sea salt

1 thick slice red onion, peeled
and roughly chopped

1 small fresh red chilli, seeded
and finely chopped

4 coriander sprigs

Ceviche can come to the table as a communal dish or as individual serves. Whichever way, offer a spoon as well as a knife and fork to enjoy the 'tiger's milk'. I have made one significant change. In Peru, the fish was cut into large chunks; I prefer raw fish sliced quite thinly. Another popular Peruvian raw fish dish is *tiraditos*, where the fish is sliced thinly, similar to Japanese sashimi. Here I present ceviche with its delicious *leche de tigre* cut in the manner of *tiraditos*. And because it was available at the fishmongers, I used red tuna and white blue-eye trevalla. Many Peruvian dishes are garnished with 'washed red onion'. This is actually thinly sliced red onion soaked in iced water, then drained to lessen its bite.

To make the marinade, blend the lime juice, fish stock, fish trimmings, celery, ginger, garlic, salt, onion, chilli and coriander in a blender to form a smoothish mixture; it will still have interesting green and red flecks in it. Transfer to a bowl, cover with plastic film and refrigerate to chill.

Cut the fish into 5 mm-thick slices, place in a shallow bowl and toss lightly with the salt. Cover with plastic film and refrigerate to chill for 20 minutes. Place the fish slices on a sheet of plastic film, leaving space between them. Cover with a second sheet of plastic film and very gently flatten the slices a bit more, using a very gentle action with a wooden mallet. Lift the plastic film with the fish sandwiched between the layers and transfer to a baking tray. Refrigerate until you are ready to assemble the dish.

Put the sliced onion into a bowl of iced water and a few ice cubes and leave for 15 minutes, then transfer to a plate lined with paper towel to drain. Chill 6 serving plates.

While the fish and onion are chilling, cook the sweet potato in a pan of lightly salted simmering water over medium heat for 10 minutes or until cooked. Drain and set aside to cool.

Divide the flattened fish evenly among the chilled plates. Generously spoon over the *leche de tigre*. Scatter with some of the drained onion and the coriander sprigs. Place a slice or two of sweet potato and a lime wedge on the side of each portion.

Braised lamb shanks with coriander and quinoa with peas

Seco de cordero

1 bunch coriander (weighing approximately 200 g), leaves and fine stems picked and soaked in cold water for 10 minutes

1 cup (250 ml) water

6 lamb shanks, frenched

sea salt

¼ cup (60 ml) olive oil

1 red onion, finely chopped

4 cloves garlic, finely chopped

1 tablespoon *aji amarillo* (yellow chilli paste, see recipe introduction) or other chilli paste

3 tablespoons oregano leaves, chopped

1 tablespoon ground cumin

2 cups (500 ml) Beef/veal Stock (see page 506)

18 small carrots, peeled

butter, to serve

QUINOA WITH PEAS

200 g mixed red, white and brown quinoa (see page 512)

1½ cups (375 ml) Chicken Stock (see page 505)

1 clove garlic, very finely chopped

1 cup (160 g) green peas (500 g peas in pod to yield 175 g)

coriander sprigs, to serve

This is my version of the Peruvian favourite *seco de cordero*, which means 'lamb stew'. It is a perfect way of serving lamb shanks with the unusual combination of coriander puree, *aji Amarillo* (a paste made from hot yellow chillies) and the warm, spicy note of cumin seed. I found the yellow chilli paste without any difficulty at a supermarket that specialises in products for the Spanish and Portuguese communities. You could substitute a paste from red chillies, which is widely available. 'Frenched' lamb shanks means that the butcher has cut around the end of the leg bone, freeing the tendons, so the meat will shrink back into a compact and neat shape during cooking, leaving the end of the shank bone exposed.

I like to serve this with quinoa (see picture on pages 238–239). Traditionally the vegetables are cooked in the stew – I think they are nicer cooked separately.

Lift the coriander from the water and transfer to a colander to drain, discarding the rinsing water. Rinse the bowl and repeat the soaking and draining. Transfer to a blender with the water, then blend to form a bright green puree. You should have about 2 cups (500 ml).

Season the shanks with salt. Heat half of the olive oil in an enamelled cast-iron or other heavy-based flameproof casserole dish over medium heat and brown the shanks on all sides. Transfer to a plate, then discard this oil. Add the remaining olive oil, the onion, garlic and yellow pepper paste and cook over low heat, stirring for 5 minutes or until well softened. Add the oregano, cumin and half of the coriander puree and stir to mix. Return the shanks to the pan and add half of the stock. Cover and simmer for 30 minutes, then stir.

Preheat the oven to 180°C.

Add the remaining stock and coriander puree, stir and taste the sauce for salt, then season if desired. Cover and transfer to the oven to cook for 30–45 minutes or until the shanks are quite tender; test them after 30 minutes. (They can be cooked several hours before dinner, or even the day before, then gently reheated in a 160°C oven.)

To cook the quinoa, put the quinoa into a fine-mesh sieve and rinse well under cold running water. Place the stock and garlic in a small heavy-based saucepan over medium heat and bring to simmering point. Add the washed quinoa and stir, then return to simmering point. Cover tightly and reduce the heat to low, then simmer for 20 minutes or until the quinoa has absorbed all the liquid and is fluffy. (Cooked quinoa can be successfully reheated in a microwave.)

Cook the peas in a pan of boiling water for 4 minutes, then drain. Either mix the peas through the quinoa immediately if you are ready to serve, or if the quinoa is to be reheated, toss the cooked peas in a spoonful of butter to warm through before mixing with the reheated quinoa.

To serve, warm a large ovenproof platter and 6 serving plates in a 110°C oven.

Steam the carrots in a steamer basket over a pan of simmering water for 8 minutes or until just tender. Lift into the warmed dish and add the butter. Toss to mix through.

Plate up the shanks, vegetables and quinoa individually on warm plates. Alternatively, spoon the quinoa and peas on the middle of the platter, then arrange the shanks around. Place the carrots among the shanks and ladle over the sauce. Garnish with coriander sprigs and serve the remaining sauce in a jug.

Custard apple and ginger mousse cannoli with tropical fruit salad

1⅔ cups (250 g) plain flour, plus extra for dusting

15 g caster sugar

pinch fine salt

100 ml white wine, at room temperature

1 free-range egg, separated

1 tablespoon lard, at room temperature

grapeseed oil, for deep-frying

CUSTARD APPLE
AND GINGER MOUSSE

1 ripe custard apple, peeled and carefully seeded (about 550 g, to yield approximately 1 cup seeded puree) *or* 550 g pureed banana

4 free-range egg yolks

75 g caster sugar

⅓ cup (80 ml) milk

1¼ cups (310 ml) thickened cream

1 tablespoon grated ginger

4 gelatine leaves (see page 512)

juice of 1 lemon

This dessert was inspired by one I ate at the restaurant Rafael in Lima, Peru. I did not like to ask chef Rafael Osterling for his recipe, and I am sure his is much more complex than my version. I did ask pastry chef and friend Natalie Paull of Beatrix Bakes for her recipe for cannoli shells, and she generously obliged. If you plan to make the cannoli, you will need eight cannoli tubes to mould the dough. Because they are fragile it is a good idea to make one or two extra in case of breakages. Alternatively, the mousse can be served in small bowls without cannoli shells – top each mould of mousse with whipped cream and serve with a fruit salad–filled passionfruit shell alongside. Place a small pile of finger lime flesh either on top of the fruit salad or the plate. (See recipe picture on pages 242–243.)

To make the cannoli shells, place the flour, caster sugar and salt in a bowl and whisk briefly to combine. Place the wine, egg yolk and lard in the small bowl of a food processor and process for 1 minute. Add the flour mixture and pulse to form a ball. Tip the dough onto a floured workbench and give it a quick knead, then wrap in plastic film and leave to rest for a minimum of 15 minutes or up to 24 hours in the refrigerator; remove before using to come back to room temperature.

Using a pasta machine, roll the dough to the second last notch; you may wish to halve and roll each piece separately. Cut into 12 cm lengths; this is enough to roll loosely around a cannoli tube with enough overlap for the seam. (The width of dough in a standard pasta machine is around 14 cm, which is just right for a standard cannoli tube.) Roll the dough around the cannoli tubes. Seal the edges with some egg white.

Heat grapeseed oil for deep-frying in a deep-fryer or heavy-based saucepan until it registers 170°C on a deep-fry thermometer. Fry the cannoli shells for 1–2 minutes or until blistered but *not* coloured. Carefully lift the tubes from the hot oil, slip the cannoli from the moulds and return them to the oil for 3 minutes or until deep gold. Lift out onto a baking tray lined with paper towel and leave to drain and cool.

To make the mousse, ensure there are no seeds in the custard apple (even one will make a mess in the food processor). Force the

MERINGUE

MERINGUE

3 free-range egg whites

30 g caster sugar

TROPICAL FRUIT SALAD

¼ small pink papaya, seeded and peeled

2 bananas

4 passionfruit, cut in half, pulp removed and shells reserved

flesh of 2 finger limes (if available)

flesh through a coarse-mesh sieve just to be sure no seeds lurk, then puree the flesh in a food processor or blender and set aside.

Using an electric mixer or hand-held electric beaters, beat the egg yolks with the caster sugar until thick and foamy. Place the milk, cream and ginger in a small heavy-based saucepan and bring just to the boil over medium heat, stirring from time to time. Add the hot milk gradually to the egg and sugar mixture.

Rinse out the pan and return the egg mixture, then cook over low heat, stirring continuously for about 5 minutes or until the mixture coats the back of a wooden spoon. Strain through a fine-mesh sieve resting over a large heatproof bowl. Soak the gelatine in a small bowl of cold water to soften for a few minutes. Squeeze the gelatine and drop into the hot custard, then whisk to make sure it has completely dissolved and leave to cool for a few minutes. Whisk in the custard apple puree until completely blended with the custard. Stir in the lemon juice. Continue to stir occasionally until the custard is quite cold and has just started to thicken around the edge of the bowl. (If the bowl of custard is placed over a bowl of crushed ice, then swirled continuously, it will thicken quite quickly – about 10 minutes – otherwise it may take up to 20 minutes to cool and thicken.)

To make the meringue, using an electric mixer or hand-held electric beaters, whisk the egg whites to soft peaks. With the motor running, add the caster sugar, then beat to form a glossy meringue. Fold the meringue into the cold, thickening custard. If intending to fill cannoli shells, leave the mousse to set in the bowl in the refrigerator. (If serving in individual bowls, ladle evenly into the bowls, cover with plastic film and refrigerate until set.)

For the fruit salad, cut the papaya and bananas into 1 cm dice and mix with the passionfruit. Spoon into the reserved shells. Refrigerate until needed.

To serve, spoon the mousse into a piping bag with a plain nozzle and fill the cannoli shells, piping mousse into each end of the shell (any leftover mousse can be refrigerated in an airtight container for up to 3 days). Place one cannoli shell and one filled passionfruit shell on each plate. Squeeze the flesh from the finger limes and place a small pile either on top of the fruit salad or on the plate.

TIMETABLE
FOR THE COOK

ONE WEEK BEFORE

- Check **Ingredients List** and note what needs to be purchased
- Check specialist equipment needed (mandoline, deep-fry thermometer, cannoli tubes, piping bags and plain nozzle)
- Advise provedores of special requests (custard apple, green plantain, tropical fruit, yellow chilli paste) – visit a Latin American food store

THREE DAYS BEFORE

- Decide on table setting, including serving dishes
- Inspect tablecloth and napkins
- Decide on wine – order if necessary
- All shopping, including flowers
- Order fish

TWO DAYS BEFORE

- Make chicken stock and beef/veal stock or purchase best-quality stock

ONE DAY BEFORE

- Wash and dry 2 bunches coriander – divide into 2 containers (some sprigs to garnish ceviche and shanks, plus 1 bunch for lamb shank sauce) – refrigerate

Ceviche
- Collect fish
- Remove from packaging, place on a wire rack over a plate – refrigerate

Lamb shanks
- Cook and cool lamb shanks – refrigerate
- Prepare carrots – refrigerate

Cannoli
- Make dough – refrigerate

MORNING OF

Ceviche
- Cook sweet potato
- Slice, flatten and chill fish
- Make *leche de tigre*
- Cut lime wedges
- Chill plates

Cannoli
- Roll dough, shape shells around moulds and fry
- Make custard apple mousse – put into bowls or a larger bowl, if piping
- Halve passionfruit (keep shells to use as serving containers)
- Make and cover tropical fruit salad – refrigerate

- Chill wine, if necessary
- Set table

AFTERNOON OF

Plantain crisps
- Season oil and set up baking trays

Ceviche
- Soak red onion in water
- Assemble on chilled plates, then cover (don't add *leche de tigre* yet) – refrigerate
- Section limes

Lamb and quinoa
- Remove shanks from refrigerator
- Prepare quinoa dish

Green salad
- Wash, dry and crisp salad leaves
- Prepare salad dressing in salad bowl with crossed salad servers ready to toss before serving

ONE HOUR BEFORE

Plantain crisps
- Preheat oven to 180°C
- Slice plantains
- Bake for 15 minutes (set timer); watch closely
- Cool

Lamb shanks
- Reduce oven temperature to 160°C
- Reheat lamb shanks
- Reduce oven temperature to 110°C
- Steam carrots and transfer to warm serving dish in oven

Cannoli
- Transfer mousse into piping bag with nozzle ready on plate in refrigerator

- Warm plates and serving dishes (see page 512)
- Get changed

DINNER IS SERVED

FIRST COURSE

- Serve plantain crisps

- Meanwhile, put pan of lightly salted water on to cook peas

SECOND COURSE

- Sauce ceviche with *leche de tigre*, scatter with onion slices and coriander sprigs
- Serve with lime wedges and sweet potato alongside

- Cook peas, drain, add butter
- Reheat quinoa in microwave and add peas
- Arrange quinoa in middle of serving platter, place shanks around, add sauce and carrots, scatter with coriander sprigs
- Serve with extra sauce offered in a jug
- Toss green salad and serve

DESSERT

- Pipe mousse into each end of cannoli shells
- Place one filled cannoli, one filled passionfruit shell and one squeeze of finger lime on each plate (alternatively, place fruit salad and finger lime pearls on top of individual serves)
- Serve

INGREDIENTS LIST

PANTRY

- Sea salt
- Fine salt
- Australian extra virgin olive oil
- Grapeseed oil, for deep-frying
- Red wine vinegar
- Plain flour
- Caster sugar
- Gelatine leaves
- Quinoa (red/white/brown)

SPICE SHELF

- Black peppercorns
- Cayenne pepper
- Ground cumin
- Smoked paprika
- Chilli paste (yellow *aji Amarillo*)

REFRIGERATOR

- Milk
- Butter
- Free-range eggs
- Lard
- 310 ml thickened cream
- Good-quality purchased fish stock (if making, see page 506)
- Good-quality purchased beef/veal stock (if making, see page 506)
- Good-quality purchased chicken stock (if making, see page 505)

GREENGROCER/FARMERS' MARKET (OR GARDEN)

- Coriander
- Oregano
- Small fresh red chillies
- Garlic
- Ginger

- 2 red onions
- 2 green plantains (extra in case some burn)
- 1 sweet potato
- 1 lemon
- 6 limes
- 1 stick celery
- 18 small carrots
- 500 g peas in pod (to yield 175 g podded)
- Selection of salad leaves
- 1 ripe custard apple (about 550 g) or 550 g bananas
- 4 passionfruit
- 2 bananas
- ¼ small pink papaya
- 2 finger limes (if available)

BUTCHER

- 6 lamb shanks, Frenched

FISHMONGER

- 500 g firm white fish, such as blue-eye trevalla, snapper, mulloway (or 300 g firm white fish [as above] plus 200 g sashimi-grade tuna)

BAKER

- Bread for the table

CELLAR

- White wine for cannoli shells
- Wine for the table
- Soft drink

LAKE
DISTRICT

A DINNER FOR 6

BUCKWHEAT BLINIS
with SMOKED SCOTTISH SALMON

SEARED
VENISON NOISETTES
with
ESCOFFIER'S SAUCE GRAND-VENEUR

MEG DODS'
MINCEMEAT PIES

STEAMED POTATOES & BUTTERED SPROUTS

BLACKBERRY JELLY

CHILLED
LEMON SOUFFLE

GRASMERE GINGERBREAD

14 Ullswater in England's Lake District has to be one of the loveliest landscapes anywhere. I was visiting my cousin who lives amidst this beauty. The sun shone and the green was of an intensity that we never see in Australia, the hills, oops sorry, the 'fells', looked majestic and the lakes sparkled. Waterways are in fact 'meres' or 'water' not 'lakes'. There were plenty of ramblers and climbers enjoying the spring sunshine. I loved the dry stone walls that stretched away as far as the eye could see and, in the fields, black and white sheep were munching on the velvety green grass. The roads were very narrow, requiring anticipation and courtesy – someone has to pull over to allow overtaking. On one occasion, all traffic stopped, as ahead were three horse-drawn gypsy caravans clopping along. Motorists waited patiently for a suitable place to pass.

There was a thriving farmers' market in nearby Penrith. To sell at the market, the displayed charter stated that produce on sale must have been, *'grown, reared, caught, brewed, pickled, smoked or processed by the stallholder in a 60 mile radius of the market'*. And the produce can only be sold by someone involved in its actual production. This is, of course, a huge bonus for the shopper, as one collects all sorts of advice and special hints, *'Try the smoked garlic grated directly onto a salad.'*; *'These undyed smoked kippers are the first of the season.'*; *'Try the damson gin as a sauce for wild duck or venison.'*

The absence of fruit and vegetables was noticeable, as the growing season is slower in the north. The stalls were dominated by sausages and pies – traditional coils of pure pork Cumberland sausage, black pudding, pork pies and other hand pies – and a wide range of smoked and cured meat and fish. Several stalls specialised in venison. I tasted cheese made with nettles; sloe and damson gin (and this was 10 a.m.); elderflower cordial; and a delicious creamy fudge.

We all remember Wordsworth and his 'host of golden daffodils'. This is Wordsworth country, so I duly visited the cottage at Grasmere where he lived with his doting sister, Dorothy. I tasted the famous Grasmere gingerbread, which was absolutely wonderful and quite unlike any gingerbread I had tasted before or since. We bought it at Sarah Nelson's Grasmere Gingerbread Shop, said to have produced this product since 1854. I bought a packet of local postcards expressly for the recipe for Grasmere gingerbread. I have just made a batch and, although the chunky biscuits are delicious, they are definitely not up to Sarah Nelson's standard!

My cousin's wife arranged a Cumbrian food tour led by local Annette Gibbons, which was quite marvellous. It was a lovely thing to do, and added a whole new dimension to our stay in the Lake District. The area was still suffering from the financial and emotional aftermath of foot and mouth disease, and she told us many stories of those dark days. Annette arranged a visit to the inspiring Jane Maggs, who created and made marvellous preserves under her label, Wild and Fruitful. At the time Jane lived in a charming stone house surrounded by a very wild garden. When I visited, preserves were made in a small kitchen, with two stoves and two assistants. Boxes of jams, jellies and relishes were stored under the dining room table. In her former life, she was a landscape architect, until captivated by the possibilities of her local produce. I bought her Hedgerow Chilli Jelly, made from rosehips, hawthorn haws and wild crabapples; Blackcurrant and Lavender Jelly; and Strawberry and Rosepetal Conserve. Jane picked her fruit locally or made friends with locals with an interesting fruit bush or tree, and grew some in her own garden. Each preserve was only made in small quantities.

On the way back to my cousin's home, we paused outside a venison farm and saw a mighty stag with enormous antlers. He inspired a venison dinner, and I could see at once an appropriate use for the hedgerow chilli jelly as an accompaniment (without this hedgerow jelly, I might have used local damsons). Back home, wanting to expand on my venison dinner and without access to damsons, I made a delicious dark jelly from wild blackberries.

My mother collected old cookery books, and amongst them I have *The Cook and Housewife's Manual* 6th edition, published in 1837, said to be the work of 'Mistress' Margaret Dods. ➤

There is much bibliographical evidence that this was the pseudonym of Christian Isobel Johnstone, who lived and wrote in Edinburgh at this time. My maternal grandmother came from that part of the world, and I have faded memories of the currants and mixed peel that featured in most of her pies and tarts. Moving past the controversy as to the real identity of 'Meg Dods', I started looking for a traditional mincemeat recipe that combined spices, citrus peel and meat. I found it in this work, the antecedent of what we know as mincemeat, used at Christmastime to fill pies or tarts. Somehow, a mincemeat pie combining venison trimmings and all sorts of spices seemed the perfect accompaniment for my venison noisettes.

Buckwheat blinis
with smoked Scottish salmon

1 cup (250 ml) milk

⅔ cup (100 g) buckwheat flour

⅔ cup (100 g) plain flour

1 teaspoon fine salt

2 teaspoons instant dried yeast

2 free-range eggs, separated

⅔ cup (160 g) sour cream

125 g clarified butter
(see page 511)

smoked salmon, smoked eel *or*
salmon roe, to serve

creme fraiche *or* sour cream and
dill sprigs, to serve

The batter for these blini can be prepared a few hours in advance, then refrigerated. Just be sure to allow one hour for the batter to return to room temperature before cooking. Cooked blini can be reheated for a few minutes in an oven set at 160°C, covered with baking paper.

Heat the milk in a small heavy-based saucepan until lukewarm; do not let it boil.

Mix the flours, salt and yeast in a large bowl and make a well in the centre. Whisk the egg yolks and sour cream into the warm milk, then tip into the flour mixture and mix well. Cover and leave in a warm place to rise for about 1 hour. Using an electric mixer or hand-held electric beaters, beat the egg whites to soft creamy peaks and fold into the batter. Leave to rest for another 1 hour.

Preheat the oven to 160°C.

Melt the clarified butter in a heavy-based frying pan and fry tablespoonfuls of the batter for about 2 minutes on each side or until golden brown. Keep the blinis warm on a baking tray in the oven until all the batter is used.

Serve at once, topped with generous slices of smoked salmon, smoked eel or salmon roe. A tiny dollop of creme fraiche or sour cream is lovely, too. Dill is especially good with smoked fish – it could be a sprig on top or coarsely chopped and stirred through the preferred cream.

Seared venison noisettes
with Escoffier's *Sauce grand veneur*

1 × 1 kg piece of venison strip loin, removed from the refrigerator 1 hour before cooking, packaging discarded and patted dry with paper towel

2 tablespoons extra virgin olive oil

freshly ground black pepper

Meg Dods' Mincemeat Pies (see page 261), assembled but not baked

Blackberry Jelly (see page 262), to serve

Green Salad (see page 503), to serve (optional)

SAUCE GRAND VENEUR

1.5 litres strong Beef/veal Stock (see page 506)

1½ cups (375 ml) red wine, plus extra to deglaze

⅓ cup (80 ml) thickened cream

1 tablespoon Blackberry Jelly (see page 262) *or* redcurrant jelly

sea salt and freshly ground black pepper

GARNISHING VEGETABLES

12 new potatoes, peeled

12 small Brussels sprouts, trimmed

butter, as needed

Venison is quite delicious; the premium cuts should be served medium–rare and deserve a good sauce. This lean meat is extremely tender and cooks very quickly. I find it mystifying that it is so little used – I suppose one reason is that it is hard to locate. In Victoria, and probably elsewhere, venison farming is a precarious business. David and Rose Laird of Hartdale Park Red Deer Farm sell their prime venison only at farmers' markets. Venison is almost always sold already trimmed and vacuum-packed. Check the 'use by' date on the pack and store it in the coldest section of your refrigerator. The great chef Auguste Escoffier's teachings underpin many preparations still executed in even the most modern professional kitchen. In his seminal work, *Le Guide Culinaire*, the detail is extraordinary. It is difficult to imagine anyone would follow his instructions to the letter any more, for instance, to make the *Sauce grand veneur* would take several days. I have modified his method, while respecting his flavour profile. You will still need to make the sauce in advance, as a little of it is needed for the pie filling. (See recipe picture on pages 256–257.)

To make the sauce, place the stock in a heavy-based saucepan, then simmer over high heat for 10 minutes or until reduced to 1 cup (250 ml). Meanwhile, place the red wine in a small heavy-based saucepan and simmer over medium heat for 5 minutes or until reduced to 2 tablespoons (40 ml).

Add the stock to the red wine and bring to the boil over high heat. Boil fiercely while whisking in the cream. When well combined and bubbling, reduce the heat to low–medium and stir in the jelly, stirring continuously until the jelly has melted. Taste the sauce for seasoning (it may reduce again a little bit) and season with salt and pepper, if desired. Set aside. (The sauce can be made in advance and stored, covered, in the refrigerator for up to 3 days. There should be 1 cup [250 ml] sauce; remember to set aside ¼ cup [60 ml] for the pie filling.)

If there is any remaining silver skin on the venison, remove with a sharp knife. Cut the strip loin widthwise into 8 equal-sized noisettes. Rub the venison with olive oil and grind over pepper.

Preheat the oven to 200°C.

Place the assembled pies on a baking tray lined with baking paper and baked for 10 minutes. Reduce the oven temperature to 180°C and continue to bake the pies for another 10 minutes. Remove the pies and set aside to reheat just before serving.

To prepare the vegetables, steam the potatoes in a steamer basket over a pan of simmering water for 10 minutes. Add the sprouts and steam for another 5 minutes or until just tender; test with a skewer; it should slip in to both a potato and sprout easily. The vegetables steam whilst the noisettes are in the hot oven.

Meanwhile, heat a heavy-based ovenproof frying pan (mine is Fonte, see page 511) over high heat until very hot. Seal the venison very well on all sides, then transfer the pan to the oven to cook for 5–8 minutes (depending on thickness). When rare, it should yield to pressure with some resistance when pressed with your thumb. If your thumb encounters no resistance and can be pushed in almost through the middle, you need to cook it for another 2 minutes, then check again. Reduce the oven temperature to 120°C. Once the oven temperature has adjusted, place the venison on a heatproof plate, cover loosely with foil and return to the oven, along with the pies to reheat.

Drain the potatoes and sprouts. Place a good lump of butter in a shallow ovenproof dish. Roll the cooked potatoes and sprouts in the buttered dish and keep warm in the oven until needed.

Wipe out the frying pan very well with paper towel. Deglaze over high heat with a splash of red wine and, when bubbling fiercely, tip in the reserved *sauce grand veneur*. Bring the sauce to the boil over high heat. Turn off the heat and add the venison noisettes to the sauce, turning to coat them on all sides. Leave the venison to sit for a minute while you retrieve the vegetables and pies. Serve the venison noisettes, vegetables, pies and sauce on warmed plates with the blackberry jelly alongside. If you like, offer an extra spoonful of blackberry jelly as a condiment. Follow with a green salad, if desired.

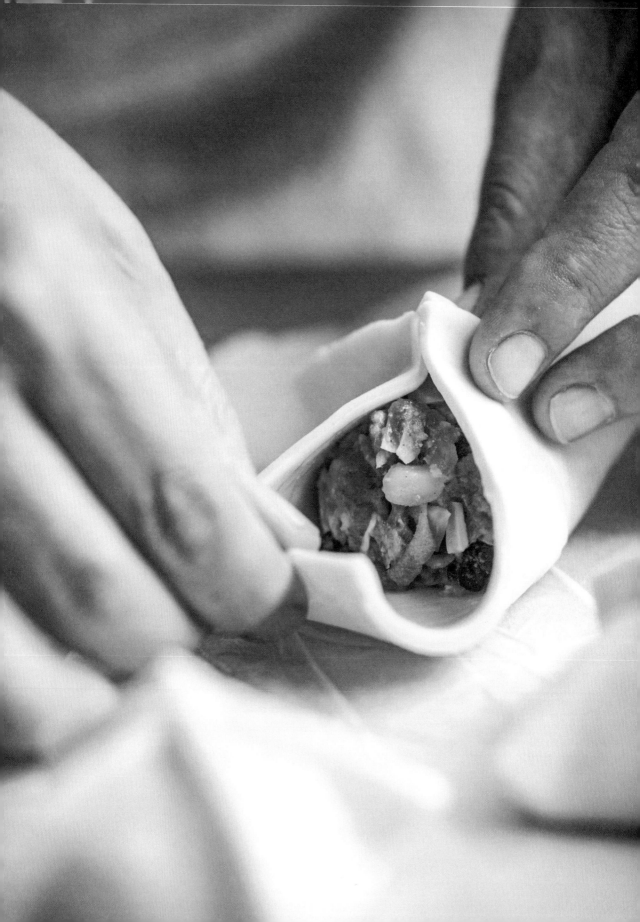

Meg Dods' mincemeat pies

250 g minced venison
(either buy mince or extra strip
loin and mince it yourself)

200 g minced pork

80 g currants

1 eating apple, unpeeled, cored
and grated

60 g blanched almonds,
coarsely chopped

30 g mixed peel

¼ teaspoon ground cinnamon

¼ teaspoon ground cloves

¼ teaspoon ground allspice

1½ teaspoons fine salt

finely grated zest and juice of
1 lemon

2 tablespoons vino cotto
(see page 513) *or* good quality
balsamic vinegar *or* port

freshly ground black pepper

¼ cup (60 ml) *Sauce grand veneur*
(see page 258)

1 tablespoon thickened cream

1 × 445 g roll Câreme sour-cream
shortcrust pastry (or make your
own Shortcrust Pastry, see page 508)

plain flour, for dusting

1 free-range egg, lightly beaten

The recipe for 'Superlative Mince-pies' in Mistress Margaret Dods' 1837 book, *The Cook and Housewife's Manual*, starts with instructions for scraping and salting a 'fat bullock's tongue'. This recipe then is a loose adaptation of the original, and I have greatly reduced the quantities. Even so, it is not feasible to make just four. I suggest freezing the extra pies in a good-quality airtight container, then baking them straight from the freezer and serving them as a hand-around treat on some other occasion. Here I have made square pies but, if preferred, you could cut the pastry into 10 cm rounds, then fold over and pinch to seal like a very small pasty.

The pies need a hot oven for a longer period of time than the venison. Once cooked, they can rest, then be reheated in the low oven while the meat and vegetables are resting. The texture of the pies is best if they are baked just an hour or so before dinner.

Mix the venison, pork, currants, apple, almonds, mixed peel, spices, salt, lemon zest and juice, vino cotto and pepper to taste in a large bowl; I find this easiest to do with my hands or using an electric mixer fitted with the paddle attachment. Stir in the sauce and cream, cover with plastic film, then refrigerate to chill for at least 1 hour to firm it up.

Roll the pastry on a floured workbench to approximately 2 mm thick. Using a sharp knife, cut into twelve 9 cm squares. Brush each square well with beaten egg. Divide the filling evenly into 12 portions and place one portion on the centre of each dough square (you should have approximately 35–40 g filling per pie). Without delay, pull up the corners of each dough square and seal into a square shape. Place on a baking tray lined with baking paper. Brush all over with beaten egg. Chill in the refrigerator for at least 20 minutes before baking. Freeze any not needed (bake 1 extra to allow for 1 to burst).

Preheat the oven to 200°C.

Bake the number of pies required for 10 minutes. Reduce the oven temperature to 180°C and bake for a further 10 minutes. Set aside to cool, then reheat when needed. Just before serving, reheat the pies in the 120°C oven with the vegetables (see page 259). (If the pies are cold, reheat in a 180°C oven.)

Blackberry jelly

2 tart apples (Pink lady or similar)

2½ cups (625 ml) water

500 g blackberries

1 cup (220 g) white sugar,
or as needed

juice of 1 lemon

When I was in Cumbria, there were plenty of blackberries or brambles and damson plums at the autumn farmers' market I visited. Back home, damsons are not easy to come by, but we have lots of blackberries. They are generally regarded as a menace by farmers, so it is harder to find them in the wild. Luckily, commercial rubus (raspberry and blackberry) growers have responded by bringing new blackberry varieties to the market. This blackberry jelly (see picture on pages 256–257) was a lovely accompaniment to the rare-roasted strip loin of venison noisettes we enjoyed when I prepared this menu for friends. You will need to strain the jelly for at least 8 hours, or overnight.

Core the apples, but do not peel. Place in a food processor and chop coarsely. Transfer to a heavy-based saucepan with 1½ cups (375 ml) of the water and cook, covered, over medium heat for 20 minutes or until quite soft, stirring from time to time to prevent the apple sticking. Tip in all the blackberries and the remaining 1 cup (250 ml) water and stir. Cover the pan and bring to the boil over high heat. Reduce the heat to low and simmer for 30 minutes or until the apple and blackberry mixture is really mushy.

Set a coarse-mesh sieve over a large bowl and line with a wrung-out doubled piece of muslin large enough to hang well over the sides of the sieve. Tip the fruit into the muslin-lined sieve and leave at room temperature without disturbing overnight, or for at least 8 hours.

The next day, lift the sieve and muslin away from the strained juice. Discard the fruit. Measure the juice and set aside. For every 1 cup (250 ml) juice measure out ½ cup (110 g) white sugar; I had 2 cups (500 ml) juice so needed 1 cup (220 g) sugar.

Place the sugar and lemon juice in a heavy-based saucepan. Heat over low heat, stirring until the sugar has dissolved; have a pastry brush and a cup of cold water ready to brush down the side of the pan in case any sugar starts to crystallise. As soon as the sugar has dissolved, add the strained apple and blackberry juice, then stir and bring quickly to the boil. Boil over high heat for 15 minutes or until a teaspoonful placed on a chilled saucer holds its shape when you drag your finger through it.

Preheat the oven to 120°C.

Warm your selected clean jars in the oven so they are ready to fill as soon as the jelly is ready (see page 513). Bottle the jelly without delay, then seal. (Providing your jars are scrupulously clean, the jelly will probably last for one year – I have never had enough to test this. As with all preserves, refrigerate opened jars and always remove jelly or jam with a clean spoon. An opened jar will keep in the refrigerator for at least a month.)

Chilled lemon souffle

almond oil or other neutral oil, for brushing

3 gelatine leaves (see page 512)

2 tablespoons boiling water

finely grated zest and juice of 2 lemons

125 g caster sugar

3 free-range eggs, separated

ice cubes

200 ml thickened cream

½ cup (40 g) flaked almonds, toasted *or* 6 Grasmere Gingerbread Biscuits (see opposite)

This lovely dessert is wonderfully light, which is achieved by some old-fashioned elbow grease. The lemon juice, sugar and egg yolks need to be whisked for at least 10 minutes in a heatproof bowl over simmering hot water. I have suggested setting this in a traditional straight-sided souffle dish with a paper collar so that the exposed side can be decorated with either flaked almonds toasted in a 180°C oven for 5 minutes or until golden or with crushed Grasmere gingerbread biscuits. Alternatively, it can also be set in a pretty glass bowl and be scooped onto dessert plates with berries on the side. (See recipe picture on pages 264–265.)

Brush the side of a 3 cup-capacity (750 ml) souffle dish with oil. Cut a doubled sheet of baking paper long enough to line the souffle dish; it should stand above the edge by 3–4 cm. Wrap the baking paper strip around the outside of the souffle dish and brush the inside surface of the paper with oil. Secure the edge with a large heatproof elastic band.

Soak the gelatine leaves in a bowl of cold water for a few minutes, then squeeze. Transfer to a small bowl and dissolve the gelatine in the boiling water. Place a large heatproof mixing bowl over a pan half-filled with hot water, making sure the bowl does not touch the water, over medium heat. Put the lemon juice, sugar and yolks into the bowl and whisk hard until the mixture triples in volume; this will take at least 10 minutes. Add the dissolved gelatine to the egg/sugar mousse, then whisk to mix.

Remove from the heat and place over another bowl half-filled with ice cubes. Whisk over the ice until thickened and cool; remove from the ice as soon as it starts to thicken. Stir in the lemon zest.

Whip the cream until softly whipped. Set aside. Using an electric mixer or hand-held electric beaters, beat the egg whites to firm peaks. Fold the cream into the mousse, then the egg whites. Transfer the mousse to the prepared souffle dish, then refrigerate for at least 1 hour, maybe 2, until set.

Place the toasted flaked almonds on a plate (or crush the gingerbread to form coarse crumbs). Using a flexible knife or spatula dipped into a jug of hot water, very gently ease the paper away from the souffle. Press the almonds or gingerbread crumbs against the exposed edge of the souffle, then serve.

Grasmere gingerbread

100 g unsalted butter

125 g plain flour

60 g soft brown sugar

2 teaspoons ground ginger

¼ teaspoon baking powder

For those readers who have been fortunate enough to visit Grasmere in the Lake District, and have probably walked where Wordsworth walked, and even admired the host of golden daffodils, I confess at once that the following recipe is *not* the gingerbread sold in Sarah Nelson's Grasmere Gingerbread Shop. That confection is absolutely unique and the recipe is jealously guarded. The gingerbread has a sticky, chewy layer, and a crunchy buttery layer – do not leave Grasmere without buying a tin. However, this recipe, based closely on one given by Jane Grigson in her excellent book *British Cookery* and another recipe featured in a local postcard, is very buttery and crunchy and will delight fans of gingery biscuits. (See recipe picture on pages 264–265.)

Preheat the oven to 170°C.

Melt the butter in a small heavy-based saucepan, then leave to cool for 1 minute. Brush a 22 cm × 12 cm baking tin with a little of the melted butter.

Sift the flour, sugar, ginger and baking powder into a bowl, then add the melted butter and stir to combine well. Using your hands, press lightly into the prepared tin.

Bake the gingerbread for 25–30 minutes. Cool a little, but while it is still warm, mark into fingers. When completely cold, store in an airtight container and eat within a few days.

TIMETABLE FOR THE COOK

THREE WEEKS BEFORE

- Any chance of a visit to a farmers' market for the venison – if feasible, plan a visit to a venison farm or order from your butcher
- Check **Ingredients List** and note what needs to be purchased
- Advise provedores of special requests (fillet of venison, venison mince, blackberries)

ONE WEEK BEFORE

- Purchase vacuum-packed venison strip loin and package of venison mince – refrigerate

Blackberry jelly
- Buy blackberries and apples
- Sterilise jars
- Start blackberry jelly and leave to drain overnight
- Finish blackberry jelly (next day or after 8 hours)

THREE DAYS BEFORE

- All remaining non-perishable shopping
- Buy veal bones and brisket
- Make beef/veal stock or purchase best-quality stock
- Reduce stock by two-thirds – refrigerate in airtight container
- Decide on table setting, including serving dishes
- Inspect tablecloth and napkins
- Decide on wine – order if necessary

TWO DAYS BEFORE

- Make venison mincemeat filling – refrigerate
- Make gingerbread biscuits
- Crush a few biscuits for soufflé edge or toast flaked almonds
- Buy perishables, including flowers

ONE DAY BEFORE

Venison
- Thaw puff pastry overnight in the refrigerator
- Make *sauce grand veneur*

MORNING OF

Blinis
- Clarify butter
- Chop or sort dill into sprigs
- Separate slices of salmon or skin smoked trout and portion

Venison
- Prepare potatoes and Brussels sprouts

Green salad
- Wash, dry and crisp salad leaves
- Prepare salad dressing in salad bowl with crossed salad servers ready to toss before serving

Lemon soufflé
- Make lemon soufflé – chill
- Remove paper lining and press crumbs or flaked almonds onto side

- Set table
- Chill wine

AFTERNOON OF THE DINNER

Blini
- Make batter; do not add egg whites yet – refrigerate

Venison
- Make venison pies and freeze those not needed (bake an extra one in case one bursts in the oven)
- Remove venison from wrapping, wipe, portion, oil and season
- Prepare egg wash for pies

ONE HOUR BEFORE GUESTS ARRIVE

Blinis
- Remove batter from refrigerator to come to room temperature
- Whip and fold in whites for blini batter

Venison pies
- Bake for 10 minutes at 200°C
- Reduce oven temperature to 180°C and bake for another 10 minutes
- Remove pies and keep warm, loosely covered with foil

- Get changed

GUESTS ARRIVE

- Warm plates for blini and venison courses (see page 512)
- Set up steamer and bring to simmering ready to heat vegetables

DINNER IS SERVED

FIRST COURSE

- Preheat oven to 160°C
- Cook blini and keep warm on a baking tray in oven
- Meanwhile, reheat pies
- Garnish with salmon, creme fraiche and dill sprigs
- Serve

- Meanwhile, increase oven temperature to 200°C

SECOND/MAIN COURSE

- Preheat cast-iron frying pan on high heat and seal noisettes, then transfer to oven for 5 minutes (set timer) – check if ready
- Turn noisettes, return to oven for additional 5 minutes (set timer)
- Retrieve noisettes from oven and rest in warm spot
- Reduce oven temperature to 120°C
- Reheat *Sauce grand veneur* in a small pan and set nearby
- Cook vegetables in steamer basket
- Add the noisettes and any juices to the *Sauce grand veneur* and turn to coat
- Return pies and noisettes in sauce to oven to keep warm
- Test vegetables, then drain into buttered, heated serving dish
- Toss green salad and serve

DESSERT

- Serve lemon souffle with ginger biscuits and raspberries alongside

INGREDIENTS LIST

PANTRY

- Sea salt
- Fine salt
- Australian extra virgin olive oil
- Almond oil
- Vino cotto or balsamic vinegar
- Red wine vinegar
- Plain flour
- Buckwheat flour
- Baking powder
- Instant dried yeast
- Gelatine leaves
- White sugar
- Caster sugar
- Brown sugar
- Blanched almonds
- Flaked almonds (optional)
- Currants
- Mixed peel
- Redcurrant jelly (if not making blackberry jelly)

SPICE SHELF

- Black peppercorns
- Ground cinnamon
- Ground cloves
- Ground allspice
- Ground ginger

REFRIGERATOR

- Milk
- Unsalted butter
- Clarified butter
- Sour cream
- Creme fraiche
- Thickened cream
- Free-range eggs
- Sour-cream shortcrust pastry
- Good-quality purchased beef/veal stock (if making, see page 506)

GREENGROCER/FARMERS' MARKET (OR GARDEN)

- Dill
- Lemons
- 12 new potatoes
- 12 small Brussels sprouts
- Selection of salad leaves
- 3 apples, such as Pink lady
- 500 g blackberries

BUTCHER

- 1 kg venison strip loin
- 250 g minced venison
- 200 g minced pork

FISHMONGER

- Smoked salmon (or smoked eel or salmon roe)

CELLAR

- Dry red wine for sauce
- Wine for the table
- Soft drink

A
DELICATE
DINNER

FOR

DAINTY APPETITES

A DINNER FOR 4

SEASONED FRESH
GOAT'S CURD

SALMON
with SAUCE VIERGE

FRENCHED
LAMB CUTLETS
with ANCHOVY, MINT & YOUNG PEAS

STEAMED WAXY POTATOES

GREEN SALAD

BLOOD ORANGE JELLY
with MANDARIN BAVAROIS

15

There are times when even the most dedicated gourmand yearns for a delicate dinner. Once upon a time, when visiting the Dordogne in France to receive accolades for my book *Cooking and Travelling in South-West France*, my daughter and I were showered with hospitality and, at the same time, we were almost drowned in duck fat and foie gras. A terrine or pate of foie gras is made from the fattened livers of ducks and is a traditional specialty of South-West France. Equally traditional is duck confit, the method of cooking parts of a duck slowly in duck fat. This cuisine is absolutely delicious but very rich – it can be indigestible to the uninitiated and is certainly not considered everyday fare. Despite that, these dishes are found on every bistro, cafe and restaurant menu in the region. Tourists beware – over-indulgence can lead to a *crise de foie*! How we would have loved to have been offered this menu as a respite.

There was another occasion at the famous bistro Benoit in Paris, where I simply could not attempt the huge slab of wild duck that arrived on my plate, dark-red, as solid as liver, and with a very gamey *odeur*. I was overwhelmed with embarrassment and had to endure the curled lip of the waiter, no doubt reinforcing his opinions about *'les anglais'*. There was nowhere to hide it – no convenient pot plant, and I simply had to say that I was feeling ill. I blamed my reluctance to tuck in on too many banquets. My daughter saved our reputation by thoroughly enjoying her poached veal shank in light broth. I have returned to Benoit since and loved my dinner. Fortunately, the same waiter was not to be seen.

But a delicate dinner does not need to be bland or devoid of exciting flavour and texture. The starter here is a little known specialty of the French town Lyon, which was once the centre of the silk industry. This dish, *cervelle de canut* (see page 275), translates as 'silkworkers' brains'! Not an altogether delightful image, it refers to the slightly bumpy curds of the cheese used.

A Delicate Dinner for Dainty Appetites

I use very fresh goat's curd and mix it so that it is almost completely smooth. Serve it with either a platter of separated witlof leaves or a basket of very thin, crunchy crackers.

And then onto the salmon. Salmon is particularly succulent when cooked medium–rare. The centre will be a glassy rose-red and steaming or poaching is the best method of achieving this. Meat or fish that is to be poached or steamed is best seasoned after cooking. The flakes of salt added to the fish before serving are absolutely essential; this is the moment for the very best flaked sea salt. Common kitchen salt will just not do – it lacks crunch and subtlety. The very best extra virgin olive oil is a seasoning element in the dish also, and combined with the dice of really ripe tomatoes and torn basil becomes *sauce vierge*. The portion I have suggested on page 276 is no more than 100 grams.

Perfectly trimmed lamb cutlets will always be one of my favourite foods, especially in late winter and early spring when they are quite small and delicately flavoured. I have a ridged grill pan that comes into its own for cutlets or a single steak. However, if I was cooking this for four or more I would go to the barbecue. The crushed peas and mint are a classic match with lamb. I always shell the peas myself but have to admit that others will prefer to buy frozen baby peas. These days we can choose our preferred potato variety as readily as we choose our favourite apple. If I am steaming potatoes I go for a waxy variety, probably Kipfler, those odd-shaped long ones (see page 278).

And to finish this delicate meal I think a tiny bit of creaminess is in order. The 'shell' of sharp blood orange jelly hides a classic Bavarian cream, infused with mandarin zest and, if possible, a few blossoms from an orange or other citrus tree. Without the blossoms, the bavarois will still taste delectable (see page 281).

Seasoned fresh goat's curd

Cervelle de canut

400 g fresh goat's curd

100 ml thickened cream

1 small clove garlic,
very finely chopped

1 tablespoon red-wine vinegar

2 tablespoons walnut oil

1 tablespoon chopped
flat-leaf parsley

1 tablespoon chervil leaves

1 teaspoon chopped chives

1 teaspoon very finely chopped
French shallot

sea salt and freshly ground
black pepper

witlof spears, inner celery sticks
or crackers, to serve

**This dip is very easy to make. Its charm depends on selecting
very fresh soft goat's curd. Chervil is such a special herb and
is only available in the springtime. Its tiny triangular heads are
best nipped from the stalks and torn into tiny pieces, rather
than chopped to an anonymous green dust. Serve with witlof
spears, or soaked inner sticks of celery or with thin crackers.**

Combine the goat's curd, cream, garlic, vinegar, walnut oil, parsley,
chervil, chives and shallot in a bowl or pulse in a food processor.
Taste and adjust the seasoning with salt and pepper.

Serve with witlof, celery or crackers.

Salmon with sauce vierge

Saumon frais au gros sel

1 carrot, peeled, sliced lengthwise and cut into 3–4 cm-long julienne

1 Lebanese (small) cucumber, peeled, halved, seeded and cut into 3–4 cm-long julienne

2 slices through a medium-sized bulb fennel, trimmed to 3–4 cm-long julienne

1 zucchini (courgette), unpeeled, sliced lengthwise and cut into 3–4 cm long julienne

handful slender green beans, topped

ice cubes

fine salt

1 × 400 g salmon fillet, skinned and pin-boned

2–3 tablespoons sea salt

ice cubes

SAUCE VIERGE

2 tomatoes, finely diced

sea salt and freshly ground black pepper

extra virgin olive oil, for drizzling

a few stems of basil, finely chopped

Modest-sized portions of skinned salmon are steamed for just a few minutes, topped with a pretty scattering of crisp-cooked vegetables, and sauced with a simple *sauce vierge* and crunchy sea salt. I have suggested a combination of vegetables but really it is up to the cook to add, subtract or change. There are very fancy steamers available, so by all means use one if you have one. I prefer to use my wok half-filled with hot water into which I put a large bamboo steamer basket with a lid. The food to be steamed sits on an enamel plate inside the bamboo basket, with or without a trace of oil (or soy, ginger and garlic on another occasion), the lid goes on and the cooking is very fast. Use the best sea salt flakes for this. In Australia, I use Murray River Gourmet Salt or Maldon; in France I would use a salt with damped largish grains, such as *fleur de sel*.

Cook all the vegetables separately in a pan of boiling salted water for 2–4 minutes, until barely tender (2 minutes only for the cucumber and zucchini). Refresh each batch in iced water, quickly drain and transfer to a baking tray covered with a clean folded tea towel to drain.

To make the sauce vierge, place the tomato in a large sauceboat and season with salt and pepper. Cover with olive oil, sprinkle with basil and leave to stand at room temperature.

Cut the salmon into 4 equal pieces. Bring water in the bottom half of a wok to the boil, then put the fish onto an enamel plate inside a steamer basket, leaving space between the pieces. Cover and steam for 5–6 minutes, turning the salmon once. (Alternatively, if you are using a steamer, place the fish in the top half of the steamer.) After 5 minutes, add all the drained vegetables; they will be hot in 2 minutes.

Arrange the salmon and vegetables prettily on 4 warmed plates, (see page 512), mixing up the colours of the different vegetables. Serve immediately, accompanied by the sauce vierge and a generous quantity of sea salt.

Guests help themselves to the sauce and coarse salt according to their taste. It is vital to add the salt only at the last moment and it should be sprinkled evenly over the salmon.

Frenched lamb cutlets
with anchovy, mint and young peas

8 small waxy potatoes,
such as Kipfler, washed

salt

2 teaspoons extra virgin olive oil,
plus extra for drizzling

8 lamb cutlets, frenched (all fat
removed and bones scraped)

Green Salad (see page 503),
to serve

ANCHOVY, MINT AND
YOUNG PEAS

2 cloves garlic, finely chopped

sea salt

4 anchovy fillets in olive oil,
chopped

1 teaspoon soft brown sugar

20 g unsalted butter

100 g shelled peas *or*
frozen baby peas

¼ cup (60 ml) thickened cream

10 mint leaves, finely shredded,
plus extra to serve (optional)

**Lamb cutlets are a favourite choice for a speedy evening meal.
Often I do little more than grill them and assemble a green salad,
but I am prepared to go to a bit more trouble when it is early
spring and the cutlets are particularly sweet. The anchovies in this
sauce should be good-quality ones. Do not use remnants at the
bottom of a jar of nameless oil that you have had for months.**

Preheat the oven to 110°C and put 4 ovenproof dinner plates inside
to keep warm, plus an extra one for the cutlets to rest on before
serving and a dish for the potatoes.

Put the potatoes into a saucepan of lightly salted water and bring
to the boil. Reduce the heat to low and cook until the potatoes are
tender when tested with a fine skewer. Drain the potatoes and peel,
then tip back into the hot pan and drizzle with a little olive oil. Tip
into the warmed dish and keep warm in the oven until needed.

To make the anchovy paste for the peas, crush the garlic to a paste
with a tiny pinch of salt and mix with the anchovy and sugar. Cook
in a small heavy-based frying pan over medium heat, stirring until
the anchovy has almost melted. Add the butter and stir to form
a smooth sauce. Set the sauce aside at this point.

Bring a small saucepan of water to the boil. Cook the peas for
3 minutes or until tender. Refresh the peas quickly under cold water,
reserving 1 tablespoon of the cooking water. Drain and reserve.

Brush the cutlets with the olive oil. Heat a ridged chargrill pan or
barbecue grill plate over high heat and sear the cutlets for 2 minutes
on each side. Place a teaspoon of the anchovy paste on top of each
cutlet and transfer to one of the warm plates in the oven to rest
while you finish the sauce.

Add the cream, mint and peas to the remainder of the anchovy
paste and heat over low heat, stirring. If the sauce is too thick, add
a spoonful of the reserved pea cooking water; the peas should just
be very lightly coated and still look bright green.

Generously spoon the anchovy and pea mixture evenly onto the
warmed plates and place 2 cutlets on each one. Add the potatoes
and garnish with a few mint leaves, if desired. Serve with a green
salad alongside.

Blood orange jelly
with mandarin bavarois

2⅓ cups (580 ml) strained blood orange juice (if fresh blood oranges are unavailable, use purchased blood orange juice instead)

½ cup (110 g) caster sugar, or to taste

½ cup (125 ml) sweet vermouth

12 gelatine leaves (see page 512)

blood orange segments, to serve (optional)

MANDARIN BAVAROIS

finely grated zest of 2 mandarins (if possible, choose fruit with tight skins as they are much easier to grate)

150 g caster sugar

4 free-range egg yolks

350 ml milk

6 gelatine leaves

50 ml strained mandarin juice

ice cubes

350 ml thickened cream, softly whipped

This jelly is very refreshing. It can either be served on its own, surrounded by segments of assorted citrus or, as here, used to fill jelly moulds that are then hollowed, leaving a thin-ish shell. The centres are filled with luscious mandarin bavarois. It is best to prepare the jelly lining a day or two in advance, as the scooped-out centres can be re-melted and will yield another one or two moulds. I find thin metal jelly moulds unmould much more satisfactorily than porcelain or plastic ones.

The bavarois recipe is about as classic as French desserts get. More luscious than a panna cotta, a bavarois should be velvety in texture. It is always tricky to calculate just the amount of gelatine needed to set the mix; too much will make the bavarois rubbery. If you are using the bavarois recipe as the surprise filling in the middle of the blood orange jellies, you will need less of it. There will be enough left to fill a few moulds with plain bavarois for the following day.

This will make five as it is difficult to make this in a smaller quantity, so there will be one leftover to enjoy the next day.

Bring the orange juice and sugar to the boil in a small heavy-based saucepan, stirring until the sugar has dissolved. Stir in the vermouth and return to simmering point. Meanwhile, soak the gelatine leaves in cold water. Squeeze and drop into the hot orange juice mixture. Stir until completely dissolved (this will take less than a minute). Ladle the jelly mixture into five 150 ml moulds and set in the refrigerator overnight. (You will have one extra in case of an accident when removing the centre and the remaining jelly can also be set in a separate mould.)

The next day, take a very sharp teaspoon and have a small pan of simmering water nearby. With great care, carve out the centre of each jelly, leaving a wall of even thickness, about 1 cm thick. (The excess jelly can be remelted and reset.) Return the hollowed jellies to the refrigerator while making the bavarois. (They can stay overnight without any problem.)

To make the bavarois, mix the mandarin zest with one-third of the sugar. Bruise well together with the back of a spoon. ➤

recipe continues.

Briefly whisk the rest of the sugar with the egg yolks. Place the milk and sugar/zest mixture in a small heavy-based saucepan and bring just to the boil over high heat. Pour immediately onto the egg yolk/sugar mixture and stir to combine. Return to the washed-out pan and cook over medium heat, stirring continuously until the custard has thickened: if you use a kitchen thermometer it will thicken at around 83°C. Strain the custard through a fine-mesh sieve into a bowl.

Soak the gelatine in cold water for a few minutes. Meanwhile, bring the mandarin juice to a simmer in a small heavy-based saucepan. Squeeze the gelatine and drop into the mandarin juice, then swish to ensure it has dissolved. Pour the juice mixture into the custard. Mix to combine. Cool the custard quickly over a bowl of ice. When completely cold and just starting to thicken at the edges, fold in the softly whipped cream.

To assemble the dessert, spoon the bavarois into the centre of the jelly shells in the moulds, filling right to the top of each mould (or fill moulds with the bavarois on its own). (The texture is best if the bavarois is served on the day it is made.)

Refrigerate for a few hours for the bavarois to set.

To serve, dip each mould into hot water for a few seconds, then invert onto a cold plate. Serve as is or with sections of blood orange or poached fruit, or even a tiny sprig of citrus blossom as a garnish.

TIMETABLE FOR THE COOK

TWO DAYS BEFORE

- Check **Ingredients List** and note what needs to be purchased
- Advise provedores of special requests (blood oranges)
- Check specialist equipment needed (do you have or can you improvise the size steamer required; jelly moulds)
- Decide on table setting, including serving dishes
- Inspect tablecloth and napkins
- Decide whether to barbecue or grill lamb cutlets – clean barbecue and check fuel, if using
- Decide on wine – order if necessary
- All shopping (except fish), including flowers
- Pick all leafy herbs – refrigerate in separate paper towel–lined airtight containers

Blood orange jellies
- Make and put into moulds

DAY BEFORE

Salmon
- Buy salmon, remove from packaging, place on a wire rack over a plate and cover – refrigerate
- Cut vegetables for garnish and cover – refrigerate

Goat's curd
- Decide whether to serve at the table or as a hand-around appetiser

Blood orange jellies
- Carve centres from jelly, re-melt and reset

MORNING OF

Blood orange jellies
- Make bavarois and fill jelly-lined moulds

Goat's curd
- Make seasoned goat's curd – refrigerate

Salmon
- Chop tomatoes for sauce vierge

Lamb
- Prepare all ingredients for anchovy and mint paste

Green salad
- Wash, dry and crisp salad leaves
- Prepare dressing in bowl with crossed salad servers ready to toss before serving

- Set table
- Chill wine

AFTERNOON OF

Salmon
- Blanch-cook all vegetables, then refresh and arrange vegetables on paper towel – refrigerate

Lamb
- Oil cutlets

Blood orange jellies
- Carefully unmould jellies onto serving plates – refrigerate

TWO HOURS BEFORE GUESTS ARRIVE

- Take lamb out of refrigerator
- Mix sauce vierge
- Set out pre-dinner drinks
- Have witlof spears or crackers ready for goat's curd
- Put potatoes into pan with water ready to be turned on when you put the salmon in steamer
- Get changed

DINNER IS SERVED

- Put on steamer with plate in position with plenty of water underneath
- Heat grill pan (or barbecue) on low
- Warm plates for salmon and lamb (see page 512)

FIRST COURSE

- Goat's curd offered with witlof and/or crackers

- Meanwhile, put salmon into steamer for 5–6 minutes (set timer) and potatoes on for lamb
- Put vegetables into steamer for 2 minutes (set timer)
- Check if potatoes are tender, drain, peel, oil and put into oven

SECOND COURSE

- Serve salmon with sauce vierge

THIRD/MAIN COURSE

- Increase heat under grill pan
- Cook cutlets (set timer), make anchovy sauce and cook peas (set timer)
- Serve lamb, sauce and potatoes
- Toss green salad and serve
- Meanwhile, remove jellies from refrigerator

DESSERT

- Serve jellies

INGREDIENTS LIST

PANTRY

· Sea salt
· Fine salt
· Australian extra virgin olive oil
· Walnut oil
· Red-wine vinegar
· Soft brown sugar
· Caster sugar
· 18 gelatine leaves
· Anchovy fillets in olive oil

SPICE SHELF

· Black peppercorns

REFRIGERATOR

· Unsalted butter
· Milk
· Double cream
· 410 ml thickened cream
· 400 g fresh goat's curd
· Free-range eggs
· 2⅓ cups (580 ml) strained
  blood orange juice
  (fresh or purchased)
· 50 ml strained mandarin juice

GREENGROCER/FARMERS' MARKET (OR GARDEN)

· Flat-leaf parsley
· Chervil
· Chives
· Basil
· Mint
· Selection of salad leaves
· Garlic
· 1 French shallot
· 1 witlof (or 1 stick celery)
· 1 red witlof
· 1 carrot
· 1 Lebanese (small) cucumber
· 1 bulb fennel
· 1 zucchini (courgette)
· 1 handful slender green beans
· 2 tomatoes
· 8 small waxy potatoes,
  such as Kipfler
· 300 g peas in pods (to yield
  100 g shelled peas; or frozen
  baby peas)
· Blood oranges
· 2 mandarins (with tight skins,
  if possible)

BUTCHER

· 8 lamb cutlets, frenched
  (all fat removed and
  bones scraped)

FISHMONGER

· 1 × 400 g salmon fillet,
  skinned and pin-boned

BAKER

· Bread for the table

CELLAR

· Sweet vermouth
· Wine for the table
· Soft drink

ANDALUCIA

A DINNER FOR 4

DEEP-FRIED
CAPERBERRIES

SPANISH-STYLE
ROASTED ALMONDS

GRILLED SARDINES
A LA PLANCHA *with* ALIOLI

———

CHICKEN
IN SAFFRON SAUCE

POTATOES *with* CHORIZO

GREEN SALAD

———

SEVILLE ORANGE
CREAM POTS

SEVILLE ORANGE
BUTTER BISCUITS

16 For my first visit to Spain, a friend and I had read about
a retreat operated by two food-loving Australian men at Almeria,
deep in the forgotten corner of Andalucia. It sounded like the
perfect base for exploration. We flew into Almeria and, after
a fast drive into the night, following a few sketchy instructions,
we miraculously found the Cortijo Grande and a most welcome
sign indicating that the small guesthouse we were aiming for was
somewhere nearby. A far-off twinkling light further encouraged
us, and finally we drove onto the gravel drive of a long, low,
softly lit building, and heard a welcoming murmur of voices
and clink of glasses.

Traveller's anxiety dissolved with a cool glass of La Mancha
white wine and a cushioned chair. With our pre-dinner wine
we had the first of many wonderful almonds, a slice of the juiciest,
palest peach-fleshed, green-skinned melon, and fat caperberries.
Almond trees grow wild here, as well as pomegranates and capers.
Most of us are more familiar with the flower buds of the caper
bush, *Capparis spinosa*, than these berries, which are the fruit of
the bush. They are served pickled with their stems still attached.

Our first proper Andalucian dinner included chicken richly
stewed with garlic and saffron. We were urged to buy saffron to
take home, as the local produce is so good and very reasonably
priced. Saffron, the dried stigmas of a cultivated species of crocus
(*Crocus sativus*), is essential in many Spanish dishes. Apparently
the saffron appears overnight during the middle of October,
when the fields around La Mancha are covered with a purple
carpet of the flowers – I would love to see this one day. Saffron is
expensive as it takes about 70 000 flowers to yield 500 grams of
the stigmas. The flowers are gathered by hand and each stigma
is then extracted, thread by thread – 60–90 grams is considered
a good day's work! The finest stigmas are bright red and over
2.5 cm long, with a yellow tail end. It is very powerful, so only
a little need be used – we were advised to use about five threads
in 600 ml liquid for a dish for four. Later, much later, after our

delicious dinner came sleep, blissful sleep – shutters drawn, a fan whirring, covered with just a cotton sheet.

Restored, the next day a fish lunch seemed an attractive idea, so we headed off to Garrucha, 'our' seaside town, where there was not a tourist in sight. All along the waterfront, restaurants and simple bars each had a heavy iron hotplate, bottled gas and a refrigerated display of *pescados y mariscos* (fish and shellfish). On offer were dishes *a la plancha*, meaning 'on the grill'. This is, of course, the very best way to cook really fresh fish – and eminently portable. The cook needed just a bucket of seawater to wash the fish and his hands, a chopping board, a knife, a jug of olive oil and a bowl of salt.

Mussels were tossed on *la plancha* with a bowl upturned over them, so that they steamed and grilled at the same time. We chose razor shell clams, sardines and calamari, all *a la plancha*. The grilled seafood was served with slices of hot toast spread with *alioli* (a powerful garlic mayonnaise), with juicy lemons and a saucer of *piccante* peppers, narrow chillies that were exactly that, piquant without being fiery. The sardines were twice the size of those we see at home, grilled with heads, scales and guts intact, but so sweet and fine, and not in the slightest bit bitter – the scales added extra crunch. Were we expected to peel the skin away, we wondered later? The razor shell clams were sweet like scallops, and with something of the texture of young calamari. The salt sprinkled on the clam shells mingled with the olive oil. We licked the shells very carefully, as they were very sharp!

Seville oranges grew luxuriantly in the town square, and one of our hosts gave me his recipe for Seville orange marmalade, still the very best marmalade fruit of all. The intense flavour of this citrus fruit can be used in many of the ways cooks use lemon juice. In this menu, it adds a sharp note to a creamy custard. Somehow sharp and surprising mixed with luscious seems a very Spanish combination to me.

Deep-fried caperberries

30 caperberries, drained

plain flour, for dusting

1 free range egg, beaten

1 cup (70 g) fine fresh
breadcrumbs

grapeseed oil, for deep-frying

I do love the fact that there are alumni of Stephanie's Restaurant dotted here and there across the country, all making their mark. A former apprentice of mine Nicky Riemer operates one of my favourite Melbourne restaurants, Union Dining. I have already mentioned the Ladies Night get-together dinner Nicky organised on page 109. She served these delectable little snacks with the aperitif. It took me straight back to Andalucia, although no-one I saw there had thought to present the ubiquitous caperberries in this way.

Nicky buys her locally grown caperberries from a specialist supplier. Not feasible for home use, I don't think, unless you happen to live near a caper farm. I prowled the supermarket shelves and found that there were brands of caperberries sold in jars of brine that had larger ones than others; the biggest caperberries available are what you want here. You can adjust the quantities depending on whether you want to do just a few, or a lot for a party. (See recipe picture on pages 290–291.)

Place the drained caperberries on a baking tray lined with paper towel in the refrigerator overnight.

Prepare 3 bowls for flour, beaten egg and the breadcrumbs.

Dip the caperberries first in the flour, then the egg, allowing the excess to drip back into the egg bowl, then coat in the crumbs, carefully placing them on a plate lined with paper towel as you go.

Heat a 4 cm layer of grapeseed oil in a heavy-based saucepan until it reaches 170°C on a deep-fry thermometer (see page 501). Working in batches, deep-fry the crumbed caperberries for 2–3 minutes, until golden and crunchy. Return to the paper-lined plate to drain. Serve hot.

Spanish-style roasted almonds

1 cup (160 g) raw almonds

boiling water, as needed

1 teaspoon sea salt

1 teaspoon Spanish sweet paprika

1 teaspoon extra virgin olive oil

'I had a little nut tree' goes the nursery rhyme. Well, I did too. The most beautiful almond tree that blossomed where I could see it through my study window. In its third year, it produced a huge crop of delicious, if very small, almonds. I shelled them all, used some and froze the rest. Then I moved house – the new owners cut down the almond tree, so this jar of rather petite almonds is my only memory. This Spanish way with almonds makes them quite irresistible. (See recipe picture on pages 290–291.)

Put the almonds into a small heatproof bowl and cover with boiling water. When cool enough to handle, slip the skins from the nuts, lay on a plate or baking tray lined with paper towel and leave to dry completely overnight or for several hours.

Place the salt, paprika and olive oil in a small bowl, then stir to make a paste.

Preheat the oven to 180°C.

Roast the almonds on a baking tray for 10 minutes or until golden, then toss them in the paprika paste and return to the oven for 5 minutes. Leave to cool completely before serving (or before storing in an airtight container).

Grilled sardines *a la plancha* with *alioli*

24 sardines, cleaned but not scaled

fine salt

2 tablespoons extra virgin olive oil

4 slices sourdough

Alioli (see opposite)

sea salt and freshly ground
black pepper

2 lemons, halved, to serve

**Inspired by the memory of the seaside town Garrucha, and
the appearance of super-fresh sardines at my wonderful local
fish suppliers, Kingfisher Seafood, at Camberwell Fresh Food
Market, I decided on a sardine first course for my Andalucian
lunch party. Truly fresh sardines should have a stiffly arched
body, and be brilliantly shiny with glossy eyes. They are very
perishable, which is why they will always be at their best
straight from the sea.**

**I have a flatplate on my barbecue, which more or less
replicates *la plancha* as it was in Andalucia. I made sure my
barbecue was absolutely clean and red-hot, then cleaned and
oiled the sardines, cut some slices of sourdough, made a small
quantity of *alioli*, and cut up some lemons. I made one mistake,
which solved one of my questions from Garrucha. I removed
the scales on my sardines, and the delicate skin stuck to my
scrupulously cleaned barbecue plate. Now I understand why
the Garrucha sardines were not scaled – the skin could be
peeled away after cooking. Another solution would be to use
a small hinged grill (see recipe picture on pages 290–291)
made expressly for small fish (or quail), so that the actual skin
is not in contact with the hotplate. No matter, the flavours were
great and the slightly charred garlicky toast was wonderful.**

Using kitchen scissors, cut along the belly of each sardine, leaving
the head intact, then pull out the guts. Have a bowl of cold water
alongside with a heaped spoonful of fine salt in it. Rinse the sardines
in this water and continue until all are done. Dry the sardines very
well with paper towel, then roll them in the olive oil.

Grill on a hot barbecue flatplate or chargrill pan, turning after
2 minutes. Grill the sourdough slices at the same time if your flatplate
is big enough, otherwise grill the bread first of all and keep warm.
Spread the toast with the *alioli*.

Sprinkle the sardines with salt and pepper and serve at once with
a bowl of cut lemons.

Alioli

3 cloves garlic, peeled

sea salt

1 free-range egg yolk

⅔ cup (160 ml) delicately flavoured
extra virgin olive oil (as opposed
to those labelled 'robust')

2 teaspoons lemon juice,
or to taste

Alioli, **literally meaning garlic and olive oil, is a Spanish sauce
made in some parts of Spain without egg, whereas the French
aïoli is essentially mayonnaise started with a large quantity of
garlic pounded with the initial egg yolks. The egg-less sauce
is much less stable and has a frighteningly large amount of
garlic in it. Better to make the French version and claim
authenticity in the manner of its use. Use a small bowl with
a round base and make this small quantity by hand.**

Using a mortar and pestle, grind the garlic with a pinch of salt to form
a paste. Transfer to a bowl and work in the egg yolk with a whisk.
Continuing to whisk, start adding the oil drop by drop, building
the sauce bit by bit as you would for mayonnaise. After one-third
of the oil has been added, add the remaining oil in a thin, steady
stream, whisking all the time; it will become very thick. Towards the
end, taste for salt and add lemon juice to taste. Cover closely with
plastic film and refrigerate.

Chicken in saffron sauce

Pollo en pepitoria

¼ cup (35 g) plain flour

sea salt and freshly ground
black pepper

1 × 1.8 kg free-range chicken

½ teaspoon saffron threads

200 ml aromatic white wine
or fino sherry

2 tablespoons flaked almonds

¼ cup (60 ml) extra virgin olive oil

1 onion, finely chopped

2 cloves garlic, chopped

1 cup (250 ml) Chicken Stock
(see page 505)

1 fresh bay leaf

1 small sprig thyme

1 stalk flat-leaf parsley

1 free-range egg

2 tablespoons coarsely chopped
flat-leaf parsley

Potatoes with Chorizo
(see opposite) and Green Salad
(see page 503), to serve

**In Spain, this dish and all dishes like it, would be cooked
in a terracotta casserole dish that is glazed on the inside,
known as a *cazuela*. These dishes are beautiful to look at and
extremely cheap in all Spanish markets. The great regret of
food-loving travellers in Spain is that one cannot fill one's
suitcase with a selection of the large platters and casseroles that
are available for a few dollars. New terracotta casserole dishes
must be soaked in water for 24 hours before using to prevent
them cracking when placed over a direct flame. Brown toasted
flour is sold in shops in Spain ready for use, but I have included
instructions for making it here. (See recipe picture on page 298.)**

Preheat the oven to 180°C.

Spread the flour in a thin layer on a baking tray and bake for
about 15 minutes or until pale brown. Leave to cool, then store in
a screw-top jar until needed. Place the toasted flour, salt and pepper
in a clean plastic bag.

Cut the chicken into 12 pieces (2 wings, 2 thighs, 2 drumsticks,
breast cut into 6 pieces) and place in the bag with the seasoned flour.
Give it several good shakes so every piece is well coated.

Place the saffron and wine in a small bowl and leave to steep.

Toast the almond flakes on a baking tray in the oven for 5 minutes
or until golden.

Heat 2 tablespoons of the olive oil in a large saute pan or flameproof casserole over medium heat. Fry the chicken pieces, skin-side
down, for 10 minutes or until the skin is golden brown, then remove
each piece to a plate (you only brown the skin side). Add the remaining
olive oil and tip in the onion and garlic. Stir to mix, then cook, covered,
over medium heat for 10 minutes or until the onion has softened.
Remove the lid, add the saffron and wine, the chicken stock, and the
bay leaf, thyme and parsley tied together with kitchen twine to form
a bouquet garni. Bring to simmering point, stirring. Return the chicken
pieces to the pan, then cook, covered, in the oven for 30 minutes.

Pierce the thigh and ensure the juices run clear with no signs
of pink; if not, bake for a further 15 minutes or until they run clear.
Reduce the oven temperature to 110°C and warm the serving plates.

To finish the dish, transfer the chicken pieces to a baking dish and keep warm in the oven. Reduce the sauce over high heat if very thin. Whisk the egg in a bowl and add a ladleful of the chicken sauce, then mix well. Remove from the heat, add the egg mixture to the sauce and shake and stir to thicken the sauce a little.

Return the chicken to the sauce and scatter with the flaked almonds and the parsley, then serve at once, with the potatoes with chorizo and green salad alongside.

Serves 4

Potatoes with chorizo

1 kg waxy potatoes
(such as Kipfler or Nicola)

extra virgin olive oil, for cooking

½ onion, finely chopped

3 cloves garlic, chopped

200 g semi-matured spicy chorizo, skin removed and cut into 4 pieces

½ teaspoon Spanish sweet paprika

1 fresh bay leaf

1 fresh hot red chilli, seeded and thinly sliced

sea salt

This lively potato dish (see picture on page 298) is intended to be served warm alongside the chicken. On another occasion, it can be a dish in its own right, served with a green salad. Ideally it would be slowly cooked in a flameproof terracotta pan (*cazuela*) that has a well-fitting lid on top of the stove.

Peel the potatoes and cut into small chunks, the size of large garlic cloves. Cover the bottom of a flameproof casserole with a 5 mm layer of olive oil and add the onion, garlic and chorizo. Cook for 3–4 minutes or until the onion has started to soften. Add the potato, paprika, bay leaf and chilli, then barely cover with cold water. Add a pinch of salt and bring to the boil over medium heat.

Reduce the heat to low and simmer, covered, for 30 minutes or until the potato is tender and the liquid has thickened. Remove from the heat and leave to stand for 20 minutes. Taste for salt and season, if desired.

Seville orange cream pots

finely grated zest and juice of
1 bright-skinned Seville orange

½ cup (110 g) caster sugar

2 tablespoons brandy

2 cups (500 ml) thickened cream

2 free-range eggs,
plus 2 extra yolks

unsprayed orange blossom
(optional), to garnish

Seville oranges have a short season and seem to have lost favour with many retailers, although there are still trees in many well-established home gardens. As keen cooks know, they make superb marmalade, and here they add their perfume and wonderful bitter notes to a creamy custard. I zest the fruit with a fine Microplane grater and prefer to leave the zest in the custard mixture. If you have zested the orange with a coarse zester, you may prefer to strain the custard before putting it into the oven. Choose attractive ovenproof custard pots or ramekins, as these are served in their cooking vessel. It is difficult to make less than this quantity. There will be one or two left over as a treat for the cook the next day perhaps. I like to serve these cream pots with a crisp biscuit – the orange-flecked butter biscuits opposite are perfect. (See picture on page 299.)

Finely grate the orange zest into a bowl, then add the strained juice, caster sugar and brandy. Leave to macerate for 1 hour.

Preheat the oven to 140°C.

Pour the cream into a heavy-based saucepan and heat over low heat to just below boiling point. Whisk the eggs and yolks to just mix well. Add the eggs to the orange mixture in the bowl and gently whisk in the hot cream. Ladle the mixture evenly into four 200 ml capacity (or six ½ cup/125 ml-capacity) moulds and arrange in a roasting pan. Gently pour enough boiling water into the pan to come halfway up the sides of the pots.

Carefully place the roasting pan in the oven, then bake for approximately 40–45 minutes; the custards will still have a slight wobble. Remove from the water bath to a wire rack and leave to cool. These are best served lightly chilled, so plan to make them at least 2 hours before serving. Remove from the refrigerator 30 minutes before serving.

Serve topped with orange blossom, if desired, with the biscuits alongside.

Seville orange butter biscuits

125 g unsalted butter, softened

½ cup (110 g) caster sugar

1 free-range egg yolk

1 tablespoon thickened cream

1 cup (150 g) plain flour

pinch of fine salt

½ teaspoon baking powder

finely grated zest of
1 Seville orange

2 teaspoons strained Seville
orange juice

raw sugar, for scattering

This dough can be made in minutes in a food processor. Use softened butter and do not over-process the mixture. On another occasion, the dough can be flavoured with sweet orange and lemon juice and zest or vanilla bean seeds. The dough is formed into a log or divided into two logs, which can then be frozen. When needed, cut very thin slices and bake quickly. These biscuits are at their best freshly baked and go very well with custards, such as the Seville orange cream pots opposite, or with a cup of tea.

Place the butter, caster sugar, egg yolk, cream, flour, salt, baking powder and orange zest and juice in a food processor. Pulse to form a soft dough as quickly as possible.

Turn the dough out onto a long sheet of baking paper and roll up, twisting firmly at each end to make a roll about 5 cm in diameter. Chill for several hours or, better still, overnight.

Preheat the oven to 200°C.

Cut the dough into 5 mm-thick slices. Place on a baking tray lined with baking paper, leaving at least 5 cm between them to allow for spreading, then scatter evenly with raw sugar. Bake for 7 minutes or until the biscuits are just browning at the edges. Leave to firm up on the tray for a minute, then lift onto a wire rack and leave to cool completely.

The biscuits can be stored for a few days in an airtight container. (The key with storing any sort of butter biscuit is to keep them in a cool spot away from sunlight, which can turn the butter rancid very quickly.)

TIMETABLE FOR THE COOK

TWO–THREE DAYS BEFORE

- Check **Ingredients List** and note what needs to be purchased
- Advise provedores of special requests (sardines cleaned, heads on but not scaled; piquillo peppers from Latin American supplier)
- Check specialist equipment needed (if possible, a flameproof terracotta dish for chicken; hinged grill for sardines)
- Inspect barbecue (clean if necessary) and check fuel
- Inspect outdoor furniture
- Decide on table setting, including serving dishes
- Decide on wines – order if necessary
- Inspect tablecloth and napkins
- All non-perishable shopping, plus flowers

Seville orange biscuits
- Make dough – chill in the refrigerator overnight

DAY BEFORE

- All perishable shopping, including fish and bread
- Drain and dry caperberries – refrigerate

Almonds
- Blanch
- Make paprika paste
- Roast almonds and cover – do not refrigerate

Sardines
- Clean, leaving scales on, place on a wire rack over a plate – refrigerate
- Make and cover *alioli* – refrigerate

Chicken
- Make chicken stock (or purchase best-quality stock)
- Cut up chicken
- Brown flour
- Toast flaked almonds and cover – do not refrigerate

MORNING OF

- Cut lemons
- Slice sourdough
- Wash, dry and chop parsley
- Remove fat from stock (if using homemade), reduce stock
- Prepare chicken so it is ready to go into oven – refrigerate
- Infuse Seville orange zest
- Set table
- Chill wine

Green salad
- Wash, dry and crisp salad leaves
- Prepare salad dressing in salad bowl with crossed salad servers ready to toss before serving

Seville orange biscuits
- Bake – store in an airtight container

AFTERNOON OF

Caperberries
- Crumb

Sardines
- Have bread slices ready for grilling
- Assemble sardines for barbecue

Orange cream pots
- Make – refrigerate

- Get changed

- Preheat oven to 180°C

Chicken
- Bake for 30 minutes (set timer)
- Keep warm, covered
- Reduce chicken sauce and set aside

Potatoes with chorizo
- Start cooking
- Check potatoes are cooked and leave to stand for 20 minutes

- Reduce oven temperature to 110°C
- Turn barbecue on to high

Caperberries
- Heat oil and fry

DINNER IS SERVED

- Warm first and second course serving dishes (see page 512)

CANAPES/FIRST COURSE

- Set out roasted almonds for self-service
- Set out fried caperberries for self-service

SECOND COURSE

- Grill sardines and bread
- Spread bread slices with *alioli*
- Serve platter of sardines, *alioli*-spread croutes and cut lemons

- Warm main course plates and serving dishes (see page 512)

- Reheat and lightly thicken chicken sauce
- Return chicken pieces to sauce
- Serve chicken and sauce in shallow heated bowl, scattered with flaked almonds and parsley
- Serve potatoes with chorizo in their cooking casserole
- Toss and serve green salad

DESSERT

- Serve Seville orange pots with Seville orange butter biscuits

INGREDIENTS LIST

PANTRY

- Sea salt
- Fine salt
- Australian extra virgin olive oil
- Oil for deep-frying, such as grapeseed oil or vegetable oil
- Plain flour
- Baking powder
- Caster sugar
- Raw sugar
- Raw almonds
- Flaked almonds
- Large caperberries

SPICE SHELF

- Black peppercorns
- Sweet paprika (preferably Spanish)
- Saffron threads

REFRIGERATOR

- Unsalted butter
- Free-range eggs
- 600 ml thickened cream
- Good-quality chicken stock (if not using homemade, see page 505)

GREENGROCER/FARMERS' MARKET (OR GARDEN)

- Flat-leaf parsley
- 2 fresh bay leaves
- Thyme
- 1 fresh hot red chilli
- Garlic
- 2 onions
- 3 lemons
- 1 kg waxy potatoes (such as Kipfler or Nicola)
- Selection of salad leaves
- Seville oranges

BUTCHER/DELICATESSEN

- 1.8 kg free-range chicken
- 200 g semi-matured chorizo

FISHMONGER

- 24 sardines

BAKER

- Bread for breadcrumbs
- Sourdough bread for croutons

CELLAR

- Aromatic white wine (Albarino-style) or fino sherry
- Brandy
- Wine for the table
- Soft drink

CLASSICALLY

FRENCH

PARIS TOUJOURS

A DINNER FOR 4

ASPARAGUS
with SAUCE MOUSSELINE

———

SCALLOP TARTLETS
with JERUSALEM ARTICHOKE CREAM
& HAZELNUTS

———

SAUTE OF CHICKEN
with POTATOES & SHALLOTS

BUTTERED SPINACH

GREEN SALAD

———

STRAWBERRIES & CHERRIES
IN GRENACHE

ROSE-GERANIUM
PANNA COTTA

17

My heart lifts every time I see the curving Parisian roofline, the slates pearl-grey in the morning, and the squat delivery vans; I smell the first baguettes and hear the clatter of shutters rolling up, as the shops prepare for the day. I love the elegantly dappled trunks of the bare plane trees. I like to peer through iron-grey pickets and glimpse a tiny square of deep-green. I smile at children in puffer jackets as they head to school, and admire older Parisians looking good in their well-polished shoes, long coats, gloves, brilliant wool scarves and firmly fixed woollen hats.

Several years ago my daughter and I spent a week in Paris. What a treat! Our hotel was in the Marais, metres from the elegant Place des Vosges. It was nearly winter. From my attic bedroom I could see the gilded column in the Place de la Bastille and, at least for the first two mornings while still jet-lagged, I awoke and watched as the clouds turned from steely grey to pink–gold. On our last night, we walked along the river back to our hotel, pausing to admire the illuminated pyramid at the Louvre, the Christmas decorations, the snaking lights up the Champs-Elysees and the glitter from the puddles on the procession of bridges over the Seine. The white parapets of the bridges gleamed softly in the moonlight. The night breezes whipped up wavelets on the water. The Hôtel de Ville was floodlit.

Friend and former colleague Janni Kyritsis and I have shared some great times, and recently we were in Paris together – the first time for many years. We carefully considered which of our favourite small tucked-away bistros to visit, and chose the belle-epoque brasserie Le Dôme in Montparnasse. We wandered through the street market near Place de la Bastille, heady with the smell of strawberries, seemingly piled with abandon on the stalls. So much more seductive than a pile of plastic boxes! Very early June is still allowed as an 'oyster month', but only just. Our waiter wanted to know whether I preferred my oysters to be '*charnus*', that is full, fat and probably about to spawn. 'No thanks', I replied. The *fines de claire* oysters that arrived were perfect – flinty, brine-y and brimming with juice. Served with

Classically French

the traditional accompaniments of rye bread, butter and finely chopped shallot in red-wine vinegar – some things do not need to be meddled with. We moved onto an extravagant course of foie gras accompanied by cubes of sauternes jelly that melted on the tongue.

Janni insisted we finish with the house speciality, a rum and vanilla mille feuille, and it was sublime. The puff pastry shattered at the touch of a fork, the cream was silky and not too sweet. Not for the first time, I noticed how French pastry chefs cook their puff pastry until it is a toasty-brown, so that the buttery layers taste nutty.

Another Parisian holiday saw me in an apartment on the Île Saint-Louis in the city's heart – four minutes from Notre Dame, two minutes from the river. The extraordinarily gracious owners of Guest Apartment Services, Philippe and Christophe, specialise in rentals of lovely older-style apartments. A bowl of gorgeous peonies was in the room to greet us, then later a bottle of champagne appeared in the refrigerator.

I invited several friends to the apartment for dinner. One of the pleasures of being in Paris with a kitchen is shopping for ingredients. Le Bon Marché in the 7th arrondissement (Métro Sèvres – Babylone) has one of the most extensive food departments I have ever seen. Whether one is simply buying a bottle of mineral water, a jar of violet petal jam, a kilo of the finest foie gras, a baguette, some golden raspberries, wild strawberries or a live lobster, the courtesy seems universal. I bought beautiful green asparagus and fat scallops, carefully counted, lightly vacuum-packed and packaged into a chiller bag by the fish counter.

Around the corner from our apartment was butcher extraordinaire M. Jean Paul Gardil. I conferred with him about how I wanted my *poulets de Bresse* cut for a saute. *Poulets de Bresse* are protected under the French AOC (*Appellation d'Origine Contrôlée*). Only certain farmers in the Bresse region can raise these chickens, following very specific guidelines. The birds are highly valued for their rich, gamey depth of flavour, yet with tender flesh and a modest quantity of delicious fat. M. Gardil asked whether I wanted my chickens cut into four, six or eight pieces. The gizzard and liver were cleaned, and the back and neck included, so I could make a stock. Such beautiful chicken, taut-skinned and rosy-pink with firm yellow fat. ➤

I seasoned each piece, brushed it with olive oil and mustard and generously sprinkled on tarragon. Alongside were glazed shallots, slender green beans and exquisite yellow potatoes, each about the size of a large olive. All favourite tastes and hardly experimental, but I know from experience it is wise not to be too ambitious in a small and unknown kitchen. I opened the door of what I thought was the oven to find it was the dishwasher!

One of the guests brought a 1981 bottle of Penfolds Grange. The bottle opener in the apartment was not up to the task and the cork crumbled at first touch. My resourceful friend dashed downstairs to the nearest Nicolas wine store, fortunately still open at 8 p.m., where the damaged cork was drawn, and a clean cloth was proffered in case we needed to filter the wine of cork fragments. All this for a smile (and a tiny taste of the wine), which was delicious, as was the tarragon chicken it was served with.

Back home, planning my Parisian-inspired dinner, I decided oysters could wait for another day. To celebrate springtime, I chose asparagus again, served with a light *sauce mousseline*, a traditional hollandaise lightened with softly whipped cream. I could not hope to compete with Le Dôme's pastry chef, so I chose lovely strawberries and cherries as our finale.

Asparagus with *sauce mousseline*

fine salt

20 spears evenly sized asparagus, stem ends snapped off and exposed ends peeled, if you wish (I see no reason to do this if the asparagus is as fresh as it should be)

SAUCE MOUSSELINE

200 g unsalted butter

2 tablespoons white-wine vinegar

pinch coarsely ground white pepper

2 tablespoons water

3 free-range egg yolks

juice of ½ lemon, strained

sea salt

2 tablespoons thickened cream, softly whipped (or use creme fraiche)

2 teaspoons chopped chives

1 tablespoon chopped French tarragon

1 tablespoon chopped chervil

Whether one chooses green or white asparagus, it is almost universally agreed that a platter of perfectly cooked spears with a simple sauce is hard to beat as a starter before more substantial dishes. I prefer asparagus that is thick rather than pencil thin, and green rather than white. It is said that asparagus is best cooked in a tall pot so that the tips steam rather than boil. Very few people own such a pot, so I find it satisfactory to use a wide saute pan, as instructed below, deep enough so that the spears can float in the simmering water.

Hollandaise is a delicious sauce for asparagus. Here, the addition of some softly whipped cream or creme fraiche adds lightness. I start with an initial reduction of white-wine vinegar, which is not strictly correct but I like the piquancy. I also fold in some freshly chopped herbs, such as chervil, chives and tarragon.

Preheat the oven to 110°C and place 4 ovenproof serving plates inside to warm.

To make the sauce, melt the butter in a small, heavy-based saucepan over low heat and leave to cool a little. Put the vinegar, pepper and water into another small, heavy-based saucepan and reduce over medium heat to 1 tablespoon liquid; this can be prepared in advance. Transfer to a small heatproof bowl that fits comfortably over a small, heavy-based saucepan half-filled with hot water, taking care that the bowl does not touch the water. Add the egg yolks and whisk well over medium heat until thick and foamy. Whisk in a little of the cooled butter at a time. When all the butter has been incorporated you should have a bowl of thick, creamy sauce. Add the lemon juice and salt to taste.

Keep the sauce warm over the pan of hot water for up to 20 minutes and, just before serving, stir in the cream or creme fraiche and herbs.

Bring a wide pan (mine is 22 cm wide × 4 cm deep) of water to the boil with some salt. Drop in the asparagus, loosely bundled for easy retrieval, then cook for 4 minutes, keeping a very close eye on it. Immediately test for tenderness by inserting with a fine skewer or the point of a small knife. Lift out onto a warm cloth to briefly drain, then divide among the hot serving plates.

Scallop tartlets with Jerusalem artichoke cream and hazelnuts

1 sheet all-butter puff pastry
(I use Carême)

50 g hazelnuts (blanched,
if available)

1 tablespoon freshly chopped flat-
leaf parsley *or* chives, *or* a mixture

finely grated zest of ¼ lemon

sea salt and freshly ground
black pepper

cayenne pepper, to taste

hazelnut oil *or* extra virgin olive
oil, as needed

12 scallops on-the-shell, with or
without roe, as you prefer

JERUSALEM ARTICHOKE CREAM

½ cup (125 ml) thickened cream

100 ml milk

300 g Jerusalem artichokes

sea salt and freshly ground
black pepper

hazelnut oil *or* extra virgin olive
oil, as needed

These tartlets seem very tricky but they are not. Almost all the preparation can be done in advance, with the final assembly and grilling taking just a few minutes. Do read the recipe right through to the end before starting. (See recipe picture on pages 312–313.)

To make the artichoke cream, place the cream and milk in a small, heavy-based saucepan and bring to the boil. Peel and coarsely chop the Jerusalem artichokes, then immediately add to the pan and cook over medium heat for 15 minutes or until the cream has reduced and the Jerusalem artichoke is very tender. Transfer to a food processor and process to form a smooth cream. Adjust the seasoning with salt and pepper, then transfer to a bowl and add a few drops of the hazelnut oil or olive oil. (This can be prepared the day before, stored in the refrigerator and reheated when needed.)

Roll out the puff pastry to about 2 mm thick. Using a 10 cm biscuit cutter, cut out 4 rounds. Prick the rounds with a fork, place on a baking tray lined with baking paper, cover with another sheet of baking paper, then place a heavy-based baking tray on top to prevent the pastry from rising during cooking. Chill for 20 minutes.

Preheat the oven to 220°C.

Transfer the pastry with both trays in place to the oven and bake for 10 minutes or until golden. Remove the top tray and cool the rounds on a wire rack.

Reduce the oven temperature to 180°C. Place the hazelnuts on a baking tray and toast for 5 minutes or until golden. If unblanched, rub the toasted hazelnuts in a dry tea towel and separate the nuts from the skins, discarding the skins. Coarsely chop, then mix with the parsley and/or chives and lemon zest and season to taste with salt, pepper and a pinch of cayenne. Add a small amount of hazelnut oil or olive oil, just enough to bind the ingredients. Keep warm.

Remove the scallops from their shells and remove and discard the hard muscle and any dark intestinal thread. Cut the scallops in half horizontally, then toss with a few drops of olive oil and a little salt and pepper.

Classically French

Cut out four 10 cm rounds of baking paper and arrange on a baking tray. Layer 6 of the scallop slices in a circular fashion on each round of paper, creating a rosette effect. Cover with a second sheet of baking paper and refrigerate until needed.

To cook and serve, preheat the oven griller to very hot. Arrange the 4 baked tart bases on a baking tray. Spread each one with 2–3 tablespoons of the Jerusalem artichoke cream. Peel the top layer of baking paper on the scallops and invert each round of scallops over the Jerusalem artichoke cream. Drizzle with a little more olive oil.

Carefully place the baking tray under the hot griller and grill for 3–4 minutes or until the scallops are just cooked; they should be opaque. (Reduce the oven temperature to 120°C to keep the chicken and plates hot for the main course.)

Quickly transfer the tartlets to heated serving plates and scatter with the warm hazelnut mixture. Serve at once.

Serves 4

Saute of chicken
with potatoes and shallots

1 × 1.8–2 kg free-range chicken

sea salt and freshly ground
black pepper

8 small waxy potatoes *or*
large ones, cut into chunks

8 French shallots

¼ cup (70 g) Dijon-style mustard

2 tablespoons extra virgin olive oil,
plus extra as needed

generous quantity of coarsely
chopped French tarragon
(spring and summer) or stripped
lemon thyme leaves (winter)

4 cloves garlic, unpeeled

2 tablespoons dry white wine *or*
dry vermouth

Buttered Spinach (see page 321)
and/or Green Salad (see page 503),
to serve

CHICKEN STOCK

reserved chicken backbone
and any bony scraps

1 carrot, roughly chopped

1 stick celery, sliced

3 cloves garlic, crushed

1 onion, roughly chopped

a few sprigs thyme, a bay leaf,
a few flat-leaf parsley stalks

I have read that in days gone by many French homes and apartments did not have ovens, so perhaps this could be why the French have an extensive repertoire of dishes that are best cooked in heavy, covered pots on the stovetop. This requires a very large pan and, even though I used the largest enamelled cast-iron casserole I own, I needed to use a second one and divided the ingredients between them. I suggest the initial preparation of the chicken is done either the day before you wish to serve the chicken or in the morning. (See recipe picture on pages 316–317.)

The day before or morning of your dinner party, remove all the wrapping from the chicken and place it, uncovered, on a plate in the refrigerator for at least 1 hour to dry out the skin.

Carefully remove the leg and thigh joints, then separate each one into two pieces. Cut out the backbone and drop it into a stockpot. Separate the two breast fillets, keeping them on the bone and taking care not to dislodge the skin. Cut away the wing bone where it joins the breast meat, to separate the breasts and wings. Add the wing tips to the stockpot. You should now have 8 pieces; season well with salt and pepper.

To make the stock, add the stock vegetables and herbs to the pot with the carcass. Barely cover with cold water and bring to simmering point. Skim the surface, then reduce the heat to low and cook the stock for at least 3 hours. Strain into a bowl and chill in the refrigerator. Remove all the solidified fat. Measure 2 cups (500 ml) into a heavy-based saucepan, then reduce rapidly over high heat to 1 cup (250 ml). Reserve until needed.

If using large potatoes, parboil for 5 minutes in a pan of simmering salted water, then drain. Put the shallots into a small pan of cold water and bring to the boil. Drain and peel. (The dish can be prepared to this point several hours before dinner.)

When ready to start cooking, select an enamelled cast-iron casserole or very wide saute pan with a tight-fitting lid that will comfortably hold the chicken pieces and the vegetables in a single layer, without extra space (or select two pans). Lightly oil the pan/s with extra olive oil.

Mix the mustard with the olive oil in a small bowl. Using your hands, massage the mustard mixture into all sides of each chicken piece and under the skin. Heat the oiled pan/s over medium heat for 1–2 minutes. Transfer the chicken pieces to the pan/s, skin-side up. Scatter over the herbs. Tip in the potato, shallots and garlic and cook over medium heat for 20 minutes. Using an egg lifter or spatula (not tongs), turn all the pieces carefully and shake the vegetables loose. Cover and saute for a further 20 minutes, then turn once more; the chicken pieces should be skin-side up again. Remove the lid/s and saute for a further 10–15 minutes or until the skin looks golden brown and the juices run clear from the thigh pieces when pierced with a fine skewer.

Meanwhile, preheat the oven to 110°C and place a large ovenproof serving dish and 4 dinner plates inside to warm.

Transfer the chicken, vegetables and garlic to the heated serving dish. Pour off the fat from the saute pan/s. Deglaze with the wine over high heat, letting it bubble up, stirring well to dislodge all the yummy bits. Add the reserved stock and stir and scrape until reduced; you should have a small quantity of very delicious sauce. Strain and spoon this over and around the chicken pieces, vegetables and garlic.

Serve the sauteed chicken, vegetables and garlic at once with the buttered spinach and/or a green salad alongside.

Buttered spinach

1 bunch spinach with large leaves (approximately 850 g, to yield around 475 g after removing the stems)

60 g unsalted butter

sea salt and freshly ground black pepper

Spinach bunches with larger leaves are less work and give a better yield. It is necessary to remove the stem from each leaf as described; this makes all the difference between a silky-smooth forkful or a stringy one. I choose smaller leaves for salads or a last-minute toss with cooked pasta; even so, I carefully remove the excess stalk and stem. If cooking a single bunch, the water clinging to the well-washed leaves will be sufficient. If cooking two or three bunches, plunge the well-washed leaves into a pan of lots of boiling water for 2 minutes, then drain well.

To remove the stem from each leaf, fold in half and pull the stem up and along the leaf, a bit like pulling up a zipper. Put the leaves into a large bowl of cold water. Swish with your hands. Lift the spinach leaves onto a baking tray, tip away the water, rinse the bowl and repeat the process. (If the spinach is very muddy, repeat.)

Transfer the washed leaves, still dripping, to a wide saute pan with a lid. Place over high heat and cook, covered, until steam escapes from the lid. Lift the lid and stir to ensure all the leaves are collapsing evenly. Cook for 1 more minute, then tip the spinach into a colander in the sink. Press the water out with the back of a saucer or similar.

If you want a puree, immediately transfer the hot spinach to a food processor with the butter and process to form a smooth green puree. Taste and adjust the seasoning with salt and pepper. This puree can be quickly reheated either in a small saucepan or in a microwave. To add extra flavour, reheat the spinach with a spoonful of the chicken roasting juices. Taste for seasoning.

Èpinards en branche

If intending to serve the spinach *en branche* (meaning left as whole leaves rather than pureed), plunge the drained cooked leaves into very cold water to cool. Squeeze gently but firmly and lay on a plate. Cover and, when ready to serve, reheat with a knob of butter. Season with salt and pepper.

Strawberries and cherries in Grenache with rose-geranium panna cotta

3 gelatine leaves (see page 512)

sweet almond oil *or* other tasteless oil, for brushing moulds

1 cup (250 ml) milk

1 cup (250 ml) thickened cream

¼ cup (55 g) caster sugar

3 unsprayed rose-geranium leaves, plus extra to serve (optional)

STRAWBERRIES AND CHERRIES
IN GRENACHE

1½ cups (375 ml) Grenache *or* other medium-bodied red wine

½ cup (110 g) caster sugar

1 teaspoon cornflour, dissolved in 1 tablespoon water

150 g best cherries, pitted

250 g best small–medium strawberries, hulled

Simple fruit desserts are always welcome, especially after a rich multi-course dinner, such as this one. Be warned that if you are using a hand-held cherry pitter there is almost always a spray of cherry juice that will stain clothing – wear an apron. If you do not have a cherry pitter, carefully gouge out the pips with a sharp knife.

To prepare the strawberries and cherries, place the wine in a stainless-steel saucepan and bring to the boil over high heat. Simmer for 10 minutes or until reduced by half. Stir in the sugar until it has dissolved and add the cornflour mixture. Cook, stirring for less than a minute to lightly thicken. Add the cherries and return to boiling point. Reduce the heat to low and cook for 1 minute. Leave to cool. (The cherries can stand for a few hours or overnight. The strawberries should be added just before serving as they may become soggy.)

Select four ½ cup (125 ml-capacity) moulds (demitasse coffee cups are ideal) and arrange on a baking tray that fits in the refrigerator.

Soak the gelatine leaves in a bowl of cold water for several minutes. Brush the moulds very lightly with the oil.

Place the milk, cream, sugar and rose-geranium leaves in a small, heavy-based saucepan over low heat, stirring from time to time until the sugar has dissolved and the mixture reaches simmering point. Squeeze the gelatine leaves and drop into the hot milk mixture, then stir to dissolve completely. Turn off and leave to infuse for 10–15 minutes. Strain into a jug and carefully fill the moulds. Refrigerate until set – at least 2 hours, but you could make these a day ahead.

To serve, dip the moulds into hot water for a few seconds. Using fingers, gently ease each panna cotta away from the edge of its mould and invert onto a cold serving plate, then give a firm shake and very gently lift off the mould.

Add the strawberries to the cooled cherry mixture and lift gently to coat them with the syrup. Serve at room temperature.

Spoon the cherries and strawberries around the panna cotta and spoon the syrup over the fruit and around the panna cotta. (I prefer to leave the panna cotta unadorned and just trembling.) Garnish each plate with a rose-geranium leaf, if you wish.

TIMETABLE FOR THE COOK

TWO DAYS BEFORE

- Check **Ingredients List** and note what needs to be purchased
- Check specialist equipment needed (cherry pitter)
- Decide on table setting, including serving dishes
- Inspect tablecloth and napkins
- Decide on wine – order if necessary
- All shopping (except scallops), including flowers

DAY BEFORE

Scallop tarts
- Make Jerusalem artichoke cream
- Buy and trim scallops – refrigerate
- Prepare puff tartlet rounds, prick and assemble on a lined baking tray – refrigerate

Chicken
- Joint chicken – refrigerate
- Make stock with chicken bones and scraps and cool (or decide to use purchased stock)
- Once cold, reduce stock – refrigerate

Buttered spinach
- Wash, stem and cook spinach (puree if desired) – refrigerate in microwave-safe container

Panna cotta
- Pit cherries – refrigerate
- Make grenache and cherry syrup
- Make panna cotta – refrigerate

- Chill wine, if appropriate

MORNING OF

- Chop herbs – refrigerate each one in a separate paper towel–lined airtight container

- Set table

Asparagus
- Make vinegar reduction for *sauce mousseline* – transfer to heatproof bowl that fits over a saucepan and set aside
- Squeeze lemon

Scallop tarts
- Slice scallops and assemble on baking paper rounds – refrigerate

Chicken
- Parboil potatoes
- Blanch and peel shallots
- Rub mustard mixture over chicken, assemble in 1 or 2 flameproof casserole dishes – refrigerate

AFTERNOON OF

Asparagus
- Measure butter and cream for *sauce mousseline*

Scallop tarts
- Bake tartlet bases – do not refrigerate
- Toast hazelnuts and mix with herbs, oil etc – do not refrigerate

Panna cotta
- Hull strawberries, slice if large

Green salad
- Wash, dry and crisp salad leaves
- Prepare salad dressing in salad bowl with crossed salad servers ready to toss before serving

ONE HOUR BEFORE GUESTS ARRIVE

- Add strawberries to cherry mixture
- Get changed

THIRTY MINUTES BEFORE GUESTS ARRIVE

- Warm plates for asparagus (see page 512)
- Assemble scallop tartlets
- Start cooking chicken – turn after 20 minutes (set timer)

GUESTS ARRIVE

- Preheat oven to 220°C

DINNER IS SERVED

FIRST COURSE

- Have water simmering to cook asparagus
- Finish *sauce mousseline*
- Cook asparagus

Meanwhile, for the chicken
- Turn chicken again and cook for 20 minutes (set timer)

- Heat griller

SECOND COURSE

- Bake scallop tartlets
- Sprinkle with hazelnut mixture and serve

- Meanwhile, reduce oven temperature to 110°C
- Warm main course plates (see page 512)

Chicken and buttered spinach
- Transfer chicken and vegetables to serving platter in oven
- Deglaze chicken cooking pan and make sauce
- Reheat spinach
- Serve chicken, vegetables and spinach

Green salad
- Toss salad and serve

DESSERT

- Unmould panna cotta and serve with cherries and strawberries

INGREDIENTS LIST

PANTRY
- Sea salt
- Fine salt
- Australian extra virgin olive oil
- Hazelnut oil
- Almond oil
- White-wine vinegar
- Red-wine vinegar
- Dijon mustard
- Gelatine leaves
- Caster sugar
- Cornflour (wheaten)
- Blanched hazelnuts

SPICE SHELF
- White peppercorns or ground white pepper
- Cayenne pepper
- Black peppercorns

REFRIGERATOR
- Milk
- Butter
- Free-range eggs
- 415 ml thickened cream
- All-butter puff pastry

GREENGROCER/FARMERS' MARKET (OR GARDEN)
- Flat-leaf parsley
- Chives
- French tarragon (if in season) or lemon thyme
- Chervil
- 8 unsprayed rose-geranium leaves
- Garlic
- 20 thick asparagus spears
- 1 lemon
- 300 g Jerusalem artichokes
- 8 small waxy potatoes, such as Dutch cream or Kipfler
- 8 French shallots
- 1 large bunch spinach (not baby spinach)
- Selection of salad leaves
- 250 g small–medium strawberries
- 150 g cherries

If making chicken stock:
- 1 carrot
- 1 stick celery
- 1 onion
- Thyme
- Fresh bay leaf

BUTCHER
- 1 × 1.8–2 kg free-range chicken

FISHMONGER
- 12 scallops, on half-shell

CELLAR
- Dry white wine or Vermouth
- Grenache for syrup
- Wine for the table

FEEDING
·A·
CROWD

A DINNER FOR 8–10

LAMB SHOULDER
MOUSSAKA

LASAGNE
with PRESERVED ARTICHOKES,
PESTO & RICOTTA

STICKY
PORK RIBS
with BARBECUE SAUCE

RADICCHIO,
WHITE BEAN, WALNUT &
PECORINO SALAD with TORN CROUTONS

WARM ROAST
CAULIFLOWER,
CHICKPEA & QUINOA SALAD

———

LA TROPÉZIENNE

18

The sort of crowd I am thinking of here is a group that has come together for a shared purpose.

A book group, a sporting team, a support group, a community gathering – probably people who may not know each other as close personal friends. It may be a group that is meeting in order to get to know one another better? Of course you could ask everyone to bring a dish, however, this helpful tradition makes me nervous. Unless someone steps in to make a list and is suitably dictatorial, you risk ending up with three dishes of lasagne and no salads. There is no denying the appeal of a baked pasta dish, so I have included one. I have suggested food that is interesting but not overly challenging, that is fun to serve and eat – not easy to be too formal when gnawing on spare ribs. All the preparation is done in advance – all that is needed at the last moment are a hot oven and hot barbecue.

The lamb moussaka has proved to be a huge success at my place and, on one occasion, I served it as individual portions in hollowed-out eggplant (aubergine) shells rather than in one large dish. I have included recipes for both versions. The cauliflower salad and radicchio salad are sufficiently substantial that an unexpected non-meat eater will be happy, and both salads will come to no harm – in fact will improve – if dressed an hour ahead of dinner time. There is enough choice so that a guest who does not eat pork can have a good time also. The addition of a seasonal fruit platter is an excellent idea whenever there are first-time guests, and there is always the option of providing a selection of cheeses instead of, or as well as, the delicious brioche-based cake.

Your guests will probably bring a bottle of wine and, here again, the flavours are sufficiently varied that whatever they bring, all will be well. For this type of occasion, it is a good idea to offer several sitting spots rather than a formal dining setting, if you can organise loose arrangements of chairs and perching spots. Your guests will return more than once to the serving table and may want to chat to a different person next time round.

Once the cooking is complete and the dishes set out on the serving table, the table is ready with plenty of plates and large napkins to cope with the ribs (or even damp tea towels), the host or hostess is free to participate without having to appear and disappear into the kitchen. And, most importantly, have fun!

Lamb shoulder moussaka

⅓ cup (80 ml) extra virgin olive oil, plus extra as needed

1 × 2 kg lamb shoulder on-the-bone (including neck) or 8 forequarter (barbecue) chops

5 onions, sliced

6 cloves garlic, chopped

⅓ cup (90 g) tomato paste (puree)

3 cups (750 ml) Chicken Stock (see page 505)

1 × 400 g tin crushed tomatoes

1 stick cinnamon

large bouquet garni (lots of thyme, lemon zest, fresh bay leaf and flat-leaf parsley stalks tied with kitchen twine)

2–3 large (500 g) waxy potatoes, cut into 1 cm-thick slices

sea salt and fresh ground black pepper

3 eggplants (aubergines), cut into 1 cm-thick slices

CHEESE SAUCE

2 cups (500 ml) milk

50 g butter

⅓ cup (50 g) plain flour

50 g finely grated parmesan

75 g haloumi, grated

sea salt and freshly ground black pepper

freshly grated nutmeg

This dish repays the effort to prepare; once done, it is delicious and very handsome. I have a much loved round porcelain ovenproof dish that I always use for it (see opposite). I have also included instructions for serving the moussaka in hollowed-out eggplant 'boats' on page 332.

Heat ¼ cup (60 ml) of the olive oil in an enamelled cast-iron or other flameproof casserole with a lid over high heat. Brown the lamb well and set aside. Tip off the fat. Add the remaining tablespoon of olive oil to the casserole, reduce the heat to medium and saute the onion and garlic, stirring for 10 minutes or until translucent. Add the tomato paste and stir, then add the stock, tomato, cinnamon stick and bouquet garni and bring to a simmer. Return the lamb to the dish and cover, then simmer over low heat for 2 hours or until tender. Add the potato and continue to cook for a further 30 minutes or until the potato is tender and the lamb is meltingly tender.

Scoop the lamb and potato from the liquid. When the lamb is cool enough to handle, strip all the meat from the bones and place in a large bowl with the potato. Discard the bones and any sinewy bits. Moisten the meat and potato with enough of the cooking liquid to keep it moist but not sloppy. Season with salt and pepper. (Refrigerate any remaining liquid for a fantastic soup another time.)

Heat a little extra olive oil in a heavy-based frying pan over medium heat. Fry the eggplant slices, turning until golden and tender. Drain on paper towel.

To make the cheese sauce, heat the milk to scalding point in a small heavy-based saucepan and set aside. Melt the butter in another heavy-based saucepan and stir in the flour. Cook, stirring, until you have a smooth, golden paste. Gradually work in the hot milk and stir until the sauce thickens and is very smooth. Continue stirring until the sauce boils. Stir in both cheeses. Cook for a further 5 minutes on a simmer mat over low heat. Season to taste with salt, pepper and nutmeg. Proceed with assembling the moussaka; it's easier to assemble if the sauce is a bit warm (Reheat in the microwave if made in advance). ➤

recipe continues.

Preheat the oven to 180°C.

Select a 2 litre-capacity gratin dish. Place the eggplant on the bottom, pushing the slices together to make a compact layer, then add the lamb/potato mixture and juice, then top with the cheese sauce. Grate over a little nutmeg and drizzle the sauce with a few drops of olive oil.

Bake for about 20 minutes or until well browned and bubbling. If the finished moussaka has been refrigerated for some time, it will take at least 40 minutes to reheat. Meanwhile, warm the dinner plates (see page 512). Cut into pieces and serve.

Individual eggplant variation

To serve this as individual portions, omit the step of frying eggplant slices on page 331 and omit the cheese sauce. Instead, cut six 14 cm-long eggplants in half lengthwise. Score the flesh side in a crisscross pattern quite deeply, without cutting through to the skin, leaving a 1 cm-thick wall intact around the edge. Brush the flesh side with 1½ tablespoons extra virgin oil and bake in a preheated 180°C oven for 20–30 minutes or until the flesh feels fairly soft (it should not be cooked as you do not want the eggplant cases to collapse). Leave the eggplant to cool a bit, then scoop out the centres with a spoon. Chop roughly. Heat another 1½ tablespoons olive oil in a wide heavy-based frying pan. Add 4 cloves chopped garlic and stir for a moment, then add the eggplant flesh. Saute for 5 minutes, stirring well. Add 30 mint leaves and a large handful of chopped flat-leaf parsley and season with salt and pepper.

Ensure that the lamb/potato mixture is not too sloppy. (Drain in a colander over a bowl, if necessary, and use the reserved juices for a soup another time.) Stir the sauteed eggplant mixture into the lamb mixture, then divide among the eggplant halves. Scatter over fresh breadcrumbs, if you wish, and cook in a 200°C oven for 10–15 minutes or until golden and bubbling.

Lasagne with preserved artichokes, pesto and ricotta

500 g dried lasagne sheets, cooked (see page 501)

salt

PESTO

150 ml extra virgin olive oil, or as needed

2 cups (2 large handfuls) firmly packed basil leaves

1 clove garlic, finely chopped

60 g pine nuts

60 g finely grated parmesan

sea salt and freshly ground black pepper

RICOTTA LAYER

750 g fresh ricotta, drained in a coarse-mesh sieve over a bowl for 20 minutes

1 large free-range egg, plus an additional egg yolk

freshly grated nutmeg

1 cup (250 ml) thickened cream

sea salt and freshly ground black pepper

1 × 500 g jar artichoke hearts marinated in extra virgin olive oil, drained and coarsely chopped

Sadly, we do not have freshly prepared artichoke hearts in our marketplaces in spring, as I have seen in Istanbul and Italy. What a luxury that is! If you are willing to prepare about 12 fresh globe artichokes, your lasagne will have the edge on this version. I have included instructions for sauteing freshly prepared artichoke hearts on page 501, just in case. Otherwise, this recipe relies on best-quality artichoke hearts preserved in extra virgin olive oil, such as can be found in our farmers' markets in springtime. Similarly, do not be tempted to use commercial pesto; it is so simple to make from fresh ingredients. Many dried lasagne sheets are described as pre-cooked. In my experience, the finished lasagne will always be much more tender if the sheets are briefly cooked as described on page 501.

To make the pesto, put half of the olive oil and the basil, garlic and pine nuts into a blender. Blend until you have a thick, green paste. Add extra oil carefully; you may not need to use it all. Tip the pesto into a bowl and stir in the parmesan. Taste for salt and pepper and season if required.

To make the ricotta layer, place the ricotta, egg and extra yolk and nutmeg to taste in a food processor and process until smooth. Add the cream and process to form a smooth cream. Transfer to a bowl. Taste and adjust the seasoning. Stir in the artichoke.

Preheat the oven to 180°C.

To assemble the lasagne, select a lasagne dish (approximately 30 cm × 25 cm). Spread a thin layer of pesto over the base, then cover with a layer of pasta. Spread one-third of the ricotta mixture over the pasta, then spread one-third of the remaining pesto over the ricotta. Repeat twice more with the pasta, ricotta mixture and pesto, finishing with a layer of ricotta. Cover the dish with foil and bake for 20 minutes. Uncover and cook for a further 15–20 minutes or until the lasagne is golden. Leave to stand for 15 minutes before cutting. Meanwhile, heat the dinner plates (see page 512), if necessary.

Cut into pieces and serve.

Sticky pork ribs with barbecue sauce

3 kg American-style baby back pork ribs (approximately 30 ribs)

1½ cups (375 ml) red-wine vinegar

3 teaspoons cayenne pepper

1½ tablespoons sweet paprika

1½ tablespoons ground cumin

2 tablespoons hot chilli sauce (see page 511)

2 tablespoons ground ginger

3 cups (750 ml) Homemade Tomato Sauce (see page 502) *or* good-quality commercial passata

1½ cups (525 g) pure maple syrup

sea salt

3 litres Beef/veal Stock (see page 506) *or* 1.5 litres stock and 1.5 litres water

BARBECUE SAUCE

4 cloves garlic, coarsely chopped

2 cups (720 g) pure maple syrup

1½ cups (375 ml) light soy sauce

1½ cups (375 ml) Homemade Tomato Sauce (see page 502) *or* good-quality commercial passata

1 tablespoon Tabasco *or* hot chilli sauce (see page 511)

These ribs are deliciously sticky and just ask to be eaten with the fingers. They are messy so do supply wet towels for finger wiping afterwards. The number of serves suggested will vary depending on whether the meal is mainly about ribs, or there will be other substantial dishes as well.

Cut the pork ribs into sections, with 3–4 ribs in each piece, then place these in a large, wide heavy-based saucepan. Add the vinegar, cayenne, paprika, cumin, chilli sauce, ginger, tomato sauce or passata and maple syrup and season with salt. Pour over enough of the stock or stock/water mixture to generously cover the meat but not drown it.

Place the pan over medium heat and cover. Simmer, stirring occasionally, for 1 hour or until the pork ribs are tender but the meat is not falling off the bone. Leave to cool in the liquid, then lift onto a deep plate, cover and refrigerate. (If you have a useful quantity of the liquid remaining, save it in the refrigerator to use in a soup or braise some soaked dried beans. Use within 2 days.)

Meanwhile, to make the barbecue sauce, place the garlic, maple syrup, soy sauce, tomato sauce or passata and chilli sauce in a heavy-based saucepan and stir to combine. Simmer, stirring frequently, over low heat for 15 minutes or until thickened. Remove from the heat and set aside to cool. (Makes about 1.25 litres.)

Twenty minutes before barbecuing, remove the ribs from the refrigerator. Pour the barbecue sauce over the ribs and turn them to coat well.

Preheat a barbecue grill plate to high. Reduce the heat to medium and cook the ribs, brushing with the sauce, for 2–3 minutes on each side or until warmed through and charred on the outside. Meanwhile, warm an ovenproof serving dish and dinner plates, if necessary (see page 512).

Transfer to the warm serving dish, then serve.

Radicchio, white bean, walnut and pecorino salad with torn croutons

1 head radicchio, quartered lengthwise

500 g baby spinach leaves, washed, spun dry and stems trimmed

40 walnut halves

1 × 400 g tin cannellini beans, drained *or* 400 g cooked cannellini or butter beans

1 teaspoon red-wine vinegar

1½ tablespoons extra virgin olive oil

sea salt and freshly ground black pepper

150 g pecorino

TORN CROUTONS

1 baguette

1 tablespoon extra virgin olive oil

This extremely simple yet delicious salad can be made larger or smaller; the quantities I have given should be plenty for eight to ten people who are enjoying the salad as part of a large selection of dishes. Heads of radicchio are furled so tightly they are ideal for slicing when whole and, other than removing any damaged outer leaves, I find they do not need washing. Because radicchio is such a sturdy salad ingredient, it will stand being dressed well ahead of time; the spinach leaves will not. If you want to prepare the salad in advance, add the spinach leaves and croutons at the last minute for a final toss and plate up before adding the shaved cheese.

Cut each radicchio quarter into 1 cm-thick slices and put into a large mixing bowl. Add the spinach leaves.

Preheat the oven to 180°C.

To make the croutons, cut the crust from the baguette, then cut into 2 cm-thick slices and tear each slice into rough croutons. Place the bread in a bowl and toss with the olive oil. Spread on a baking tray and bake for 10 minutes or until the croutons are just starting to look golden. Leave to cool for a few minutes, then add to the bowl with the leaves.

Toss the walnuts in the oily crouton bowl, then place on the baking tray and toast in the oven. Watch carefully and check after 5 minutes – toasted walnuts are delicious, burnt walnuts are not. Cool and add to the salad bowl. Add the drained beans.

Mix the vinegar with the olive oil and drizzle over the salad. Season with salt and pepper, then lift and toss with your hands. Pile the salad onto a wide platter so that every guest can get some of all the good bits. Shave the pecorino over evenly, then serve.

Warm roast cauliflower, chickpea and quinoa salad

200 g white or brown quinoa
(see page 512)

1½ cups (375 ml) water

sea salt

1 whole large cauliflower
(about 800 g), trimmed and
cut into small florets

2 cloves garlic, finely chopped

1 teaspoon ground cumin

1 × 400 g tin chickpeas, drained
and rinsed

1 teaspoon ground coriander

finely grated zest and juice of
2 lemons

½ cup (125 ml) extra virgin
olive oil

freshly ground black pepper

2 large onions, thinly sliced

1 cup (large handful) coarsely torn
flat-leaf parsley, washed and dried

1 cup (large handful) coarsely torn
mint leaves, washed and dried

1 tablespoon sherry vinegar

4 sections preserved lemon
(optional)

Cauliflower has been a much underrated vegetable, yet salads such as this one are becoming very popular in modern cafes, so maybe its reputation is on the rise. Cauliflower should retain some crispness and not be cooked to a mush. Cooking the onions until they are very dark brown may surprise, but they are a lovely garnish, especially when combined with the faintly Middle Eastern spicing. An especially delicious addition would be finely diced preserved lemon rind scattered over the salad to finish.

Preheat the oven to 200°C.

Rinse the quinoa under cold running water for a few minutes, then place in a heavy-based saucepan with the water and 1 teaspoon salt. Bring to the boil, then reduce the heat to medium and simmer, covered, for 20 minutes or until all the water has been absorbed and the grains are swollen. Spread on a baking tray to cool.

Meanwhile, combine the cauliflower, garlic, cumin, chickpeas, coriander, lemon zest and 2 tablespoons of the olive oil in a bowl. Season to taste with salt and pepper and spread in a large, shallow roasting pan. Roast for 15–20 minutes or until golden and tender, shaking the pan from time to time to ensure that nothing is sticking.

Meanwhile, fry the onion in another 2 tablespoons of the olive oil over medium heat, stirring and turning, for 10 minutes or until very dark brown. Transfer to a plate lined with paper towel to cool.

Combine the parsley, mint, vinegar, lemon juice and remaining olive oil in a large bowl, then add the warm cauliflower, chickpeas and quinoa, season to taste and toss to combine.

Serve on a wide platter, scattered with the onion. (If you have some preserved lemon, peel away and discard the flesh, cut each piece of rind into small dice and scatter over the salad.)

La Tropézienne

BRIOCHE DOUGH

30 g caster sugar

1 cup (250 ml) milk

2 teaspoons instant dried yeast

6 free-range egg yolks,
lightly beaten

3⅓ cups (500 g) plain flour

1 teaspoon fine salt

150 g unsalted butter, chopped,
plus extra for buttering

1 free-range egg yolk, mixed with
1 teaspoon water, as egg wash

pure icing sugar (optional),
for dusting

PASTRY CREAM

2 cups (500 ml) milk

1 vanilla bean, split

2 gelatine leaves (see page 512)

6 free-range egg yolks

¾ cup (165 g) caster sugar

⅓ cup (50 g) cornflour

1 cup (250 ml) thickened cream

2 teaspoons rum

TOPPING

30 g soft butter

30 g white sugar

30 g ground almonds

La Tropézienne is reputed to have been a favourite of Brigitte Bardot when she was filming *And God Created Woman* in St Tropez, or so I've heard. In any case, it has a certain mythic quality, and apparently every bakery in St Tropez has its own version. My first taste of this dessert was bought from a small French pastry shop in Australia's Byron Bay many years ago now. Its charm is that it is lush and creamy but not very sweet. Do let the finished Tropézienne sit at room temperature to soften so that it is suitably squidgy when it is cut. I have used rum to flavour the pastry cream; other options would be orange flower water or even kirsch. Many bakers scatter coarse pearl sugar over the top crust before baking – I do not.

Start the brioche 4 hours beforehand. Heat the sugar and milk to lukewarm in a small heavy-based saucepan. Sprinkle over the yeast and leave for 10 minutes to froth. Add the egg yolk to the warm milk/yeast mixture and mix lightly with a whisk or fork.

Sift the flour and salt into a large bowl, form a well in the centre and pour in the milk mixture. Beat well using an electric mixer fitted with a dough hook. Add the softened butter in several lots, beating well after each addition. Continue to beat until the dough is shiny, smooth and comes away cleanly from the side of the bowl. Transfer to a lightly buttered bowl. Cover with a damp cloth and leave to rise in a warm place, away from draughts, for 2–2½ hours; it should have doubled in size.

Punch down the dough gently, then flatten on a lightly greased baking tray to form a round about 24 cm in diameter and no more than 1 cm in height. Cover with a dry tea towel and leave in a warm, draught-free place to recover for 1 hour.

Meanwhile, to make the pastry cream, scald the milk with the vanilla bean in a small heavy-based saucepan. Soak the gelatine leaves in a bowl of cold water for a few minutes to soften, then squeeze out the excess water, drop into the scalded milk and whisk lightly to mix. In a bowl, beat the egg yolks with the sugar and cornflour until thick. Pour in the milk mixture and whisk until smooth. Return the mixture to the rinsed-out saucepan and stir ➤

recipe continues.

continuously over medium heat until the pastry cream has thickened, become smooth and come to a boil. Using a wooden spoon, beat vigorously for 1 minute. Pour through a coarse-mesh sieve resting over a bowl. Wash and dry the vanilla bean and reserve for another use. Press plastic film onto the pastry cream to prevent a skin forming, then refrigerate to chill. Use the pastry cream when it is cold.

Once the pastry cream is quite cold, whip the cream until quite stiff. Using a whisk, vigorously whisk the cold pastry cream to lighten it, folding in the rum and whipped cream. For a perfect texture, force this lightened cream through a fine–medium-mesh sieve resting over a bowl.

Preheat the oven to 190°C.

For the topping, mix the butter, sugar and ground almonds in a small bowl. Lightly brush the brioche all over with the egg wash and scatter evenly with the topping mixture.

Bake for 20 minutes or until the topping is a deep gold. Slide the brioche onto a wire rack and leave to cool. When the brioche is quite cold, using a long serrated knife, split through the centre horizontally; the base should be a little bit thicker than the top layer.

To assemble, place the bottom layer of the Tropézienne on a flat serving platter. Pile a generous layer of the pastry cream on top. Settle the brioche top onto the cream, pressing it gently with the palm of your hand to ensure that it connects with the cream. Dust with icing sugar, if you wish.

Leave for 1 hour at room temperature before cutting it into wedges. (Refrigerate any leftovers, but bring them back to room temperature before eating within 2 days. Cold, hard brioche is very unappealing.)

TIMETABLE FOR THE COOK

ONE WEEK BEFORE

- Check **Ingredients List** and note what needs to be purchased
- Advise provedores of special requests (order lamb shoulder on bone, including neck, sawn into large pieces; and American-style baby back pork ribs from butcher)

THREE DAYS BEFORE

- All shopping, including flowers and baguette for croutons
- Decide on table setting, including serving dishes
- Inspect tablecloth and napkins
- Decide on wine – order if necessary
- Make homemade tomato sauce, if using

TWO DAYS BEFORE

Moussaka
- Make all components
- Assemble – refrigerate

Pork ribs
- Make barbecue sauce
- Cook ribs in stock – leave to cool
- Transfer ribs to deep dish – refrigerate

DAY BEFORE

Lasagne
- Prepare lasagne sheets
- Make pesto/ricotta layer components
- Prepare fresh artichokes (if using)
- Assemble lasagne – refrigerate

Pork ribs
- Cook ribs in barbecue sauce – refrigerate

La Tropézienne
- Make pastry cream
- Whip cream, then lighten pastry cream

MORNING OF

- Set table
- Chill wine
- Zest and juice lemons

La Tropézienne
- Make brioche – 2-hour rise
- Knock down brioche – shape and recover for 1 hour

Warm cauliflower salad
- Cook quinoa
- Fry onions until dark brown
- Slice preserved lemon
- Chop garlic, cover with olive oil
- Pick herbs, wash and dry – refrigerate in paper towel–lined airtight containers

Radicchio salad
- Prepare radicchio and spinach leaves
- Tear and bake croutons
- Bake walnuts
- Shave pecorino – cover plate

AFTERNOON OF

La Tropézienne
- Preheat oven to 190°C
- Make topping for brioche and bake
- Split cooled brioche and fill – leave for minimum 1 hour

Moussaka and lasagne
- Remove from refrigerator before putting into oven

- Prepare fruit platter

TWO HOURS BEFORE GUESTS ARRIVE

Radicchio salad
- Assemble, leaving out spinach, croutons and pecorino

- Get changed

ONE HOUR BEFORE GUESTS ARRIVE

- Heat barbecue

Radicchio salad
- Add spinach, croutons and pecorino

Cauliflower salad
- Preheat oven to 180°C
- Roast cauliflower and chickpeas
- Assemble

Lasagne and moussaka
- Cover and put into oven

Ribs
- Remove from refrigerator and pour over barbecue sauce, turn

- Warm plates and serving dishes (see page 512)

TO SERVE DINNER

- Uncover moussaka, remove when bubbling and allow to settle
- Uncover lasagne, remove when bubbling and allow to settle
- Wearing an apron, grill ribs, brush with sauce, turn, brush again

DINNER IS SERVED

- Add final garnishes to both salads
- Assemble all dishes on buffet table, including piles of plates and napkins, for self-service

DESSERT

- Cut La Tropézienne into wedges and serve

INGREDIENTS LIST

PANTRY

· Sea salt
· Fine salt
· Australian extra virgin olive oil
· Red-wine vinegar
· Sherry vinegar
· Plain flour
· Cornflour (wheaten)
· White sugar
· Caster sugar
· Pure icing sugar
· Ground almonds
· Dried yeast
· 2 gelatine leaves
· 500 g dried lasagne sheets
· White or brown quinoa
· Pine nuts
· Tomato paste (puree)
· 1.25 litre tomato passata
  (or Homemade Tomato
  Sauce, see page 502)
· 1.25 kg pure maple syrup
· Light soy sauce
· 1 × 400 g tin crushed tomatoes
· 1 × 400 g tin cannellini beans
· 1 × 400 g tin chickpeas
· Preserved lemons (optional)

SPICE SHELF

· Black peppercorns
· 1 stick cinnamon
· Tabasco or chilli sauce
· Nutmeg (whole)
· Cayenne pepper
· Sweet paprika
· Ground cumin
· Ground ginger
· Ground coriander
· 1 vanilla bean

REFRIGERATOR

· 1.25 litres milk
· 230 g unsalted butter
· 2 cups/500 ml thickened cream
· 15 free-range eggs
· 150 g parmesan
· 150 g pecorino
· 75 g haloumi
· 750 g fresh ricotta
· 750 ml good-quality
  chicken stock (if making
  homemade, see page 505)
· 3 litres good-quality beef stock
  (if making homemade, see page
  506) (or 1.5 litres stock,
  1.5 litres water)
· 1 × 500 g jar artichoke hearts
  marinated in extra virgin olive
  oil (or 12 fresh artichokes;
  see below)

GREENGROCER/FARMERS' MARKET (OR GARDEN)

· Flat-leaf parsley
· Thyme
· 1 fresh bay leaf
· Basil (to yield 2 cups/2 large
  handfuls firmly packed)
· Mint
· Garlic
· 7 onions
· 2–3 large (500 g) waxy
  potatoes
· 3 eggplants (aubergines)
· 1 head radicchio
· 12 fresh artichokes (if available)
· 500 g baby spinach leaves
· 1 large cauliflower (about 800 g)
· 3 lemons
· 40 walnut halves
· Fruit selection for platter

BUTCHER/DELICATESSEN

· 1 × 2 kg lamb shoulder on-
  the-bone (including neck) or
  8 forequarter (barbecue) chops
· 3 kg American-style baby
  back pork ribs

BAKER

· 1 baguette
· Bread for crumbs (if needed)
· Bread for the table

CELLAR

· Rum
· Wine for the table
· Soft drink

FATHER'S
DAY
DINNER

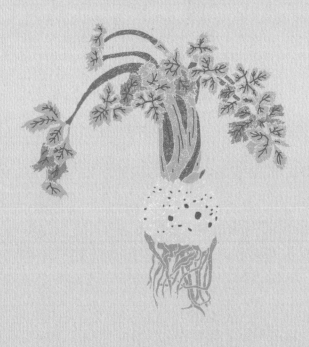

A DINNER FOR 6

CHICKEN LIVER
CROSTINI

———

CELERIAC & PARSLEY SOUP
with SAFFRON GNOCCHETTI

———

BEEF CHEEKS
IN RED WINE *with* CARROTS
& MASHED POTATO

CRISP-FRIED BROCCOLINI
with ANTHONY SIMONE'S BATTER

GREEN SALAD

———

JOCELYN'S
LEMON MERINGUE TART

19

My father and mother had a fine partnership. They were great
friends as well as partners, and it was always obvious that they
enjoyed each other's company. When they travelled, Mum noted
down what they ate, and painted watercolour miniatures of
the landscape. Dad did the planning and driving, and took the
home movies. Their perfect days always ended with a meal in
a friendly restaurant and a glass or two of wine. In latter years,
the memories of those trips were very sustaining for Dad once
he was alone.

I loved my mother and cannot ever repay the debt I owe
her for all she taught me about my life's passion – good food –
but somehow I felt emotionally closer to my father. Even now,
20 years after his death, I think of him every day and wish we'd
had more time together. Dad was a fount of knowledge, with
a wise understanding and long view of the world and its issues.
He read very widely and his values became my values. He was
very special not just to his children but also his grandchildren.

Dad gave me uncritical support in all my ventures, sometimes
even when perhaps he ought not to have. He was embarrassingly
proud of everything I wrote and kept an album of press cuttings
of reviews of both my restaurants and my books.

This is a serious preamble to celebrating Father's Day. I don't
know that we celebrated it very often as a family, so here is
a dinner my father would have enjoyed very much, consisting of
some of his favourite dishes. Almost to the very end of his life,
he enjoyed a glass or two of red wine with dinner, and this dinner
will go well with one of his beloved reds from Rutherglen, Victoria.

Before the soup I have selected to serve *crostini di fegatini
di pollo* – a platter of crunchy toasts topped with sauteed, then
chopped chicken livers. During the two months I spent in Tuscany
in 1997, almost every restaurant meal started in this fashion.
The crostini came to the table, often unordered. A perfect
accompaniment to that first sip of wine, and very few Italians
drink without eating. Two bites and they disappeared, so before
one knew it, the platter was empty.

The lovely celeriac and parsley soup, with its slippery soft golden dumplings, or *gnocchetti*, is a lovely combination of grass-green from the parsley and gold from the saffron.

And the braised beef cheeks are simply a winner for any dad who loves red meat and red wine. Make it one or two days in advance and gently reheat. Because of the textural difference between the braised beef cheeks and crisp broccolini, I like to serve the broccolini in its own heated dish, to be enjoyed with, or even after, the saucy beef cheeks.

The lemon meringue pie is a classic and, when well made with a fluffy meringue top and sharp lemon curd filling, is always popular. I took inspiration from Jocelyn Hancock, a former colleague and renowned Brisbane baker (see page 365). Jocelyn tops her tart with Italian meringue, which requires making a sugar syrup. If you prefer, just serve the cooled lemon tart with extra cream or berries, then it well be *tarte au citron*, the French take on lemon tart. My tart is a bit smaller than Jocelyn's, so I have reduced her quantities. I used a 22 cm fluted tart tin with a removable base. Interestingly, we both swear by the shortcrust recipe made famous by Damien Pignolet. My dad would have loved it!

Chicken liver crostini

Crostini di fegatini di pollo

12 slices bread, cut from
a baguette or sourdough loaf

⅓ cup (80 ml) extra virgin olive oil

1 red onion, finely diced

1 × 100 g piece smoked bacon,
rind removed and discarded, diced

1 clove garlic, finely chopped

500 g trimmed chicken livers
(weighed after removing all
connective tissue)

150 ml vin santo *or* other
full-bodied white wine

1 tablespoon salted capers,
well rinsed and drained

4 anchovy fillets in olive oil,
chopped *or* 2 tablespoons
anchovy paste

sea salt and freshly ground
black pepper

This Italian recipe specifies vin santo, the very special wine of Tuscany made from grapes allowed to dry to concentrate their sweetness before being transferred to oak barrels for several years. Your favourite late-picked wine will give a hint of its grapey flavour. If you don't have one, do not despair, use a full-bodied dry white wine. The mix can be made several hours before dinner, providing you have a very hot grill to quickly reheat the crostini.

Brush the bread slices with olive oil and grill under a hot oven griller or in a chargrill pan over medium heat.

Heat the remaining oil in a wide heavy-based frying pan over medium heat and cook the onion, bacon and garlic for 3–5 minutes. Add the chicken livers and saute quickly; they should be seared on the outside but still a little pink in the centre. Tip in the wine and increase the temperature to high, then cook, stirring to prevent sticking, for 2–3 minutes or until the wine has reduced rapidly but the contents of the pan are still quite moist; you want the cooking to be fast.

Transfer the liver mixture to the bowl of a food processor, then add the capers and anchovies or anchovy paste and pulse quickly to form a very coarse paste. Season with salt and pepper to taste.

Spread each piece of grilled toast evenly with the mixture. Pile onto a platter and offer at once.

Serves 6

Celeriac and parsley soup
with saffron *gnocchetti*

30 g butter

1 large leek, white part only, sliced into rounds and well washed

500 g celeriac (weighed after peeling), cut into 5 cm pieces

1 litre water

3 cloves garlic, peeled

150 ml thickened cream

1 cup (large handful) well-packed flat-leaf parsley leaves

boiling water, as needed

sea salt and freshly ground black pepper

few drops Tabasco

1 quantity Saffron *Gnocchetti* (see opposite) and crusty bread (optional), to serve

I do love this soup with its subtle flavours of celeriac and softly cooked garlic and the brilliant green from the parsley. The little marbles of saffron *gnocchetti* are a delightful surprise. (See picture on pages 354–355.)

Melt the butter in a large heavy-based saucepan over medium heat. Add the leek, cover the pan and sweat for 10 minutes or until really soft without taking on any colour. Add the celeriac and water, bring to a simmer, then reduce the heat to low, re-cover and cook gently for 20 minutes or until tender.

Meanwhile, put the garlic into a small heavy-based saucepan, cover with cold water and bring slowly to the boil over low heat. Drain. Repeat twice more. Return the drained garlic to the pan and tip in the cream. Bring to a simmer over low heat, then simmer slowly for 10 minutes or until the garlic has softened. Set aside.

Preheat the oven to 110°C and place 6 ovenproof bowls inside to warm.

Put the parsley leaves into a large heatproof bowl and pour the boiling water over. Leave for 30 seconds, then drain; do not refresh the parsley.

Immediately transfer the hot cream, garlic and parsley to a blender, then blend to form a smooth bright-green sauce; this will take a few minutes. Transfer to a bowl and set aside. Without washing the blender, blend the celeriac soup to form a smooth puree (depending on the size of your blender, you may have to do this in two batches). Tip through a coarse-mesh sieve over a bowl, stirring with a wooden spoon to ensure there are no lumps. Add the green mixture to the soup and whisk gently to mix well, then taste and adjust the seasoning with salt, pepper and Tabasco. The soup should be a smooth, bright spring green; if it is too thick, add a little extra boiling water.

Ladle into the warmed bowls, then top with saffron *gnocchetti* and serve with crusty bread, if desired.

Saffron *gnocchetti*

⅔ cup (160 ml) milk

60 g unsalted butter

½ teaspoon saffron threads

1 tablespoon boiling water

⅔ cup (100 g) plain flour, plus extra for dusting

1 large free-range egg

100 g goat's curd *or* fromage frais

sea salt and freshly ground black pepper

This mixture is best when made one day in advance and needs to be made at least eight hours before poaching. Excess dough can be frozen but will need to be gently thawed in the refrigerator before poaching.

Place the milk and 30 g of the butter in a small heavy-based saucepan. Place the saffron in a small bowl, then pour the boiling water over and leave for 2–3 minutes to infuse. Add the saffron liquid to the milk, then bring to the boil. Add all the flour at once and beat with a wooden spoon until blended; the mixture will be very thick. Cook over medium heat, beating constantly, for 2 minutes or until the mixture is very dry and comes away from the side of the pan. Remove from the heat and leave to cool for a couple of minutes. Add the egg and beat it into the mixture until incorporated.

Melt the remaining 30 g butter. Transfer the dough mixture to an electric mixer fitted with the paddle attachment. Add the melted butter and goat's curd or fromage frais and beat for at least 3 minutes or until smooth and compact; it should be very like the texture of choux pastry. Season to taste with salt and pepper. Transfer to a bowl, cover with plastic film and leave for at least 8 hours.

To serve, preheat the oven to 110°C. Place a plate in the oven in case you have to poach the *gnocchetti* in batches. *Gnocchetti* should not sit around for more than a minute or two after poaching or they risk losing their lightness.

Pinch off small portions, roll into Ligurian olive–sized (1.5 cm) balls with your hands and set out on baking paper. Select your widest saucepan and fill with lightly salted water. Bring the water to a simmer and have the soup hot in a pan before starting to poach the *gnocchetti*. Poach the *gnocchetti* for 3 minutes or until they rise to the surface, then scoop out with a slotted spoon. Transfer to the warmed plate while you ladle the soup into the warmed bowls. Slip evenly into each serve of soup.

Serves 6

Beef cheeks in red wine
with carrots and mashed potato

6 beef cheeks

¼ cup (60 ml) olive oil

2 tablespoons brandy

6 turnips, cut into bite-sized chunks

6 medium–large carrots,
cut into bite-sized chunks

bouquet garni of bay leaf,
thyme and flat-leaf parsley
stalks tied with kitchen twine

2 cups (500 ml) Beef/veal Stock
(see page 506), or as needed
to barely cover

freshly ground black pepper

Green Salad (see page 503),
to serve

MARINADE

1 × 100 g piece smoked bacon,
cut into 2 cm × 1 cm lardons

1 onion, sliced

1 carrot, sliced

2 sprigs thyme

6 stalks flat-leaf parsley

1 fresh bay leaf

2 wide pieces orange zest

4 cloves garlic, bruised

5 juniper berries

½ teaspoon black peppercorns

2 cups (500 ml) red wine

This is such a good slow-cooked dish – it takes two days to achieve a great result. Start on Friday and invite your dad and the family for Sunday dinner. Uncooked, these largish lumps of very hard muscle (hopefully already denuded of very tough silver skin by your butcher), do look rather unpromising, yet after several hours of slow braising they are transformed to soft, savoury mouthfuls with a unique gelatinous texture. Mashed potato is a perfect accompaniment, or another option is a chunky pasta that will soak up the sticky juices. (See recipe picture on pages 358–359.)

If your butcher has not already done so, strip the tough membrane from the beef cheeks – the technique is the same as for skinning a fish fillet. Slip a sharp knife between the membrane and the flesh, hold the membrane tightly with one hand and zigzag the knife close to the chopping board and along the beef cheek. Discard the membrane.

Place the skinned cheeks in a large glass or other non-reactive bowl and add the marinade ingredients: bacon, onion, carrot, thyme, parsley, bay leaf, orange zest, garlic, juniper, peppercorns and red wine. Stir to mix, then cover with plastic film and refrigerate overnight.

The next day, place a colander over a large bowl, then drain the meat and marinade, reserving the liquid. Extract the cheeks and bacon lardons and pat dry with paper towel. Discard the vegetables, herbs, orange zest, garlic and spices.

Heat one-third of the olive oil in a heavy-based frying pan over high heat and, working in batches, seal the cheeks for 5 minutes or until well coloured on both sides. Add the brandy and carefully tip the pan to light the brandy and turn the meat; take care as the brandy will flame. Transfer to an enamelled cast-iron casserole. Continue until all meat is browned and flamed. Brown the lardons for 5 minutes and transfer to the casserole.

Preheat the oven to 140°C.

Tip the strained marinade into the frying pan, then bring to the boil over high heat and boil for 10 minutes or until reduced by half. Pour into the casserole.

MASHED POTATO

1 kg Nicola *or* desiree
potatoes, peeled and cut
into even-sized chunks

salt

1 cup (250 ml) milk

100 g unsalted butter

sea salt and freshly ground
black pepper

Add the turnip, carrot, bouquet garni and enough stock to barely cover, then season with pepper. Cover with a doubled sheet of baking paper and the lid and cook in the oven for 2½–3 hours, until the cheeks are very tender. Leave to cool.

To make the mashed potato, put the potato into a pan with lightly salted cold water. Bring to simmering point over medium heat and cook until the potato is completely tender when tested with a fine skewer. Meanwhile, bring the milk to the boil in a small heavy-based saucepan. Drain the potato and return to the pan over medium heat for a moment to dry off any moisture. Press the potato, a few chunks at a time, through a potato ricer into a stainless-steel bowl. Whisk in the butter, then the boiling milk. Press the potato puree through a medium-mesh sieve, using the pestle from your mortar or a strong flexible scraper to remove any last little lumps; the mashed potato should be reasonably fluid – if it is too thick add a little extra hot milk. Season with salt and pepper to taste. (Mashed potato can be made well in advance and refrigerated, then reheated in a microwave or steamer over simmering water until hot.)

Spoon off and discard any solidified fat on the surface of the casserole; there will be very little, if any. Reheat gently over low heat. If the sauce is too thin, pour it into a heavy-based saucepan, then boil rapidly over high heat, skimming off any froth that rises to the surface, until reduced and sticky; you want enough to moisten the meat very generously and to flow a little into the mashed potato.

Preheat the oven to 110°C and place 6 plates inside to warm.

Meanwhile, return the reduced sauce to the casserole and stir to mix.

Spoon mashed potato onto the centre of each warmed plate, then place a beef cheek on top and pour the sauce over and around, like a moat; make sure you distribute the vegetables and lardons evenly. Serve with the green salad alongside.

Crisp-fried broccolini
with Anthony Simone's batter

12 stalks broccolini, trimmed, washed and well dried

olive oil, for deep-frying (see page 501)

sea salt

ANTHONY SIMONE'S BATTER

1 cup (150 g) self-raising flour

1 cup (150 g) cornflour

400 ml sparkling mineral water

As a broccoli-lover, I find it surprising that so many do not like this vegetable, although I suspect broccolini, with its tender stalk and smaller head, has converted many. During a weekend in Victoria's Ovens Valley, my friend and I dined at Simones Restaurant in Bright, where my good friends Patrizia Simone and her husband George have presided over the kitchen and front-of-house since 1986. In the best European tradition, son Anthony has moved into the kitchen to relieve Patrizia (who, I hasten to add, is still a force to be reckoned with and continues to call the shots as to how much red pepper to add to the annual salami mix). Anthony is doing a great job, and I enjoyed a memorable meal. I especially recall the beautifully crisp vegetables, and Anthony has kindly given me his batter recipe. Don't restrict this batter to broccolini; I love it with very young zucchinis (courgettes) or zucchini flowers, too. It is best kept cold, and can be stored for a few days in the refrigerator. Before using you will need to whisk it to a smooth consistency.

To make the batter, sift both flours into a bowl. Slowly whisk in half of the mineral water. (Anthony suggests using your hands for the next bit, but I managed well with a whisk!) Add the remaining mineral water in two batches, whisking to form a smooth consistency. The batter can be used at once or refrigerated and whisked when required.

Preheat the oven to 110°C and put an ovenproof serving dish inside to warm.

Heat the olive oil in your selected pan (see page 501) until it reaches 170°C on a deep-frying thermometer. Dip 6 of the broccolini stalks into the batter, allowing the excess to drain back into the bowl, then deep-fry for 5 minutes or until light golden and crisp. Lift out and drain well on a baking tray lined with paper towel. Transfer to the serving dish to keep warm in the oven while you coat and fry the next batch. Repeat with the remaining broccolini and batter.

Sprinkle with salt, then serve at once.

Jocelyn's lemon meringue tart

6 free-range eggs

240 g caster sugar

finely grated zest and juice
of 3 lemons

200 ml thickened cream

1 quantity Sweet Shortcrust Pastry
(see page 508)

1 free-range egg white,
lightly beaten

ITALIAN MERINGUE

4 free-range egg whites

1 teaspoon liquid glucose

2 tablespoons water

240 g caster sugar

There are many versions of this popular dessert pie, and many of them, especially in Australian kitchens, involve cornflour-thickened fillings, which can be rather solid. I was starting to feel like Goldilocks as I had made one tart that was too solid and one that was too runny – the lemon filling oozed everywhere once it was returned to the oven to brown the meringue topping. By chance, scrolling through Instagram, Jocelyn Hancock (see page 351) announced on that very day she had included her favourite recipe for lemon meringue in her *Courier Mail* column. I followed this up and subsequently thanked Jocelyn for what has been voted a winner. The Italian meringue is worth the extra effort to make over a conventional meringue topping; this could be the moment to invest in a sugar thermometer (see page 513). Make the filling mixture several hours before, or ideally chill it overnight.

For the lemon filling, crack the eggs into a large bowl. Break up with a whisk, then add the sugar and whisk to combine well. Add the lemon juice and zest, whisk through, then add the cream and stir through. Chill for several hours or overnight. Stir and then strain through a coarse-mesh sieve into a bowl before using.

Roll out the pastry on a lightly floured workbench until 3 mm thick, then use it to line a 22 cm flan tin with a removable base; I let the excess pastry drape over the edge to avoid any concern about shrinkage. Line the pastry with baking paper or foil and fill with baking weights or dried beans. Chill for 20 minutes.

Preheat the oven to 200°C.

Bake the pastry shell for 10 minutes, then remove the baking paper or foil and weights. Paint the base and side of the shell with the lightly beaten egg white. Return to the oven and bake for a further 5 minutes; the base should be golden brown. Leave to cool in the tin, then shave off the excess pastry from the rim or cut off with kitchen scissors.

Reduce the oven temperature to 150°C.

Put the tin with the baked shell onto a baking tray and pour in the strained lemon filling. Bake for 45 minutes, then check; ➤

recipe continues.

the filling should have just the merest tremble when you gently shake the tin. Turn off the oven and leave the tart inside for a further 5 minutes, then remove and leave on a wire rack to cool completely.

To make the meringue, put the egg whites into the bowl of an electric mixer fitted with the whisk attachment. Put the glucose and water into a small, heavy-based saucepan, then pour the caster sugar on top. Bring to the boil over medium heat, stirring until the sugar has dissolved. Attach a sugar thermometer to the side of the pan and boil undisturbed until the mixture reaches 115°C. When soft ball stage is reached, start whisking the whites and continue to cook the syrup until it reaches 121°C. Remove the syrup from the heat and, with the motor still running, slowly pour the syrup over the stiffly whipped whites; the whites will become thick, glossy and increase in volume. Continue to beat for another 15 minutes or until the meringue has cooled to 30°C.

Spoon the meringue over the cold tart in big blobs. Brown gently with a kitchen blowtorch or under a hot oven griller for 3 minutes or until the meringue peaks are golden and a bit scorched here and there. Cut into wedges and serve.

TIMETABLE FOR THE COOK

ONE WEEK BEFORE

· Check **Ingredients List** and note what needs to be purchased
· Advise provedores of special requests (beef cheeks, vin santo)
· Check specialist equipment needed (candy/sugar thermometer, kitchen blowtorch, potato ricer, electric mixer with a paddle and whisk attachments)

THREE DAYS BEFORE

· Decide on table setting, including serving dishes (note the main course really needs *assiettes creuses* [see page 511] or deep plates)
· Inspect tablecloth and napkins
· Decide on wine – order if necessary (including another try for vin santo, if necessary)
· All shopping, including flowers
· Marinate beef cheeks – refrigerate

TWO DAYS BEFORE

· Braise beef cheeks, then cool – refrigerate
· Slice baguette for crostini – store in an airtight container

DAY BEFORE

Soup
· Make soup – refrigerate

Beef cheeks
· Remove any fat from surface
· Check if sauce needs reducing; reduce if necessary and strain back over cheeks in clean pan – refrigerate
· Make mashed potato, place, covered, in a microwave-safe container or bowl that fits neatly over pan of hot water – refrigerate

Gnocchetti
· Make dough – refrigerate

Lemon meringue tart
· Make, chill, bake and seal pastry shell for lemon meringue tart (set timer)
· Make filling – refrigerate

MORNING OF

Green salad
· Wash, dry and crisp salad leaves – refrigerate
· Prepare salad dressing in salad bowl with crossed salad servers ready to toss before serving

Lemon meringue tart
· Fill and bake lemon tart

· Chill wine, if necessary
· Set table

AFTERNOON OF

Crostini
· Make topping mix – do not refrigerate
· Grill croutons

Soup
· Shape *gnocchetti* onto baking paper-lined tray – refrigerate

Broccolini
· Make batter
· Set up pan for deep-frying alongside paper towel–lined tray

Lemon meringue tart
· Prepare Italian meringue and add to tart

TWO HOURS BEFORE GUESTS ARRIVE

Beef cheeks
· Preheat oven to 160°C
· Slowly reheat beef cheeks, then transfer to low heat on stovetop, so that oven temperature can be increased

ONE HOUR BEFORE GUESTS ARRIVE

Crostini
· Pile crostini mix onto croutons and arrange on baking tray

Soup
· Slowly reheat in pan
· Put water in another pan to poach *gnocchetti*

Beef cheeks
· If mash is to be steamed, set up to heat

Lemon meringue tart
· Blowtorch or grill meringue on tart

· Get changed

GUESTS ARRIVE

Crostini
- Increase oven temperature to 220°C
- Heat crostini

- Warm plates and serving dishes (see page 512)

DINNER IS SERVED

FIRST COURSE

- Serve crostini

SECOND COURSE

Soup
- Poach *gnocchetti*
- Serve soup with *gnocchetti*

THIRD/MAIN COURSE

Beef cheeks
- Check that mash is really hot
- Serve warmed beef cheeks on hot mash

Broccolini
- Fry broccolini and transfer to hot serving dish
- Serve broccolini

Green salad
- Toss and serve

DESSERT

- Cut tart into wedges and serve

INGREDIENTS LIST

PANTRY
- Sea salt
- Fine salt
- Australian extra virgin olive oil
- Plain flour
- Self-raising flour
- Cornflour (wheaten)
- Caster sugar
- Glucose
- Salted capers
- Anchovy fillets in olive oil

SPICE SHELF
- Black peppercorns
- Saffron threads
- Juniper berries
- Tabasco

REFRIGERATOR
- Milk
- 250 g unsalted butter
- Free-range eggs
- 350 ml thickened cream
- 100 g goat's curd or fromage frais
- 2 cups/500 ml good-quality beef/veal stock (if making, see page 506)

GREENGROCER/FARMERS' MARKET (OR GARDEN)
- Flat-leaf parsley
- 2 fresh bay leaves
- Thyme
- Garlic
- 1 red onion
- 1 onion
- 1 leek
- 500 g celeriac
- 6 turnips
- 7 carrots
- 1 kg potatoes, such as Nicola or desiree
- 12 broccolini stalks
- 3 lemons
- Selection of salad leaves
- 1 orange

BUTCHER/DELICATESSEN
- 6 beef cheeks
- 500 g chicken livers
- 200 g smoked bacon

BAKER
- Baguette or sourdough for crostini
- Bread for the table

CELLAR
- Brandy
- Vin santo
- Red wine for beef cheeks
- Wine for the table dinner
- Sparkling mineral water
- Soft drink

MEZZE
IN
ISTANBUL

A FEAST FOR 6

Melon
with WHITE CHEESE

Artichoke Salad
with BROAD BEANS & DILL

CIVAN'S
Carrot & Ginger Dip

Smoky Eggplant
with YOGHURT & POMEGRANATE

BURGHUL & SOUR CHERRY-STUFFED
Vine Leaves

Turkish Tomato Salad

A BOWL OF OLIVES

YOGHURT FLATBREAD

———

CIVAN'S
Burnt Bottom Pudding

20

When planning to visit a new city, I like to read something about it – preferably a novel or cookery book that brings places to life, rather than a history book. I want to anticipate its atmosphere and people, become familiar with the names of areas and monuments and, of course, be introduced to its food. Sybille Bedford captivated me with her stories of the South of France, Colette led me deep into the countryside of Burgundy, Simenon's Maigret stories left an indelible impression 50 years ago, when I first visited Paris and, more recently, I loved Elena Ferrante's quartet of family life in Naples. Then there are food writers, such as Pierre Koffmann, who writes beautifully of his early life in Gascony, and the doyenne, Elizabeth David, who captured the essence of the Mediterranean. Just a handful of my favourites . . .

I knew embarrassingly little about Turkey, other than a few scattered facts, including that it straddles Europe and Asia; the fall of Constantinople in 1453; the rise of Ataturk as the first president of the republic (reinforced after reading *Birds Without Wings* by Louis de Bernières), and the ensuing secularisation of the country; the expulsion of Greeks in the 20s; and, of course, the challenging story of Australia's involvement in the battle at Gallipoli. Place names such as Hagia Sophia, the Blue Mosque and the Golden Horn were subliminally familiar. Not a great deal to go on . . . I knew a bit more about Turkish food thanks to the diversity of Australia's population.

So when I was recommended *The Museum of Innocence* by Orhan Pamuk, and told it was about everyday life in Istanbul from the 70s to the 80s, it seemed a perfect introduction. I had no idea what I was letting myself in for. Six hundred pages later, and overwhelmed by the story of Kemal's obsessive love for Füsun, set amid the mores of middle-class Istanbul, I was determined to visit the museum conceived of and constructed at the same time as the book. Even the very existence of the Museum of Innocence was hard to grasp. The ambiguity of the fictional hero telling his story to the author in a building where this hero has a bedroom and the author has a chair beside the bed, and whose experience in many ways echoes incidents and places in the story – what is real, what is fictional? And does it ultimately matter?

Yet I was utterly captivated by my visit to the Museum of Innocence. Every wooden box or vitrine is named and numbered to connect it to a specific chapter in the book. The premise is that everyday objects have the power to evoke memory and bring forth unprecedented thoughts and emotions in the observer. And so they do. I remember quite disconnected objects from the book: the barrette with pink rosebuds Kemal stole from Füsun's house; the photographs of ships on the Bosphorus; the montage of 4213 cigarette butts, each one dated and annotated; the raki glasses; the pearl earrings that Kemal's father kept to give to his mistress; burnt matches marking the passage of time; a porcelain broken heart; a quince grater; and on it goes . . . Quite a lot of food is mentioned in the book. Early in the story, Kemal spends many evenings with his old friends and consumes an astonishing quantity of raki, accompanied by small mezze.

In Istanbul I enjoyed the custom of choosing from an array of mezze, and grew to appreciate a glass of the powerful aniseed-flavoured raki diluted with ice. Over many evenings, what started as a few tastes before going on to dinner became dinner itself, as the parade of dishes went on and on. I ate lots of eggplant, quite a lot of green leafy vegetables in yoghurt – sometimes tender and spinach-like, sometimes crunchy purslane and sometimes samphire, sauteed simply in olive oil. I have cooked samphire many times and have always been defeated by the thin core of hard string in the middle of every piece. The Turkish chef explained that the samphire was boiled for a surprisingly long time, up to 45 minutes depending on its youth, then the green fleshy 'leaf' was stripped away from its stringy centre, just as we might strip leaves from a sprig of thyme. Every visit to a recommended *lokanta* (restaurant) offered dishes with hitherto unknown combinations; spicy meatballs with long green peppers, *kokoreç* (skewered intestines spiced with oregano and cumin) for the adventurous, liver kebabs and octopus in various ways. A bowl of olives, fresh local cheeses and a basket of flatbread were constants, alongside the fancier dishes.

What a healthy diet it is. Breakfast was almost always white cheese, tomatoes, cucumber, olives, bread, jam and tea. ➤

The street food was similarly fresh and interesting. My first *gözleme* was filled with nettles and curd cheese. Brightly painted handcarts on every corner sold either sesame-coated bread rings known as *simit*, roasted chestnuts or roasted corn cobs, trays of stuffed mussels or barbecued mackerel. And nothing is more refreshing than a freshly squeezed glass of pomegranate juice.

The traditional name for the pudding on page 388 is *kazandibi*, meaning 'the bottom of the pot'. There are many sweet dishes from this part of the world made from semolina or ground rice, and even cornflour. Some are intended to be softly set, even to wobble like a belly-dancer's tummy, I was told by a former resident of Istanbul. Others are firmer, intended to be cut into pieces to serve, such as the one I've included on page 388.

Sitting on one of the many rooftop bars at sunset looking over the Golden Horn, drinking raki with ice or a glass of wine, with illuminated mosques and the Galata Tower in the foreground, is a never-to-be forgotten experience. Istanbul is a rich and seductive city. Its monuments are breathtakingly beautiful, the waterways busy and teeming with craft of all sizes, the gulls cry loudly, the bazaars are glittering, and the labyrinth of narrow streets utterly fascinating. I will return.

Melon with white cheese

1 honeydew melon, absolutely ripe

200 g ricotta salata *or* other fresh white cheese, cut into 6 slices

1 lemon, cut into 6 wedges

freshly ground black pepper

bowl of olives (such as Kalamata olives), to serve

It was late summer when I visited Istanbul, and the weather was marvellous. Still very warm but with balmy evenings just made for eating outdoors. The simple cafes were irresistible. Inside the door were generally a selection of cold dishes, colourful and mostly vegetarian. Self-service was often encouraged. Later a waiter would ask if you wanted any hot mezze. Usually we had been so greedy, and had eaten quite a lot of bread, as well as copious helpings of every cold dish, that we could not manage any more.

I was intrigued by this lovely and very simple cold mezze. The melons offered were pale green and so sweet and juicy. Success depends on choosing a really ripe melon and a silky smooth cheese. Turkey is very proud of its local cheeses and I am afraid I do not know what we were served. The white cheese was like ricotta salata or a very soft young pecorino. There was a pepper grinder on the table and a wedge of lemon on the side – and that was it. (See recipe picture on pages 376–377.)

Halve the melon and discard the seeds. Cut into slices and cut away the skin.

Serve on a very cold plate, with a slice of cheese alongside each slice of melon and wedges of lemon. Offer the pepper grinder, and a bowl of olives alongside, if desired.

Artichoke salad
with broad beans and dill

2 lemons

6 large globe artichokes

1 cup (110 g) shelled broad beans

ice cubes

2 cups (2 large handfuls) rocket
leaves, trimmed

½ cup (small handful) fresh
dill sprigs

½ cup (small handful) flat-leaf
parsley, very coarsely chopped

2 tablespoons extra virgin olive oil

2 teaspoons pomegranate molasses

60 g salty cheese, such as ricotta
salata *or* young pecorino

sea salt and freshly ground
black pepper

**Alas, we do not have perfectly prepared globe artichokes in
our farmers' markets. But come spring we do have very fresh
artichokes; this is when it is worth the considerable effort to make
this salad. Our artichokes are smaller than those I saw in Istanbul,
so you may need to prepare a couple more. The broad beans add
an extra bit of substance. Artichokes discolour quickly, so once
the leaves have been pared to reveal the heart they need to be
submerged in a bath of cold water acidulated with a squeezed
lemon. Do not attempt the final assembly until all the other dishes
are ready for the mezze table. (See recipe picture on pages 376–377.)
And do wash your hands very well after handling artichokes,
as the raw leaves leave a very unpleasant taste on the skin.**

Fill a stainless-steel or glass bowl with cold water and add the juice of
1 of the lemons. Tear off all the dark outer leaves from each artichoke,
until you get to the very pale inner leaves. Hold each one on its side
and use a serrated knife to cut away the top two-thirds. Halve the
second lemon and use one half to rub all over the exposed artichoke.
Use a small, sharp paring knife to trim the base of all the dark nubby
bits; they should be uniformly pale and rubbed with the lemon.

Halve each artichoke bottom and, using a sharp teaspoon, remove
any prickly, pointy, pink-tinged leaves and the tuft of inedible fibrous
matter. Rub quickly with lemon and drop into the acidulated water.
This all takes much longer to describe than do – if only we had those
clever people trimming artichokes for us!

Drop the broad beans into a pan of simmering water for 1 minute.
Drain, refresh in iced water for 30 seconds, then dry and double-peel.

To assemble, choose a beautiful platter. Spread half the trimmed
rocket leaves (no long stems, please) and most of the dill and parsley
over it. Slice the artichokes very thinly, either using a very sharp knife
or, better still, a mandoline or vegetable slicing gadget. Drop the
artichoke into a bowl with the olive oil and add the broad beans. Toss
to mix and coat lightly. Scatter the artichoke and broad beans over
the greens, then drizzle with the pomegranate molasses. Shave strips
of cheese and scatter over the salad, then season lightly with salt and
pepper. Finish with the remaining rocket, dill and parsley, and serve.

Civan's carrot and ginger dip

300 g carrots, peeled and cut
into chunks

¼ cup (60 ml) extra virgin olive oil

20 g ginger, finely chopped

1 clove garlic, finely chopped

½ teaspoon sea salt

½ teaspoon cumin seeds, toasted
and pounded using a mortar
and pestle

¼ teaspoon cayenne pepper

juice of ½ lemon

40 g fresh walnuts, coarsely
chopped

Yoghurt Flatbread (see page 96),
to serve

For my first evening in Istanbul, I was taken to Yeni Lokanta, a bistro-style cafe whose young and handsome chef, Civan Er, served an enticing array of mezze dishes. This was one of my favourites and Civan generously shared the recipe (see picture on pages 380–381). To my great surprise, he also asked me to sign a copy of my own book *The Cook's Companion*, so obviously we got on well!

Preheat the oven to 200°C.

Roll the carrot chunks in a little of the olive oil and place on a baking tray, then roast for 40 minutes or until quite soft and a little bit coloured. Leave to cool.

Transfer the carrot to the small bowl of a food processor and process with the ginger, garlic, salt, cumin, cayenne, lemon juice and remaining olive oil, stopping to scrape down the bowl from time to time until coarsely pureed; the aim is not a completely smooth puree, so there should still be texture. Scrape into a bowl and fold in the walnuts. Taste for salt, lemon juice and olive oil and adjust if necessary.

Serve with yoghurt flatbread.

Mezze in Istanbul

Smoky eggplant with yoghurt and pomegranate

3 (about 1 kg) eggplants (aubergines)

½ cup (150 g) natural Greek-style yoghurt

1 clove garlic, chopped to a paste

sea salt

juice of 1 lemon, or to taste

freshly ground black pepper (optional)

3 tablespoons roughly chopped flat-leaf parsley

½ cup (100 g) pomegranate seeds, for scattering (from an average pomegranate weighing 300 g)

2 tablespoons extra virgin olive oil

Yoghurt Flatbread (see page 96), to serve

Despite the ubiquitous presence of eggplant in some form on every mezze table, it is always one of the first dishes selected from an offered tray. There is no question that the smoky flavour of this dish is a central part of its charm. This can only come from a barbecue or a very hot grill plate. It is universally loved – maybe because it's so good spread on a piece of flatbread (see picture on pages 380–381). With the addition of tahini, this salad becomes baba ghanoush, the popular dish served as a dip in Australia.

Heat a barbecue grill plate until hot. (Alternatively, balance a wire rack over a medium–high gas flame and roast the eggplant over this; the rack may have to be reserved for this purpose in the future, as it may well buckle.) Roast the eggplant, turning 2–3 times so that they roast evenly, for 15 minutes or until the skins have charred and they feel quite soft. Remove with tongs and leave to cool a little.

Using a paring knife, peel away the charred skin. Wipe the eggplant free of any remaining charred fragments with paper towel. Halve lengthwise and put into a colander resting over a plate to catch the draining juices, so they can easily be discarded. Leave to drain for 10 minutes, then press the halved eggplant to extract more of the juices (or squeeze in a clean dry cloth).

Chop the flesh and put it into a large mixing bowl.

Whisk the yoghurt with the garlic and salt, then add to the eggplant. Stir in half of the lemon juice and the parsley and taste. Add more salt and/or lemon juice and some black pepper, if needed.

Spread the smoky eggplant into an attractive bowl or platter and scatter over the pomegranate seeds, then drizzle with the olive oil.

Serve at room temperature. (If made in advance and refrigerated, bring it back to room temperature before serving. Eat within 3 days.)

Serve with yoghurt flatbread.

Burghul and sour cherry–stuffed vine leaves

34 vine leaves, either fresh *or* preserved in brine

juice of 1 lemon

400 ml Chicken Stock (see page 505) *or* tomato juice, if menu is vegetarian

natural Greek-style yoghurt (optional), to serve

BURGHUL AND SOUR CHERRY STUFFING

⅔ cup (160 ml) water *or* Chicken Stock (see page 505)

75 g butter

2 tablespoons pine nuts

½ onion, very finely chopped

½ teaspoon ground cinnamon

¼ teaspoon ground cloves

½ teaspoon sea salt

1 cup (160 g) medium burghul

freshly ground black pepper

150 g drained preserved sour cherries

3 tablespoons finely chopped mint

finely grated zest and juice of 1 lemon

I am indebted to Nevin Halici's *Turkish Cookbook* for explaining that in Turkey a *dolma* is a container – usually a vegetable or fruit – into which a filling is put, such as stuffed sweet peppers (capsicums). Whereas a *sarma* is something wrapped up, often in a vegetable leaf. This recipe is technically a *sarma*, despite the fact such vine leaf–wrapped products are usually sold as *dolmas*, and were in fact so described on menus in Istanbul. Fresh vine leaves are only suitable for stuffing in this manner in the spring, when they are fully opened and pliable, before they harden and crisp in the summer sun. At all other times of the year you will need to buy preserved vine leaves. Preserved leaves in brine or salt need to be boiled for 1 minute only; in both cases snip away any stalks. Burghul is another spelling for bulgur (cracked wheat). You may have leftover stuffing; if so, freeze it for another batch sometime, or serve as a side dish within a day or two alongside grilled or barbecued lamb or fish.

To make the stuffing, place the water or stock in a heavy-based saucepan and bring to the boil. Keep warm.

Melt half of the butter in a heavy-based saucepan over low heat and cook the pine nuts, stirring, for 5 minutes or until pale-gold. Remove and set aside. Add the rest of the butter and the onion to the pan and cook over low heat for 5 minutes or until well softened but not browned. Add the spices, salt and burghul and cook for 2–3 minutes, stirring. Add the hot stock or water and cover, then quickly bring to boiling point over high heat. Reduce the heat to low–medium and cook for 10 minutes or until the liquid is absorbed and holes appear on the surface of the burghul. Reduce the heat to low and place a thick folded pad of paper towel or dry tea towel between the surface of the burghul and the lid and cook for another 10 minutes. Turn off the heat and leave to cool, covered. Taste for salt and pepper and season, if desired. Stir in the cherries, pine nuts, mint and lemon zest and lemon juice to suit your taste. ➤

recipe continues.

Choose a saute pan with just enough room to hold 24 tightly rolled parcels in a single layer. Line the pan with 4–5 of the vine leaves to prevent the rolls sticking. Spread out 24 of the leaves on a clean workbench and divide the stuffing among them, including 2–3 sour cherries in each roll. Roll tightly, tucking the ends in neatly. Arrange the rolls in the pan. Cover with more of the remaining leaves. Pour on the hot stock or tomato juice. Hold the rolls down by placing a small heatproof plate upside down in the pan. Cover and cook very gently over low heat for 35–40 minutes. Remove the lid and leave to cool.

These could be served with natural Greek-style yoghurt, or you could crush a garlic clove to a paste and mix it with a little yoghurt and smear it on the serving plate before setting out the rolls.

If using fresh vine leaves...

Bring a pan of water to the boil with the juice of a lemon. Working in batches, drop in the leaves for 4 minutes, then remove, rinse under cold water and lay out on a clean dry cloth, shiny-side down, then proceed with the recipe.

Turkish tomato salad

½ red onion, finely chopped

6 ripe tomatoes, peeled and seeded (to yield approximately 600 g)

1 long green pepper (capsicum), seeded or ½ red pepper (capsicum), seeded

1 Lebanese (small) cucumber, peeled and seeded

1 clove garlic, finely chopped

½ cup (handful) flat-leaf parsley, coarsely chopped

¼ cup (small handful) mint, chopped

sea salt

1 teaspoon hot chilli paste (see page 511)

pomegranate seeds *or* small mint sprigs, for scattering (optional)

Yoghurt Flatbread (see page 96), to serve

POMEGRANATE DRESSING

2 tablespoons extra virgin olive oil

1 tablespoon strained lemon juice

1 teaspoon pomegranate molasses

The distinctive features of this salad are that the ingredients are very finely chopped and it is quite wet, so it is best enjoyed with a spoon. At Zübeyir, a deservedly popular Istanbul *kebap* restaurant with its central open grill, guests are served a flat plate of this salad without asking for it, and versions appeared at every mezze selection I was offered in Istanbul. I ate many such salads and am sure they varied, but the constants were tomatoes, mint, long green peppers and more or less hot chilli. The dressing usually included a little pomegranate molasses and plenty of lemon juice. This version (see picture on page 389) works for me.

Soak the onion in a bowl of water for 20 minutes. Drain, wrap in paper towel and squeeze dry, then finely chop.

Chop the tomatoes, pepper and cucumber as finely as you can, then place in a bowl. Add the garlic, parsley and mint. Tip the salad into a coarse-mesh sieve over a bowl and leave for 30 minutes to drain any excess juices.

Tip the salad into a clean bowl, season with salt to taste and add the chilli paste.

To make the dressing, mix the ingredients together and stir through the salad. Taste again for balance of flavours and seasoning; adjust if necessary.

Spread the salad onto a shallow wide plate and decorate with some pomegranate seeds, if you like. If unavailable, dot the salad with a few little mint sprigs, then serve with flatbread.

Civan's burnt bottom pudding

3 cups (750 ml) milk

350 g caster sugar

1 piece mastic (see page 512), crushed (optional)

100 g ground rice

fine salt

ground cinnamon, for sprinkling (optional)

orange blossom, to serve (optional)

ORANGE BLOSSOM SYRUP (OPTIONAL)

2 tablespoons water

½ cup (180 g) honey

juice of ½ lemon

few drops orange flower water

This recipe is firmly based on one given to me by Civan Er, the chef from Yeni Lokanta restaurant in Istanbul. I have included a more detailed method than I received to encourage cooks to give it a go. To achieve the scorched burnt bottom, it is imperative to select an appropriate pan. It should not have a non-stick coating but be highly polished and very smooth. I used a heavy-based enamelled cast-iron Le Creuset frying pan, but a perfectly clean pressed steel frying pan would do. The pudding needs to be refrigerated for at least 6 hours (or overnight) in the pan, so choose something that fits in your refrigerator (no super-long handles). If you cannot find mastic, the recipe will still work. Ensure you have bought ground rice, *not* rice powder.

Put the milk, sugar, mastic, if using, ground rice and a pinch of salt into a heavy-based saucepan and whisk to combine. Heat over medium heat, whisking until the mixture comes to the boil. Simmer, stirring continuously until the mixture has thickened. Strain through a coarse-mesh sieve into another pan to remove any tiny lumps.

Heat your 'burnt bottom' pan over medium heat, then spoon in a couple of ladlefuls of the pudding mixture. Reduce the heat to low and carefully start burning the bottom; to get a thoroughly burnt bottom, use the back of a large metal spoon to keep spreading the mixture round and round so that there is a good layer of 'scorch'. When you can see that there is an even layer of 'burnt bottom', pour the rest of the pudding mixture into the pan and tap it on the workbench a few times to get a smooth top. Leave to cool at room temperature until cold, then refrigerate for at least 6 hours; better still if left overnight.

To make the syrup, if using, boil the water, honey and lemon juice in a small, heavy-based saucepan until thickened. Cool and flavour with a little orange flower water.

Using a wet flexible metal spatula, cut the pudding into wedges. (I sacrificed a slim wedge to work my wet spatula right underneath the bottom). Place a wedge upside down on a plate; sprinkle some cinnamon on it if you like (or spoon over a little syrup), then serve with an orange blossom, if desired.

TIMETABLE FOR THE COOK

THREE DAYS BEFORE

- Check **Ingredients List** and note what needs to be purchased
- Select a supplier for freshest spices – suggest visiting a Middle Eastern food store
- Advise provedores of special requests (mastic, preserved sour cherries)
- Check specialist equipment needed (pressed steel frying pan with undamaged surface for pudding; see page 388)

TWO DAYS BEFORE

- Decide on table setting, including vibrant serving dishes – ensure you have enough plates
- Inspect tablecloth and napkins
- Decide on wine – order if necessary
- All shopping, including flowers

ONE DAY BEFORE

- Juice 6 lemons and finely grate zest of 2 of the lemons – keep separate from the juice (see page 512)
- Chop 6 cloves garlic, set aside in small bowl covered with extra virgin olive oil (see page 512)
- Wash and sort best dill leaves, then cover – refrigerate in a paper towel-lined airtight container
- Wash and sort youngest parsley leaves to leave whole, then cover – refrigerate in a paper towel-lined airtight container
- Chop mint – refrigerate in a paper towel-lined airtight container
- Chill wine, if necessary

Artichoke salad
- Wash and trim rocket leaves and cover – refrigerate

Carrot dip
- Roast and cool carrots – refrigerate
- Chop ginger – refrigerate
- Toast and chop walnuts (do not refrigerate)
- Toast cumin seeds and pound to a powder, leave in an airtight container (do not refrigerate)

Eggplant dish
- Extract pomegranate seeds and cover – refrigerate

Stuffed vine leaves
- Toast pine nuts
- Stuff and cook vine leaves – refrigerate in an airtight container

Burnt bottom pudding
- Make and cover – refrigerate

MORNING OF

- Chop lots of parsley – set aside
- Set table

Melon platter
- Cut lemon wedges

Artichoke salad
- Prepare artichokes and drop into acidulated water – weight to keep under water
- Blanch and peel broad beans

Tomato salad
- Soak onion, drain and chop
- Chop tomatoes, peppers and cucumbers, strain
- Make pomegranate dressing – set aside at room temperature

Eggplant dish
- Make (do not add pomegranate seeds), transfer to an airtight container – set aside at room temperature unless weather is hot

Carrot dip
- Blend carrot with all ingredients, except walnuts

Burnt bottom pudding
- Make orange blossom syrup (if using)

Flatbread
- Make dough

- Get changed

THIRTY MINUTES BEFORE SETTING OUT MEZZE DISHES

Melon platter
- Slice ricotta salata, if using
- Slice melon

Artichoke salad
- Finish making
- Combine greens for artichoke salad in a serving bowl

Carrot dip
- Transfer to serving dish and fold in walnuts

Stuffed vine leaves
- Assemble stuffed vine leaves on a yoghurt-smeared plate

Eggplant dish
- Place on a shallow platter or bowl and scatter with pomegranate seeds

Tomato salad
- Assemble and put onto the serving dish

Burnt bottom pudding
- Carefully cut wedges invert onto cold plates – refrigerate

- Cook flatbread
- Arrange all platters on table for self-service

MEZZE IS SERVED

DESSERT

- Serve – remember orange blossom syrup, if using

INGREDIENTS LIST

PANTRY

- Sea salt
- Fine salt
- Australian extra virgin olive oil
- Caster sugar
- Artichokes preserved in olive oil (if no fresh ones)
- Tomato juice (if using for vine leaves)
- Pine nuts
- Burghul (medium)
- Ground rice
- Pomegranate molasses
- Preserved vine leaves (if fresh unavailable)
- 175 g honey
- Preserved sour cherries

SPICE SHELF

- Black peppercorns
- Cumin seeds
- Cayenne pepper
- Ground cinnamon
- Ground cloves
- Hot chilli paste
- Mastic
- Orange flower water

REFRIGERATOR

- Milk
- Butter
- 260 g ricotta salata or young pecorino or other young, fresh cheese
- Natural Greek-style yoghurt
- Good-quality purchased chicken stock, if using (if making, see page 505)

GREENGROCER/FARMERS' MARKET (OR GARDEN)

- Flat-leaf parsley
- Dill
- Mint
- 1 onion
- 1 red onion
- Garlic
- Ginger
- 7 lemons
- 6 large artichokes (if in season)
- 200 g broad beans
- 2 handfuls rocket
- 300 g carrots
- 3 eggplants (aubergines) (about 1 kg)
- 6 tomatoes
- 1 long green or red pepper (capsicum)
- 1 Lebanese (small) cucumber
- 1 honeydew melon
- 1 pomegranate
- Fresh vine leaves (if available, if not, purchase preserved)
- Citrus blossom (if available)
- 40 g fresh walnuts

CELLAR

- Soft drink
- Raki
- Wine (if serving)

ELIZABETH

DAVID

A DINNER FOR 6

A BASKET OF
CRUDITES
ANCHOVY DIPPING SAUCE

———

QUICHE LORRAINE

———

NAVARIN OF LAMB
with SPRING VEGETABLES

GREEN SALAD

———

CHOCOLATE
& ALMOND CAKE

21   Elizabeth David was born in 1913 and died in 1992.
She is remembered as the author of eight books about food
and culture, and for many short essays and magazine pieces,
most of them collected and published by her friend, editor
and literary executor, Jill Norman.

It is difficult to think of anything to say that has not been
written by others, myself included. Quite simply, she changed
the landscape in Britain and beyond as far as food appreciation
and practice went. Her influence continues to this day. We very
nearly met. In 1990 I was invited to do a week-long promotion
at a London hotel. In my memoir, *A Cook's Life*, I recall that:

> . . . at the end of one lunchtime during this promotion, I was being
> interviewed for a fairly lightweight magazine when out of the
> corner of my eye I saw a stately woman with a faintly familiar
> profile and white upswept hair being escorted from the dining room
> by two solicitous companions . . . I was aghast!. It was Elizabeth
> David. The queen of food writers had chosen to come to lunch
> to taste my mussel soup, my boned and stuffed rabbit and I was
> trapped, answering some rather mundane questions . . . and
> missing the opportunity to do . . . what? What would I have
> said I have often asked myself? Stammered some form of thanks
> for a lifetime of inspiration?

Elizabeth David once wrote me a letter commenting
favourably on my very first book. Back home, and remembering
my close encounter that had an unsatisfactory ending, I went
to read it once again. The letter had disappeared. It has never
been seen again.

Despite the temerity of this statement, I identify with certain
of my mentor's characteristics, and I am very sad we never met
properly. Elizabeth was hard on herself and I am critical of my
achievements, both of us were capable of intense concentration
and focus, we share a very real need for privacy, and yet both of
us were and are intensely loyal and nurturing of our deep close
friendships. I have read that Elizabeth kept notebooks. I have
notebooks in the hundreds.

Her writing can give me goosebumps. I can pull one of her books from the shelves (and often do) and let it open anywhere; there I will read not just a recipe, but a detail of a special pot, or a quick word picture that evokes a place, or some detail of domestic life that colours in the background of a recipe. She puts in the people, describes the journey, and even suggests the weather. The reader is being given so much more than a list of ingredients and a few sentences of how-to-do-it. And here and there a cautionary note of what not to do. And who would not sympathise with her plea in *Is There a Nutmeg in the House?* to serve good bread, rather than 'a skimpy little wedge of white winceyette placed with boarding-house gentility underneath a folded napkin upon a side-plate'?

In my own file of cuttings relating to Elizabeth David, I have a beautiful photograph of her wearing a crisp white cotton shirt, and next to it, from *The World of Interiors* magazine from August 1993, three pages of photographs of Elizabeth's two kitchens, which look as if Elizabeth has just stepped out for a moment. The table is cluttered with a pottery mixing bowl, a cheeseboard with cut cheeses, notebooks, pencils in an old jam jar, a glass of wine, a system box of cuttings and more and more. On the wall hangs a collection of grills and her wooden plate rack (she eschewed modern appliances and had no dishwasher). I have numerous obituaries and a picture of another much-admired writer Sybille Bedford attending Elizabeth's memorial service in London.

After her death, there was an auction of the contents of her kitchens. Wooden spoons went for surprising sums of money as England's food-lovers competed for their own little bit of culinary history. I think it was Prue Leith who bought the kitchen table!

For this menu I decided to choose dishes from regional France. It was to France that Elizabeth's writings first sent me; Italy came later. Despite the enormous changes in restaurant food in the past 30 years, good home cooking still must fit with busy lives and, for most of us, fairly straightforward equipment and appliances. This dinner must end with the very famous Chocolate and Almond Cake (see page 406) found in several of Elizabeth's books and in the works of many food writers, including *The Cook's Companion*, as well as in cafes all over the English-speaking world.

A basket of crudites

Presenting a still-life of raw vegetables is an exciting challenge for the cook. It can look absolutely glorious – a mixture of colours and shapes – or rather sad. I like to choose a platter or basket that allows all the shapes to be seen. Every guest should have a large plate and a very sharp knife. Crudites are probably best suited to serving during spring or summer, when the crispest carrots and radishes and most luscious tomatoes are in season. In Elizabeth's book *French Provincial Cooking*, her description of the delights of a simple starter of raw vegetables, asks that, when serving radishes, they be '. . . washed, trimmed of excess greenery but left otherwise as God made them, rather than disguised as water lilies'. So please take note of these comments regarding over-trimmed radishes. Leave the broad beans and peas in their very young pods so that guests shell their own. The fronds should be left waving on the fennel. And a few inner celery leaves are lovely. (See recipe picture on pages 396–397.)

Possibilities include:

· asparagus	· cucumber	· salad leaves
· avocados	· fennel	· tomatoes
· button	· peas	· witlof
mushrooms	· peppers	· zucchini
· carrots	(capsicums) –	(courgettes)
· cauliflower	yellow, orange	
· celeriac	and red	
· celery	· radishes	

Bouquets of herbs would include:

· basil	· mint	· tarragon
· dill	· parsley	

And don't forget a bowl of lemon wedges and a bowl of olives.

Anchovy dipping sauce

½ small onion, finely chopped

2 tablespoons red-wine vinegar

6 anchovy fillets in olive oil, chopped

3 teaspoons capers (either salted or in brine)

½ cup (small handful) flat-leaf parsley, chopped

¾ cup (180 ml) extra virgin olive oil

freshly ground black pepper

Alongside the crudites there should be bottles of olive oil in easy reach, as well as bowls of sea salt and freshly ground pepper and bouquets of herbs, arranged like pots of flowers. More elaborate sauces to accompany the crudites are also permitted, such as the parmesan cream on page 420, or the anchovy sauce given here.

Place the onion and half of the vinegar in a small bowl and leave to stand for 15 minutes, then drain, discarding the vinegar.

Put the anchovy, capers, drained onion, parsley and remaining vinegar into a blender and blend. With the motor running, dribble in the olive oil until emulsified, then add pepper to taste.

Serve this in small bowls, as it is very intense.

Quiche Lorraine

1 quantity Shortcrust Pastry
(see page 550)

plain flour, for dusting

125 g (2–3 rashers) streaky bacon,
rind removed and thickly sliced

4 free-range egg yolks, plus 2 eggs

1½ cups (375 ml) thickened cream

freshly grated nutmeg

sea salt and freshly ground
black pepper

witlof salad *or* Green Salad
(see page 503), to serve

There is a rather acerbic essay by Elizabeth berating cookbook writers for telling their readers that any open tart is a 'quiche', which name she feels has a tradition and expectation of being made with eggs, cream and maybe bacon, but not cheese, at least not in Lorraine. Given this, here is the classic combination of bacon, cream, eggs and no cheese. Small *quiches Lorraine*, just big enough to hold in your hand, are a favourite picnic item when on any road trip in country France. And while I do respect tradition and will not call any open tart a quiche Lorraine, it is useful for a cook to know that the formula of 4 egg yolks, 2 eggs and 1½ cups (375 ml) cream can be the basis for many other vegetable-based tarts. And one can include a handful of grated gruyere, just as long as the tart is not called a quiche Lorraine!

Like all custard-based dishes, the filling must not cook too quickly (that is, at too high a temperature) or it will have holes.

When required, roll out the pastry, dusting the workbench generously with flour as necessary. Line a 22 cm flan tin with a removable base with the pastry and refrigerate to chill for 20 minutes. (The rolled-out pastry shell could be frozen for the next day; there is no need to thaw it before the initial baking. It may take an extra 5 minutes in the oven.)

Meanwhile, preheat the oven to 200°C.

Line the pastry case with foil or baking paper and baking weights or dried beans and bake for 20 minutes. Remove from the oven and leave to cool. Remove the foil or baking paper and store the baking weights. Brush the base with lightly beaten egg white and return to the oven for a further 5 minutes or until lightly browned.

Reduce the oven temperature to 170°C.

Gently fry the bacon in a heavy-based frying pan over low–medium heat until crisp, turning once. Cut the bacon into small pieces and scatter over the pastry case. Whisk together the egg yolks, eggs, cream and seasonings. Season to taste, if desired.

Place the pastry shell in the tin on a baking tray. Pour the egg mixture over the bacon and bake the quiche for 20–25 minutes or until firm and golden. Cool to lukewarm before eating.

A Book of Mediterranean FOOD

by Elizabeth David

Navarin of lamb
with spring vegetables

1 × 1.5 kg boned shoulder of lamb, trimmed of excess fat, blade bone and shank reserved (to yield approximately 1.25 kg meat)

extra virgin olive oil, for cooking

sea salt

60 g butter

1 large onion, diced

1 large carrot, diced

1 leek, white part only, washed and sliced

2 thick slices celeriac, peeled and diced *or* 1 stick celery, sliced

1 teaspoon white sugar

¼ cup (35 g) plain flour

2½–3 cups (625–750 ml) Chicken Stock (see page 505)

3 cloves garlic, peeled

bouquet garni (bay leaf, thyme, flat-leaf parsley stalk and rosemary sprig tied together with kitchen twine)

freshly ground black pepper

A navarin is essentially a stew of cut-up lamb with spring vegetables. (See recipe picture on page 403.) Elizabeth gives a very general recipe in her book, *French Country Cooking*. My version incorporates a couple of thoughts from another of my literary mentors, the late food writer Richard Olney, and it has delighted family and friends over the years.

Preheat the oven to 200°C.

Place the shank and blade bone in an enamelled cast-iron casserole with 2 tablespoons olive oil, then roast, covered, for 30 minutes.

Meanwhile, trim the lamb into 4 cm cubes, removing any excess fat. Rub the lamb with 1 teaspoon salt and set aside.

Remove the casserole from the oven, reduce the temperature to 180°C, then add 40 g of the butter, onion, carrot, leek and celeriac or celery. Cover again and return to the oven for a further 20 minutes or until the vegetables are well softened. Place over medium–high heat on the stovetop and stir frequently for 10 minutes or until the vegetables are well coloured. Tip all the vegetables and the bones into a coarse-mesh sieve resting over a large bowl and press firmly on them to retrieve as much of the buttery juices as possible. Reserve the shank. Discard the blade bone and vegetables. Wipe out the casserole with paper towel, ensuring there are no specks of onion left that could burn.

In the same casserole, brown the lamb in batches over medium–high heat, dribbling in the buttery juices; if necessary, add a little more olive oil. When all the lamb has browned, return it to the casserole, increase the heat to high and sprinkle in the sugar, turning the meat to caramelise the sugar. Add the flour, stirring well to coat every piece. Gradually add the stock, stirring to create a sauce-like consistency. Once the sauce looks smooth, add the garlic, bouquet garni and the reserved shank. Reduce the oven temperature to 170°C, then cover and bake for 1¼ hours or until the lamb is tender.

Scoop the lamb into a large bowl and strain the sauce over. The navarin can be refrigerated overnight or for several hours. (The shank adds important gelatinous juices to the sauce. You can decide to remove it and eat it separately with a small salad the next day, or alternatively cut the meat from the shank and add it to the navarin.)

12 small waxy potatoes,
such as Kipfler

12 small carrots, peeled

3–6 small turnips, halved or
quartered, according to size

½ cup (80 g) shelled peas

2 tablespoons chopped
flat-leaf parsley

Reheat the navarin at 160°C for 45 minutes. Meanwhile, prepare the garnishing vegetables. Parboil the potatoes in a saucepan of simmering water for 10–15 minutes or until three-quarters cooked. Drain. Heat the remaining butter in a heavy-based saucepan over medium heat, then cook the carrot and turnips, covered, for 5 minutes. Add the potatoes, carrots and turnips to the casserole and cook for a further 20 minutes. During the final 5 minutes, pour boiling water over the peas, then drain and add to the navarin. Taste the sauce for salt and pepper and season if necessary. Warm the serving bowls (*assiettes creuses*; see page 511) as described on page 512.

Serve in the warmed bowls and scatter each portion with chopped parsley. It would be a good idea to set each place at the table with a spoon as well as a knife and fork.

Chocolate and almond cake

125 g bittersweet/dark chocolate (70 per cent cocoa solids), roughly chopped

1 tablespoon brandy

1 tablespoon strong black espresso coffee

100 g unsalted butter, softened

½ cup (110 g) caster sugar

¾ cup (90 g) ground almonds

3 free-range eggs, separated

pure icing sugar, for dusting

double cream and raspberries or strawberries (optional), to serve

This well-known recipe is based on the French classic *Reine de Saba*, or Queen of Sheba's cake, made famous by Elizabeth David. Apart from its deliciousness, I love this recipe because it requires no fancy mixers, and can be made most satisfactorily with nothing more high-tech than a wooden spoon and a whisk. This excellent cake has been included in several of my own books. It is ideal for those who love rich chocolate cakes that are not too sweet and are easy to make on a whim. I prefer this cake served as a dessert with double cream, and maybe some raspberries or strawberries.

Preheat the oven to 160°C. Butter an 18 cm round cake tin and line with baking paper. (If you are sure your springform cake tin does not leak, you might prefer to use it, as this cake is very fragile and often cracks when turned out.)

Combine the chocolate, brandy and coffee in a heatproof bowl that fits snuggly over a saucepan of simmering water, making sure the base of the bowl does not touch the water, then heat without stirring until melted. Stir when melted and add the butter and sugar. Mix well. Add the ground almonds and stir very well. Remove from the heat.

Lightly beat the egg yolks and stir into the chocolate mixture. Beat the egg whites until firm but not dry. Lighten the chocolate mixture with a spoonful of egg white, then fold in the rest of the white and spoon the batter into the prepared tin.

Bake for 40–45 minutes. The cake will still test a little gooey in the centre. It will have developed a crust and be very fragile. Cool completely in the tin, then carefully turn out onto a flat plate and invert onto a serving plate. (If using a springform tin, release the side and turn out.) Dust with icing sugar.

Cut into slices and serve with cream and berries, if desired, to the side.

TIMETABLE FOR THE COOK

ONE WEEK BEFORE

- Check **Ingredients List** and note what needs to be purchased
- Consider holding your party on a day that can include a morning visit to a farmers' market for the finest ingredients for your basket of crudites
- Advise provedores of special requests (order a boned shoulder of lamb from your butcher, request the blade bone and shank be included in your parcel)

TWO DAYS BEFORE

- All shopping, including flowers
- Decide on table setting, including serving dishes (ideally *assiettes creuses* [see page 511] for navarin and large under-plates for salad)
- Inspect tablecloth and napkins
- Decide on wine – order if necessary

DAY BEFORE

- Pick parsley, wash and dry – refrigerate in paper towel–lined airtight container

Navarin
- Cook at 170°C for 1¼ hours
- Strain sauce over meat – refrigerate

MORNING OF

Crudites
- Hopefully visit farmers' market for the freshest crudites
- Trim all crudites – refrigerate
- Decide on presentation
- Make anchovy sauce

Navarin
- Prepare garnishing vegetables

Quiche
- Make and blind-bake shortcrust pastry

Chocolate cake
- Check berries for garnish

- Chill wine
- Set table

AFTERNOON OF

Chocolate and almond cake
- Bake and cool

Quiche
- Chop and saute bacon – leave to cool
- Make custard filling – refrigerate

Navarin
- Chop parsley garnish

Witlof/green salad
- Wash, dry and crisp salad leaves
- Prepare dressing in bowl with crossed salad servers ready to toss before serving

ONE HOUR BEFORE GUESTS ARRIVE

Quiche
- Preheat oven to 170°C
- Put bacon into tart shell, pour over custard and bake
- Rest on wire rack at room temperature

Navarin and vegetables
- Reduce oven to 160°C
- Reheat

- Get changed

DINNER IS SERVED

FIRST COURSE

- Arrange basket of crudites as a beautiful still-life for self-service with all sauces and accompaniments

- Meanwhile, warm second and main course plates (see page 512)

SECOND COURSE

- Serve quiche

THIRD/MAIN COURSE

- Serve navarin with garnishing vegetables
- Toss salad and serve

DESSERT

- Slice chocolate cake and serve with berries and cream

Remembering Elizabeth David

INGREDIENTS LIST

PANTRY

· Sea salt
· Fine salt
· Australian extra virgin olive oil
· Red-wine vinegar
· Plain flour
· Caster sugar
· White sugar
· Pure icing sugar
· Ground almonds
· Anchovy fillets in olive oil
· Capers (either salted or in brine)
· 125 g bittersweet/dark chocolate (70 per cent cocoa solids)
· Espresso coffee beans

SPICE SHELF

· Black peppercorns
· Nutmeg (whole)

REFRIGERATOR

· Unsalted butter
· 375 ml thickened cream
· Double cream (optional)
· Free-range eggs
· 750 ml chicken stock (if making homemade, see page 505)

GREENGROCER/FARMERS' MARKET (OR GARDEN)

· Flat-leaf parsley
· Fresh bay leaf
· Thyme
· Rosemary
· Selection of seasonal produce for crudites, which could include: asparagus; avocados; button mushrooms; carrots; cauliflower; celeriac; celery; cucumber; fennel; peas; peppers (capsicums) – orange, red and yellow; radishes; salad leaves; tomatoes; witlof; zucchini (courgettes); basil; dill; mint; flat-leaf parsley; French tarragon
· Garlic
· 2 onions
· 1 large carrot
· 12 small carrots
· 12 small waxy potatoes, such as Kipfler
· 1 leek
· Celeriac (or 1 stick celery)
· 6 small turnips
· 250 g peas in pod (to yield 80 g shelled peas)
· Witlof or selection of salad leaves
· Strawberries or raspberries (optional)

BUTCHER/DELICATESSEN

· 1 × 1.5 kg boned shoulder of lamb, trimmed with blade bone and shank reserved
· 2–3 sliced rashers streaky bacon

BAKER

· Bread for the table

CELLAR

· Wine for the table
· Brandy
· Soft drink

A
CHRISTMAS
EVE

FAMILY GATHERING

A DINNER FOR 8

BOUDIN BLANC
with BEURRE BLANC

———

FISH & POTATO
TORTINO

WARM PEPPERED
FILLET OF BEEF
with PARMESAN CREAM,
KIPFLER POTATOES
& SLOW-ROASTED TOMATOES

SALADE AUX LARDONS

———

RASPBERRY SOUFFLES

22

It seems that Christmas Eve gatherings have become more significant, as the concept of family has broadened to include former partners, in-laws and children of different unions, bringing with it the associated logistics of organising several generations at the table at the same time. When children and/or their parents have to go in different directions on Christmas Day, it seems even more important to be all together the night before, so this is a pretty festive menu.

The *boudins blanc* (meaning 'white sausage') on page 415 are included in many French Christmas dinners. I consumed many during the academic year when I lived in the Loire Valley. Having dinner one evening with chef Bruno Loubet at the Zetter Hotel in London, I tasted his beautiful *boudin blanc* and he murmured the word '*panade*'. A panade is rarely used in cookery these days, but can be useful. Almost always made from bread soaked in milk and cream, here the term refers to a cooked paste of flour, water and butter combined as if to make choux pastry. This clue sent me back to my library, where I perused treasured books by Escoffier and Raymond Oliver and, having an afternoon to spare, worked on a recipe that resulted in an ethereal and luxurious sausage, and was really not that hard to make.

For a French Christmas, the *boudin* would be studded with winter truffles. Instead, I like to add coarsely chopped French tarragon, which grows luxuriantly in temperate Australia at Christmas time. If you are attempting this dish for a Christmas in July celebration, search out a fresh black truffle from the rapidly expanding Australian industry; mine came from Manjimup in Western Australia. And do make the *boudins blanc* at least once during truffle season! Simply omit the tarragon and add 30 g chopped black truffle instead. However, the sausages are still delicious without the truffle.

The recipe for the raspberry souffles on page 427 is one I clipped from the pages of the inimitable French magazine *Cuisine et Vins de France*. This recipe advises that the basic preparation can be frozen for one week! I have tested this and would say that, although the flavour was still superb after one week in the freezer, and undoubtedly there are times when this would be very convenient, the souffle did not rise nearly as well as when baked from fresh. But then, how important is the height of the souffle compared with the stress levels of the cook?

I used to subscribe to *Cuisine et Vins de France* during the late 70s, when it was absolutely sensational. One of its early contributors was one of my food heroes, the late Richard Olney, whom I've mentioned several times in this book (see pages 6, 404 and 475). His monthly column, *Un Américain à Paris*, commenced in 1964 and continued for 10 years. In his autobiography, *Reflexions*, he has much to say about the magazine's history and importance.

In 1961, *Cuisine et Vins de France* was the first French magazine devoted to food and wine, and found a dedicated (read, small) audience under the brilliant direction of the co-owner Madeleine Decure. They organised fantastic wine- and food-tasting dinners at the most revered Paris restaurants, and three-day gastronomic adventures into the wine-growing districts of France. Richard's accounts of the sensational dinners and extraordinary wines that accompanied each course make jaw-dropping reading for wine and food obsessives, or those interested in the design of formal dinners in many of the great restaurants of France. These meals were wildly extravagant and quite beyond the capacity of most of us to manage, far less enjoy, today. *Cuisine et Vins de France* never made a profit and was sold to a large American company in 1979; it very quickly lost its integrity. I no longer subscribe to it but still have a small collection of special issues I cannot bear to part with.

So back to our family Christmas Eve gathering.

Once the preparation of the *boudin* and souffles is out of the way, the rest of the menu is easy to manage. Do order your fish well in advance, as at my fish market Christmas Eve resembles the very worst day at the Boxing Day department store sales; ordered parcels have priority!

I have included a dish of beef fillet as well as the simple fish and potato pie. Some families will cook both, and others may choose one or the other. And a portion of the *salade aux lardons* could be assembled without the belly bacon to accommodate non-meat eaters. You may wish to serve a simple biscuit with the souffle. If so, the Seville orange butter biscuits on page 301 can be made using lime zest.

Boudin blanc with beurre blanc

20 g butter

1 onion, very finely chopped

2 tablespoons dry white wine
(or heavily reduced chicken stock;
see page 505)

600 g free-range chicken breast
fillet or tenderloins, free of all skin
and sinew, cut into 1 cm pieces
and well chilled (trimmed weight)

2 tablespoons roughly chopped
French tarragon

1 teaspoon sea salt

½ teaspoon freshly ground
white pepper

½ teaspoon freshly grated nutmeg

1 free-range egg, separated,
plus 1 free-range egg white

1½ cups (375 ml) thickened cream

250 g clarified butter
(see page 511), melted

1½ cups (105 g) fine fresh white
breadcrumbs, for coating

Beurre Blanc (see page 417),
to serve

French tarragon sprigs,
to serve (optional)

PANADE

300 ml water

50 g butter

½ teaspoon salt

⅔ cup (100 g) plain flour

I have made several versions of this melt-in-the-mouth delicacy over the years, but this is the best. We cannot obtain black truffles at Christmas time as the French can – ours are in season during our winter – so I use aromatic French tarragon instead. I have suggested accompanying this with a classic beurre blanc. Best of all would be to make the beurre blanc reduction using tarragon vinegar.

You will need an electric mixer with a mincing attachment that has both fine and coarse discs and two piping bags without nozzles for this recipe. Many recipes include a quantity of pork fat, or breadcrumbs soaked in milk or cream to bind the mixture together – known as a panade in culinary terminology (see page 412). Once poached, the sausages can be refrigerated for up to two days. The quantities can easily be doubled if you are cooking for a crowd.

To prepare the panade, place the water, butter and salt in a heavy-based saucepan and slowly bring to simmering point over low heat. Remove from the heat, tip in the flour and stir vigorously. Return to low heat and cook, stirring frequently, for 5 minutes or until the paste leaves the side of the pan. Tip onto a plate, cover with plastic film and refrigerate until well chilled. (This could be made the day before mixing with the minced chicken if well covered.)

Heat the butter in a small heavy-based frying pan over low heat, then cook the onion for 5 minutes or until well softened. Add the wine or chicken stock and continue to cook, stirring, over low heat for 3–5 minutes or until the onion is quite dry. Transfer to a plate, cover with plastic film and refrigerate until chilled.

Using an electric mixer with the coarse mincing disc attachment, mince the chicken with the onion mixture, tarragon, salt, pepper and nutmeg. Change the mincing disc to the fine one. Mince the chicken mixture and egg yolk (add the truffle now, if using) until well combined. Cover with plastic film and refrigerate until well chilled.

Transfer the chilled mince to the bowl of the electric mixer and attach the paddle beater. Gradually beat in the egg whites; the mixture should look glossy at this point. Beat in the chilled ➤

panade, continuing to beat until the mixture is smooth. With the motor on medium speed, gradually beat in the cream. Check the seasoning by poaching a tiny ball of the mixture in a pan of simmering salted water. Taste and make any adjustments. Chill the finished mixture once more, before shaping and poaching.

Place half of the chicken mixture each into 2 piping bags without a nozzle. (The mixture must be kept as cold as possible, so refrigerate one bag while you work with the other.) Working with one piping bag at a time, pipe 2 fat sausages onto a sheet of plastic film, pressing firmly on the piping bag; each sausage should be approximately 20 cm long × 3 cm wide. Cut the plastic film generously around each sausage so each one can be rolled firmly in several layers of plastic film, twisting the ends of the plastic film to force the sausage mix to be compact without air holes and to seal. (Once poached, the sausages can be cut in half, so think that each length you pipe will be two sausages.) Repeat with the remaining chicken mixture in the second piping bag. You should have 4 fat sausages each about 20 cm long. Chill the wrapped sausages in the refrigerator for 30 minutes.

Have ready a shallow flameproof baking dish with simmering lightly salted water over low heat. Gently slip the wrapped sausages into the water and poach for 6 minutes. Turn the sausages over and turn off the heat. Leave the sausages in the water for a further 6 minutes to finish cooking. Remove and drain on a clean, dry tea towel. Return to the refrigerator until needed.

Just before serving, remove the plastic film. Cut each sausage in half. Roll the sausages in the melted clarified butter and fine fresh breadcrumbs.

Heat a film of clarified butter in a heavy-based frying pan over medium heat and gently fry the sausages, turning, for 10 minutes or until golden and warmed through. Serve at once with beurre blanc, topped with a French tarragon sprig, if desired.

Makes about ½ cup (125 ml)

Beurre blanc

1 tablespoon finely chopped
French shallot

½ cup (125 ml) tarragon vinegar
or dry white wine

coarsely ground white pepper

100 g unsalted butter,
cut into 6 chunks

few drops lemon juice

sea salt and freshly ground
black pepper

**While I generally make beurre blanc with a white wine
reduction, I think it is best to use tarragon vinegar here
to accompany the boudin blanc on page 415.**

Place the shallot, vinegar or wine and white pepper in a small heavy-
based saucepan and simmer over medium heat for 5 minutes or
until the mixture is a mush without obvious liquid. Start whisking
in the butter, a chunk at a time, whisking until all the butter is
incorporated. Season with lemon juice, salt and pepper. Remove
from the heat and rest in a warm place. Serve with the boudin blanc.

If using black truffle in the *boudin blanc* . . .

Place 1 chopped black truffle and ¼ cup (60 ml) of the thickened
cream in a small heavy-based saucepan over low heat for
5 minutes to infuse, stirring. Cool completely. Include the
cold truffle-infused cream to the total cream quantity when
beating the cream into the boudin mixture.

Fish and potato *tortino*

1 kg waxy potatoes,
such as Kipfler, scrubbed

2 cloves garlic, finely chopped

3 tablespoons chopped
flat-leaf parsley

sea salt and freshly ground
black pepper

1 fresh long red chilli,
finely chopped

⅔ cup (160 ml) extra virgin
olive oil

2 tablespoons picked
oregano leaves

2 tablespoons finely grated
lemon zest

1 teaspoon fennel seeds, crushed
using a mortar and pestle

1 cup (250 ml) Homemade Tomato
Sauce (see page 502) *or* good
quality commercial tomato passata

1.5 kg very fresh fish fillets (I used
1.5 cm-thick John Dory fillets),
skinned or not, as you prefer

2 tablespoons chopped basil

1 cup (70 g) coarse breadcrumbs
or panko breadcrumbs

My fish *tortino* (a lovely Italian word meaning 'little pie') was inspired by a version cooked by Faith Willinger, author, traveller, cook and raconteur, recalling this dish she had enjoyed more than once at the celebrated Cibrèo Ristorante in Florence. While Faith used swordfish, my favourite fish for this is sweet John Dory fillets. If you do not have fennel seeds in your spice cupboard, go for a walk alongside a river bank or on any quiet lane and you may spy wild fennel; just be sure your local council or rail authority hasn't sprayed it. Pick a seed head or a flower head, shake it over a plate and you will have all the fennel flavour (and more) than you need.

Cook the potatoes in a saucepan of simmering water until tender. Leave until cool enough to handle, then cut into thick slices. Dress them with the garlic, 1 tablespoon of the parsley, salt, pepper, a pinch of the chilli and one-quarter of the olive oil, then stir to combine. Place the potato mixture in a single layer in a 30 cm × 24 cm baking dish (mine is oval).

Mix the oregano with the lemon zest and crushed fennel seeds, then sprinkle half over the potato. Spoon over half of the tomato sauce. Place the fish in a single layer over the tomato sauce to completely cover. Season with salt and pepper, then scatter over the basil and the remaining chilli, oregano mixture, parsley and tomato sauce. Top with the breadcrumbs and drizzle with the remaining olive oil. Cover with plastic film and refrigerate until you are ready to bake the *tortino*.

Preheat the oven to 220°C. Remove the *tortino* from the refrigerator to come to room temperature.

Bake the *tortino* for 20–25 minutes, depending on the thickness of the fish, until the breadcrumbs are browned, the fish is cooked through and the pie bubbles around the edges. Serve hot or at room temperature.

Serves 8

Warm peppered fillet of beef
with parmesan cream, kipfler potatoes
and slow-roasted tomatoes

1 tablespoon black peppercorns

¼ teaspoon whole allspice

1 teaspoon smoked paprika

½ teaspoon sea salt

1 × 1.5 kg beef eye fillet, trimmed of all sinew

1 tablespoon extra virgin olive oil

8 Kipfler potatoes, washed

butter, chopped flat-leaf parsley and chopped chives, to serve

Slow-roasted Tomatoes (see opposite), to serve

PARMESAN CREAM

3 free-range eggs

1 clove garlic

sea salt

2 anchovy fillets in olive oil, chopped

1 tablespoon red-wine vinegar

2 teaspoons Dijon mustard

1 teaspoon lemon juice

2 tablespoons finely grated parmesan

½ cup (125 ml) extra virgin olive oil

freshly ground black pepper

I have specified Kipfler potatoes but if unavailable choose another waxy variety. Although there will be more parmesan cream than needed, it is difficult to make less in the food processor. It keeps, covered, for a week in the fridge, and can be used to dress a Caesar salad. (See the recipe picture on pages 422–423.)

To make the parmesan cream, boil the eggs for 4 minutes exactly, then immediately cool under cold running water and, as soon as you can, crack the eggs and, using a teaspoon, scoop the contents into a food processor. Process the eggs until fairly smooth. Crush the garlic with a pinch of salt and add to the food processor, along with the anchovy, vinegar, mustard, lemon juice and parmesan. Process until well combined, scraping down the side of the bowl once. With the motor running, gradually dribble in the olive oil; the sauce should be thick and creamy. Taste and adjust for salt and pepper. Cover tightly with plastic film and refrigerate. Bring to room temperature before serving.

Preheat the oven to 230°C.

Using a mortar and pestle, crush the peppercorns and allspice coarsely. Mix with the paprika and salt. Brush the beef fillet with some of the olive oil and roll in the spice mixture.

Heat a heavy-based ovenproof frying pan over high heat until very hot. Film with a few drops of olive oil. Seal the fillet on all sides. Transfer to the oven and roast for 15–20 minutes, turning once; the meat should feel quite springy when it is removed and will be rare. Wrap the pan loosely in foil and set aside to rest for at least 15 minutes.

While the beef is roasting and resting, place the potatoes in a pan of lightly salted cold water and bring to the boil. Reduce the heat to medium and cook for 15 minutes or until tender. Drain the potatoes and, when cool enough to handle, peel. Return to the saucepan and toss with the butter, parsley and chives and season well with salt and pepper. Keep warm. Meanwhile, warm 8 dinner plates (see page 512).

Scoop some of the parmesan cream into a squeezy bottle, if desired. Slice the fillet thickly and arrange on a large platter, surrounded by the tomatoes. Squeeze squiggles of parmesan cream over each slice of beef, if you like, and serve with the potatoes, with the remaining parmesan cream in a small bowl alongside.

A Christmas Eve Family Gathering

Slow-roasted tomatoes

¼ cup (60 ml) extra virgin olive oil

16 long stalks basil

8 large roma (plum) tomatoes, halved lengthwise

16 cloves new-season's garlic, peeled

sea salt and freshly ground black pepper

1 tablespoon vino cotto (see page 513)

As you need to cook these tomatoes at 150°C, they need to be completed before the fillet goes into a much hotter oven. And as they take about two hours to cook, they can be roasted well before dinner. I really like the contrast of hot beef, warm potatoes and almost chilled oily tomatoes. Choose meaty tomatoes that are ripe but firm – oval roma (plum) or similar varieties are perfect. On another day, these tomatoes make a lovely contribution to a cold summer lunch buffet.

Preheat the oven to 150°C. Select a baking dish that will hold the tomatoes comfortably in a single layer.

Drizzle some of the olive oil into the baking dish and strew with half of the basil sprigs, then settle the tomato halves, cut-side up, on top. Tuck the garlic among the tomatoes. Scatter with the rest of the basil. Drizzle with the remaining olive oil, then season generously with salt and pepper.

Roast for 2 hours or until the tomatoes have collapsed a bit and look very juicy. Cool and drizzle with the vino cotto. Serve dressed with the pan juices, basil and garlic, which will be soft and melting.

Salade aux lardons

3 cups (3 large handfuls) baby spinach leaves, stems trimmed, washed and dried

3 cups (3 large handfuls) crunchy salad leaves (the heart of frisee is the best, next comes sliced witlof, then maybe the inner leaves of cos), washed and dried

4 slices sourdough *or* other substantial bread

1 clove garlic, halved

4 × 5 mm-thick belly bacon slices, cut into 5 mm-thick matchsticks (lardons)

½ cup (125 ml) extra virgin olive oil

sea salt

8 small very fresh free-range eggs

1 tablespoon red-wine vinegar

freshly ground black pepper

Lardons **is the French term for small sticks of belly pork (usually smoked) generally cut at least 5 mm thick. In Australia, the best substitute for** *poitrine fumée* **(French-style smoked bacon) is smoked bacon purchased from a quality supplier; I get mine from my local farmers' market. Smoked belly bacon or kaiserfleisch is available at many delicatessens. Ask for it to be cut 5 mm thick. I would not bother with this delicious salad if all that was available was the bacon sold in supermarkets – which in my experience is wet, flabby, thinly cut and without its all-important edge of fat.**

Line a clean tea towel with a long piece of paper towel and tip the prepared greens on top. Wrap into a loose parcel and refrigerate to crisp until needed.

Preheat the oven to 100°C. Warm 8 serving plates in the oven.

Rub the bread lightly with the cut garlic clove, then tear into rough 1 cm croutons.

Film a non-stick heavy-based frying pan with water and drop in the bacon. Saute over medium heat for 5 minutes or until the fat starts to run and each matchstick starts to colour and crisp a little. Using a slotted spoon, scoop from the pan and transfer to a baking tray in the oven to keep warm.

Add half the olive oil to the pan and saute the bread over medium heat for 5 minutes or until golden on all sides. Transfer to the baking tray in the warm oven. Push the pan to one side but do not wash it.

Bring a wide saucepan of lightly salted water to the boil. Working in batches, break each egg into a small cup, slide it into the water and cook until the white has just set, then scoop out and leave to sit in a bowl of warm water. Just before serving, reheat in a saucepan of simmering water, then drain well.

Arrange the greens on a platter, scatter over the bacon and croutons and top with the eggs. (Alternatively, divide the greens, croutons, bacon and eggs among the 8 warmed plates.)

Quickly reheat the frying pan over medium heat, add the remaining olive oil and the vinegar and stir, then spoon the dressing over. Grind over some black pepper and serve at once.

Raspberry souffles

750 g raspberries, plus 24 extra

275 g caster sugar

1½ cups (375 ml) water

10 free-range egg whites

pure icing sugar, for dusting

extra raspberries, to serve (optional)

TO PREPARE THE MOULDS

60 g butter

70 g caster sugar

PASTRY CREAM

2 cups (500 ml) milk

1 vanilla bean, split

6 free-range egg yolks

¾ cup (165 g) caster sugar

⅓ cup (50 g) cornflour

1 tablespoon raspberry eau-de-vie *or* brandy (optional)

Twenty years ago, my friend and former colleague Janni Kyritsis gave me a smooth chunk of wood, barrel-shaped, about 10 centimetres in diameter with a slightly rounded end, just the right size to fit into my hand. It is absolutely the perfect tool for forcing anything through a sieve – if you have a handy friend or partner I would urge you to acquire such a thing. Otherwise, the vital step in this recipe – forcing raspberry mixture through a sieve to yield the pulp without a single seed – can be quite difficult. Try using a flexible pastry scraper or the pestle from a mortar or the back of a large tablespoon.

As I mentioned on page 412, these souffles can be prepared in advance and frozen for up to one week, then baked straight from the freezer for about 15 minutes just before serving. They will not be as spectacular – or rise as high – as when freshly baked, but the host may feel it is worth the loss of height to have no last-minute beating and folding. This recipe makes 12, so if you only require eight, freeze the remainder to bake another time. The last time I made them I used frozen berries, and a mix of raspberries and blackberries. The souffles were just as delicious.

To prepare the moulds, melt the butter and brush eight 8 cm-wide × 4 cm-high (200 ml-capacity) moulds very well. Tip the sugar into one mould, then roll around and tip out into the next mould. Continue until all the moulds are coated. Chill the moulds in the refrigerator until needed.

To make the pastry cream, place the milk and vanilla bean in a small heavy-based saucepan and bring to simmering point over medium heat. Using an electric mixer or hand-held electric beaters, beat the egg yolks, sugar and cornflour in a bowl until thick. Pour the milk into the yolk mixture and whisk until smooth. Transfer the mixture to the rinsed-out saucepan and stir continuously over medium heat until the pastry cream has thickened, become smooth and has come to the boil. Add the raspberry eau-de-vie or brandy, if using. Beat the cream vigorously with a wooden spoon for 1 minute. Press through a coarse-mesh sieve resting over a bowl. Wash and dry the vanilla bean and reserve for another use. ➤

recipe continues.

Press plastic film directly onto the surface of the pastry cream to prevent a skin forming. Refrigerate until cold.

Put the raspberries into a stainless-steel saucepan with 250 g of the caster sugar and the water. Bring to the boil and simmer for 5 minutes. Set a fine–medium mesh-sieve over a bowl and pour the berry mixture through it. You now need to work the residue really firmly to extract all the pulp, leaving the seeds behind. Set aside a scant cup (250 ml) of this puree to serve as a sauce. Return the rest to the pan and boil, stirring all the time, over high heat for 8 minutes or until well reduced and starting to look like raspberry jelly. Leave to cool.

Preheat the oven to 220°C.

Transfer the cooled pastry cream to a large bowl and leave to return to room temperature. Work with a whisk to loosen it. Whisk in the cooled raspberry jelly until well combined. Using the clean and dry bowl of the electric mixer, beat the egg whites until they start to foam. Immediately add the remaining 25 g of caster sugar and continue to beat until you have firm but soft peaks. Gently fold into the raspberry base.

Half-fill the moulds and place 2 raspberries in each one. Finish filling the moulds and level the surface with a spatula. Firmly run the point of a small sharp knife (or the tip of your finger!) around the circumference of each mould, place in a baking dish and bake straightaway for about 12 minutes; they should have risen.

Serve with a sprinkling of icing sugar on the top and extra raspberries alongside, if desired. Offer a little of the raspberry sauce on the side.

TIMETABLE FOR THE COOK

ONE WEEK BEFORE

· Check **Ingredients List** and note what needs to be purchased
· Advise provedores of special requests (a truffle if making *boudin* in winter?)
· Check specialist equipment needed (mincing attachment for electric mixer; 2 piping bags; heavy pan for cooking beef)

THREE DAYS BEFORE

· Decide on table setting, including serving dishes
· Inspect tablecloth and napkins
· Decide on wine – order if necessary
· Complete all shopping, including flowers
· Order fish
· Visit butcher – buy trimmed, centre-cut and vacuum-packed beef fillet, free-range chicken (reserve breast fillets for *boudin*; freeze thighs to cook on another occassion) and carcass for stock

Boudin blanc
· Make chicken stock, if using, from wings/bones – freeze in 2 cup/500 ml quantities
· Reduce 2 cups/500 ml of the chicken stock to 50 ml – label and refrigerate
· Chill chicken
· Make panade – refrigerate
· Make onion mix – refrigerate

TWO DAYS BEFORE

Boudin blanc
· Mince, mix and chill
· Pipe, wrap and poach

Beef dish
· Make parmesan cream – refrigerate

DAY BEFORE

· Collect beef and fish
· Remove fish from packaging, place on a wire rack over a plate – refrigerate

Boudin blanc
· Melt clarified butter – refrigerate

Salade aux lardons
· Cut belly bacon into lardons – refrigerate
· Cut/tear sourdough into croutons

Beef
· Slow-roast tomatoes – refrigerate

Raspberry souffles
· Make raspberry base ('jelly' and sauce) – refrigerate
· Make pastry cream – refrigerate

MORNING OF

· Chop 3 cloves garlic (see page 512)
· Chop flat-leaf parsley
· Strip oregano leaves
· Chop chilli
· Grate lemon zest
· Tear basil leaves
· Set table
· Chill wine

Boudin blanc
· Unwrap *boudins*, then roll in clarified butter and fine breadcrumbs – refrigerate

Salade aux lardons
· Wash, dry and crisp salad leaves

AFTERNOON OF

Tortino
· Assemble and cover – refrigerate

TWO HOURS BEFORE GUESTS ARRIVE

Beurre blanc
· Make reduction
· Chop butter

Beef
· Season, cover with a cloth and leave at room temperature

Salade aux lardons
· Poach eggs, slide into warm water

Raspberry souffles
· Prepare moulds
· Remove pastry cream to come to room temperature
· Whisk raspberry 'jelly' into pastry cream
· Place souffle dishes in baking dish
· Put raspberry sauce into sauce jug

· Get changed

ONE HOUR BEFORE GUESTS ARRIVE

Tortino
· Preheat oven to 220°C and remove *tortino* from refrigerator
· Bake *tortino* for 25 minutes (set timer) – rest in warm spot

Beef
· Seal on all sides

Salade aux lardons
· Saute bacon and sourdough croutons – do not wash pan

· Warm plates and serving dishes (see page 512)

DINNER IS SERVED

FIRST COURSE

- Finish beurre blanc – leave in bowl over warm water
- Gently fry *boudins blanc*
- Serve with a spoonful of beurre blanc, garnished with extra tarragon
- Meanwhile, increase oven temperature to 230°C

SECOND/MAIN COURSE

Beef | Tomatoes | *Tortino*
- Put beef into oven for 15 minutes (set timer), remove, rest, loosely covered with foil while first course enjoyed
- Remove tomatoes from refrigerator
- Cook and season potatoes for beef; keep warm
- Reduce oven temperature to 150°C and return *tortino* to oven for 15 minutes (set timer)
- Serve *tortino*
- Slice beef and serve with warm potatoes and roasted tomatoes
- Drizzle beef with parmesan cream
- Meanwhile, set oven temperature to 220°C for souffles

THIRD COURSE

- Reheat poached eggs in a small saucepan of simmering water
- Deglaze bacon and crouton pan and pour over greens
- Assemble individual *salade aux lardons* or serve on a platter

DESSERT: 20 MINUTES BEFORE YOU WISH TO SERVE

- Prepare and bake souffles
- Have under-plates ready
- Dust souffles with icing sugar

INGREDIENTS LIST

PANTRY

- Sea salt
- Fine salt
- Plain flour
- Australian extra virgin olive oil
- Tarragon vinegar
- Vino cotto
- Red-wine vinegar
- Dijon mustard
- Caster sugar
- Pure icing sugar
- Cornflour (wheaten)
- Tomato passata (or ingredients to make Homemade Tomato Sauce, see page 502)
- Coarse breadcrumbs or panko breadcrumbs
- Anchovy fillets in olive oil

SPICE SHELF

- White peppercorns
- Black peppercorns
- Nutmeg (whole)
- Fennel seeds
- Allspice (whole)
- Smoked paprika
- Vanilla bean

REFRIGERATOR

- Milk
- Butter
- Clarified butter
- 2 dozen free-range eggs
- Thickened cream
- Parmesan

GREENGROCER/FARMERS' MARKET (OR GARDEN)

- Flat-leaf parsley
- French tarragon
- Oregano
- Basil
- Chives
- 1 fresh long red chilli
- 2 heads garlic
- 1 onion
- 1 French shallot
- 1 lemon
- 2 kg waxy potatoes, such as Kipfler
- 8 large roma (plum) tomatoes
- 3 cups (large handfuls) baby spinach leaves
- 3 cups (large handfuls) salad leaves (include frisee if possible)
- 1 kg raspberries
- Black truffle (optional)

BUTCHER/DELICATESSEN

- 1 × 1.5 kg beef fillet, trimmed
- 4 × 5 mm-thick slices belly bacon
- 600 g free-range chicken breast fillets or tenderloins (without skin)
- chicken carcass and wings for stock

FISHMONGER

- 1.5 kg × 1.5 cm-thick fish fillets, such as John Dory

BAKER

- White loaf for breadcrumbs
- Sourdough loaf for salad croutons
- Bread for the table

CELLAR

- Dry white wine for *boudin blanc*
- Raspberry eau-de-vie or brandy (optional)
- Wine for the table
- Soft drink

CHRISTMAS
DAY
LUNCH

A LUNCH FOR 6

PARMESAN
SPONGE CAKE

———

DUCK GALANTINE
with PICKLED WATERMELON RIND

WATERCRESS SALAD

BARBECUED
ROCK LOBSTER
with MANGO SALAD

———

WINE TRIFLE
SEMIFREDDO

AN ASSORTMENT OF
FRESH BERRIES

23

If ever a menu is needed that can be prepared well in advance
it is for Christmas Day lunch. Even the best-laid plans seem to
disappear in the rush to this day when we are all urged to relax
with our nearest and dearest.

For many years I worked on Christmas Day so that others
could gather around a table in my restaurant to enjoy family
and friends without fuss. My own Christmas tended to involve
collapsing onto the couch in the early evening, with some toast
and a couple of glasses of wine, followed by a big sleep, before
offering a massive feast to my friends and their children on
Boxing Day – dishes almost exclusively the result of superior
leftovers from the restaurant.

For many years post-restaurant, the Boxing Day tradition
continued. And it was fun. In later years I relented, allowing
friends to contribute a dish, which made it easier on me, and my
refrigerator. Babies grew into schoolchildren, then teenagers, and
then brought babies of their own. When I moved house recently,
the tradition came to an end.

So for the first time I had to plan like everyone else for
a festive Christmas Day lunch that would allow me to enjoy
it myself, that is, where timing didn't matter at all. If we wanted
to linger over the unwrapping of presents (as decreed by my
younger daughter), none of the dishes would spoil.

This menu can be started well in advance. The biscuits and
charcuterie can be completed several days, even a week before
Christmas, and the semifreddo should be in the freezer one or
two days before Christmas Day. The only last-minute shopping
(and that can happen two days before the big day) is for berries,
mango and salad leaves. Oh, and the decision needs to be made –
rock lobster salad at room temperature or barbecued rock
lobster served straight from the grill? I have given instructions
for both options.

I am fortunate to have outstanding fishmongers, Kingfisher
Seafood at Camberwell Fresh Food Market. We had a long
discussion about rock lobster tails. I'd decided to barbecue rock
lobster and serve it with mango. Did I need to buy live lobsters
on Christmas Eve, and attempt to drown them myself? I was not

looking forward to this. My fishmonger assured me that he had organised a store of lobsters that had been snappingly fresh when they were individually wrapped and frozen in his very cold freezer.

Some years earlier I had had a dreadful experience while holidaying on the Victorian coast. I bought what I hoped were excellent rock lobster tails. Once home and on the barbecue it was soon obvious that the tails had almost certainly been taken from dead or dying animals found in local lobster pots. They were flabby, pasty and quite inedible, and they put me off rock lobster for years.

This time my trust paid off. I took possession of the two rock lobsters I needed a week beforehand, carried them home in a chiller bag and each one was carefully rewrapped in a thick pad of newspaper inside a freezer bag. I did not take them from the freezer until very early on Christmas morning and the texture was perfect. If you are disinclined to buy rock lobster, options might be bug tails, grilled in just the same way.

The cheesey parmesan sponge cake goes very well with a good sparkling wine and can be served warm from the oven or made earlier then sliced and toasted. It will prevent tummy rumbles while presents are distributed.

The charcuterie course will elicit much admiration. The galantine takes time to prepare but the result is decidedly worth it. The pickled watermelon rind is a very old fashioned preserve, but excellent with the duck. And if you have any of your own spiced fruit (cherries, quinces or similar) offer them also with the galantine.

Don't forget to preheat the barbecue to very hot!

Parmesan sponge cake

125 g self-raising flour

½ teaspoon baking powder

½ teaspoon sea salt

¾ cup (60 g) finely grated parmesan

60 g semolina

freshly ground black pepper

90 g butter, melted and cooled, plus extra for brushing

3 free-range eggs, separated

175 ml milk

This is a cheese cake in the literal sense – a light, cheese-flavoured spongy cake, not a creamy, sweet cheesecake. I like to grate the parmesan on a Microplane so that it stays loose and fluffy, rather than in a food processor, where it is ground very finely. It is at its best served whilst still warm or, if made in advance, sliced and toasted.

Preheat the oven to 190°C. Line a 20 cm cake tin with baking paper.

Sift the flour into a bowl with the baking powder and salt. Mix in the parmesan, semolina and some pepper to taste. Make a well in the centre and pour in the butter, egg yolks and milk. Mix well to form a loose batter. Using an electric mixer or hand-held electric beaters, whisk the egg whites until stiff peaks form, then gently fold into the mixture.

Pour the mixture into the prepared tin and bake for 30 minutes or until firm and nicely browned. Cool for a few minutes in the tin, then turn out on to a wire rack to cool a little. Brush with a little extra butter and serve warm.

Duck galantine

1 × 2 kg organic duck, boned with leg bones intact (ask your butcher or poultry supplier to do this or follow the recipe instructions)

sea salt and freshly ground black pepper

1 teaspoon extra virgin olive oil, plus extra for oiling

Pickled Watermelon Rind (see page 442) and Watercress Salad (see page 505), to serve

ORANGE AND PISTACHIO STUFFING

650 g duck breast (includes weight of breast fillets from the boned duck, plus 3–4 extra breast fillets to make up 650 g total), cut into 2 cm chunks

600 g boneless skinless pork belly, cut into 2 cm chunks

200 g pork back fat, cut into 2 cm chunks

finely grated zest of 1 orange

2 cloves garlic, chopped

¼ cup (35 g) unsalted pistachio kernels

2 teaspoons sea salt

1 teaspoon freshly ground black pepper *or* quatre-epices

1 tablespoon O-Gin (from Kangaroo Island Spirits) *or* brandy

This galantine is a showstopper. What is not eaten on Christmas Day will make excellent leftovers in a few days' time (you will probably not want to eat such a fancy dish two days in a row).

My duck came from a Vietnamese organic poultry supplier, with head, neck and feet intact. I saved the neck and froze it to stuff and confit another day. I own a small vacuum-packing machine, which is invaluable for items such as this. You will need a mincing attachment for your electric mixer, a trussing needle or a craft needle to sew up the duck and a ball of kitchen twine. I was introduced to O-Gin on Kangaroo Island where it is made by Kangaroo Island Spirits. O-Gin has interesting herbal flavours including Coastal Daisybush (*Olearia axillaris*), as well as citrus and exotic peppers. I have suggested brandy as an alternative if you cannot find the special gin.

Remove the wishbone from the duck. Cut the skin of the duck right down the backbone and carefully remove it completely, as well as removing the thigh bones and first joint of the wings (see pictures on page 441). Open out the boned duck and carefully strip away the breast fillets, then reserve these to use in the stuffing. Lightly season the inside of the duck skin with salt and pepper, then fold it up, put onto a plate, cover with plastic film and refrigerate until needed.

To make the stuffing, place the duck breast, pork belly, back fat, orange zest, garlic, pistachios, salt, pepper and gin in a bowl and mix very well. Cover with plastic film and chill for at least 1 hour; the mixture needs to be kept very cold when you are handling it.

Using the coarse blade of a mincer, mince the stuffing mixture. Fry a small patty of this mixture, leave to cool, taste and adjust the seasoning if necessary. Chill the mixture again.

Using an electric mixer with the paddle attachment, beat the stuffing mixture for 2–3 minutes or until it becomes a bit sticky; this step is essential to make a galantine that will hold together and slice well without crumbling. ➤

recipe continues.

Preheat the oven to 200°C.

Lay the opened out duck, skin-side down, in a lightly oiled roasting pan. Sew up the back vent using a trussing needle or craft needle and kitchen twine. Pack the filling into the opened-out duck skin. Pin with skewers and then sew the duck up.

Turn the duck breast-side up, in the roasting pan, brush with the olive oil and roast for 1 hour, basting once or twice with the pan juices. Test that it is ready by pricking the thigh with a fine skewer; if the juices run clear it is cooked. Leave the galantine in the roasting pan until cool enough to handle, then wrap tightly in doubled foil to keep it in a good shape. Refrigerate until needed.

Cut into 1 cm-thick slices with a very sharp knife (*not* an electric knife) and serve with the pickled watermelon rind and the watercress salad.

Pickled watermelon rind

1 kg watermelon rind,
cut into 6 cm × 1 cm strips,
leaving a blush of the pink flesh

¼ cup (30 g) sea salt

1 litre water

PICKLING SYRUP

1 kg white sugar

600 ml white-wine vinegar

600 ml water

1 lemon, thinly sliced

1 stick cinnamon

1 teaspoon cloves

1 teaspoon whole allspice

This old-fashioned preserve is good with most meats, particularly brawn or pâtés, and is perfect with the galantine on page 439. It keeps well for at least six months, so can be made weeks in advance of Christmas Day. Once when lunching at a favourite London restaurant, Clarke's in Kensington Church Street, I spied an item on that day's menu – 'sliced parma ham served with Stephanie Alexander's watermelon rind pickle'. I was absolutely thrilled with the compliment, as Sally Clarke's perfectly conceived menus have delighted me several times on visits to London.

You will need to buy an average-sized watermelon and scoop out the flesh. Either puree it to make juice and use or freeze, or refrigerate the flesh to eat fresh.

Soak the rind overnight in a glass or other non-reactive container in the salt and water at room temperature.

The next day, drain the rind and transfer to a heavy-based saucepan, then cover with cold water and simmer over medium heat for 30 minutes or until the head of a pin easily pierces the skin. Drain, discarding the water, then set aside.

To make the pickling syrup, place the sugar, vinegar, water, lemon, cinnamon stick, cloves and allspice in a heavy-based saucepan, then bring to a simmer over medium heat, stirring to dissolve the sugar. Simmer for 10 minutes. Add the rind and boil rapidly for 10 minutes or until the rind is translucent. Fill two 2 cup (500 ml) or one 1 litre-capacity hot sterilised jar/s (see page 513) with the rind, lemon and spices and pour over the syrup. Using a spoon or a skewer, ease pieces of the rind away from the edge of the jar to release any trapped air bubbles. They will bubble to the surface and disappear. Seal while hot.

Leave for at least 1 week to mature before eating (it is even better if you leave it for a month, and is still delicious months later).

Barbecued rock lobster
with mango salad

2 ripe mangoes, cut into 1.5 cm dice

juice of 1 lime

4 × 800 g raw rock lobsters

sea salt and freshly ground
black pepper

3 handfuls young watercress sprigs

HERB BUTTER

200 g unsalted butter,
at room temperature

1 clove garlic, finely chopped

juice of 1 lime

2 tablespoons freshly chopped
flat-leaf parsley

2 teaspoons finely chopped chives

1–2 teaspoons hot chilli sauce
(optional, see page 511)

sea salt and freshly ground
black pepper

On page 435 I have described the care with which my fishmongers prepare and freeze rock lobster tails so that their customers get the best product. As is often the case when it comes to cooking, a first-class, knowledgeable supplier is the best friend you can have.

If you catch your own rock lobsters, you will know how to despatch them with a stab through the tail on the underside where the tail meets the head. You can ask your fishmonger to do this, but a killed rock lobster starts to deteriorate quickly (within a few hours), so it is not feasible to request this unless you are barbecuing the creature very soon – which will not be the case for Christmas Day. Alternatively, drown the lobster in a trough of cold water; this can be upsetting as it will flap around for about 20 minutes. Whichever method you choose, rock lobsters are very expensive. Frozen bug tails are more affordable, and will barbecue in about one-third of the time. The herb butter and mango salad would be perfect with them also. Allow three bug tails per person and expect them to take 10 minutes to barbecue. The herb butter can be prepared an hour or so before attending to the barbecue and left at room temperature. If you'd like to prepare it in advance and store it in the refrigerator, then you'll need to remove it an hour before barbecuing to return to room temperature. (See recipe picture on pages 446–447.)

To make the herb butter, mix the butter, garlic, lime juice, parsley, chives, chilli paste, if using, and salt and pepper to taste to form a smooth greenish paste; this can be done in a small food processor or you can use a small bowl with a fork. Set aside.

Sprinkle the mango with the lime juice. Set aside. Ensure the barbecue grill plate is very hot. Place the lobsters on the grill plate, turning them every 5 minutes until all sides are uniformly bright red; a whole rock lobster of this size will take about 20 minutes.

Transfer the lobsters to a baking tray and leave to rest for 5 minutes. Cut them in half lengthwise, then extract and discard the intestinal thread and the head sac. Press a spoonful of the 'mustard' from inside each head through a fine-mesh sieve into a small bowl and incorporate into the herb butter.

As the meat of the rock lobster clings tenaciously to the shell, for easy eating, using a very sharp knife, cut around the tail meat to extract it from the tail shell. Spoon a little herb butter into the shell. Cut across the tail meat to make thick chunks or slices. Return the chunks or slices to the shell and brush and spoon the herb butter generously all over the cooked flesh, allowing time for it to melt and ooze around and between each piece.

Arrange the lobster halves on a long platter, then fill the heads with some of the mango and watercress sprigs, with any extra mango offered in another bowl. Season to taste. Sprinkle with the remaining watercress sprigs, then serve.

Rock lobster and mango salad

The texture and temperature is best of all if you have bought a live rock lobster and cooked it yourself in simmering salted water. To do this, bring a very roomy stockpot filled with at least 8 litres well-salted water to the boil (allow 40 g kitchen salt to every litre of water). Slip in the just-killed or asleep rock lobsters and return the water to boiling point. Reduce the heat until the water is just under boiling point and start timing the cooking – the rock lobsters will take 8 minutes for every 500 g, plus an extra 5 minutes; for an 800 g lobster that would mean about 17 minutes.

Shell and chop the lobsters as soon as you can handle them, so that the flesh is faintly warm before you mix it with 1 cup (300 g) Homemade Mayonnaise (see page 502) combined with 2 tablespoons chopped flat-leaf parsley, any additional herbs and a little of the lobster 'mustard', if desired. Serve on a platter with the mango and watercress sprigs.

Wine trifle semifreddo

12 sponge fingers, broken into
bite-sized pieces

500 g mixed berries (select
from blackberries, blueberries,
raspberries and strawberries;
the strawberries should be
hulled and quartered)

⅓ cup (75 g) caster sugar

juice of 1 lemon

½ cup (125 ml) fino *or*
amontillado sherry

1½ cups (375 ml) thickened cream

extra blueberries and sliced
strawberries, to serve

CUSTARD

6 free-range egg yolks

¾ cup (180 ml) milk

200 g caster sugar

**Sometimes I buy Italian preserved morello cherries, sold in a very
pretty blue and white ceramic pot with the cherries in a delicious,
very thick syrup. A few of these glistening cherries and a little of
the syrup goes very well with a portion of this semifreddo. This
makes a generous amount, but leftovers will be greatly appreciated.**

Place the sponge fingers in a bowl.

Place the berries, sugar and lemon juice in a wide, heavy-based
frying pan and heat over medium heat, stirring once or twice until
the sugar has dissolved. Cover and cook for 5 minutes or until there
are plenty of juices. Uncover, tip in the sherry and increase the heat
to high, then boil rapidly for 1 minute. Tip the sponge fingers into
the pan and stir to mix; not all of the biscuit should disintegrate
completely. Set this berry/biscuit mush to one side to cool completely.

To make the custard, using an electric mixer, whisk the egg yolks
until very thick. Meanwhile, heat the milk and sugar in a small
heavy-based saucepan over medium heat, stirring until the sugar has
dissolved. Simmer for 2 minutes, then with the motor still running,
pour the milk mixture onto the egg yolks and continue to beat until
the mixture is almost cold. Spoon this thick mixture into a large
mixing bowl, wash and wipe the bowl of the electric mixer and whip
the cream until soft peaks form. Fold the berry mixture and the
cream into the custard. Fold lightly but thoroughly. Tip into
a 2 litre-capacity bowl (or a bowl and a loaf tin, or two 1 litre-
capacity bowls). Cover with plastic film and freeze.

Slice and serve with blueberries and strawberries, and some
preserved morello cherries, if using.

TIMETABLE FOR THE COOK

TWO WEEKS BEFORE

· Check **Ingredients List** and note
what needs to be purchased
· Advise provedores of special
requests (rock lobster, duck,
pork back fat)
· Locate Italian preserved
morello cherries
· Check specialist equipment
needed (trussing needle, mincing
attachment, preserving jars,
semifreddo/bombe mould)
· Make pickled watermelon rind
to serve with duck

THREE DAYS BEFORE

· Decide on table setting, including
serving dishes
· Check barbecue (clean if
necessary) and check fuel
· Check outdoor furniture
· Inspect tablecloth and napkins
· Decide on wine –
order if necessary
· Collect frozen rock lobsters –
take chiller bag and immediately
transfer to your freezer
· Collect duck and duck stuffing
ingredients

Duck galantine
· Bone, stuff and roast duck
for 1 hour
· Cool and wrap tightly – refrigerate

TWO DAYS BEFORE

· All shopping, including flowers

Semifreddo
· Make and freeze

ONE DAY BEFORE

Parmesan cake
· Weigh all ingredients
· Prepare tin

Lobster
· Make herb butter and cover
tightly – refrigerate

· Wash, dry and crisp salad leaves,
including watercress
· Chill wine
· Set table

CHRISTMAS MORNING

Lobster
· Remove rock lobster from
freezer to tray to thaw at
room temperature
· Squeeze lime juice
· Cut mango and mix with lime
· Remove herb butter from
refrigerator

Parmesan cake
· Mix and bake

· Put watermelon pickles (and other
accompaniments) into bowls
· Prepare salad dressing in salad
bowl with crossed salad servers
ready to toss before serving
· Get changed

LUNCH IS SERVED

FIRST COURSE

· Serve parmesan cake whilst
presents are shared

Lobster
· Cook lobsters on hot barbecue,
then rest

MAIN COURSE

Duck galantine
· Slice and serve with pickled
watermelon rind
· Toss and serve salad

Lobster
· Split lobster, ease flesh from
shell, line shells with butter,
replace meat
· Season mango
· Fill lobster heads with mango
salad and watercress sprigs
· Put extra mango salad into bowl
· Serve

DESSERT

· Turn out semifreddo and
cut into wedges
· Put morello cherries into
a small bowl
· Serve semifreddo with extra
berries alongside

INGREDIENTS LIST

PANTRY

· Sea salt
· Fine salt
· Australian extra virgin olive oil
· Red-wine vinegar
· White-wine vinegar
· Self-raising flour
· Baking powder
· Semolina
· Caster sugar
· White sugar
· 12 sponge fingers
· Unsalted pistachio kernels
· Italian preserved morello cherries

SPICE SHELF

· Black peppercorns
· Quatre-epices (optional)
· 1 stick cinnamon
· Cloves
· Allspice (whole)
· Hot chilli sauce (optional)

REFRIGERATOR

· 290 g butter
· Milk
· 2 cups/500 ml thickened cream
· 60 g parmesan
· 9 free-range eggs (plus 2 extra if making mayonnaise)

GREENGROCER/FARMERS' MARKET (OR GARDEN)

· Flat-leaf parsley
· Chives
· Garlic
· 1 orange
· 2 lemons
· 2 limes
· young watercress sprigs
· 1 bunch watercress
· 2 large handfuls small, choice, mild-flavoured salad leaves (such as baby spinach and soft-leaf mignonette)
· 1 average-sized watermelon (to yield 1 kg watermelon rind)
· 2 ripe mangoes
· 500 g mixed berries (blackberries, blueberries, raspberries and strawberries)
· Strawberries

POULTRY SUPPLIER/BUTCHER

· 1 × 2 kg organic duck, boned (ask for it to be opened down the back with leg bones intact)
· 650 g duck breast (includes weight of breast fillets from the boned duck, plus extra to yield 650 g total)
· 600 g boneless skinless pork belly
· 200 g pork back fat

FISHMONGER

· 4 × 800 g raw rock lobsters

CELLAR

· O-Gin (from Kangaroo Island Spirits) or other artisanal gin or brandy
· Fino or amontillado sherry
· Wine for the table
· Soft drink

A WEEKEND AT
CAPE COD

***

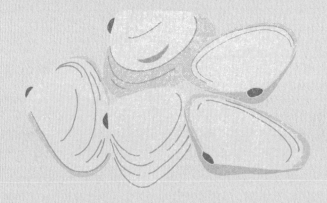

A DINNER FOR 4

STEAMED CLAMS OR PIPIS
with MELTED BUTTER & HERBS

———

FLATTENED
SOFTSHELL CRAB

———

WHOLE SNAPPER
BAKED IN A PAPER PARCEL

POTATOES
BAKED IN PAPER PARCELS

PICCOLO FRITTO
OF FRIED MUSHROOMS, LEMONS,
CAPERS & RADICCHIO

———

CHOCOLATE CHIFFON TART

24 We set out for a long weekend in Provincetown on Cape Cod, having rented a holiday cottage. The food experiences as one travels the US highways are predictably dismal. Choose from Bob's Big Boy, Roy Rogers, Mrs Fields, Dunkin' Donuts and many more: huge helpings; piles of unnecessary 'sides'; coleslaw (sweet); grated plastic cheese; fried tacos; fried chips; giant paper cups of soda (sweet); paper cups of dressings and sauces (all sweet); and everything served on paper plates with plastic knives and forks and paper cups.

I had a moment of nostalgia for the auto-grills in Italy and France, with their steaming espresso, grilled and pressed ham and mozzarella sandwiches, light-as-air sugared pastries, and pushed the memory away . . .

The roads were crowded with holidaymakers. Once in Cape Cod, most houses had the attractive, distinctive architecture of high gabled roofs and cedar shingle walls, which had faded to a lovely silver-lavender. The window and door sashes were painted in various soft colours, and in the front gardens were riotous displays of spring flowers.

At Rock Harbor we visited Cap't Cass Rock Harbor Seafood, where Cass and Betty have run a restaurant for over 40 years, serving real food. It could not have been more of a contrast to the depressing highway offerings; my spirits lifted immediately. We shared a plate of 'steamer' clams served with one bowl of hot water for rinsing and another of melted butter, plus a flavoursome clam chowder generously filled with minced clam and pieces of pork and potato. This was followed by a lobster or crab roll that advertised 'no filler, just meat'. Summer seemed just around the corner on this sunny day.

Our little house sat just a few metres from the sand, and from our picture window we had a view of the boardwalk, the waiting Adirondack chairs and a fluttering umbrella, and beyond, Cape Cod Bay. It was very peaceful. Essential items for a foodie holiday here were a very sharp knife for filleting fish, a good corkscrew, a firm chopping board and an unblemished non-stick pan.

A Weekend at Cape Cod

At Clem and Ursie's Fish Purveyors (sadly now closed), I bought a whole bass with roe intact. I used the head and tail to make a simple fish stock with an onion and a few parsley stalks, then wrapped the fish in buttered foil and baked it. Clem had suggested a dusting of cornmeal or flour for the roe, but sold neither, so I had to improvise. I quartered some button mushrooms and tossed them quickly in butter and added the roe. Once the roe appeared to be nearly cooked and the mushrooms had coloured nicely, I sliced the roe, squeezed over lemon juice, then finished with some pepper and plenty of parsley. This made a very sophisticated and lovely topping for each portion of baked bass. I was very pleased with this meal.

I also bought softshell crabs from Clem and Ursie. We had them for breakfast the next morning. Again following their instructions, I cleaned and dried them most carefully and sauteed them over high heat in a little olive oil with sliced ginger, flattened in the pan with a second pan on top; a brick was suggested but none was to hand. I finished them with a few drops of chilli sauce, roughly chopped coriander and a squeeze of lime juice. They were full of meat and very crunchy! Had we been better provisioned, I might have dipped the crabs in cornmeal or flour or my favourite batter, then fried them for a deliciously crisp crust.

Without a pantry, I could not make anything sweet. I regretted not having bought a slab of good dark chocolate – we decided to wait for coffee and pie at a main street bakery the next day. Echoes of American popular culture led me to think the range of pies would be outstanding. Maybe because it was a holiday weekend, the choice was limited. I think my recipe for chocolate chiffon tart (see page 468) is far better than the very stodgy version I tried. And the coffee was like water!

A few years down the track, we were together again in Australia, so I invited my friends for a nostalgic get-together. I found plenty of local clams, and softshell crabs from Malaysia. We do not have bass with or without its roe, so I decided on snapper, showered with plenty of herbs, wrapped in baking paper rather than foil, partnered with the tiniest waxy potatoes baked in their own garlicky buttery parcel. I did add a warm side salad, inspired by a memory from right across the United States. At San Francisco's Zuni Café I was once offered a delectable little *piccolo fritto* of deep-fried sliced flat mushrooms and thin slices of Meyer lemon with crisp wedges of fried radicchio. And I made another chocolate tart.

Steamed clams or pipis
with melted butter and herbs

150 g unsalted butter

2 tablespoons coarsely chopped
flat-leaf parsley

1 tablespoon coarsely chopped dill

1 tablespoon finely chopped chives

1 kg clams (vongole) *or* pipis

1 red onion, very finely chopped

2 cloves garlic, very finely chopped

1 cup (250 ml) dry white wine

sea salt and freshly ground
black pepper

This is such a simple but such a delicious way to enjoy pipis, clams or vongole, whatever you want to call them. With their increasing popularity it is now rare to find sand or grit in the shellfish, so I assume they must undergo purging somewhere between seabed and fishmonger. Although there are some variations in their size and shape, in my experience these make little difference to the cooking method, although the largest may take an extra few minutes to steam. I have improved on the recipe I tasted in Cape Cod by substituting the strained cooking liquor for the water, and using our superior-flavoured unsalted butter and plenty of very fresh herbs. Provide large napkins that can be tucked into collars, and be prepared with damp tea towels or facecloths for finger wiping at the end of this delicious feast.

Preheat the oven to 110°C and place a heatproof bowl inside to keep the clams warm while you finish the cooking liquor. Have ready 2 large bowls, 8 small bowls and 4 warmed soup plates.

Melt the butter in a small heavy-based saucepan over low heat. Set aside and stir in the herbs. Keep warm.

Place the clams or pipis in a wide (minimum 24 cm) deep frying pan or saute pan with a tight-fitting lid. Add the onion, garlic and wine. Cook, covered, over low heat until a gush of steam lets you know all the shellfish have opened. Push the pan off the heat, then scoop the shellfish into one of the large warmed bowls; bits of onion will be transferred but that is good. Reheat the cooking liquor, then strain through a paper-lined strainer into the other large bowl, discarding the solids.

Divide the cooking liquor among 4 of the small bowls. Divide the melted herb butter among the remaining small bowls. Serve the hot clams in the soup plates and encourage guests to start at once.

Pick up a clam, swish it in the hot broth, then in the melted butter and slurp it up.

Flattened softshell crab

4 softshell crabs, thawed on
a paper towel-lined plate in the
refrigerator overnight

1 tablespoon extra virgin olive oil

3 tablespoons thinly sliced ginger,
cut into julienne

lime or lemon wedges and
your favourite chilli sauce
(see page 511), to serve

handful of coriander sprigs,
for scattering

Softshell crab is rightly considered a delicacy in crab-loving parts of the world – it certainly is in Cape Cod and Louisiana in the US, two places I have enjoyed them. Every crustacean sheds its shell regularly as it grows. If a crab is caught at this stage, the shell does not harden and the entire crab can be eaten, after a little bit of cleaning. I have been served softshell crab in tempura batter, and once soaked in buttermilk, then dusted in flour and pan-fried, but I think Clem and Ursie (see page 455) had the best advice, and the cooking method used here is so easy. In Australia, almost all softshell crab is imported from South-East Asia and sold frozen. Early attempts at developing a softshell crab industry in Queensland seem to have stalled. You will need to thaw the crabs in the refrigerator overnight and provide large napkins and damp cloths for wiping fingers afterwards when you serve them.

Preheat the oven to 110°C and place 4 ovenproof plates inside to warm.

Pull away the back flap from each crab, remove and discard the feathery gills, then rinse and dry the crabs well. Rinse away the 'yellow or brown' matter if you wish (many chefs do not, preferring to retain all the flavours).

Have everything ready as the cooking is very fast. You need a heavy-based frying pan that holds the crabs in one layer without crowding and a second frying pan that fits inside the first to flatten the crabs. (Clem and Ursie recommended a house brick. If available, wrap it well in foil and lightly oil the foil before using it.) If your pan is not big enough, cook 2 crabs at a time and transfer the first batch to the oven to keep warm.

Brush the crabs with olive oil. Heat a few drops of olive oil in the bottom frying pan over high heat. Carefully add the crabs, scatter with half of the ginger and place the second pan (or brick) on top. Cook for 3 minutes, then lift the second pan (or brick) and turn the crabs. Replace the second pan (or brick) and cook for another minute.

Serve the crabs on the warmed plates, with the remaining ginger, wedges of lime or lemon, small dishes of chilli sauce and coriander sprigs alongside.

Whole snapper baked in a paper parcel

2 × 800 g whole snapper, cleaned and scaled

sea salt and freshly ground black pepper

100 g butter, melted

Potatoes Baked in Paper Parcels (see opposite) and Green Salad (optional, see page 503), to serve

AROMATIC BED

40 g butter

2 French shallots, finely diced

1 large carrot, finely diced

1 stick celery, finely diced

2 cloves garlic, finely chopped

2 tablespoons dry vermouth *or* dry white wine

sea salt

HERB GARNISH

3 tablespoons finely chopped flat-leaf parsley

2 tablespoons finely chopped chives

1 tablespoon finely chopped chervil, dill *or* oregano

⅓ cup (80 ml) fruity extra virgin olive oil

finely grated zest of 1 lemon

We do not catch bass in our waters but do have marvellous snapper. The recipe is intended for whole fish, each one sufficient for two generous serves. I have included instructions for adapting the recipe for individual snapper fillets opposite. (See recipe picture on pages 462–463.)

Preheat the oven to 200°C.

Check the fish carefully for scales. Season inside and out with salt and pepper, then slash in 3 places across the thickest part of each side of the body to ensure even cooking. Trim away the fins and tail. Refrigerate until needed.

Roll out a length of baking paper for each fish 2½ times the length of the fish. Brush with some of the melted butter.

For the aromatic bed, heat the butter in a heavy-based saucepan over low heat and saute the shallot, carrot, celery and garlic for 3 minutes, covered. Uncover and add the vermouth or wine and allow to bubble together. Set aside to cool for a few minutes. (Half of the mixture forms a bed for each fish and half is spooned into the cavity of each fish.) Place a fish on each paper sheet, centred over the vegetables. Divide the remaining vegetables between the cavities of the fish, then brush the skin-side with melted butter. Fold the paper parcels in half and tightly fold the edges several times to form a tight seal. Place on one or two baking trays, without overlapping.

Bake the fish for 35 minutes or until the parcels are puffed.

Just before serving, make the herb garnish. Combine the herbs, olive oil and lemon zest in a small bowl.

Take the parcels to the table intact on a warmed flat plate (see page 512). Encourage your guests to slit open the parcels and inhale the lovely aroma. The fish and their juices can now be enjoyed directly from the parcels or divided, and portions of fish and garnish can easily be slid onto an extra warmed plate. Spoon over the herb garnish.

Offer the puffed parcels of tiny potatoes separately, with a green salad to the side, if desired.

Potatoes baked in paper parcels

16–20 very small Kipfler potatoes, washed and dried

80 g unsalted butter, barely melted

sea salt and freshly ground black pepper

4 cloves garlic, unpeeled

The quantities are up to the cook and will depend on the size of potatoes available and how many you are cooking for. Do not bother with this method if your potatoes are larger than a walnut or longer than your finger. And wrap each portion separately in a much smaller version of the paper 'butterfly' described below. If these are to accompany the paper-wrapped fish, as here, check you have the oven space to accommodate all the parcels. They will take longer than the fish and could be moved to the bottom oven shelf for the final 15 minutes while the fish is still cooking (see recipe picture on page 463).

Preheat the oven to 200°C.

Roll the potatoes in the butter, then sprinkle with salt and pepper and toss with the garlic. Make individual parcels of buttery potatoes and garlic using baking paper (see below). Fold the edges firmly a couple of times to form a tight seal. Bake for 40 minutes; the paper parcels should be browned and puffy.

Serve the potatoes in their parcels on a side plate. Your guests will enjoy tearing open the parcels and inhaling the delicious aroma.

If using snapper fillets . . .

Use four 200 g fillets; check carefully for scales and trim any fins. Season with salt and pepper. Melt 100 g butter. On baking paper, trace around 2 medium-sized dinner plates slightly overlapping, like butterfly wings, then cut out. Repeat 3 times and brush with melted butter. Prepare the Aromatic Bed opposite and place half evenly underneath the fish fillets on the baking paper and the rest on top. Prepare the herb garnish and set aside until needed. Tightly fold the paper edges several times to form a tight seal. Place on baking tray/s, without overlapping. Bake at 200°C for 15 minutes, until the parcels are puffed. Serve slit parcels on warmed plates, with the herb garnish spooned over the fish.

Piccolo fritto of fried mushrooms, lemons, capers and radicchio

8 flat mushrooms, thickly sliced

¼ round radicchio, outer
leaves discarded, cut into
1 cm-thick slices

2 lemons, preferably Meyer,
washed, ends discarded and
cut into very thin slices,
seeds flicked out

2 tablespoons capers
in brine, drained

4 handfuls baby spinach leaves,
washed, dried and wrapped in
a cloth

2 handfuls baby salad leaves,
washed, dried and wrapped in
a cloth

1 cup (250 ml) buttermilk

⅔ cup (100 g) plain flour

⅔ cup (110 g) fine semolina

sea salt and freshly ground
black pepper

2 litres grapeseed oil,
for deep-frying

1 tablespoon best-quality
extra virgin olive oil

In 2013, I was saddened to read of the death of Judy Rodgers, head chef of the legendary Zuni Café in San Francisco, far too soon at the age of 57. My memories include tasting Rodgers' famous roast chicken with bread salad, roasted in the brick oven directly in front of those guests with an oven-side seat. On my last visit, the restaurant, as usual, was extremely busy. Judy saw me and my friends waiting at the bar and brought us a bowl of her *piccolo fritto* salad to nibble on. It was absolutely delicious and such a generous gesture. This abbreviated version will give some idea of the dish. The lemon slices are a revelation. Judy writes at length about *piccolo fritto* and its almost infinite variations in her splendid book *The Zuni Café Cookbook*. Given that this will take last-minute attention from the cook, it may be a good idea to serve it as a separate course, rather than trying to orchestrate simultaneous service of the fish, potatoes and *piccolo fritto*.

Set out the mushrooms, radicchio and lemon slices on a baking tray and place the capers in a small bowl. Refrigerate the spinach and salad leaves. Place the buttermilk in a shallow bowl. Mix the flour and semolina on a baking tray, then season with salt and pepper.

Have a baking tray nearby for the coated food before frying and a third tray lined with plenty of paper towel for draining the fried food. (All of these trays can be prepared hours beforehand.)

Heat the grapeseed oil in a deep heavy-based saucepan until it reaches 170°C on a deep-fry thermometer (see page 501).

Working in batches, dip the mushrooms in buttermilk, coat with the flour mixture, shaking to remove any excess, then place on the second baking tray. Repeat with the radicchio and lemon.

Working in batches, start deep-frying the coated food; do not prod or poke. Lift out and drain on the paper towel–lined tray as soon as each piece is lacy and crisp. Deep-fry the capers in a heatproof fine-mesh sieve so that they are not lost in the oil; they will burst open like little flowers.

Place the spinach and salad leaves on a wide serving plate, then drizzle with the olive oil and pile on the fried bits. Sprinkle with salt and serve immediately.

Chocolate chiffon tart

3 gelatine leaves (see page 512)

120 g bittersweet/dark chocolate
(70 per cent cocoa solids),
broken into pieces

⅓ cup (80 ml) strong
espresso coffee

3 free-range eggs, separated

80 g caster sugar

½ teaspoon pure vanilla extract

unsweetened whipped cream
and sliced strawberries sprinkled
with a little caster sugar (optional),
to serve

CHOCOLATE PASTRY

125 g unsalted butter,
plus extra for buttering

80 g caster sugar

1 cup (150 g) plain flour

50 g good-quality Dutched cocoa

**This superb recipe will make you lots of friends. As the filling
contains no butter or cream, it is much more enjoyable to eat
than those tarts filled with pure ganache, which leave me feeling
faintly ill no matter how good the chocolate used. The pastry is
child's play to make (and in fact, would be perfect for a young
assistant cook), as it is pushed into the tin with fingers and
knuckles, just as one does for the crumb crust of a cheesecake.**

**On one occasion I dropped the pre-baked shell and it
cracked badly. Undeterred, I put the pieces in the food
processor, gave them a quick pulse, then put a layer of loose
chocolate crumbs into a shallow bowl, poured the chiffon
mix on top and topped it with cream, resulting in some
sort of trifle. Afterwards, I thought I should have added
a layer of coffee jelly before the cream. When available, this
tart is extra-special with a spoonful of sliced, lightly sweetened
strawberries alongside for a textural contrast. (See recipe
picture on pages 466–467.)**

To make the pastry, butter a 23 cm tart tin lightly. Using an electric
mixer with a paddle attachment, cream the butter and caster sugar
until very pale. Stop the motor. Sift the flour and cocoa and tip
into the butter mixture. Drape a tea towel over the mixer or use the
plastic guard. Turn on the motor to low speed and incorporate
the flour mixture into the butter mixture. Stop the motor as soon
as the dough is well combined; it will be very moist and crumbly.

Immediately tip the mixture into the prepared tin and work the
dough over the base and up the side. Using your knuckles, press in
well to ensure the pastry comes well up the side of the tin. (Try to
make a very thin layer, as this pastry is very crunchy and a bit like
chocolate shortbread.) Smooth the base and side with the bottom
of a tumbler or similar. Refrigerate for 1 hour to chill.

Preheat the oven to 190°C.

Bake the pastry shell for 15 minutes. Remove and, using a clean
dry tea towel, press the pastry back up the side of the tin if it has
slipped down during baking. Leave to cool completely before adding
the filling.

To make the filling, soak the gelatine leaves in a small bowl of cold water for 5 minutes. Combine the chocolate and coffee in a heatproof bowl that fits snugly over a saucepan of simmering water, making sure the base of the bowl does not touch the water, then stir from time to time until the chocolate has melted and the mixture is smooth.

Remove the bowl from the pan and set aside, then tip out almost all of the hot water, leaving just 2 tablespoons in the pan. Squeeze the gelatine leaves and drop them into the water left in the pan, then swish to dissolve. Pour into the chocolate mixture and stir well.

Using an electric mixer or hand-held electric beaters, beat the egg yolks, half of the caster sugar and the vanilla until thick and pale. Whisk in the chocolate mixture, ensuring that it is all well mixed together. Refrigerate to chill for 15 minutes, whisking once or twice, until the mixture starts to thicken a little around the edge.

Wash the bowl and beaters and dry very thoroughly.

Using the electric mixer, beat the egg whites until soft peaks form. Gradually beat in the remaining sugar until you have a glossy meringue. Fold into the chocolate mixture and pile into the chocolate pastry case.

Leave to set. (In hot weather, place the tart in the refrigerator. Otherwise, leave to set at room temperature.) Serve with the whipped cream, and sweetened strawberries alongside, if desired.

TIMETABLE FOR THE COOK

ONE WEEK BEFORE

- Check **Ingredients List** and note what needs to be purchased
- Advise provedores of special requests (softshell crabs will be frozen)
- Check specialist equipment needed (deep-fry thermometer, fine-mesh sieve, filter paper)

TWO DAYS BEFORE

- Decide on table setting, including serving dishes
- Decide on wines – order if necessary
- Inspect tablecloth and napkins (you need large napkins)
- Inspect barbecue (clean if necessary) and check fuel (wood, gas or charcoal?)
- Check outdoor furniture
- All shopping, including flowers
- Order fish and clams

ONE DAY BEFORE

- Collect seafood – remove fish from packaging, place on a wire rack over a plate – refrigerate
- Thaw crabs in refrigerator
- Chop 4 cloves garlic and cover in extra virgin olive oil (see page 512) – refrigerate
- Chop ginger – refrigerate

Clams
- Chop red onion – refrigerate

Snapper
- Cook vegetable aromatic bed – refrigerate

Chocolate chiffon tart
- Bake and cool tart shell

MORNING OF

- Wash, dry and chop parsley, chives and dill – refrigerate in separate paper towel-lined airtight containers
- Wash, dry and pick coriander sprigs – refrigerate in paper towel–lined airtight container
- Wash, dry and stem spinach leaves – refrigerate in paper towel–lined airtight container
- Wash, dry and crisp salad leaves, if serving Green Salad
- Prepare salad dressing in salad bowl with crossed salad servers ready to toss before serving, if required
- Cut lemon wedges
- Clean crabs – refrigerate
- Set table

Snapper and potato parcels
- Melt butter
- Wrap fish parcels – refrigerate
- Wrap potato parcels – do not refrigerate

Chocolate chiffon tart
- Make filling
- Fill tart – do not refrigerate unless very hot weather

AFTERNOON OF

Piccolo fritto
- Slice radicchio, lemons and mushrooms
- Prepare trays
- Place oil in suitable pan for deep-frying with thermometer clipped to side

Chocolate chiffon tart
- Whip cream, put into bowl for serving and cover – refrigerate
- Slice strawberries, if using

- Get changed

ONE HOUR BEFORE GUESTS ARRIVE

Clams
- Put clams into suitable pan
- Arrange filter-paper strainer over bowl nearby
- Melt butter

Softshell crab
- Set out garnishes – dishes of chilli sauce, bowls of lime wedges and sprigs of coriander

DINNER IS SERVED

- Warm bowls for clams and plates for crab (see page 512)

FIRST COURSE

Clams
- Dampen towels for sticky fingers, roll and heat in microwave for 1 minute
- Melt butter and stir in herbs – divide among 4 warm bowls
- Cook clams
- Divide cooking liquor among 4 bowls
- Divide clams among 4 larger bowls
- Have large bowl in centre of table for empty shells

SECOND COURSE

Softshell crabs
- Fry crabs
- Serve on warmed plates with garnishes
- Offer more wet, warmed towels for fingers

- Warm main course plates and serving dishes (see page 512)

Snapper, potatoes and *piccolo fritto*

· Increase oven temperature
  to 200°C
· Bake potato parcels on lower shelf
  for 40 minutes (set timer)
· Bake fish parcels on top shelf for
  35 minutes (set timer)

· Meanwhile, heat oil for *piccolo
  fritto* and assemble trays and
  ingredients
· Have serving platter or individual
  plates ready with spinach and
  salad leaves
· Fry *piccolo fritto*, drain on paper
  towel–lined tray
· Serve fish and potatoes on
  separate platters
· Pile *piccolo fritto* onto leaf-lined
  platter and season to taste
· Fry capers and scatter over
· Serve *piccolo fritto*

DESSERT

· Slice chocolate chiffon tart
  into wedges
· Offer whipped cream and
  sliced strawberries

INGREDIENTS LIST

PANTRY

· Sea salt
· Fine salt
· Australian extra virgin olive oil
· Fruity extra virgin olive oil
· 2 litres grapeseed oil
· Red wine vinegar (optional)
· Capers in brine
· Plain flour
· Fine semolina
· Caster sugar
· 3 gelatine leaves
· Good-quality Dutched cocoa
· 120 g bittersweet/dark
  chocolate (70 per cent
  cocoa solids)
· Espresso coffee beans

SPICE SHELF

· Black peppercorns
· Hot chilli sauce
· Pure vanilla extract

REFRIGERATOR

· 500 g butter
· Buttermilk
· Thickened cream
· Free-range eggs

**GREENGROCER/FARMERS'
MARKET (OR GARDEN)**

· Flat-leaf parsley
· Dill
· Oregano
· Chives
· Chervil (optional)
· Coriander
· Garlic
· Ginger
· 1 red onion

· 2 French shallots
· 4 lemons
· 1 lime (optional)
· 1 large carrot
· 1 stick celery
· 16–20 very small
  Kipfler potatoes
· 8 flat mushrooms
· 1 round radicchio
· 4 handfuls baby spinach leaves
· 2 handfuls small salad leaves
· Selection of salad leaves
  (optional)
· Strawberries (optional)

FISHMONGER

· 4 softshell crabs
· 1 kg clams (vongole) or pipis
· 2 × 800 g snapper,
  cleaned and scaled or
  4 × 200 g snapper fillets

CELLAR

· Dry white wine for clams
· Dry vermouth or dry white
  wine for snapper
· Wine for the table
· Soft drink

SYBILLE BEDFORD

INSPIRED

NEW YEAR'S DAY

DINNER

A DINNER FOR 4

OYSTERS
with SEAWEED BISCUITS

———

WHITING QUENELLES
IN CLASSIC BEURRE BLANC

———

TURKEY ROLL
with CHESTNUTS
& BRUSSELS SPROUTS

WATERCRESS SALAD

———

ICE-CREAM BOMBE
with CHOCOLATE SAUCE

25

I was captivated by reading Sybille Bedford's fictionalised memoir *Jigsaw*, and later her actual memoir *Quicksands*, published in 2005, just a year before her death at the great age of 95. She must have accumulated notes and stories throughout her life, as the energy and vigour of her writing is quite remarkable, as are her powers of recall.

What a life she lived; what adventures; what marvellous friendships she had! How modern and forward-thinking she was; how independent; and seemingly at home no matter where she lived, be it as a paying guest in England, in a rooftop apartment in Rome, on the Italian Lakes, in New York, or wherever she found herself. Both books are captivating but challenging to read, as Sybille swoops from one location to another, rarely including a date, flitting from one decade to another, without immediately obvious connections. However, the books combine to form a whole recounting a dazzling, stimulating life story, encompassing a childhood in Germany, eccentric family life, both world wars, the idyll of the south of France between the wars, and wild adventures at every point, together with much comment on the human condition up to and including the horror of September 11, 2001.

In both books, Sybille writes of Sanary-sur-Mer in the south of France, where she spent several long summers during her late teens in the late 20s and early 30s. The reader is drawn into that intense time in her life, its significant dark shadows mingled with loves and the presence of other strong personalities. It is a truly wonderful account of a France that has largely disappeared. In *Quicksands*, her description of Sanary as it was on first acquaintance makes my heart beat a little faster

> . . . *the waterfront with boats and quays and coils of rope, the crouching menders of nets, the unceasing clank of some* parties de boules, *and beyond it the backdrop, 'la place' lieu of markets and encounters . . .' '. . . the foothills of the Provençal Alpes – empty country of harsh earth, sun-baked and fruitful barely scarred by a scattering of low ageless stone-built human habitations, thyme-scented, terraced with olive, narcissi, wines. Sanary. As it was.*

Sybille Bedford loved food and wine and they were a pivotal part of a well-lived life. She does not dwell on meals enjoyed – they just provide colour and authenticity as the stories unfold. She offers vivid glimpses of life as it was; of small shopkeepers, including the vanished *bonnetiers*, where one bought thread, beach hats and canvas shoes; of the market each morning; and of the daily catch of the local fishermen, whose wives mended the nets and children gathered sea urchins and mussels in the shallows. She mentions the rosé of Bandol, one of my favourite wines decades later, which makes me think of food writer Richard Olney, who made this same section of Mediterranean coast his home from 1960 onwards. In Richard's own autobiography, *Reflexions*, there are many mentions of his friendship with Sybille Bedford. He writes this beautiful paragraph describing a meal they shared:

> *We began with scrambled eggs and truffles, with the chops I served a salad of garden lettuces spiced with a few salt anchovy fillets and chopped hyssop and finished with a platter of cheeses.*

Richard also writes in *Reflexions* of how, to Sybille:

> *In her autobiographical novels (*A Legacy, A Favourite of the Gods, A Compass Error, Jigsaw*), a passion for the table . . . is woven through the treacherous tales of imperfect love, heartbreak and desolation, a steadying and voluptuous thread of joy.*

I wish I had written that – it rings true for me too. I remember a lunch I shared with Richard who, whilst so amazingly hospitable to an admiring food-lover from faraway Australia, was quite shy. He produced a small sack of broad beans and suggested I peel them. Our luncheon salad included quite a lot of hyssop gathered from his extensive herb borders.

The menu here is my present-day interpretation of a meal described in Sybille's book *Jigsaw*, enjoyed by her and some friends one New Year's Day in the early 30s at Sanary-sur-Mer. ➤

PLATTER OF *FRUITS DE MER*
Seafood platter

QUENELLES DE BROCHET
Fish quenelles

DINDONNEAUX
Turkey

CHESTNUT PUREE

SALAD OF WATERCRESS

BOMBE À GLACE
Ice-cream bombe

One should spare a moment's thought for the chef who prepared the quenelles for Sybille and friends. At that time, the *brochet* (pike, a freshwater fish much prized in France), would have been forced through a fine-mesh sieve by hand, then the cream would have been incorporated slowly over ice. The whole thing was recognised as a big deal, so when *quenelles de brochet* was on a menu, it would have been much appreciated.

This feast also involved roasting a whole turkey and carving it at the table, with a chestnut puree offered alongside. Here I've created a dish that honours the flavours and sense of ceremony but is easier to achieve. Having been a great fan of period dramas such as *Downton Abbey*, my cook's heart starts to beat very fast whenever I see one of those scenes where a table of guests is served endless plates of this and that by servants. I just know that everything will be stone-cold! If the turkey is to be served hot, it is important that everything is hot, including the serving plates, the serving dish the turkey roll is transferred to for resting and the vegetables, which should be served directly from the very hot baking dish – not transferred to a cold serving dish to be passed around.

Oysters with seaweed biscuits

54 freshly shucked oysters
(9 per person)

SEAWEED BISCUITS

1 free-range egg

pinch fine salt

1 × 375 g packet Carême all-butter
puff pastry

1 × 25 g packet toasted nori sheets

**It has been a long battle in the Australian hospitality industry
(over 30 years in my experience), to convince serious restaurateurs
that the oysters they offer should be identified by region, that
they should be opened to order, then served spread out in their
shell with all juices intact, rather than being cut from the shell,
washed and flipped. A plate of properly opened oysters is a treat.
If you are willing to give it a go, you could order unopened
oysters and open them on the afternoon of your party. Practise
with a smaller number a week or so beforehand. These seaweed
biscuits go well with them and are a delicious nibble at other
times. I buy commercial all-butter puff pastry made by the
South Australian company Carême for these biscuits. In keeping
with the spirit of Sybille Bedford's classic menu (see page 476),
I've deliberately kept this course simple.**

To make the biscuits, lightly mix the egg with the salt. Cut four
8 cm-wide pieces of puff pastry from the roll.

Roll each pastry piece between two sheets of baking paper to
form a 12 cm-wide rectangle. Place on a baking tray lined with
baking paper and refrigerate to chill for 20 minutes. Brush two of
the puff pastry rectangles with egg wash. Cover with a piece of nori
cut the same size as the pastry rectangle. Brush the nori very lightly
with the egg wash and cover it with the remaining puff pastry.

Using a very sharp knife, cut the pastry and nori 'sandwich' into
3 mm-wide strips. Gently lift and twist each strip, then place on the
lined baking tray. Continue until all the pastry is cut and twisted.
Refrigerate to chill for 20 minutes.

Preheat the oven to 200°C.

Bake the biscuits for 8 minutes or until golden. Transfer to
a wire rack and leave to cool a little.

Serve warm, if possible, with the freshly shucked oysters alongside.

Whiting quenelles in beurre blanc

300 g King George whiting fillets, skinned and boned (to yield about 250 g flesh)

2 free-range egg whites (60 ml)

sea salt

Tabasco *or* freshly ground white pepper

⅓ cup (4 tablespoons) diced vegetables (carrot, asparagus or peeled broccoli stalk and celeriac make a good combination), cut into 3 mm dice, blanched

150 ml chilled thickened cream

2 tablespoons finely chopped herbs, such as dill, chives and tarragon

1 quantity Beurre Blanc (see opposite)

The French word *quenelle* means a small piece of food, shaped between two spoons. Nowadays it might also be a spoonful of cream or ice-cream. Here the quenelles are made from mousseline, usually pureed raw fish or shellfish bound with egg white with cream added. This mixture is then scooped between two spoons into a fat almond-shaped quenelle, and slid into simmering liquid to cook, where they swell to a wonderful lightness. The shaped quenelles can be placed on a baking tray lined with baking paper and refrigerated until ready to cook. Other than the classic presentation here, it can be used as a pasta filling or layered with other ingredients and baked as a terrine, while tiny quenelles, made with teaspoons, can be poached and slipped into a consomme or delicate soup. (See recipe picture on pages 480–481.)

Puree the fish in a food processor, then gradually blend in the egg whites and season with salt. Add Tabasco or white pepper to taste. Process until very shiny, then transfer to a bowl, cover with plastic film and refrigerate to chill for 1 hour. Return to the cleaned and chilled processor bowl and gradually work in the cream. Stop the processor midway through and scrape down the bowl to make sure every bit of fish is mixed with the cream. With the motor running, continue to add the rest of the cream. Transfer to a bowl, then fold in the vegetables and most of the herbs at this point. Cover with plastic film and chill until needed.

Preheat the oven to 110°C. Place an ovenproof plate and a serving dish inside to warm.

Bring a pan of lightly salted water to simmering point. Working in batches, shape spoonfuls of the mousseline using two dessertspoons, then gently slip each quenelle into the water. Continue until all the mixture is used. Turn the quenelles over after 2 minutes. The quenelles will be poached in about 4–5 minutes, depending on their size. Lift out with a slotted spoon to drain on the warmed plate lined with paper towel or a clean dry tea towel, then transfer to the warmed serving dish.

Spoon the sauce over the quenelles and scatter with the remaining herbs, then serve.

Classic beurre blanc

1 tablespoon finely chopped
French shallot

½ cup (125 ml) dry white wine

coarsely ground white pepper

100 g unsalted butter,
cut into 6 pieces

few drops lemon juice, to taste

sea salt and freshly ground
black pepper

This classic white butter sauce causes needless anxiety, however, it is simplicity itself once it is understood that the butter must be added to the reduction quite quickly, so that it remains a creamy emulsion and doesn't overheat and turn to oil. When made with Australian butter (from grass-fed cows), beurre blanc will be distinctly yellow. Made from the butters of Normandy and the Loire, where the butter is a pale-cream colour, the sauce is much lighter in colour, hence the name.

Simmer the shallot, wine and pepper in a small heavy-based saucepan over medium heat for 5 minutes or until the mixture is a mush without obvious liquid. (This can be done an hour or so in advance.) Start whisking in the butter pieces, a chunk at a time, over medium heat, until the butter has melted and incorporated. Strain through a fine-mesh sieve (or not, as you wish). Season to taste with lemon juice, salt and pepper.

Beurre blanc will hold in a warmed jug or small bowl resting over warm, not boiling, water for at least 30 minutes. Cover it closely with plastic film until you wish to serve it.

Turkey roll with chestnuts and Brussels sprouts

1 × 4 kg free-range turkey

100 g butter, plus 40 g melted butter for brushing

2 cloves garlic, finely chopped

finely grated zest of 1 lemon

sea salt and freshly ground black pepper

3 tablespoons coarsely chopped flat-leaf parsley

1 tablespoon finely chopped French tarragon

6 waxy potatoes

30 Brussels sprouts, trimmed

30 vacuum-packed roasted and peeled chestnuts

Watercress Salad (see page 505), to serve

TURKEY STOCK

reserved turkey bones (including neck, if present), chopped

1 onion, roughly chopped

1 carrot, roughly chopped

1 stick celery, roughly chopped

1 bouquet garni (6 stalks flat-leaf parsley, 4 sprigs thyme, 2 fresh bay leaves)

¾ cup (180 ml) dry white wine

water, to cover

This turkey roll is one for a true food-lover who enjoys a challenge and is prepared to spend a bit of preparation time getting all the work done in advance. However, there are several specialist suppliers who prepare already boned and rolled turkeys at Christmas time, so all is not lost if you just cannot face this. As almost all Christmas turkeys are sold frozen, and the thawing will take at least two days in the refrigerator, I think it unlikely that your local poultry supplier would offer to bone the turkey for you and save the skin. You will need a piece of muslin and kitchen twine to wrap the roll for cooking. When it comes to serving, this is an ideal moment to offer a jar of spiced fruit (peaches or quinces are my favourites) or a sharp savoury jelly made with blackcurrants or sour cherries. (See recipe picture on pages 484–485.)

When boning the turkey, the aim is to end with a large unbroken piece of skin, which becomes the wrap for the breast-meat roll. (It is harder to describe than do.) Once you have started, as long as you keep the knife angled into the bone and carefully feel your way with your fingers, boning a bird in this manner is not that difficult. Using a small sharp knife and with the turkey on a chopping board, cut down one side of the backbone and proceed, using your fingers to separate the skin from the flesh. Cut between the breast and the wing joint to separate the joint from the carcass; the skin will be separated from the thigh and can then be carefully pulled away from the drumstick. Cut the skin free and start again on the other side of the bird. Carefully holding the loose skin taut, separate the skin from the breast meat. Cut the wings away from the bird. Spread out the skin on the board and inspect it – there is a lot of skin on a turkey, so even if you have a couple of holes, there should still be plenty of skin.

Remove the two breast fillets (each will weigh around 600 g). Cut out the sinew that is easily visible in the under-fillet. Save the skinless leg meat to mince or chop into a pie filling another time (weigh, bag, label and freeze for up to 1 month) and use the bones in the stock.

To make the stock, place the reserved carcass, the onion, carrot, celery, bouquet garni, wine and water to cover in a large stockpot or heavy-based saucepan and bring to a simmer. Simmer for 2–3 hours, then strain and refrigerate until needed. When cold, remove any fat from the surface, then boil over high heat until reduced by half. Chill. (Freeze whatever is left in small containers. Label and date, then use within a month.)

Place the 100 g butter and the garlic in a small heavy-based saucepan over low heat, stirring until the butter has melted and the garlic is fragrant but not coloured. Remove from the heat, leave to cool for a minute, then stir in the lemon zest. Spread out the turkey skin with the inner surface uppermost. Brush the skin with some of the garlic butter. Place 1 breast fillet on the buttered skin, season well with salt and pepper and brush liberally with more of the garlic butter. Scatter with half of the herbs. Season the second fillet with salt and pepper, brush all over with the garlic butter and position it 'top to tail' over the first fillet. Brush with the remaining garlic butter. Cut away any excess skin, making sure you have enough to cover the roll. Pull up the skin to cover the breasts and tie securely with kitchen twine at 5 cm intervals.

Cut a piece of muslin large enough to fully encase the roll in a single layer. Wet the muslin, wring it out, then dip it in the remaining melted butter. Wrap the entire roll firmly in the buttered muslin, secure it with kitchen twine, then weigh it; it will probably be about 1.3–1.5 kg. Put it into a baking dish large enough to contain the turkey and potatoes, then refrigerate until ready to cook. (This can be prepared to this stage up to 24 hours in advance and refrigerated.)

When planning, allow 40 minutes roasting time per kg, plus 20 minutes resting time, and remove the turkey roll from the refrigerator 30 minutes before roasting. Preheat the oven to 200°C.

Arrange the potatoes in a single layer around the turkey roll. Pour ½ cup (125 ml) of the turkey stock or water into the baking dish and roast for 30 minutes, then add a little more stock or water to prevent the juices burning. Carefully turn the potatoes. Roast for another 30 minutes, then test the turkey. Pierce the centre with a thin skewer; the juices should run clear. If using a meat thermometer, ➤

recipe continues.

the internal temperature should be 75°C. If cooked, transfer the roll to a warmed plate and cover loosely with foil. If not, continue to roast and test after another 15 minutes, then remove as above.

Meanwhile, cook the Brussels sprouts in a pan of lightly salted simmering water for 3 minutes or until just tender. Drain and refresh in cold water for 1 minute, then drain very well.

Add the chestnuts and Brussels sprouts to the baking dish with the potatoes, which should look sticky and crisp. (They should hopefully have mixed with some really great roasting juices.) Add an extra spoonful of turkey stock if the baking dish looks at all dry.

Reduce the oven temperature to 150°C, return the baking dish to the oven and roast with the sprouts for 10 minutes. Remove the foil and return the turkey to the baking dish so all the juices mingle. Snip off the twine and ease the muslin from the turkey roll. The turkey and vegetables will stay hot for 30 minutes out of the oven and will continue to improve. Warm the serving plates (see page 512).

Using a sharp knife, cut thick slices from the roll. Spoon over any cooking juices. Serve a portion of potatoes, chestnuts and sprouts with each slice on each warmed plate, with the watercress salad alongside.

Churn-free ice-cream bombe
with chocolate sauce

Making an ice-cream bombe is fun, although it takes organisation and the cook needs to allow enough time for each layer to freeze before adding the next one. I have selected recipes that do not need churning in an ice-cream machine, but you will need to buy a sugar or candy thermometer.

There are three layers to this bombe: coffee ice-cream, nougat ice-cream and apricot parfait (see pages 492–494). The textures of each layer should be similar to allow for easy cutting. The bombe needs to be taken out of the freezer 30 minutes before you want to serve it to soften just a little. Another time, make just one of these flavours and set it in a log or other shaped mould. Alternatively, you could layer the flavours in a log mould, then serve slices. Nigella Lawson's coffee ice-cream is well known, and is an absolutely foolproof recipe; I have adjusted the quantities slightly. My nougat ice-cream, originally published in *The Cook's Companion*, takes more work, as does the apricot parfait.

Some elements can be made in advance, simplifying the assembly. The praline, the apricot syrup and the puree can be finished before you start on the first ice-cream. And you will only use half of the apricot parfait and just over half of the nougat ice-cream for the bombe; you can freeze the rest in an airtight container or loaf tin, together or separately, for another day. Serve a chocolate sauce (see page 492) alongside, if you wish. When this arrives at the table, expect to be overwhelmed with applause! ➤

Nigella's coffee ice-cream

2 tablespoons instant espresso granules (I use Moccona Classic Dark Roast Instant Coffee)

1 tablespoon boiling water

300 ml thickened cream

175 g sweetened condensed milk

30 ml espresso liqueur

1 teaspoon almond *or* other neutral oil

In the UK, Nigella uses espresso coffee powder, which is not currently available in Australia. Instead I use Moccona Classic Dark Roast Instant Coffee, and follow the note on nigella.com that, 'If you are using another type of instant coffee then we would suggest you dissolve the coffee granules in as little hot water as possible. You would need to use slightly more and we would suggest 2 tablespoons of instant coffee dissolved in 1 tablespoon of water from a just-boiled kettle.' It is useful to note that Nigella's instructions use a UK tablespoon, which is 15 ml, whereas I use an Australian tablespoon, which is 20 ml.

Make this ice-cream the day before the others. Dissolve the coffee powder completely in the boiling water in the bowl of an electric mixer fitted with the whisk attachment. Cool. Add the cream, condensed milk and liqueur and whisk together until the whisk leaves trails of soft peaks in the bowl and you have a gorgeous caffe-latte-coloured airy mixture.

To assemble the bombe, select a 1.5 litre-capacity bowl, brush with the oil and line it with 4 layers of plastic film, leaving enough film extending over the rim to make the bombe easier to remove. Smooth the film as well as you can as any wrinkles will appear on the surface of the finished bombe.

Spoon the coffee ice-cream into the mould and squash it up the sides by inserting a 1.25 litre-capacity bowl into the bowl. Place the doubled bowl into the freezer overnight or for at least several hours, until the first layer is firm enough so that the second bowl does not move around too easily.

Make the praline for the nougat ice-cream now (see opposite).

Chocolate sauce

125 g bittersweet/dark chocolate (70 per cent cocoa solids)

½ cup (125 ml) thickened cream

½ cup (125 ml) milk

1 teaspoon honey

Grate the chocolate in a food processor, then place in a small heavy-based saucepan with the cream, milk and honey. Heat gently over low heat, stirring for 5 minutes or until quite smooth. The sauce will thicken as it cools; if it becomes too thick, warm it in a microwave for 30 seconds.

Nougat ice-cream

¼ cup (55 g) caster sugar

30 g liquid glucose

¼ cup (90 g) honey

4 free-range egg whites

400 ml thickened cream, softly whipped

90 g glace fruit, chopped

45 g candied peel, chopped

ALMOND PRALINE

¼ cup (20 g) flaked almonds

1 teaspoon almond *or* other neutral oil, for brushing tray

¼ cup (55 g) caster sugar

To make the praline, preheat the oven to 180°C. Place the almonds on a baking tray and toast in the oven for 10 minutes or until pale golden.

Have ready an oiled baking tray or pizza tray. Place the sugar in a small heavy-based saucepan over medium heat to dissolve; brush the side of the pan with cold water to prevent the sugar crystallising. When the sugar has dissolved and is golden, add the almonds and immediately pour the mixture onto the oiled tray, then leave to set.

Break the praline into large pieces and pulverise in a food processor or with a meat mallet until fine crumbs form. Store in an airtight container until needed.

Put the caster sugar, glucose and honey into a small heavy-based saucepan over medium heat. Bring to a simmer and stir once or twice until the sugar has dissolved. Boil until the mixture registers 116°C on a sugar thermometer. When the syrup is nearly ready, beat the egg whites in the bowl of an electric mixer until they hold stiff peaks. With the motor running, pour the syrup onto the egg whites, then beat until the mixture is cold; this can take up to 20 minutes. Fold the cream into the cooled nougat mixture, then fold in the glace fruit, candied peel and praline. Put into the freezer until you are ready to add this layer to the bombe (don't delay too long or it will be too hard to mould).

Remove the doubled bowl from the freezer and ease out the inner bowl; a flexible metal spatula dipped in hot water may help it to detach. Alternatively, wring out a cloth in boiling water and use it to rub the inside of the inner bowl to loosen it. Fill the centre with the nougat ice-cream, pressing it up the side of the bowl with a 2 cup (500 ml-capacity) bowl. Place in the freezer with the small bowl inside for several hours, covered with a lid or a doubled layer of plastic film.

Apricot parfait

125 g Australian dried apricots

2 cups (500 ml) water

juice of ½ lemon

1 cup (250 ml) thickened cream

SYRUP

250 g white sugar

⅔ cup (160 ml) water

Ensure you use Australian dried apricots, as Turkish apricots won't yield the vibrant orange colour needed. Check the label as many commercial products combine the two.

Soak the dried apricots in a bowl with the water overnight. Next day, drain and puree the apricots in a blender; you should have approximately 150 ml puree. Add the lemon juice.

To make the syrup, put the sugar and water into a small heavy-based saucepan over low heat. Stir continuously until the sugar has dissolved but do not allow the syrup to come to the boil. (You only need 150 ml of this syrup. Save the rest in the refrigerator for brushing over sponge fingers to set the unused portion of parfait in a mould for another day, if desired.)

Place 150 ml of the sugar syrup and the apricot puree in a large bowl and whisk together. Cover with plastic film and refrigerate to chill.

Whip the cream to soft peaks. Whisk half of the cream into the apricot mixture to lighten it, then fold in the remaining cream. Cover with plastic film and put into the freezer until ready to assemble the bombe.

Remove the bombe from the freezer once the nougat layer is quite firm, then ease out the second bowl; a flexible metal spatula dipped in hot water may help it to detach. Alternatively, wring out a cloth in boiling water and use it to rub the inside of the bowl to loosen it.

Fill the remaining space in the mould with apricot parfait. Smooth the top of the bombe with a palette knife, then fold over the overhanging plastic film. Freeze for at least 6 hours before unmoulding.

To unmould the bombe, remove it from the freezer for 30 minutes before serving to soften. Run a flexible metal spatula around the outside of the plastic film lining. Invert onto a flat plate and ease out the bombe. Remove the plastic film and smooth the exterior, if you wish, using a palette knife dipped in hot water.

Cut out wedges of the bombe and serve with chocolate sauce, if desired. Return any uneaten portion to the bombe mould, re-cover and store in the freezer.

TIMETABLE
FOR THE COOK

THREE WEEKS BEFORE

(Note that, as many suppliers close immediately after Christmas, planning for a New Year's Day special dinner can be tricky.)

- Check **Ingredients List** and note what needs to be purchased
- Check specialist equipment needed (sugar thermometer, meat probe, muslin, bombe mould, oyster shucker)
- Advise provedores of special requests (whole small turkey, thawed, to be collected on a pre-determined day; unopened oysters; toasted nori sheets)

THREE DAYS BEFORE

- Decide on table setting, including serving dishes
- Inspect tablecloth and napkins
- Decide on wine – order if necessary
- All shopping, including flowers
- Order 1 dozen unopened oysters for a practice run or plan to serve opened oysters
- Collect thawed turkey

Ice-cream bombe
- Soak apricots
- Make praline
- Make syrup for apricot parfait
- Prepare bowl for bombe
- Make coffee ice-cream

TWO DAYS BEFORE

Ice-cream bombe
- Make nougat
- Make nougat ice-cream
- Make apricot parfait
- Assemble bombe – freeze

DAY BEFORE

- Collect fish and shellfish, including opened oysters, if using
- Remove fish from packaging, place on a rack over a plate – refrigerate
- Chop garlic (see page 512)

Turkey roll and watercress salad
- Melt butter
- Bone turkey
- Assemble, wrap and tie turkey – refrigerate
- Make and reduce turkey stock – freeze any extra
- Soak, dry and pick watercress – refrigerate

MORNING OF

Oysters
- Thaw puff pastry
- Make seaweed biscuits

Quenelles
- Make whiting mousse – refrigerate
- Scoop quenelles onto a baking paper–lined baking tray – refrigerate
- Cut and blanch vegetables for mousse – refrigerate
- Prepare reduction and cut butter for beurre blanc

Ice-cream bombe
- Make chocolate sauce – store in a small saucepan or microwave-safe container for quick reheating

Watercress salad
- Wash, dry and crisp leaves
- Prepare salad dressing in salad bowl with crossed salad servers ready to toss before serving

AFTERNOON OF

Turkey roll
- Prepare vegetables

Oysters
- Open oysters (if using unopened)

- Set table

TWO HOURS
BEFORE GUESTS ARRIVE

- Have pan ready with lightly salted water for poaching quenelles
- Blanch Brussels sprouts
- Get changed

ONE HOUR
BEFORE GUESTS ARRIVE

Quenelles
- Place heatproof bowl over hot water to keep beurre blanc warm so it doesn't split

Turkey roll
- Preheat oven to 200°C and roast turkey and potatoes for 30 minutes (set timer)
- Turn potatoes and cook for another 30 minutes (reset timer)
- Test turkey – if cooked, remove from oven, cover loosely with foil and continue to roast potatoes and add sprouts and chestnuts; if not, cook for another 15 minutes (set timer)
- Loosely cover turkey and vegetables with foil and rest in a warm spot

Sybille Bedford-inspired New Year's Day Lunch

DINNER IS SERVED

FIRST COURSE

· Serve oysters and seaweed biscuits

SECOND COURSE

· Warm bowls for quenelles
  (see page 512)
· Make beurre blanc and keep warm
· Poach quenelles, scoop out
  with slotted spoon, drain briefly
  on paper towel and then into
  warmed bowl
· Spoon over beurre blanc, scatter
  with herb garnish and serve

THIRD/MAIN COURSE

· Warm plates and serving dishes
  (see page 512)

Turkey roll
· Set oven temperature to 150°C
· Uncover turkey roll, remove twine
  and transfer turkey roll to platter
  with vegetables, return to oven for
  20 minutes (set timer)
· Deglaze roasting pan with extra
  stock as needed to make sauce
· Slice turkey and serve with
  potatoes, chestnuts and sprouts,
  spoon on cooking juices

Watercress salad
· Toss and serve

Dessert
· Reheat chocolate sauce, if using
· Dip a palette knife in hot water,
  then use to ease the bombe
  from mould
· Slice bombe into wedges and
  place on plates
· Offer chocolate sauce separately

INGREDIENTS LIST

PANTRY

· Sea salt
· Fine salt
· Australian extra virgin olive oil
· Almond oil
· Red-wine vinegar
· Caster sugar
· White sugar
· Liquid glucose
· Honey
· 90 g glace fruit
· 45 g candied peel
· 125 g Australian dried apricots
· Flaked almonds
· 125 g bittersweet/dark
  chocolate (70 per cent
  cocoa solids)
· Toasted nori sheets
· 2 packets vacuum-packed
  roasted and peeled chestnuts
  (to yield 30)
· Espresso coffee granules
· 1 × 400 g tin sweetened
  condensed milk

SPICE SHELF

· Black peppercorns
· White peppercorns or
  ground white pepper
· Tabasco

REFRIGERATOR

· Milk
· 500 g unsalted butter
· Free-range eggs
· 1.225 litres thickened cream
· All-butter puff pastry

**GREENGROCER/FARMERS'
MARKET (OR GARDEN)**

· Flat-leaf parsley
· Dill
· Chives
· French tarragon
· Thyme
· Fresh bay leaves
· Garlic
· 1 onion
· 1 French shallot
· 2 lemons
· 2 carrots
· 1 celeriac
· 1 stick celery
· 2 asparagus spears
· 1 broccoli stalk
· Watercress
· Baby spinach leaves
· Mignonette lettuce
· 8 waxy potatoes,
  such as Dutch cream
· 30 Brussels sprouts

POULTRY SUPPLIER/BUTCHER

· 1 × 4 kg turkey, thawed

FISHMONGER

· 300 g King George whiting
  fillets
· 54 unopened Pacific or
  Sydney Rock oysters

CELLAR

· Dry white wine for beurre
  blanc and turkey stock
· Wine for the table
· Soft drink
· Espresso liqueur

BASICS

Sauteing fresh artichokes

If using freshly prepared artichoke hearts in the recipe on page 334, trim 12 artichokes down to the heart, then slice each heart into 1 cm-thick slices. Heat a little olive oil in a heavy-based frying pan over medium heat and saute the artichoke pieces for 5 minutes or until they start to look golden, stirring once or twice. Cover the pan and reduce the heat to low, then saute for a few more minutes. Test by inserting with a skewer; they are ready when a skewer pierces them easily. Cool before folding into the ricotta mixture, then proceed with the recipe.

Cooking lasagne sheets

500 g dried lasagne sheets

salt

Bring a very large saucepan of well-salted water to the boil. Drop in the sheets, a few at a time. Have ready alongside the stove a basin half-filled with very cold water and a tray lined with a clean dry tea towel. After 2 minutes, lift the cooked pasta sheets from the boiling water (I use a wooden spoon) and drop them into the cold water. Give them a quick swish, then lift them out and spread on the tea towel to drain; ensure the sheets do not touch or they will stick and tear.

How to deep-fry

A word of caution regarding deep-frying. The best deep-frying is done in olive oil – while expensive, the flavour is worth it. I prefer to use a deep heavy-based saucepan rather than a counter-top deep-fryer, as the saucepan will do a good job with far less oil. If you have a depth of 5–6 cm oil, it will be satisfactory for broccolini (see page 362). Any ingredient to be dipped in batter must first be dry. Fry the food in batches and do not crowd the pan. You can test the oil with a cube of bread, but a deep-fryer thermometer is a far better idea. Start frying when the oil registers 170°C, always ensure the room is well ventilated and have a paper towel–lined tray nearby (but not too near). Once the oil has cooled completely, strain it through a funnel into a glass bottle, then label and keep as frying oil for a few more batches.

Homemade tomato sauce

1 kg ripe tomatoes, cored,
seeded and roughly chopped

3 cloves garlic, chopped

1 onion, roughly chopped

1 fresh bay leaf

½ cup (125 ml) extra virgin
olive oil

Preheat the oven to 180°C.

Place the tomato, garlic, onion and bay leaf in a roasting pan
and drizzle with the olive oil. Roast for 2 hours; the tomato mixture
should be very soft.

Discard the bay leaf. Press the tomato mixture through a food
mill or tomato mill; the sauce will be a lovely red-gold colour. Blend
in a blender for an extra-smooth texture. Refrigerate for up to 3 days
or transfer to an airtight container, label, date and freeze for up to
one month.

Homemade mayonnaise

2 free-range egg yolks

pinch of sea salt

1 tablespoon lemon juice,
or to taste

200 ml extra virgin olive oil

freshly ground white pepper *or*
Tabasco, to taste

Choose a bowl and rest it on a damp cloth, so it cannot slip around.
Work the egg yolks with the salt and lemon juice for 1 minute, until
smooth. Using a wooden spoon or whisk, gradually beat in the olive
oil, adding the first few tablespoons one at a time and whisking well
after adding each one. After one-third of the oil is in, the rest can be
added in a thin, steady stream, beating all the while. Taste for acidity
and adjust with drops of lemon juice, salt and pepper or Tabasco.
Press plastic film directly onto the surface to prevent a skin forming,
then refrigerate. Return to room temperature before using or before
adding any additions such as sour cream, extra lemon or cut herbs.
(Leftovers can be stored in an airtight container in the refrigerator
for up to 1 week.)

Bechamel sauce

600 ml milk

50 g butter

⅓ cup (50 g) plain flour

sea salt and freshly ground
black pepper

freshly grated nutmeg (optional)

40 g finely grated parmesan
or gruyere (optional)

Heat the milk over high heat to scalding point in a small heavy-based saucepan and set aside. Melt the butter in another heavy-based saucepan over medium heat and stir in the flour. Cook, stirring, until you have a smooth golden paste. Gradually work in the hot milk and stir until the sauce thickens and is very smooth. Continue stirring until the sauce boils. Cook for a further 5 minutes on a simmer mat over low heat, stirring from time to time. Season to taste with salt and pepper. Keep warm or, if the assembly is delayed, warm the sauce briefly in a microwave; it must be easily spreadable, if using as a lasagne layer.

Green salad

A green salad accompanies almost every meal I prepare. I keep a salad storage container in my refrigerator, so that it is the work of seconds to extract a couple of handfuls of washed and dried leaves, dress them with the best Australian extra virgin olive oil and season with a small amount of sea salt and freshly ground pepper.

The leaves vary with the season. I grow some soft leaves, but not enough to keep me in salad every day. I like a mix of textures, so I add witlof and torn radicchio with softer leaves, such as frilly mignonette lettuces, with maybe a handful of rocket for a bit of bite. Hearts of cos lettuce are a good choice. While baby spinach leaves are delicious, in my experience, they do not last as well in my salad storage bowl.

Whether the leaves are from the market or my garden, I fill a large bowl with cold water. I consign any damaged outer leaves to the compost bin. I break up whole lettuces or tear strips from leaves unfurled from a head of radicchio, nip long stalks from the rocket and soak everything in the water for no longer than 30 minutes.

I then line my salad storage container with a couple of layers of paper towel, and dry small handfuls of leaves at a time, using a salad spinner, taking care to use it gently. Once all the leaves are dried, I add a couple more sheets of paper towel and snap on the lid – there it is, beautiful salad for several days.

When I prepare a salad for just myself, I do not use red-wine vinegar or any acid because I find that a gloriously fruity olive oil gives all the flavour and balance I need. If I am making a larger ➤

bowl of salad to share, I make a simple dressing directly in the salad bowl. In goes a pinch of sea salt flakes and maybe a teaspoon of aged red-wine vinegar. Then I add a puddle of extra virgin olive oil (maybe 2 tablespoons) and a few turns of the pepper mill. I mix this together lightly with a spoon and taste it for balance and acidity. This quantity of dressing is plenty for 6 handfuls of mixed leaves, enough for 4 enthusiastic salad eaters.

And I have one dislike – dressings made with balsamic vinegar. Usually the balsamic purchased is of poor quality and too much is used, so that the balance is destroyed and the flavour is harsh.

There are many possible variations. These are my favourites:

· for the oil component of the dressing, use a ratio of
  one-third walnut oil to two-thirds extra virgin olive oil
· use Spanish sherry vinegar in place of red-wine vinegar
· use a little bit of vino cotto instead of red-wine vinegar
  for a touch of sweetness
· include shavings of parmesan or pecorino or cubes
  of gruyere
· include toasted fresh walnuts
· include croutons that have been lightly rubbed
  with a cut clove of garlic and baked with olive oil
· include cubes of avocado
· include shreds of celeriac
· add some petals from edible flowers and herbs
  (not too many and petals only – no-one can eat
  a whole nasturtium or calendula flower) –
  try calendula, heartease, nasturtium, chives

Basics

Watercress salad

1 bunch watercress (to yield
about 2 cups [2 large handfuls]
lightly packed sprigs)

2 cups (2 large handfuls) small,
choice, mild-flavoured salad
leaves, such as baby spinach
and soft-leaf mignonette

sea salt

½ teaspoon red-wine vinegar

1 tablespoon extra virgin olive oil

freshly ground black pepper

**The sharp almost mustard-like bite of watercress is very
welcome served alongside dishes that are very buttery or rich.
A little bouquet of leaves looks wonderful tucked around grilled
or roasted poultry or in a salad bowl mixed with about the same
quantity of other fresh leaves and turned with just a few drops
of extra virgin olive oil, sea salt and freshly ground pepper.**

Pick the smallest, greenest watercress sprigs. Discard all thick stems
and yellow leaves. Wash well and dry in a salad spinner, then wrap
gently in a paper towel–lined tea towel and refrigerate until needed.

Wash and dry the other salad greens. Plan to serve the leaves in
a wide salad bowl, so that their shapes can be admired and the turning
required to coat with the dressing will be minimal.

Place a few grains of sea salt in the selected shallow salad platter
and add the vinegar to dissolve the salt. Mix with the olive oil and
a grind of black pepper. Leave in the bottom of the platter with
crossed salad servers over the top just until the moment of service.

Tumble in the greens and lift gently to coat with the dressing.

Makes about 1 litre

Chicken stock

1 chicken backbone and
any bony scraps

1 carrot, roughly chopped

1 stick celery, sliced

3 cloves garlic, crushed

1 onion, roughly chopped

a few sprigs thyme, a fresh bay leaf,
a few flat-leaf parsley stalks

Place the bones, vegetables and herbs in a stockpot. Barely cover
with cold water and bring to simmering point. Skim the surface,
then reduce the heat to low and cook the stock for 3 hours. Strain
into a bowl and chill. Remove all the solidified fat. Reduce rapidly
over high heat by half. Reserve until needed. Label and freeze any
extra stock in an airtight container for up to 1 month.

Makes about 1½ litres

Simple beef/veal stock

500 g beef brisket on the
bone, chopped

500 g veal shank, chopped

2 carrots, roughly chopped

2 sticks celery, sliced

2 onions, roughly chopped

3 cloves garlic, crushed

a few sprigs thyme, a bay leaf,
a few flat-leaf parsley stalks

Put the bones, vegetables and herbs into a stockpot and cover well
with cold water. Bring to a simmer, then skim the surface well.
Return to simmering point. Skim the surface, then reduce the heat
to low and cook the stock for 3 hours. Strain into a bowl and chill.
Remove all the solidified fat. Reduce rapidly over high heat by half.
Reserve until needed. Label and freeze any leftover stock in an
airtight container for up to 1 month.

Makes about 3 cups (750 ml)

Fish stock

heads and bones of 2 flathead

1 onion, sliced

1 carrot, sliced

1 leek, white part only,
well washed and sliced

2 outside layers of a bulb of
fennel, sliced

3 stalks flat-leaf parsley

1 fresh bay leaf

1 sprig thyme

6 black peppercorns

150 ml dry white wine

freshly ground white pepper

freshly grated nutmeg, to taste

Wash the bones well, scraping away any blood, then cut out
and discard the gills. Chop the bones into a few pieces. Put the
bones, onion, carrot, leek, fennel, herbs, peppercorns and wine
into a stockpot and cover well with cold water. Bring very slowly
to simmering point over low heat, then skim the surface to remove
any impurities. Simmer for 20 minutes. Have ready a strainer lined
with damp muslin resting over a large bowl. Ladle the stock into the
muslin-lined strainer, then leave the stock to cool; discard the solids.
Refrigerate in an airtight container for up to 2 days or label, date
and freeze for up to 1 month. Season with white pepper and nutmeg.

Pork and pistachio boiling sausage

1 kg boneless pickled pork shoulder, cut into 3 cm cubes

300 g hard back fat, cut into 3 cm cubes

⅓ cup (45 g) shelled unsalted pistachio kernels

2 tablespoons Cognac

1 tablespoon sea salt

½ teaspoon freshly ground black pepper

¼ teaspoon freshly grated nutmeg

finely grated zest of 1 orange

1 teaspoon finely chopped garlic

This recipe dates from the early days of Stephanie's Restaurant. It was usually served as the centrepiece of a luncheon salad with hot waxy potatoes dressed with capers, lots of parsley and chives and a handmade mayonnaise, with a green salad alongside.

If you cannot buy a good-quality boiling sausage, this makes a reasonable substitute. It does require a meat mincing attachment to an electric mixer. You will need to give your butcher notice that you require pickled pork shoulder and hard back fat. If you have an extremely obliging butcher, they may be prepared to put your mix into wide natural casings. If not, several layers of tightly wrapped plastic film and a sheet of muslin will do. Start this recipe two days ahead of serving.

Put the pork and fat into a large bowl with the pistachios, Cognac, salt, pepper, nutmeg, orange zest and garlic. Mix well. Cover with plastic film and refrigerate overnight.

Put the mixture through the coarsest blade of an electric mixer fitted with a meat mincer attachment. Refrigerate overnight again.

The next day, fry a small meat patty to taste for seasoning, then make any adjustments. Place the chilled mixture in the bowl of the electric mixer fitted with the paddle attachment and beat for several minutes, until the mixture is sticky and homogenous. (This is the moment to return to the butcher with the mix – carried in a chiller pack of course – and ask them to put it into casings.)

Alternatively, divide the mixture into two or three sausages; aim for 6–8 cm diameter if the sausage is to be wrapped in brioche, otherwise please yourself. Roll each one in several layers of plastic film, twisting the ends to form a very tight roll, shaped like a Christmas bonbon. Tie each end with kitchen twine. Each sausage can be wrapped again in muslin as an extra precaution against bursting during cooking.

Lower the sausages into a large pan of simmering water and simmer over low heat for 30–45 minutes, depending on thickness. Leave to cool in the water (remembering that if the sausage is intended to be wrapped in brioche, see page 164, it should still feel warm to the touch when it is wrapped in the dough). Otherwise, once really cold, unwrap the sausages, rewrap them in clean muslin and foil and use within a few days or freeze them for up to 1 month.

Shortcrust pastry

Makes enough to line a 22–26 cm tart tin with some left over

240 g plain flour,
plus extra for dusting

pinch fine salt

180 g butter, cubed

¼ cup (60 ml) ice-cold water

Sift the flour and salt into a food processor, then add the butter. Pulse briefly to combine until the mixture looks like breadcrumbs. With the motor running, add the cold water and process until the mixture forms a rough ball. Lightly dust a workbench, then tip the dough out and knead briefly. Wrap in plastic film and chill in the refrigerator for 30 minutes.

(Leftover pastry can be labelled and frozen or rolled and used to line a smaller tin, then frozen in the tin to use another day.)

Sweet shortcrust pastry

Makes enough to line a 22–26 cm tart tin with some left over

1⅓ cups (200 g) plain flour

125 g cold unsalted butter,
cut into 1 cm dice

25 g caster sugar

1 free-range egg

2 tablespoons ice-cold water

few drops of pure vanilla extract

Place the flour and butter in a food processor, then pulse for a few seconds. Add the sugar and pulse again briefly. Lightly whisk the egg with a fork and add the water and vanilla. With the motor running, add the egg mixture and process until the dough comes together to form a ball. Give the dough a quick knead, then divide into two-thirds and one-third. Press each lump into a disc, wrap in plastic film and refrigerate for at least 1 hour (or even overnight). Remove the dough from the refrigerator 30 minutes before you wish to roll it.

(Leftover pastry can be labelled and frozen or rolled and used to line a smaller tin, then frozen in the tin to use another day.)

Basics

Glossary

Assiettes creuses

'Hollow plates' in French, which is a perfect description for these shallow bowls. These are ideal for serving any juicy and chunky casserole, pasta or any dish with a fair amount of sauce. The best ones have a 20 cm diameter hollow.

Chilli paste

Asian and Spanish food stores sell various chilli pastes, and the Indonesian sambal oelek, available in supermarkets, is a great standby. Once opened, keep the jar in the refrigerator and wipe the neck with paper towel after every use to prevent tiny specks of chilli becoming mouldy.

Chilli sauce – hot

Use your favourite brand of chilli sauce, as long as it is a hot style rather than sweet chilli sauce. Some will include other ingredients, such as ginger or garlic, and be textured. Others will be quite smooth and just hot.

Chillies – Scotch bonnet

Scotch bonnet chillies look really cute and inoffensive, yet they are said to be one of the hottest of all chillies, as measured on the Scoville Scale.

Citrus – segmenting

Cut a slice from the top and bottom of the fruit. Using a sharp knife, carve away the peel, following the curve of the fruit and slicing deep enough to remove the pith. Either cut crosswise slices or release individual segments by slicing a segment away from its membrane.

Clarified butter

This is now readily available in the refrigerator section of supermarkets. To make your own, melt and simmer butter until the solids fall to the bottom of the saucepan, then ladle the liquid butter through a damp muslin cloth into a bowl. Leave to set until solid, then refrigerate in a covered container. It will last for several weeks.

Cream

I use thickened cream in my recipes for sauces, desserts such as ice-creams and other recipes. Both pouring and thickened cream are suitable for whipping. I use double cream for serving alongside sweet tarts and other desserts. I also use sour cream and creme fraiche, where the recipe calls for it.

Extra virgin olive oil – Australian

One of the most exciting developments in Australia's food world has been the growth of an excellent olive oil industry. I urge all cooks to buy Australian. Olive oil does not mature and is at its best in the year of harvest. In most cases, local oil will be fresher than imported oils.

Farro

An ancient wheat variety that is newly rediscovered and popular. Farro is darker in colour than modern wheat, with a tougher husk that protects the grains and maintains freshness longer than other wheats. Bread made with farro is dark and nutty, with a distinctive aroma. I use Mount Zero brand.

Fonte pans

I have a new all-Australian cast-iron frying pan by Fonte, a brand that has recently become available in specialist cookware stores, and I have fallen in love with it. It never buckles, it can be heated to red-hot, it deglazes perfectly, and it is easy to care for, needing just a wash in soapy water, then being left to air dry.

Garlic – preparing in advance

When preparing garlic in advance for a number of recipes within a menu, it is useful to know that 1 clove garlic equals ½ teaspoon chopped garlic. Cover in extra virgin olive oil until required.

Gelatine

I prefer to purchase McKenzie's (Australian-owned) gelatine leaves, sold in most supermarkets in clearly marked packets containing 12 leaves, which sets 1 litre of liquid.

Lemon juice/zest – preparing in advance

When grating lemon zest and squeezing lemon juice in advance for recipes across a menu, it is useful to know that 1 lemon equals 1 tablespoon of finely grated zest and 2–3 tablespoons juice.

Mastic

This gum is used to add flavour and especially texture to Middle Eastern and Greek dishes. It is sold as small lumps that are easily crushed.

Moist flakes coconut

This McKenzie's brand product is found in the baking section of supermarkets and, as the name suggests, is moister than regular coconut flakes or desiccated coconut.

Orecchiette

These tiny ear-shaped pasta are made from semolina flour. They take longer to cook than many other dried pasta shapes, up to 15 minutes.

Persillade

This French breadcrumb and parsley mixture keeps well for a day or two in the refrigerator and leftovers can be scattered over fish to be grilled or other baked vegetables, such as halved eggplant (aubergines) or pieces of pumpkin (squash).

Piquillo peppers – preserved

These preserved Spanish peppers can be found in jars and tins in good supermarkets, and certainly in all specialist Spanish or Portuguese food stores.

Plates and serving dishes – warming

As kitchen facilities vary, you can either heat plates in a second oven, a microwave or in a sink filled with hot water. If using the oven, preheat to 110°C and put the ovenproof serving dishes inside to warm.

Potatoes – waxy

Waxy potatoes are high in moisture and low in starch. They hold their shape when boiled and are ideal for adding to salads or for eating whole tossed with butter and chopped parsley. Some waxy varieties, such as Kipfler and Pink fir apple, are long and finger-shaped. Other varieties are round. They are not suitable for mashing or for making gnocchi.

Quinoa

Quinoa is not a grain. It is a distant relative of rhubarb and sorrel and the seeds, which are the part that is eaten, are described as pseudo-grains. It comes as cream, red or brown seeds. Quinoa is gluten-free and has less fat than other seeds, is easy to digest and is rich in fibre and minerals.

Rapini

Also known as *cime di rapa* or broccoli *raab*. The parts of this leafy green Italian vegetable that are used are the thin stems with leaves and clusters of yellow flowers attached, preferably while the flowers are still in bud. When preparing, the first task is to sort the rapini, cutting and reserving the thin stems with young leaves and flower heads into 10–12 centimetre-lengths. You then give the prepared greens a really good dunk in cold water and drain them in a colander or dry in a tea towel before proceeding.

Red rice

Camargue red rice is a brown–maroon colour, with an earthy, nutty flavour and resembles wild rice in shape. When cooked, it is never fluffy but remains chewy and al dente. It is excellent in salads or pilafs.

Sea salt

This is salt that can be crumbled, such as Maldon or Murray River, which I call sea salt throughout, as well as the very special *fleur de sel* that is a French import with damp largish grains. In France it is intended for use in dishes such as the salmon with *gros sel* on page 276.

Sterilising glass jars

Wash the jars in hot, soapy water, then rinse them in hot water. Put into a stockpot of boiling water for 10 minutes, then drain upside down on a clean tea towel. Dry thoroughly in a preheated 150°C oven, then fill while still hot.

Sugar/candy thermometer

These terms are interchangeable. This thermometer measures the stages of a sugar solution during cooking, from thread stage (106–112°C) to soft ball stage, (112–116°C), hard ball (121–130°C), hard crack (149–154°C) and finally caramel (160–177°C). The same thermometer can be used to measure hot oil for deep-frying. There are several kinds, including those that clip onto a saucepan and are easy to read, as well as digital thermometers. A candy thermometer can be used as a meat thermometer, although it will register temperatures higher than is needed for meat cooking. For most meat cookery, a digital probe thermometer is easier to use.

Sumac

Sumac is a dark red spice ground from the berry of a shrub. It is used to add tartness to all manner of Middle Eastern dishes in the same way as other cultures use lemon or tamarind. When combined with sesame seeds and dried thyme it is used as a topping for flatbread and called za'atar.

Verjuice

Verjuice is the juice of unripe grapes. It is excellent for glazing poultry before roasting, deglazing baking dishes after roasting anything at all and using as a mild acidulant in sauces and dressings. It is an unfermented product and, once opened, must be stored in the refrigerator.

Vino cotto

Vino cotto or vincotto is a centuries-old condiment originating in the south of Italy. It is traditionally made from the unfermented crushed fruit and skins of red grapes, known as 'must', and produces a syrup with a sweet and sour flavour, equally useful in sweet and savoury dishes and as an ingredient in marinades and dressings or for drizzling over fruit.

Watercress

It is only the youngest, freshest leaves and their delicate stems that ought to be served. Watercress does not store well and quickly develops yellow leaves with a horrible smell. When buying a bunch inspect it closely; it should be bright-green and bouncy. Almost inevitably there will be a lot of waste. Do not even think of using the tough central stems. And one is warned about collecting watercress in the wild if it is growing in a waterway used by stock animals or near an industrial run-off, as watercress quickly absorbs pollutants.

Bibliography

Alexander, Stephanie *A Cook's Life*, Lantern, Melbourne, 2012

Alexander, Stephanie *Cooking and Travelling in South-West France*, Lantern, Melbourne, 2002

Alexander, Stephanie *The Cook's Companion*, revised edition; Lantern, Melbourne, 2004

De Bernières, Louis *Birds Without Wings: A Novel*, Secker & Warburg, London, 2004

Bedford, Sybille *Jigsaw: An Unsentimental Education*, Eland Publishing, London, 1989

Bedford, Sybille *Quicksands – a Memoir*, Penguin, London, 2005

Blanc, Georges *Ma Cuisine des Saisons*, Robert Laffont, Paris, 1984

Campbell, Joan *Bloody Delicious! A Life with Food*, Allen & Unwin, Sydney, 1998

David, Elizabeth *French Country Cooking*, Dorling Kindersley, London, 1951

David, Elizabeth *French Provincial Cooking*, Michael Joseph, London, 1960

David, Elizabeth *Is There a Nutmeg in the House?*, Penguin, London, 2002

Dods, Margaret *The Cook and Housewife's Manual*, 6th edn, Oliver & Boyd, Edinburgh, 1837

Escoffier, Auguste *The Escoffier Cookbook: A Guide to the Fine Art of Cookery*, Crown Publishers Inc, New York, 1961

Gomersall-Hubbard, Gabriella *Growing Honest Food: An Oasis of Italian Tradition in the Suburbs*, Hyland House Publishing, Flemington, 2012

Grigson, Jane *The Observer Guide to British Cookery*, Michael Joseph, London, 1984

Halici, Nevin *Nevin Halici's Turkish Cookbook*, Dorling Kindersley, London, 1989

Hopkinson, Simon *Week In, Week Out; 52 Seasonal Stories*, Quadrille, London, 2007

Lawson, Nigella *Nigellissima: Instant Italian Inspiration*, *Chatto & Windus*, London, 2015

Malouf, Greg *Turquoise: A Chef's Travels in Turkey*, Hardie Grant, Melbourne, 2007

Moran, Sean *Let it Simmer*, Lantern, Melbourne, 2006

Norwak, Mary *The Farmhouse Kitchen*, Ward Lock, London, 1975

Oliver, Raymond *La Cuisine, sa Technique, ses Secrets* Secrets of Modern French Cooking, Bordas, Paris, 1965

Olney, Richard *Lulu's Provençal Table: The Exuberant Food and Wine from Domaine Tempier Vineyard*, HarperCollins, New York, 1994

Olney, Richard *Reflexions*, Brick Tower Press, New York, 1999

Pamuk, Orhan *The Innocence of Objects*, Harry N. Abrams, New York, 2012

Pamuk, Orhan *The Museum of Innocence: A Novel*, Faber & Faber, London, 2011

Pignolet, Damien *French*, Lantern, Melbourne, 2005

Rodgers, Judy *The Zuni Café Cookbook: A Compendium of Recipes and Cooking Lessons from San Francisco's beloved Restaurant*, W.W. Norton & Company, New York, 2002

Smithers, Annie *Annie's Garden to Table: A Garden Diary Featuring 100 Seasonal Recipes*, Lantern, Melbourne, 2012

Stein, Gertrude *The Autobiography of Alice B. Toklas*, Stellar Editions, 2014

Toklas, Alice *The Alice B. Toklas Cookbook*, The Folio Society, London, 1993

Willinger, Faith *Adventures of an Italian Food Lover*, Clarkson Potter, New York, 2007

Acknowledgements

The team at Penguin have risen to the challenge and together we have worked very hard to produce this beautiful book in record time, maintaining the standards of beauty and excellence set and expected by publisher Julie Gibbs throughout the eleven years of the Lantern imprint of Penguin. If this was to be its final hurrah we all wanted to go out on an exceptional high. Thanks to Julie, we have a magnificent cover reproduced from a woodblock by the renowned artist Cressida Campbell. This kitchen portrait has all the warmth and honesty that I hope shine through my stories and recipes.

A very big thank you to Publishing Manager, Katrina O'Brien, who has kept everyone to a tight schedule. Once again, it has been a pleasure to work with editor Kathleen Gandy, whose meticulous work has ensured consistency throughout. I am thrilled with the design of the book, so thank you to Evi O and Daniel New. And thanks also to Photoshoot Producer, Cass Stokes.

The photoshoots were extensive and exhausting, and for these I thank home economist Caroline Griffiths, photographer Mark Chew and stylist Lee Blaylock. Caroline powered through long days retaining a sense of calm, as well as a sense of humour. I am especially grateful for the care and attention shown on the days when I was unable to be present.

From my own team, I would not have survived without the eagle eye and hard work of my Personal Assistant, Katie Barnett, and the skill and loyalty of my kitchen right-hand, chef Mel Schouten.

Family and friends have been involved in tasting many of the dishes. I hope it was always a pleasure.

Index

LANTERN

UK | USA | Canada | Ireland | Australia
India | New Zealand | South Africa | China

Penguin Books is part of the Penguin Random House group of companies whose addresses
can be found at global.penguinrandomhouse.com.

Penguin
Random House
Australia

First published by Penguin Random House Australia Pty Ltd, 2016

10 9 8 7 6 5 4 3 2 1

Designed by Evi O. © Penguin Random House Australia Pty Ltd
Photography by Mark Chew
Styling by Lee Blaylock
Photoshoot production by Cass Stokes
Editing by Kathleen Gandy
Typeset in Janson Text by Post Pre-press Group, Brisbane, Quuensland
Colour separation by Splitting Image Colour Studio, Clayton, Victoria
Printed and bound in China by RR Donnelley Asia Printing Solutions Ltd

National Library of Australia
Cataloguing-in-Publication data:

Alexander, Stephanie, 1940- author.
The cook's table: 130 recipes to share with family and friends/Stephanie Alexander;
photography by Mark Chew.
9781921384455 (hardback)
Includes bibliographical references and index.
Cooking.
Menus.
Entertaining.
Chew, Mark, photographer.

641.5

penguin.com.au/lantern

The publisher would like to thank
the following suppliers for generously
providing props for photography.

Perfect Pieces perfectpieces.com.au
Royal Doulton royaldoulton.com.au
Villeroy & Boch villeroy-boch.com.au
Waterford waterfordcrystal.com.au
Wedgwood wedgwood.com.au

Excerpt from *Quicksands* by Sybille Bedford
(Hamish Hamilton, London, 2005) reprinted by
permission of Penguin Random House UK.

Recipe on page 202 for neenish tartlets from
Bloody Delicious! by Joan Campbell (Murdoch,
Sydney, 1997) reprinted by permission of Allen
& Unwin and Sue Fairlie-Cunningham.

Quotes by Elizabeth David and her adapted
recipes reprinted by permission of Jill Norman.

Recipe for Nigella's coffee ice-cream on page
492 adapted from One-Step No-Churn Coffee
Ice-cream recipe from *Nigellissima* by Nigella
Lawson, published by Chatto & Windus,
reprinted by permission of The Random
House Group Ltd.

Recipe on page 100 for Strawberry Crush
Ice-cream from *Let it Simmer* by Sean Moran
(Lantern, Sydney, 2006) reprinted by permission
of Penguin Random House Australia Pty Ltd.

The author would also like the thank
the following for their kind permission
to reproduce copyright material:
Cressida Campbell, Civan Er,
Jocelyn Hancock, Jack Ingram,
Damien Pignolet, Anthony Simone
and Annie Smithers.

Where others have been quoted, every effort
has been made to contact them, and full
acknowledgement of their work has been
given in the text.

Front cover
After lunch (2002) by Cressida Campbell

Back cover
Kitchen (1989) by Cressida Campbell